The
BOOK OF
MANAGEMENT WISDOM

# ALSO AVAILABLE IN THE WISDOM SERIES

**The Book of Business Wisdom**

Offers 54 essays from such legends of commerce and industry as John D. Rockefeller, Jack Welch, Sam Walton, P. T. Barnum, J. Paul Getty, Andrew Grove, and Henry Ford.

Topics include: the essentials of good management, how to get ahead, and maintaining individuality in the corporate world.

**The Book of Leadership Wisdom**

Offers 52 essays from such legendary leaders as Andrew Carnegie, Bill Gates, Michael Eisner, H. Ross Perot, Katharine Graham, Akio Morita, and T. Coleman Du Pont.

Topics include: leading revolution, dealing with adversity, and corporate culture.

**The Book of Investing Wisdom**

Offers 46 essays from such legends of Wall Street as Warren Buffett, Peter Lynch, Abby Cohen, Bernard Baruch, John Moody, John Templeton, Charles Dow, and George Soros.

Topics include: the nuts and bolts of analysis, attitude and philosophy, lessons from notorious characters, and beyond your average blue chip.

**The Book of Entrepreneurs' Wisdom**

Offers 53 essays from such legendary entrepreneurs as Henry Ford, George Eastman, Kim Polese, Col. Harland Sanders, Lillian Vernon, Warren Avis, Richard Branson, Dave Thomas, and Steve Jobs.

Topics include: the start-up process, the maverick element, venture capital, risk and strategy, entrepreneurial management, and personal stories.

# The
# BOOK OF
# MANAGEMENT
# WISDOM

Classic Writings by
Legendary Managers

Edited by Peter Krass

John Wiley & Sons, Inc.

New York • Chichester • Weinheim • Brisbane • Singapore • Toronto

ISBN 0-471-35487-2

Printed in the United States of America.

10 9 8 7 6 5 4 3 2 1

# Contents

v

Contents

vi

Contents

# Contents

# Introduction

Every day we manage our personal life and our job, from little routines to grand plans. Taking care of ourselves poses enough problems, but consider how drastically the nature of work management changes the moment you have even one person reporting to you in some capacity. Now you have to concern yourself with another's affairs, a sure recipe for disaster unless handled deftly. The first big question: How will your relationship unfold? Will it be positive or negative? Andrew Grove, chairman of Intel, bluntly states, "Dealing with conflict lies at the heart of managing any business. As a result, confrontation—facing issues about which there is disagreement—can be avoided only at the manager's peril." But if there must be conflict, are management transgressions such as using tactics preferred by Attila the Hun or Prince Machiavelli justified? Not in the twenty-first century.

Whether you're managing one person or an entire organization, enlightened answers to the tough questions are here in *The Book of Management Wisdom*. Drawing on their experience, the great cast of managers in this collection offers a range of practical advice, case studies, and humorous anecdotes, but doesn't include discourses on org charts or balance sheets. As Harold Geneen, the legendary leader of ITT, observes in the first essay, "The key, essential element in all good business management is emotional attitude. The rest is mechanics. As I use the term, management is not a collection of boxes with names and titles on the organizational chart. Management is a *living force*."

Living force? Are we entering a mystical realm occupied by just a few great leaders? How does this realm apply to management? According to *Merriam Webster's Collegiate Dictionary* (Tenth Edition), the word *manage* means, among other definitions, "to handle or direct with a degree of skill . . . to make and keep compliant . . . to alter for a purpose." Pretty cut-and-dried; nothing mystical. However, as you read through the various essays and speeches by a spectrum of leaders from a cross section of industries, no one espouses keeping others compliant or oppressed. In fact, one of the themes that comes to the forefront is how to manage people and organizations without sounding like a crusty army general who relies on command and control.

In the good old days, the army general was, in fact, the executive model. In his 1995 book, *Managing in a Time of Great Change*, Peter F. Drucker points out that when large corporations began to emerge, only the army was available as a model. He writes, "Management as a practice is very old. The most successful executive in all of history was surely that Egyptian who, 4,700 years or more ago, first conceived the pyramid—without any precedent—designed it and built it, and did so in record time. Unlike any other work of man built at that time, that first pyramid still stands. But as a discipline, management is barely fifty years old." Now that businesses no longer treat employees like just another resource to be used up and the leftovers discarded as they were not only 3,000 years ago, but just 100 years ago, good management is crucial. It is the vital organ, which brings us back to Geneen's "living force."

The emotional attitude Geneen refers to involves directing without oppressing, and that theme echoes throughout *The Book of Management Wisdom*. Take the late Sam Walton, founder of Wal-Mart, who donned his cheerleading outfit (figuratively speaking) whenever he visited one of his stores, and led the employees in a Wal-Mart cheer that ended with "Who's number one? THE CUSTOMER!" Walton's emotional attitude motivated his people and focused them on the all-important consumer.

Odds are good that you won't find steely-eyed General Electric CEO Jack Welch in a cheerleading outfit; nevertheless his ideas also reverberate with spirit. Welch, who likes to think of himself as running a grocery store to better serve the customer, promotes the tearing down of walls between groups such as manufacturing and marketing, and even between customers and suppliers, to improve efficiencies. He calls it being "boundaryless." "Boundaryless behavior is the soul of today's GE," he writes—that's Geneen's living force, too.

Before continuing, a caveat: No business manager is perfect, and practicing best methods has proved challenging for more than a few in this collection. Just take Andrew Carnegie, who in 1886 wrote that peaceful arbitration should be used to settle differences between capital and labor. A mere six years later, he and his lieutenants mishandled the strike at their Homestead steel plant and a bloodbath resulted, with ten killed. Back in the 1890s, the press and cartoonists had a field day with Carnegie, portraying him as both devil and saint. Today's business miscues provide similar fodder for humorists such as Scott Adams, creator of the popular *Dilbert* comic strip. In his book *The Dilbert Principle*, Adams wryly lists 13 "Great Lies of Management," of which three are: "Employees are our most valuable asset"; "I have an open-door policy"; and "We're reorganizing to better serve our customers." Consider his point: Talk is cheap, which is what Carnegie and many executives since him have discovered.

To avoid the pitfall of lip service, managers must become acutely aware of the many tools and techniques that go into creating Geneen's living force. *The Book of Management Wisdom*, like the other collections in the Business Wisdom series, is broken down into eight parts to highlight those tools and techniques and how the authors put them to use. Each part has its own brief introduction that draws out the major themes. For example, Part I, "Essential Qualities of Great Managers," lays out the basic qualities managers must embody, such as right-brain thinking, the entrepreneurial spirit, and a positive attitude. To reinforce the ideas set forth in Part I, very specific daily management topics and person-to-person issues are discussed in Part II, "Empowerment, Productivity, and Conflict Management," and Part III, "Hiring, Firing, and Day-to-Day Management," such as delegating, job titles, meetings, and reports.

In Part II, Arthur Blank and Bernie Marcus, cofounders of Home Depot, explain how they empower their managers by giving them room to operate. In defining job boundaries for regional presidents, Blank and Marcus tell them to consider themselves autonomous, but also enclosed by an invisible electric fence, and the only way to find out whether they are overstepping their responsibilities is to get zapped. Fortunately, they acknowledge, "We learned together where that fence is; it is in different places for different people, and it moves all the time. . . . What works in Maine might not necessarily click in Atlanta or Seattle." Now that's emotional attitude that can't be boxed. That attitude must be protected, and according to legendary adman David Ogilvy (Part III), office politics can poison it quickly. His advice is blunt: "Fire the worst of the politicians. You can identify them by how often they send you blind copies of their poison-pen memos to their rivals." Ogilvy rewards and punishes, the key being to find that balance between the carrot and the stick.

Now if day-to-day management isn't complicated enough, throw in technology (Part IV) and global issues (Part V) and you have a real stew cooking. Technology has always driven innovation; Adam Smith, who wrote the 1776 book *The Wealth of Nations*, once said in a lecture that "two men and three horses will do more in a day with the plough than twenty men without it." New technology liberated mankind from arduous field labor, but it can also be used to control, as was portrayed so vividly in George Orwell's *1984* and his chilling concept of the all-seeing, all-knowing Big Brother. However, a good manager will use technology not to control people, but operations, by creating timely and telling reports or business models. For example, J. Willard Marriott, the hotel tycoon, uses technology to model demand for his thousands of rooms and to develop price plans. While this example is part of the mechanics of managing, technology can also perpetuate Geneen's living force. Michael Dell opens his essay by declaring, "One of the sayings around Dell is that if you want to get people to think big, you need to act big. We were certainly thinking big when we set about constructing a successful Internet model." After reading his evangelical piece, in which he describes how he poses as Uncle Sam, you'll get the Internet religion.

Technology has also made the world a smaller place, but in this context smaller means more complicated, with more variables (such as cultural differences) to be conscious of. These issues are addressed in Part V, "Lessons from around the World." The late Coca-Cola CEO Roberto Goizueta, who was born and raised in Cuba, acknowledged that consideration; however, he believed that to succeed globally, a company must have "a central theme, idea or symbol that binds together the business system, the brands and the consumers." While global variables make business more complex, looking on the bright side, one finds that there are not only more opportunities, but lessons to be learned from international business leaders. For example, entrepreneur Kenichi Ohmae, an ex–McKinsey director, explains how Japanese executives use creative insight to envision strategic plans. It's a matter of studying market realities, timing, and available resources, and then remaining extremely conscious of all these factors when contemplating a plan. Yes, the living force pervades Japan, too.

The Internet and the networked world now play major roles in the future of business; however, much of value can still be learned from the "Evolution of the Organization" (Part VI); that is, the past, which includes such icons as Carnegie; Charles R. Flint, nicknamed the father of the trust back in the 1890s; Alfred Sloan, the ingenious chief of General Motors who espoused coordinated decentralization in the 1920s; and Royal Little, who built a conglomerate a decade before it became the rage in the 1960s. These pioneers of business grappled with many issues we no longer need to consider, but they nonetheless built the templates for modern structures and theories, and have more than a few worthwhile ideas to share. For example, in decentralizing GM's management, Sloan understood that "men capable of getting the results we want will not work under orders." Sloan himself claimed to have never issued an order while chief of GM. Again, he embodied Geneen's living force.

As for broader organizational issues, eliminating layers and getting closer to the frontline have been the obsessions of top managers of the 1980s and 1990s. Returning to Drucker, in his book *Managing for the Future*, he confirms that "for 35 years, from the end of World War II until the early '80s, the trend ran toward more and more layers of management and more and more staff specialists. The trend now goes in the opposite direction." Principal reasons for this new trend are the rise of competition, both national and international, and much greater stockholder and customer expectations. Part VII, "Bashing Bureaucracy," and Part VIII, "Reengineering and Transformation," tackle the issues of organizational structure, reorganization, and the need to be more efficient.

According to management gurus such as Drucker, reengineering, which involves companies reorganizing themselves around the flow of information, is one of the most important new tools available to managers. However, beware of its effect on Geneen's living force. Humorist Adams takes a mocking, yet poignant swing at it: "Reengineering a company is a bit like performing an appendectomy on yourself. It hurts quite a bit, you might not know exactly how to do it, and there's a good chance you won't survive it. But if it does work, you'll gain enough confidence to go after some of the more vital organs, such as that big red pumping thing." His message: Watch out or you might kill the spirit of the company. To be sure, the managers in Parts VII and VIII are very conscious of that possibility. Thomas Watson, legendary leader of IBM, preaches the importance of maintaining core beliefs. John E. Martin, retired CEO of Taco Bell (and featured in Michael Hammer and James Champy's *Reengineering the Corporation*), emphasizes the importance of telling employees that changes are being made to benefit the customer, not to pay for a new suite of plush executive offices.

Management boils down to this: Whether you're into management-by-walking-around, management-by-objective, management-by-exception, or even management-by-crony, it's the attitude you bring to the job that counts most. Attitudes are not mystical. Attitudes are determined by and will determine how you use available management tools to best serve your existing customers and create new customers, which is what business is in its purest form. The legends included in *The Book of Management Wisdom* offer a complete arsenal of techniques, ideas, and instructional anecdotes to achieve that end. Choose your weapons wisely, and remember that these icons of business didn't achieve greatness by holding back anything when it came to management attitude.

The
BOOK OF
MANAGEMENT WISDOM

# PART I

# Essential Qualities of Great Managers

The primary characteristic a manager must have, declares Harold Geneen in the opening essay, is emotional commitment; otherwise, high standards will not be set and goals will not be met. The managers in Part I aren't interested in an organized desk or a meticulous day planner; they're looking for the right mind-set. For Charles Tandy, the man behind Radio Shack, that means bringing an entrepreneurial spirit to the job. For Robert Lutz, former president and vice chairman of Chrysler, it's about right-brain thinking; that is, relying on intuition and guts, not data-driven analysis. For John Fox, founder of Minute Maid, an essential quality is courage. Great managers, he writes, must have the courage to gamble, to delegate, and to be tough. Geneen likens managing to running a marathon, and the ideas presented in Part I create an excellent starting line.

# HAROLD GENEEN
## 1910–1997

Harold Geneen inherited a stodgy telecommunications company when he was recruited for ITT's presidency in 1959—he then transformed it into a multinational conglomerate powerhouse, pumping up annual sales from $766 million to $22 billion over time. Juggling ITT was not much different from his father's job of managing concert performers. Geneen was born in Britain, but his family moved to the United States when he was less than a year old. After attending a Connecticut private school, he began work as a page on Wall Street, then pursued an accounting career. Geneen held several finance jobs with such firms as American Can Co. and Bell & Howell. Then, in 1956 he was hired as an executive vice president of Raytheon. His mission: to turn around the ailing company, which he did, and after three years he was tapped by ITT.

In less than 10 years, Geneen built ITT into a conglomerate of 150 affiliated companies operating in 57 countries, managing interests that varied from the U.S. president's hotline with Moscow to Avis Rent-A-Car. Never liking the term "conglomerate," he preferred to label ITT "a unified-management, multiproduct company." People were important to his success formula: "We set out to hire the very best people in the industry that we could find. I did not want glamorous, glib-talking men who got by on their coiffured good looks or family connections."

He also understood that for a true multinational conglomerate to operate efficiently, control was everything. To personally keep track of his empire, Geneen had a dozen or so attache cases lined up in his office, each stuffed with plans and reports. At times he could be overbearing, and the discipline he inflicted on others has been likened to that of the Catholic Church or the Communist Party. His managers were subject to continuous scrutiny within a system of checks and balances. For Geneen, "the highest art of professional management requires the literal ability to 'smell' a 'real fact' from all others." He also believed that "the essential element" for all managers is "emotional attitude," which he wanted to be as intense as a nuclear explosion.

# The Essential Elements
## *Harold Geneen*

The key, essential element in all good business management is emotional attitude. The rest is mechanics. As I use the term, management is not a collection of boxes with names and titles on the organizational chart. Management is a *living force*. It is the force that gets things done to acceptable standards — high standards, if you will. You either have it in a company or you don't. Management must have a purpose, a dedication, and that dedication must be an emotional commitment. It must be built in as a vital part of the personality of anyone who truly is a manager. He or she is the one who understands that management must manage.

The attitude is a self-fulfilling one, too. The man who says, "I must do this," will stay at his task until all hours, trying again and again and again, until he finds a satisfactory answer. The answer must be, above all, satisfactory to him. And he will know it. There may be seventy-eight ways to do something and only ten of them with satisfactorily good answers. The manager will continue to probe and to seek for one of those ten answers. It may not be the best of all answers. But he won't settle for anything lower than one of those ten. The next time he will strive for yet a better answer, higher on the list, learning something new all the time, and achieving better results as he goes along. He will work this way because of his emotional attitude, more than anything else, and that attitude inevitably will be emulated by those who work with him, so that it becomes a way of life in that organization. The urge to do what must be done is powered

---

> The key, essential element in all good business management is emotional attitude. The rest is mechanics.

---

by deep-seated emotion, not logic. He might not be able to explain why he works the way he does, or why he makes this choice and not the other one. He does it because he "feels" that it is right. That feeling is transmitted to others who work for him or with him. They know his emotional commitment includes them as well as the goals of the enterprise. They are willing to follow his lead because of that "feeling" which makes him the kind of person he is.

No matter if you are managing a business, a church, a scout troop, a career, or your home life, I believe that the test of management is whether or not it achieves the goals it sets for itself; the higher the goals, the better the management. In fact, if the level of goals is too low, I wouldn't call it manage-ment at all; anyone can do it. A marathon runner is someone who can run twenty-six miles 385 yards *in a given amount of time*, whether the standard is two and a half, three, or three and a half hours. But what about the fellow who runs it in ten hours? He's not a marathon runner; he's a guy wearing short pants and a pair of running shoes who is out getting some fresh air. We are defining the runner in terms of his *per-formance*. So do we define a corporate manager.

If the manager is to accomplish his objectives, he absolutely has to get the information necessary to make the right decisions. The steps along the way define themselves as he goes toward his objectives. To surmount each step, he needs solid facts so that he can recognize the realities of situations. His decisions, if based realistically upon reliable information, will not be all that difficult. Facts are power.

---

Management is not a collection of boxes with names and titles on the organizational chart. Management is a *living force.*

---

They are crucial to good management. In order to get the straight facts in any situation, the manager must ask straight questions, and to do that he must do his homework so that he has a deep understanding of what he is encountering. If he has a good record of making the right decisions, he can help people around him to be effective and successful in their own areas, so that their total accomplishment is greater than the sum of their individual parts. That is leadership. And if the leadership is successful, it creates a momentum in the enterprise which enriches the participants with such a feeling of pride and energy that they produce results, short-term and long-term results, which they themselves never thought possible. I've separated the elements here, but in practice they all move along together, en masse, nourishing each other like the fusion in a nuclear reactor, creating the fire, the pressure, and the power which produce energy. All this is the critical emotional content of good management.

This is the emotional horsepower that drives people to do things, drives them to keep at it because they feel they *must* get the answer, drives them to push on until they get results that are satisfactory to them. Of course, you don't always succeed in every effort. But then you recognize it early on, and you get out of that situation. You cut your losses and go on to something else. If you are a manager, you don't drift.

1984

# JOHN M. FOX

As founder of Minute Maid, best known for its orange juice, John Fox had to manage through more than a few downturns, including bad harvests, bad investments, and depressed markets. Still, he built such a respectable company over 15 years that Minute Maid merged with Coca-Cola in 1960. Early in Fox's business career, entrepreneurship was not on the horizon. After graduating from Colgate University in 1934, he took a sales job with IBM. Nine years later he was a branch sales manager with his eye on a vice presidency position; however, corporate life was turning out to be less rewarding than he hoped.

To truly prove himself, Fox wanted to build a small business from the ground up, so he resigned and hooked up with a group of engineers dedicated to developing commercial uses for scientific discoveries. At the time, they were looking for someone to head a small company called Vacuum Foods that made orange juice concentrate and powder. Fox spearheaded the search and then elected himself. The early years were tough as Fox dealt with undercapitalization and constant threats of bankruptcy. To introduce the new product, advertising was crucial, and that alone ate up a huge chunk of money. Fox changed the name of the company to the more consumer-friendly Minute Maid in 1945 and became the industry leader.

Tough times hit in December of 1957 when a freeze struck Florida, threatening orange groves, and Wall Street beat up the company until its stock was trading at a mere 4⅜, a nine-year low. To save his ailing company, Fox moved the headquarters from New York City to Orlando; converted salesmen into brokers working on commissions; sold off expensive surburban Florida property to purchase more affordable rural land for groves; and used innovations to save most of the crop. Ten months later the stock was trading at 18, and two years later the company merged with Coca-Cola. In *What It Takes to Be a Manager,* Fox provides his blueprint for success, and naturally his first prerequisite is *Creative Ability.* Toward that end, he describes his own experience in tapping the subconscious mind, a power that he believed could be developed.

# What It Takes to Be a Manager
## *John M. Fox*

In selecting this subject I realize I am venturing into dangerous territory. There is very little agreement on the matter—the business school professors rarely speak from experience—merely from observation—and a lofty observation at that since they haven't been troubled with the little problem of "meeting the payroll."

The managers themselves are so busy that they rarely have time to analyze just what it is that makes them good managers. What is more, they are by nature realists and their failures and mistakes fog over the elements of successful management that they practice—much of it by instinct rather than planning.

To be at all objective about this controversial subject, one must review the three broad phases of management evolution that have developed during our own lifetime. Fifty to seventy-five years ago nearly every company in America was managed by its owner. Some of the most exciting chapters of our industrial history were written by these brilliant, far-sighted and tough-minded men like Henry Ford, [Harvey S.] Firestone, George Westinghouse and their ilk.

With the growing need for capital to expand, the ownership shifted to the public. Guidance of the companies remained for the most part in the hands, strong hands they were too, of such giants as T. J. Watson of I.B.M., Sewell Avery of Montgomery Ward, Walter Chrysler, and hundreds of others, many of whom are still running a good show in their respective companies. But a one-man show.

As our businesses have become more complex with the need for special knowledge in production, taxes, marketing, engineering and finance, the scope of running a company widened to a vista beyond the ken of any one man. The team management idea was born. It is perhaps best exemplified by General Motors—one of the earliest and probably still the most successful proponent of this scheme.

The team concept has some very real hazards, however. The very need for specialization has had the tendency to produce men who have a kinship to finance or sales or production. This often develops an over-emphasis of their specialty to the detriment of the whole operation. This was exemplified in the recent book and movie, "Executive Suite." Here we saw the company controller, who had gone "overboard" on the importance of the financial scoreboard side of the business. As the war ended, our managements awoke to the great need and the great lack of qualified top management men. Executive development plans became a fad—nearly every major company had one. "Job rotation" became the watchword. Advanced management courses at the universities were in great demand, and still are. I am not in any way belittling these efforts—some have proven very effective. Others have failed miserably. You all probably know examples of each. There is emerging, however, a feeling that finding our leaders of tomorrow is more fundamental than merely appointing a group of "crown princes" who may or may not have what it takes to be good managers.

It was my good fortune to attend a roundtable conference at Columbia recently. The subject of the discussion that took place one evening a week for two months was "Management of Expanding Enterprises." The topic that came in for a heavy concentration of study was this one of selecting and training the men who could successfully manage a growing enterprise.

From the statements and convictions of this group of successful operating executives, plus some additional observations of other business leaders who have demonstrated their ability to field competent management teams, I have extracted six fundamental qualities that are found or should be present in men destined to command in business. This list I'm sure is not complete. I must hasten to point out that all of these qualities are rarely, if ever, found to their fullest in any one man. Such a paragon of perfection probably does not exist. The list may be useful, however, to anyone who wants to climb high on the management ladder and who is willing to pay the price that the climb exacts.

The first qualification is CREATIVE ABILITY. Business is looking for *men who can think*. There are many synonyms for this quality. It is sometimes called vision—also imagination. Whatever the handle, remember that nothing starts without an idea behind it. It is the lifeblood of an organization. It is a must for success. It is an essential of all growth. To be a good manager, the ability to think creatively, constructively and clearly is essential. The leadership role in management calls constantly for resourcefulness. The fast moving, continually changing pattern of the modern competitive business world demands this quality if success and satisfactory profits are to be the goal.

There are many misconceptions about this ability to have ideas. One of the most outrageous statements on the subject that I have ever heard came from a professorial friend of mine who said that a man should change jobs and preferably businesses after he had produced ten good ideas. Quite to the contrary, it is well recognized now that the brain not only never tires, it actually becomes more productive and efficient with use. Moreover, no one has yet been able to utilize more than a small fraction of the potential in his brain.

The ability to think creatively can be developed. One of the greatest aids to this worthwhile pursuit is the faculty of turning loose the tremendous thinking power that is latent in every one of us. This is the *use of our subconscious* minds.

9

Those of you who have learned to tap this great human resource know its tremendous value. For those of you who have yet to experience the wonder of having the solution to a knotty problem reveal itself to you as you are shaving in the morning or at some other unheralded and unplanned moment, one of life's greatest thrills still lies ahead.

---

Remember above all that your superior is expecting you to bring him solutions—not problems.

---

My own first such experience took place early in my sales career with I.B.M., and before I had heard or read anything about the subconscious mind. I had sold my first installation of tabulating equipment to a textile firm in New Bedford—the Wamsutta Mills. I'm afraid that in my great anxiety to make that ice-breaking sale I oversold the customer rather shamefully. It wasn't until the machines were delivered and the installation of the accounting system was under way that I awoke to the fact that I had promised results that the machines were not designed to produce. I spent several anxious, then panic-stricken, days trying to make the equipment live up to my claims.

Finally, nearly at the end of my rope, and quite seriously wondering if I would be fired when Wamsutta learned the truth and the machines were sent back, I spent one whole evening at the New Bedford Hotel recapitulating and reviewing the elements of the problem. With no glimmer of an answer, I went to bed—exhausted and completely discouraged.

The next morning as I was sitting in the bathtub, the answers to my problem started to come to me as clearly as if they were being written on the tile wall around the tub. I jumped out and without bothering to dry myself hastily wrote down the procedure that had seemingly just popped into my mind.

Without wasting time on breakfast, I tore down to the Wamsutta office—punched up the cards needed to test the program and started up the machines. It worked exactly as I had visualized it and exactly the way the Wamsutta people wanted it!

Many years later I learned that this was a demonstration of my subconscious mind at work. I learned that it is best to feed the elements of a problem to your mind just before you retire. Then while you are in repose that night or perhaps after several nights, the solutions will come to you—almost like magic. And, what is much more important, the solutions will represent clearer and sounder thinking than you can usually produce with your everyday conscious mind. The old axiom of "Let's sleep on it" is based on this power, and I heartily recommend it to you as a valuable tool in your management kit.

Just a few other thoughts on creative ability. Be curious—ask questions—keep an open mind to the other fellow's ideas—and listen—by all means learn to listen!

Remember above all that your superior is expecting you to bring him solutions—not problems.

The second characteristic to be looked for is JUDGMENT. Webster defines this somewhat elusive quality as the "ability to judge justly or wisely, especially in matters affecting action." It is also described as "good sense." *Men who are destined for leadership must be men who can make sound and wise decisions.*

This sound-thinking qualification goes hand in hand with the previous creative thinking attribute. Sheer brilliance of innovation and invention can be disastrous without a counterbalance of common sense.

I had a superior early in my sales career who was quite famous throughout the company as a trainer of men. He had an impressive record of raw college graduates who had started under his tutelage and had become high producers and often good managers in a remarkably short time. A pet aversion of his was people who would not use their heads.

Instead of solving our problems for us when we would come running into his office with some headache that had us licked, he would tell us to turn around and read out loud the sign tacked above his door. This sign read, "AS A LAST RESORT USE COMMON SENSE."

There have been countless examples of great, earth-shaking fiascos that came about because someone in a key position failed to use good judgment—forgot the fundamentals of simple common sense.

The inventor of the modern self-service store, Clarence Saunders, fell into this trap not many years ago. After his spectacular success with the Piggly Wiggly Stores, forerunners of all of today's supermarkets, he went overboard for the completely automatic grocery store.

He called it the Keydoozle Store. His dream store worked something like this. As the customer entered, he was handed a little metal gadget that looked something like a pistol. The merchandise was racked around the store on display as single units each behind a glass panel. Under each item there was a keyhole-like aperture into which the customer poked his pistol-like key. He would pull the trigger once for each item he wanted.

This action would record on a punched tape the price of his purchase and set up the behind store machinery to assemble his order on a conveyor belt. By the time he had made his selections and would walk to the cashier who would run the tape from his hand machine through a computer, the entire order would be assembled and boxed and waiting for him in the front of the store.

Quite an idea! No pushing carts around a block-sized amphitheatre. Space would be conserved. Time would not be wasted waiting in line to check out. Labor would be saved because hard-to-maintain mass displays would be eliminated. In principle it was great, but the idea was a huge flop. Why? It took more maintenance men to keep all the machinery running than any store operator could afford, and even then it would invariably break down on Fridays or Saturdays during the heaviest shopping hours. The chaos that resulted made it a joke.

---

This sign read, "AS A LAST RESORT USE COMMON SENSE."

---

Is judgment something people are born with? I think not. I go along with an old college professor of mine who once lectured my class on how to develop judgment. It was his advice that we should take every opportunity that presented itself to practice and exercise our judgment. He recommended that we study public issues currently under discussion in Washington. Read all we could about them. Read the commentators' and columnists' opinions, but reserve our decision until we had gotten both or all sides of the argument. Then carefully weighing the evidence, the facts and opinions that we had uncovered, we should make up our minds on the issue. We should write down our considered position on the matter. Later, when time had finally brought the right answer to light, as it nearly always does, we should compare our position with what turned out to be right. "This practice, if started early enough in life, and continued for as long as you live, will develop our wisdom without paying the price of expensive mistakes," my professor said. I didn't follow his advice for very long, but I wish I had.

A final thought: on this matter of sagacity. A negative, fault-finding approach is not a substitute for judgment. Every new idea can be killed at its birth by a superior who can see nothing but the reasons why something won't work. Enthusiasm and a positive attitude are an important part of the balance required of a leader whose judgment and decision making activities will be tested from the day he assumes important managerial responsibility.

The third qualification that seems to be generally considered essential in a manager is ADMINISTRATIVE SKILL.

The good executive must be able to foresee the needs of his operation — to forecast its requirements in men, in materials, in money, and in time. He must have the talent to resolve these needs into a practical and understandable program. Modern day business must have *men who can plan.*

This is the unglamorous side to the manager's job. It requires a painstaking concern over a multitude of details; it requires more than a little "i" dotting and "t" crossing; it requires concentration and vigilance — and, above all, it requires an orderliness of mind and method. In my opinion it is an area where many otherwise top executives are the weakest. In the pressure and pace of daily operating affairs, it becomes a problem for many to find time for the planning and thinking out of the projects that have been created and decided upon by our fertile minded and decisive executive types. This failure can be, and often is, the graveyard of many worthwhile ideas with great subsequent waste of dollars and hours.

Our forefathers may have been able to operate on the "opportunistic" basis. The growth of our economy, the unlimited natural resources, and the vast untapped markets permitted and actually, in many cases, called for the fast-moving, crapshooting business swashbuckler.

Times have changed. The difficulty of creating capital wealth because of the tax structure and the competitive complexion of our current economy does not permit much leeway for such waste of either money or time.

As I said, one of the outward manifestations of this quality is orderliness. The way a man marshals his thoughts, the way he presents his arguments, the way he plans his own life, the way he keeps his working quarters — these are signs of an orderly mind — or lack of it.

Omitting the infrequent, unforeseeable emergency that can throw a curve into any of our personal lives, the good manager lives within his income, and finds ways in spite of today's inflated living costs to protect the financial security of himself and his family, to provide for their health and well-being and to spare himself the mental anguish of not being able to make ends meet. This calls for a real measure of sacrifice in most cases, and a family decision to deny itself many of the material enticements with which our society abounds.

The fourth quality that the Columbia seminar felt was important was a POSITIVE ATTITUDE. A manager must be optimistic—he must radiate confidence and enthusiasm. The business world of today and tomorrow wants leaders *who can inspire.*

---

This failure [to plan] can be, and often is, the graveyard of many worthwhile ideas with great subsequent waste of dollars and hours.

---

This positive approach cannot be a manufactured or an artificial one. It must not be merely a pose—it must be sincere and deeply felt. A company, an operation within a company, a project within an operation, must be led by a manager who has an all-abiding faith in his work and objectives. This over-riding belief is usually the secret weapon against the discouragement of difficulties and problems.

The behavior of the manager, his facial expressions, even the droop of his shoulders are all watched closely by the rank and file of employees. A discouraged and despondent executive can send a hundred or more employees' morale into the gutter. A worried looking boss can touch off a wave of fear rolling throughout an organization that starts a chain of resignations among the best people and work slowdown among nearly all of them.

You can properly ask how does a man go about developing this positive, optimistic attitude. With the problems of government regulations, taxation, cutthroat competition, strikes, personnel failures besetting him daily, most modern managers face enough grief to cause them to commit suicide once a week. How do some men develop the ability to relax in the midst of constant pressure and trouble?

An important key to the answer to this question is health. Vigorously good health is a must if a manager is going to keep up with the pace demanded by managerial responsibility. This means proper eating habits, care against overindulgence in smoking, drinking and eating, adequate rest and exercise. A sick or half-sick manager is a real handicap to a company.

All work and no play usually produces a tense and grim executive. Hobbies and outside interests actually result in a man having greater capacity and vigor in his professional role. Vacations are necessary—and no company should permit its key executives to get so swamped that they feel guilty for taking time off.

It is not easy to develop this ability to stay undisturbed when things around you are going wrong. The jokes about the ulcer incidence among business managers is no joke. Our country's consumption of aspirin is a national disgrace.

Another important weapon against worry and pessimism is FAITH—faith in the people to whom you have assigned an important job, faith in yourself, faith in God. People more often than not live up to the faith that they know you have in them. You yourself will more often than not do a good job if you believe you can.

There is a little prayer that could be labeled "The Manager's Prayer" that goes something like this:

"Oh Lord, give me the serenity to accept with grace those things I cannot change,

The courage to work and fight for those I can,

And the wisdom to know the difference."

---

A discouraged and despondent executive can send a hundred or more employees' morale into the gutter. A worried looking boss can touch off a wave of fear rolling throughout an organization.

---

In this same vein, I should like to tell you of an experience that I had during the early days of the company. It happened in the winter of 1947. Our problems had become seemingly insurmountable. The new "mousetrap" we had brought to the world had laid a giant egg—nobody, *but nobody*, was beating a path to our doorstep. Working capital had fallen to a zero level, sales were nonexistent, the frozen food industry generally was on the verge of going broke. As the saying goes, "When the tide goes out, the rocks begin to show." Everywhere I looked there were rocks!

At this juncture I decided to attend the Canners Convention in Atlantic City. This was a mistake. My gloom was merely an echo of the gloom I found on all sides down there. Misery loves company and I found a plethora of company that year on the boardwalk.

My stomach began to ache—I worried about the stock we had sold to the public—I worried about the employees we had wheedled away from secure, well-paying jobs. I went to sleep— eventually—at night worrying—I woke up early in the morning worrying—I even worried about the sleep I was losing.

My family lived in Atlantic City so I was staying with them. Besides, it saved the hotel expense which we could ill afford. One day near the end of the convention, I was asked by my father if I would like to accompany him to a Rotary Club lunch. I had little stomach for this but I knew Dad would feel hurt if I refused.

My unhappiness with the decision to go to the lunch deepened when I saw that the speaker was to be a minister of the gospel. My gloom was so abject that I was in no mood for a sermon. This minister was Dr. Norman Vincent Peale, who I soon found out was and is one of America's most inspirational and accomplished speakers. Dr. Peale announced that his subject would be "Tension—the Disease that is Destroying the American Businessman."

From the first words he uttered it was as though he were talking only to me. I knew I was the tensest man in the audience. It was a great speech and one that he has told and retold all over this country. The formula he gave for relaxing and putting aside worry I would like to repeat.

First, you relax physically. This is done by stretching out in bed or in a comfortable chair. Then you methodically and carefully concentrate on relaxing each part of your body. Start with your scalp, then your face, your neck, your shoulders and so on down until you are as loose as a pan of ashes.

Second step—you relax your mind. You recall a pleasant incident in your life—a vacation, your honeymoon, a play, a book, anything that brings back into your mind's eye a pleasant scene.

Then finally, you relax your soul. This for most of us businessmen is a little tougher. But it can be done by renewing your faith in the Lord. You get right with God. You check your fears and worries with Him. He can handle them much better than you can. You do this in prayer. If you know no other prayer, the age-old children's one will do quite well, "Now I lay me down to sleep, I pray the Lord my soul to keep."

The first thing you know you'll be fast asleep. I know because in desperation I tried it out that very night. I heard Dr. Peale tell about it. It not only worked but I awoke the next morning refreshed and renewed and convinced we would work out of our jam some way. We did.

The job of inspiring others also involves some important mechanical skills. You want men who can talk well, men who can write well, men who can be understood, men who can sell people on doing what they want them to do.

Some people have these skills quite naturally—most have to develop them painfully and laboriously. How? By practice, practice and more practice. This is why public speaking courses are desirable for an aspiring manager. He should also strive to excel in clear, concise written expression. A large measure of his success will depend on his ability to communicate.

The fifth quality to be sought is COURAGE. Managers must be *men who will gamble*—not gamble in the Monte Carlo, Churchill Downs or crapshooting sense of the word. Business is a matter of taking a risk and quite often the magnitude of the risk is a measure of the possible gain—or loss.

In nearly every business decision someone must have the courage to take positive action without having in hand *all* of the facts and data necessary to make that decision risk-free. To wait for all of the necessary information can mean missing an opportunity, can mean a more aggressive competitor will take the important initiative, can mean a timing failure. Timing in business affairs is vital. So usually someone, a manager with courage, must stick his neck out and decide to do something—now!

It takes courage to delegate. To give a subordinate the authority to perform a function, to stand aside and let him make a decision—a decision that may turn out to be wrong—takes valor. It is a fundamental precept of business management that although the work load may be distributed down the line and many decisions may and should be made down the line, the final responsibility for the success of an operation cannot be delegated. The results of a departmental decision cannot be ducked by the department head; the performance of a division is the responsibility of a division vice president; the deeds and performance, or lack of it, of every individual in a company is the responsibility of the president. *A manager can never abdicate this responsibility.*

---

Timing in business affairs is vital. So usually someone, a manager with courage, must stick his neck out and decide to do something—now!

---

Since it is a well understood code that a manager must take the blame for the mistakes of his organization—yet at the same time pass on the credit for its success—it defies a man's natural instincts not to review and approve every decision within his jurisdiction. When this happens you have no true delegation. One of the hardest lessons for a manager to learn is to learn to "let go."

The courage to delegate is particularly strained when the person to whom the job is delegated happens to be young or relatively inexperienced. I have always liked American Brake Shoe's William Given's term *"The Freedom to Fail"* as a basic management principle in this matter. Men will not take risks and make decisions if they find mistakes mean dismissal. The climate of a company, set by its top management, must allow for failures in decision-making if there is to be a development of managerial ability within the organization. We learn far more by our errors than our successes, but it takes a courageous executive to encourage this freedom.

It takes courage to be tough—to say "no" to requests that come daily to a manager's desk. It's much pleasanter to acquiesce and to be a good guy. But with every important executive position goes the unpleasant task of being a wet blanket when the good of the organization is involved.

It takes courage to ask your superior for advice. Many executives have the idea that, once given a responsibility, it will be viewed as a sign of weakness if they admit they are stumped when they are. It always takes courage for a man in an authoritative position to say "I don't know."

It takes courage to disagree with a superior. There has been a lot written and even more said about the undesirability of the "Yes" man. Nevertheless, it takes real guts sometimes for a man to say "Boss, I think you are wrong—Sir!" It takes even more guts for a manager to take action without a precedent or company policy to back him up.

When a manager is given responsibility it is not for him to complain or alibi. Nor can he wait for a decree from above when immediate action is called for.

If the action which his best judgment tells him should be taken is one that is expressly forbidden by policy or instruction from higher management, then the executive should try to get clearance for a change of the policy. When there is not enough time for the clearance to come through, he has to take action and explain or defend it afterward.

A manager is supposed to get things done—this often takes real pluck.

Larry Appley, President of the American Management Association, in one of his recent bulletins said: "A principle for the propagation of the Management Species might run as follows: *to blend with one's environment may earn survival; to oppose it risks extermination; to control and redirect it ensures progress.*"

The sixth and final quality that I am going to talk about is CHARACTER. Managers must be *men of high integrity.* The quality of integrity—the honesty, sincerity, the moral posture of a top executive must be unquestionable. This is a common ingredient of all real leaders. They may have the previously discussed five characteristics in greater or lesser degree—on this quality there can be no compromise.

Integrity manifests itself in many ways—some quite subtle, I think.

---

When a manager is given responsibility it is not for him to complain or alibi. Nor can he wait for a decree from above when immediate action is called for.

---

Leaders of integrity have humility. President Eisenhower, probably the greatest leader of men in our time, demonstrated this quality the night that he was elected President of the United States. Many of you will remember his words as he stood before his deliriously happy campaign workers, having achieved the top accolade of American life—"We should always take our jobs seriously but never ourselves."

Arrogant leaders are short-lived. Arrogant managers may survive because they own the business or have their boards of directors buffaloed. But their companies never attain their full potential because people cannot feel loyalty to arrogance. As Clarence Frances once said "You can never buy an employee's loyalty—this you have to earn."

On this same subject Disraeli wisely remarked "Every man has the right to be conceited—until he is successful." The success of every manager is so tied up with the efforts of those around him that he cannot help but be humble if he is a man of integrity.

I race sailboats for a hobby—not well, I'm afraid, but enthusiastically. In sailboat racing we have a term known as "Corinthianism" that I believe illustrates this quality of integrity.

I had the occasion to demonstrate "Corinthianism" to my children one day a couple of summers ago. The Foxes' boat by some strange fluke rounded the first mark well ahead of the fleet. This was the first time this had ever happened. By an even stranger fluke (the breezes on Long Island Sound are famous for their flukiness) we approached the second mark with our competitors out of sight under our stern. At this exultant moment, father goofed. In rounding this mark the main boom jibed over and struck the buoy a resounding thump—we had fouled out.

---

Arrogant leaders are short-lived. Arrogant managers may survive because they own the business or have their boards of directors buffaloed. But their companies never attain their full potential because people cannot feel loyalty to arrogance.

---

I turned the boat and started home for our mooring. The children who were crewing nearly had apoplexy. "Holy cow, Dad, what are you doing—the finish line is in the other direction!" I explained we had committed a foul and were required to withdraw from the race. "But no one saw us—not even in their glasses could they have seen us!"

It took a little while to point out that since we knew we had committed a foul that was all that counted. *That is "Corinthianism."*

To be a manager a man must have the confidence of his superiors that his actions will be the same whether his deeds are subject to observation or not. *This is integrity.*

I think that the development of managers is of tremendous importance—important to our children and the generations to come—important to the free enterprise system—important to our country—important to our precious American way of life. It is a profession of which I am proud to be a member—junior grade. I would be supremely happy if either of my sons or both of them would choose to aspire to and could qualify as managers.

1956

# CHARLES D. TANDY
## 1918–1978

The man who built Radio Shack was Charles Tandy, a wily Texan who always had a cigar in hand. Tandy's beginnings were inauspicious: In 1935 he flunked out of Rice University. He subsequently received a degree from Texas Christian University, and from there it was a year at the Harvard Business School and then the navy and World War II. Meanwhile his father was selling leather soles and other shoemaking supplies to shoe-repair shops, with little prospects for company growth. But young Tandy discovered that leathercraft projects were popular with the injured soldiers recuperating in hospitals, and wrote to his dad that he should expand into leathercraft supplies. When Tandy left the navy in 1947, father and son organized the Tandy Leather Company, a mail-order/retail-store operation.

Business boomed and by the mid-1950s Tandy was looking to enter new fields. He first learned of Radio Shack in 1961, but it would be another two years before he bought the small electronics retail chain. When he took over Radio Shack, there were only nine outlets, and the company's net worth was a negative $2.5 million. Fifteen years later the chain included 7,000 stores, with an amazing 594 locations opening in 1976. Needless to say, Tandy liked to move boldly and quickly. Two key factors to success were imposing strict financial inventory controls, and creating weekly reports that kept him on top of district managers and red-flagged any drop in sales. He'd berate them, "If you can't get your job done in five days, do it in seven."

Tandy also believed that money was the best motivator of men, and he set up four different profit-sharing plans for store managers. Bonuses always outweighed salary; by 1976 a variety of profit-sharing plans had made more than fifty Radio Shack millionaires. To personally stay focused and undisturbed, Tandy kept an office away from the office, with no secretary. With all the success, Tandy still considered himself an entrepreneur, a key attitude to bring to the management of a company. In the following selection, he warns, "If the CEO is the only entrepreneur in the organization, his company is not likely to set any growth records."

# The CEO as Entrepreneur
## *Charles D. Tandy*

I should explain that I interpret entrepreneurship broadly. In my opinion, the term applies not only to those who organize and manage a company, taking the risk involved, but also to those who acquire ailing companies and reorganize them, taking the risk involved. Tandy Corporation has practiced entrepreneurship both ways—and several times—and has the scars to prove it. I know of no better way to tell you my ideas about entrepreneurism than to preface my comments with a brief recital of my company's life and hard times.

### THE ENTREPRENEURIAL SPIRIT YESTERDAY

Tandy Leather Company, genesis of the present corporation, began in Fort Worth, Texas, on a shoestring back in 1918. My father, David L. Tandy—from whom I inherited my enthusiasm for selling and merchandising—formed a partnership with Norton Hinckley to sell sole leather and other shoe repair supplies to shoe repair dealers in Texas. The firm weathered the Depression's storms, gathered strength, and established a firm base in the shoe findings business during the next 25 years.

My first contribution to the company came in the form of a letter to my father while I was on navy duty in Hawaii during World War II. I suggested to him that leathercraft might offer new possibilities for growth of the shoe findings business because leather was used in large quantities in army and navy hospital units and recreation centers. Leathercraft gave the men something useful to do; and their handiwork, in addition to being therapeutic, had genuine value.

When I returned home from the service in 1947, I obtained permission to operate the small leathercraft division which my father had formed at my suggestion. One of my early moves was the opening of the first two retail stores specializing exclusively in leathercraft. These two stores opened in 1950 in El Paso and San Antonio. I felt that if these two stores could survive, with the help of direct-mail-order sales, my formula for a leathercraft chain-store operation might be successful. The venture made a 100 percent return on investment the first year.

Our first catalog, only eight pages, was mailed in response to inquiries resulting from two-inch ads which we had placed in *Popular Science* magazine. Mail-order sales of leathercraft were a vital part of our formula.

In spite of the success of the two pilot stores, Mr. Hinckley, my father's partner, was not enthusiastic about the new leathercraft division; so, in 1950, my father and I worked out an agreement whereby we pursued the leathercraft business and Mr. Hinckley took over the shoe findings business.

From 1950 on, the successful formula of retail and mail-order stores supported by direct-mail advertising was expanded into today's chain of 236 leathercraft stores. The same basic formula has been applied to all of the specialty retailing divisions later operated by the corporation.

The do-it-yourself movement prompted by consumer goods shortages and high labor costs was gaining momentum in the early 1950s. The 15 leathercraft stores opened during the first two years were successful, and our management was gaining confidence. When a handicrafts company in East Orange, N.J., became available after it had suffered a series of financial setbacks, I seized the opportunity to buy it. American Handicrafts Company became Tandy Leather Company's first acquisition. This acquisition brought a broad line of do-it-yourself handicraft products, two established retail stores in the New York area, and useful knowledge of school and institutional markets.

We began promptly to make this sick company well and to move it forward. In 1953 we opened 16 additional retail stores, all following the basic formula of the first pilot stores.

Believing then and now that good people are as vital to an organization as good merchandise, and believing further that without proper incentives neither the people nor the company will grow, we made all of the managers of the first stores partners in the organization and cut them in on the capital investment and the profits. All of the employees in the company from file clerks up were invited to buy into the new companies as they were formed and to share in the profits.

The five-year period between 1950 and 1955 was an exciting period of growth and optimism for the Tandy organization. Sales reached $8,000,000 and earnings were $523,000—all generated from leased premises in 75 cities in the United States.

---

Good people are as vital to an organization as good merchandise . . . we made all of the managers of the first stores partners in the organization and cut them in on the capital investment and the profits.

---

To cope with the estate and management problems created by a successful closely-held company—then owned by over 100 stockholder-managers—we chose to sell the company rather than go to a public underwriting. In 1955, therefore, we sold the company to the American Hide and Leather Company of Boston, which was listed on the New York Stock Exchange. It had been in the tannery business for some 54 years but had fallen into serious financial difficulty, its annual sales having dropped from $17 million to $9 million in recent years. Terms of the sale provided options for the stockholders of our Tandy Leather Company to buy 46 percent of the shares of American Hide and Leather Company stock at $4 per share over a four-year period.

Earnings of the Tandy organization, applied to the deficit of our new parent company, erased the losses and provided new cash flow for an aggressive diversification program which its management felt was vital to growth. Disposing of the tanneries and changing the name to General American Industries to dramatize the new management concept, the company in 1956 embarked on a diversification program by acquiring three companies wholly unrelated to the leather-craft business and the assets of Tex Tan of Yoakum, Texas, engaged in manufacture and sale of finished "western" goods such as saddles, belts, billfolds, and purses. This Tex Tan acquisition, it later developed, was the wisest decision made in 1956.

The high hopes and excitement brought about by the merger of our Tandy Leather Company changed to frustration and despair between 1955 and 1958. It became apparent that of the five divisions in General American Industries only two — Tandy and Tex Tan — were profitable. This presented me with the toughest challenge I had faced to date. It made me furious to see the hard-earned profits of the Tandy and Tex Tan groups used to plug the losses of the other divisions instead of being applied to growth and expansion as originally planned. Management of the other groups would not, or could not, pursue the profit-oriented practices of the Tandy and Tex Tan groups. Thus began a struggle for control of the parent company.

I used all of my resources to raise money to purchase the 500,000 shares of stock that were included in the original merger agreement. All of the key personnel in the Tandy and Tex Tan groups lent their support. A nip-and-tuck proxy fight was imminent. Only weeks before the annual stockholders' meeting that would decide the fate of the enterprise, I learned of the existence of a stockholder in a foreign country who controlled a very large block of stock and was not clearly committed to the incumbent management or to our group. Both factions sent emissaries to Europe to lay the facts on the table before this key stockholder.

The day of the stockholders' meeting was one of enormous strain and anxiety. Proxies were counted. The owner of the critical block of stock, in a perfect display of neutrality, had abstained from voting. Our Tandy group obtained management control of General American Industries.

In 1960, we sold the last of the unprofitable divisions. This was the first and only year in which our organization showed a loss ($267,000) and a drop in sales, both resulting from the costly divestitures.

During the "clean-up" year of 1960, our company emerged with the management team, marketing direction, and operating objectives that exist today. In 1961, the company name was changed to Tandy Corporation; the corporate headquarters were moved to Fort Worth; I became president and chairman of the board; and our company name was listed on the New York Stock Exchange.

We concentrated our efforts on expanding the Tex Tan Division, which manufactured and sold saddlery, riding equipment, and other finished leather goods, and the Tandy Leather Division. We acquired Craftool Company, manufacturer of precision leather tools, and Clarke and Clarke, Limited, a leathercraft firm in Barrie, Ontario.

By 1961, we were operating 125 stores in 105 cities of the United States and Canada. We were on our way again.

In that year, we acquired several new companies to complement our line of products, including a manufacturer of leather sport and western clothing, and a manufacturer and retailer of needlecraft items. It was now possible to use the resources of one division to develop new products for another.

In 1962, the Tandy organization advanced money to

Cost Plus, a West Coast importer of decorator furnishings, gourmet foods, and unusual housewares from all over the world. The firm needed capital for expansion. We received distribution rights for the remainder of the United States and the use of the name.

Because the chain-store route had already been proved several times by Tandy Corporation as a rapid and profitable means of expansion, we established our first import store outside of California in Fort Worth, and during the following months we opened additional stores. The type of marketing used by Cost Plus—later named Pier 1 Imports—was fruitful and productive, but it required considerable continuing capital investment. By 1964, another one of our new acquisitions, Radio Shack, was beginning its vigorous expansion. The management of Tandy Corporation determined that this new acquisition offered a greater opportunity for early return on our limited capital, so we sold the Pier 1 operation to that division's executive group. Pier 1 continues to be successful today.

Our policy at Tandy has always been growth through reinvestment of profits. If an idea can't be proved effective within a reasonable period, we move on to something else.

## THE ENTREPRENEURIAL SPIRIT TODAY

In 1962, I became intrigued with the potential for rapid growth in the retail electronics industry. Tandy Corporation acquired Electronic Crafts in Fort Worth as a pilot operation. The initial success of this pilot operation prompted me to seek a company in the electronics field that had the needed resources and talents for successful expansion. In 1963, I found Radio Shack in Boston, a mail-order company that had started in the 1920s by selling to ham operators and electronic buffs. Radio Shack, with nine retail stores, was in very poor operating and financial condition. It had lost

$4,500,000 the year before. It owed more than $6,000,000 to a Boston bank and $2,000,000 to an insurance company. It had a net worth of minus $2,500,000.

---

If an idea can't be proved effective within a reasonable period, we move on to something else.

---

This acquisition, more than any other in our corporate history, required me, as Chief Executive Officer, to carry out my entrepreneurial risk-taking role to the hilt—unless I've mixed a metaphor there somewhere.

When I presented the proposed acquisition to my board of directors, they were unanimously opposed to the idea. Some of them apparently thought that I had cracked up.

"Why in the world should you take on this kind of problem?" they asked. "Nobody has ever been able to make one of these electronic firms profitable enough to amount to anything."

I replied, "I believe that I can turn the situation around."

"But we don't want you to do it," they said firmly.

Here was an entrepreneur's moment of truth. I couldn't understand why all of my directors couldn't see the potential in Radio Shack that I could see. I was one director out of nine, so I couldn't outvote them. Literally with tears in my eyes, and with some emotion, I told them that I was deadly serious about acquiring Radio Shack. I pointed out that many of the inside directors had been doing what they wanted to be doing, with one of them handling the accounting, another handling this or that.

"Now, I am going to do what I want to do. If I don't get an affirmative vote on this proposed acquisition, then I will sell every share of stock that I own in our corporation and will personally acquire Radio Shack on my own hook."

I wasn't trying to run a bluff. I felt that strongly about what I could see in Radio Shack and what I could do with it.

31

I was willing to gamble that it was something I could make into a viable, strong, and prosperous company.

When the directors realized that I was really this determined about acquiring Radio Shack, they changed their minds and voted unanimously for the acquisition.

In fiscal 1975—12 years after the acquisition—our Radio Shack Division operated 2,651 stores, did 68 percent of our corporation's $724,488,293 worth of business, and made 81 percent of total divisional income.

In those 12 years since 1963, we had made a number of major changes in the Radio Shack operation and had applied some of the merchandising techniques pioneered with Tandy Leather. Almost immediately, we reduced inventories through an aggressive direct-mail campaign to existing customers, concentrating our selling efforts on items with fast turnover and broad consumer appeal. We reduced the number of stock items from 40,000 to 2,500; at the same time, we tripled the turnover. We began requiring a 25 percent down payment and later cut out credit altogether. We insisted that buyers and merchandise men work constantly to develop new ideas for exclusive products and then buy properly so that our products would be competitive. When manufacturers in the United States were inadequate for this purpose, we developed resources abroad. We expanded retail stores rapidly. Two years after we had assumed leadership, Radio Shack was profitable and was in sound financial condition with sales approaching $20 million.

We decided to open Radio Shacks in Canada five years ago. We made profits there the second year. In 1973, we began European operations using the name Tandy International Electronics. By the end of fiscal 1975 we had more than 220 stores in Europe. We also launched Radio Shack in Australia in 1973, and had 67 stores operating there by the end of fiscal 1975.

Last year, we opened a Radio Shack either in this country or abroad at the rate of one per day, and we expect to continue this pace in the year ahead. In fact, in fiscal 1975, if you include our authorized sales centers—proprietor-owned stores in cities under 20,000 population—openings of Radio Shacks were at the rate of more than two per day.

We're going to put Radio Shack around the globe. We're going to have somebody selling our products down the Nile, down the Amazon, or wherever. We're not there yet, but that is our plan.

---

I don't believe in hanging on to operations which we can't run effectively. As many Chief Executive Officers and all football coaches have learned, many of them the hard way, you can't win 'em all.

---

I think that we can do this with Radio Shack because we already manufacture more than 30 percent of our merchandise, and this percentage is steadily increasing. We intend to duplicate what we achieved with Tandy Leather—that is, to manufacture practically everything that we sell. Our motives in expanding our manufacturing activities, aside from profits, are (1) to gain the skills in design and technology required to keep us in a position of leadership; (2) to achieve product exclusivity; and (3) to reduce dependence on external suppliers.

Although Radio Shack is the fastest horse in the Tandy corporate stable, we have a score of other horses that are running quite well—plus a couple which have come up lame in the back stretch.

As the emphasis of our operations became more and more retail, rather than mail-order, we began looking for an established retail organization to merge with our expanding system. This turned out to be a full-line department store and a chain of six junior department stores in Fort Worth.

We expanded the former into 3 suburban shopping centers around Forth Worth and the latter to 74 retail outlets in North Texas and Oklahoma. When we couldn't make the operation profitable after five years of expansion effort, we sold it and took our losses.

I don't believe in hanging on to operations which we can't run effectively. As many Chief Executive Officers and all football coaches have learned, many of them the hard way, you can't win 'em all.

In the late 1960s and early 1970s, we acquired no fewer than 22 companies. Many of these companies are in businesses related to one or more of our established divisions and, where feasible, we have integrated them. We have expanded some of them into chains; have merged some of them with other divisions; and have liquidated some of them.

Our latest move is a plan to separate Tandy Corporation into three publicly held companies in order to provide more intensive and distinct management leadership of the three basic and diverse businesses in which we are engaged — consumer electronics, handicrafts, and leather products. Under the plan, now awaiting the necessary approvals by regulatory agencies, Tandy Corporation will carry on the consumer electronics (Radio Shack) operations as its sole business. The plan calls for the issuance to shareholders, in the form of a tax-free dividend, of the common stock of two new companies to be drawn from the handicrafts operations and from the leather products operations of the present corporation. It will provide shareholders in the future with three clearly defined investment vehicles, each with a simplified corporate structure and business direction.


## SOME OBSERVATIONS AND SUGGESTIONS

The most important element in our success is probably our people. Our executive and management people, for the most part, have been developed and promoted from within our organization. We have a motivation and career progress program which attracts and holds a particular type of individual—the type who delivers and expects to be paid for it. The program is simply this: Each profit center manager and executive is compensated with a nominal salary and a bonus formula which can yield him a generous portion of the annual profits of his unit. Nearly one out of every five of our 20,000 employees receives an annual bonus.

> We keep our tables of organization simple, or forget about them altogether. In my opinion, many large corporations pay too much homage to organization charts and rely on them too much.

This program has enabled us to build a management organization of seasoned, profit-oriented people who respond to the challenge of individual progress in their personal incomes and in their careers. We have never needed employment contracts or stock option programs or retirement plans with our kind of people. We do encourage ownership of company stock through our contributory Tandy Employees Investment Plan; and today, our employees own more than 20 percent of the outstanding stock of the company and will probably own an even higher percentage in the years ahead.

We run our divisions and subsidiaries with a light corporate touch, giving the presidents and managers both authority and responsibility, pegging their bonuses to their performance. This practice identifies and encourages entrepreneurship, which is basic to our American free-enterprise system.

Our corporate president earned the post primarily by bringing the three Tandy companies for which he was responsible from a $250,000 loss on sales of $12.6 million in fiscal 1970 to a $4 million profit on sales of about $50 million in fiscal 1974.

We keep our tables of organization simple, or forget about them altogether. In my opinion, many large corporations pay too much homage to organization charts and rely on them too much. A corporation with an informal and flexible organizational setup is better able to take advantage of opportunities that come along, and can take prompt action when problems arise.

Running a corporation in today's economic climate, buffeted simultaneously by inflation and recession—and keeping the corporation profitable and growing—is a full-time job for a CEO. At the same time, all CEOs are being called upon to shoulder a large part of the growing responsibilities of corporations with respect to employees, shareholders, consumers, environmentalists, minorities, bankers, investors, the press, the community, Congress, endless government agencies, and even foreign governments. I let my associates handle quite a bit of this. Granted, some external matters you have to do yourself, simply because you're the top guy. But I never forget that the corporate woods are full of companies in trouble because the CEO was not minding the store.

It goes without saying—but I'll say it anyway—a successful entrepreneur must have the courage of his convictions.

I like the title and much of the content of a recent book on entrepreneurship by Joseph Mancuso. He titled the book *Fun and Guts** —which may be overdoing things a bit—but he wanted to make the point that an entrepreneur's philosophy

---

* Mancuso, Joseph; *Fun and Guts*; Reading, Mass.: Addison-Wesley Publishing Company; 1973.

should be a cross between "fun and games" and "blood and guts." Mancuso claims that entrepreneurs are born, not made, and that you can spot them across a room. They will be the persons "talking about doubling sales and earnings, or attracting new capital, or a five-year growth program." They "would rather discuss raising capital than girls, rather talk of a new product, service, or marketing technique than eat." He cites energy as the one coefficient of entrepreneurial success. "You may have all of the ambition in the world, gobs of capital, a gambling man's soul, and business degrees covering the entire wall, but if you aren't virtually a human dynamo, forget it."

In my opinion, shared by Mancuso, entrepreneurs are individualistic and optimistic, and they prefer the 3-to-1 shot to the odds-on favorite or the horse listed at 20 to 1.

---

It goes without saying—but I'll say it anyway—
a successful entrepreneur must have the
courage of his convictions.

---

Some CEOs own all or a large piece of their companies. They risk their own money, and they are a very special brand of entrepreneur. We need more of them.

But some of our most important CEO entrepreneurs today are cast in the role of "professional manager." They may own a share of the company, and that share may even be significant for them in a personal financial sense; but the ownership share of these CEOs is insignificant in relation to the total ownership, which often is in public or institutional hands. These men are important in light of the vast portion of industrial enterprise which they shape. They, too, must have the courage of their convictions. Unfortunately, the list of these CEO-entrepreneurs is too short.

## CONCLUSION

And, now, for some closing thoughts.

Aside from the CEO, who needs the entrepreneurial spirit? We feel that in our company, line management must be made up of entrepreneurs. Even staff managers should possess a high degree of entrepreneurship to bring creativity to their assignments and to work effectively with line management.

Can the CEO cultivate entrepreneurship in an organization? Or does entrepreneurship necessarily depend on one man? "Yes" to the first question; "no" to the second. The best way to cultivate entrepreneurship is to preach, practice, appreciate, and reward it when it is demonstrated. If the CEO is the only entrepreneur in the organization, his company is not likely to set any growth records.

Where does the board of directors fit into the entrepreneurial picture? Right in the middle. There is hardly any way that a CEO can exercise much entrepreneurism unless his directors—at least a majority of them—give him the authority and the necessary support. Ideally, most of them will be entrepreneurs themselves.

---

Aside from the CEO, who needs the entrepreneurial spirit? We feel that in our company, line management must be made up of entrepreneurs.

---

I would like to express one last thought and one hope. The thought is rather old-fashioned, but I remember that when our forefathers settled this country, nobody took them by the hand. If they had a good crop, it was theirs; if they had a bad one, it was tough. That is exactly how we try to run our company and treat our people, which is a lot different from the way most large companies are run.

My hope is that the good which the Tandy team has accomplished with its entrepreneurial efforts will be an encouraging and enlightening example to others, particularly those outside the field of business activity, whose understanding of the free-enterprise system needs to be encouraged and enlightened.

1976

During a 1937 reorganization, Edouard Muller was appointed president and chairman of Nestle, one of the largest food companies in the world. The enterprise had been founded in 1867 by Henri Nestle, who had developed a cow's milk food for infants, and who later launched a condensed milk product. So, while today Nestle is best known in the United States for its chocolate, an area the company entered in the early 1900s, it actually built itself upon milk products. After Muller went to work for Nestle, one of his first big assignments was, at age 26, to market its products in Turkey. To encourage the consumption of chocolate, one of his highly successful innovations was to work with cinema owners in a promotion in which chocolate candy bar wrappers could be used for admission.

The year after the innovative Muller took the reins, the company launched Nescafe, the instant coffee, which was a result of eight years of research. Several years later Nestea, a powdered tea, hit the shelves. While successful products were introduced on his watch, Muller had the unfortunate task of guiding Nestle through World War II, which involved fending off the Nazis, and trying to manufacture products with limited or rationed resources. On the other hand, the conflict generated huge demand for powdered milk and Nescafe, which fueled revenues. Muller reflected, "These terrible years of war, with their manifold and far-reaching problems, have amply demonstrated the need for and the value of individual personality combined with wholehearted cooperation in many spheres." Indeed, Nestle expanded operations in South America, tripled its powdered milk production, and positioned itself to meet increased global demand once the war was over.

Muller, who was characterized as an energetic globe-trotter, described the qualities needed for management and managers in *Personality in Business*. He declared, "If a chief ever becomes afraid of encouraging his associates to be as good as, or better than himself, he is lost as a constructive force. His whole personality changes and, instead of thinking broadly and objectively, he tends to become egotistical, dictatorial and narrow-minded."

# Personality in Business
## *Edouard Muller*

I often think that one disadvantage of a large business—and in our own field I believe we can safely claim that distinction—is that the Chief tends more and more to lose personal contact with many of his associates. This is true even of large national companies and, in the case of an international concern such as ours, the gulf is widened by geography.

I have always been a great believer in the value of close personal contact in our business, from top to bottom. This is the best way, indeed the only way, to get to know one's collaborators properly; to appreciate their true worth and to discover those with the necessary personality and initiative for encouragement and promotion.

Every enterprise, great or small, is characterised by the personalities of those who direct it and participate in its affairs. Its development, progress and reputation are in their hands. Therefore, if I were asked what I consider to be the most important individual attribute in business, I think I should put Personality at the head of my list. The kind of personality which seeks to keep a business on a high level; the kind of personality which makes an executive exact the utmost from himself before he demands it of others and, by his own actions, sets an example for all his colleagues.

We are inclined to forget occasionally that personalities in every organization can be, and are, judged from several viewpoints. The "Boss" has to judge those under him from his position as head of affairs. On the other hand, his collaborators may have quite a different perspective, especially where they themselves are concerned. Moreover, they usually have some very definite views about the Chief himself and others senior in rank. It behooves all executives therefore, in every capacity, to see to it that these judgments or opinions—provided they are unbiased—mainly reflect their own good qualities and, to that end, the example they set day by day is worth far more than an occasional lecture.

Again, every business has very important relationships with people outside its own environment, sometimes as buyer, sometimes as seller. None of us can afford to ignore the impressions and judgments formed by these outside sources—indeed it is always interesting and frequently as illuminating to know them as it is to know the opinions of those within the organization.

---

If I were asked what I consider to be the most important individual attribute in business, I think I should put Personality at the head of my list.

---

By this I do not mean that we should depend too much on the views and opinions of others. Those who carry the responsibility must, in the end, make decisions according to the best of their own ability but they should not necessarily presume that these decisions cannot be improved. On the contrary, I think all of us should be happy and proud when we have assistants around us who have the courage of their own convictions, or to have clients who will express divergent views openly and without rancor.

I am sure that most of us will be able to recall instances when such opinions or ideas, given without thought of personal prestige, have resulted in useful changes being made in some plan or program and how, by this means, new and valuable personalities have been uncovered.

There are two sides to every business, the human and the material. In my experience the best achievement is possible only when both are interwoven into one harmonious whole. In a small company where the Chief and his managers and staff are in close daily contact, this objective is more easily attained than in a larger concern which must be split up into several parts. Nevertheless, this does not alter the fundamental role of the Chief. He still has to carry the ultimate responsibility for everything that happens in the business — good or bad — but he must adopt different methods to ensure maximum harmony and cooperation.

First he must choose efficient deputies to whom he can delegate responsibility. This tends to limit his personal contact to his closest collaborators and, more and more, he must depend upon them to carry out the broader principles and policies without losing their individual initiative or creative ability.

In our case, the problem is even more complex as the divisions or subdivisions are not only internal or departmental but external through associated companies, which themselves are frequently departmentalized. Under these circumstances it is essential that each department or section should be directed uniformly to some extent, so that each can work smoothly with the other wherever or whenever this becomes necessary. However, I feel this merely emphasizes the importance of personality as, if the wrong type of individual is chosen for a key position anywhere along the line, the effect can be harmful to the whole as well as to the part immediately concerned.

A good Chief, whether he be head of a company, division, department or section should be master of his own job and always eager to widen his knowledge. He should strive to have the best possible assistants around him and be both able and willing to give them every help and encouragement to progress. If a Chief ever becomes afraid of encouraging his associates to be as good as, or better than himself, he is lost as a constructive force. His whole personality changes and, instead of thinking broadly and objectively, he tends to become egotistical, dictatorial and narrow-minded. Pleasure in work, in initiative and the acceptance of greater responsibility by others disappears and the development of their personality value is retarded if not halted entirely.

There is nothing worse for any business, in my opinion, than the individual who can see no point of view except his own. Such personalities invariably suffer from a marked preoccupation with personal prestige. They cannot assimilate the ideas and knowledge of others; they lose contact with their associates and fail to take advantage of the initiative shown by others. I would ask every leader in our concern, and those who aspire to lead in the future, to avoid that mentality as one would the plague, since it leads only to trouble and we have enough of that commodity to handle without creating more of it ourselves.

---

A good Chief, whether he be head of a company, division, department or section should be master of his own job and always eager to widen his knowledge.

---

As I have said before, every enterprise is characterized by the personalities of those who direct its affairs. For good or ill they determine its prevailing tone and spirit and this applies equally to any part as well as to the whole. No Chief, in any capacity, should ever forget this and he should be ready always to accept responsibility for whatever goes on in his section, division or company. Where ideas or initiative are lacking, where little foresight is shown in planning ahead or in the provision of competent understudies to himself, the fault is his and be must be big enough to acknowledge it.

It is really astonishing how many excuses some men can find when things go wrong just to avoid acknowledging that they have made a mistake. Any business in which this mentality prevails is in a sorry plight. We are all human and we all make mistakes sometimes. If the leading personality is strong enough to admit that and always act unselfishly, in the best interests of the group, his subordinates will be quick to recognize this trait and strive to emulate his example in their own spheres. It is hardly necessary for me to add that they will be just as quick to recognize the opposite and will be equally liable to react accordingly.

Of course in a large business one must have good organization for, without this, cooperation is impossible. This brings me to a really significant point, as development of individual personality and organization are often mutually antagonistic. The one we are anxious to encourage but we cannot dispense with the other without causing confusion and disorder.

---

There is nothing worse for any business, in my opinion, than the individual who can see no point of view except his own.

---

Obviously no section or division of any business can operate quite independently, as in that way lies chaos. We must have certain plans, principles and general policies to which all subscribe if unified management is to be maintained and I am sure you will agree that can be assured only through the willing and thoughtful cooperation of all, chiefs and staff alike, whatever the position they hold or the type of work they do. In brief, through the fullest possible development of the human personalities on which the ultimate success or failure of these plans and policies depend.

At the same time we should never regard organization as an end in itself, only a means to an end. Organization is a dead thing and without the vital spark of human initiative—which stems from personality—it can impede progress and may gradually stifle the creative spirit on which all progress depends. We must see to it therefore, all of us, that our own organization, while strong enough to maintain important fundamentals, is always kept flexible and never allowed to become so rigid that our collaborators function as automatons.

> Let us resolve to discard egoism, ideas of personal prestige and strive instead to cultivate the kind of personality which will breed mutual trust and appreciation.

These terrible years of war, with their manifold and far-reaching problems, have amply demonstrated the need for and the value of individual personality combined with wholehearted cooperation in many spheres. Without attempting to prophesy I believe that many of our problems in the postwar years may be even greater than now, problems which will demand these same attributes as never before.

I feel, therefore, that those who now carry the responsibilities—and here I am thinking principally of the senior executives—should concentrate even more than usual on developing eventual successors. As I see it, it is up to them to pass on the benefit of their wider experience of men and methods to the younger generation; to build soundly and wisely now and endeavor to bridge the current difficulties in such a way that, when the time comes, the newcomers can go forward confidently to new horizons.

This is the season of goodwill and good resolutions. As a final message, therefore, I would say, let us all, irrespective of rank, resolve to work henceforth for the common good. Let us resolve to discard egoism, ideas of personal prestige and amour propre and strive instead to cultivate the kind of personality which will breed mutual trust and appreciation. I am sure that, with this as our goal, and if we all try hard enough, we can find sufficient talent within the ranks of our great Company to provide men and women of outstanding personality, initiative and ability, who will ensure its success in the future as others have done in the past.

1945

# Robert Galvin
## 1922–

Back in 1940, Robert Galvin quit college and joined his father's business as a humble stock clerk. The company: Motorola, whose name Paul Galvin had created in 1930 by combining "motor" with "Victrola" (phonograph), because he was manufacturing the first commercially successful car radios. As early as 1948, Robert was pushing his father to go into transistors, which Bell Labs had just invented. Galvin did, and once Robert assumed the helm in 1956, he continued to pursue leading-edge technology. Some 40 years later he witnessed the opening of the company's Florida pager plant, where the manufacturing was handled by robots. That year Motorola won the first Malcolm Baldridge National Quality Award.

Over the years, competition, especially with Japanese firms, was fierce. To prevail, Galvin knew he had to rely on every employee: "Just as thousands of Egyptian laborers—and not their pharaohs—built the pyramids, so do the bench technologists build whatever there is for us to 'manage.' Conversely, failure results from holding these people back." Galvin didn't supress his "laborers"; instead, feedback and two-way communication were crucial. "Communication does not start with what 'I' have to say," he wrote in 1996. "Rather, it starts with the other person. It starts with what I hear."

To keep ahead of the competition, Galvin required his R&D people to create detailed "technology road maps," which charted the potential of products ten years into the future. These maps directed them to discontinue consumer products such as televisions in the mid-1970s. Motorola shifted its focus to the semiconductor business and advanced electronics. Galvin calls such changes *self-renewal*. "Renewal is a great word," he says. "It is the driving thrust of our corporation. It comes trippingly off the tongues of our people." In terms of his own personal development, Galvin has found that teaching others helps him learn. Knowledge is obviously important in making management decisions; however, in the following selection, Galvin cautions that "we can overwhelm ourselves with too much knowledge on most subjects."

# Managing Knowledge toward Wisdom
## *Robert Galvin*

T he challenge of managing knowledge portends that this is the "age of the mind." Advancing societies have matured through many ages. Centuries ago, the "age of the crafts." More recently, the "age of industry." Now, the "age of the mind." Of course, crafts will continue to fill important roles. Industry will always be essential. And the imaginative and sensible use of the mind has been evident through all ages. But the "age of the mind" is ever more promising and demanding.

Tools have keyed development through each Age. Early tools enhanced the craftsman and mechanized tools and instruments drove industry. Information processing hardware, software and communications are the new tools for further managing knowledge and intellectual capital and are a worthy challenge to manage unto themselves in this the "age of the mind." But the mastery of the use of these tools, as vital and achieving as it is becoming, is more the form than the substance of the ultimate wisdom that we seek from managing knowledge and intellectual capital.

A few months ago, I was privileged to speak to a scholarly audience on the subject of knowledge. The idiom *lifelong learning* was referenced in early presentations. I elected to play on words. "Lifelong learning is important," I said, "but it implies a ponderous pace suggesting we have abundant years to achieve learning. Obviously that was not intended. But our expectation should be timely mastery, again and again."

How best do we master? Many of us think that teaching is the best of the learning processes. In fact, I played on those words also, referring to the outmoded phrasing "I'll learn you a lesson," wherein the term *learn* was employed as the synonym for the word *teach*. Indeed, we learn better by teaching and we must teach others to do similarly.

---

How could our business be truly competitive if the Chief Executive Officer of any company with whom we competed was smarter than I was?

---

I come to this challenging issue of striving to master the managing of knowledge as a business person. The challenge of doing so is no more nor less in business than other sophisticated fields. It is simply one of the fields wherein the worth and degree of mastery is substantially measurable as the business thinker and doer personally practices and applies development principles both timely and consistently. This paper suggests a dozen rewarding developmental endeavors.

## TRAINING FOR SUCCESS

Years ago business was faced again with one of those periods of struggle to improve competitive competence. In raising the question to myself, (How can we be more competitive?), I went through the conventional business analysis questions of what function and what cost we could modify in order to make our institution more competitive. Those conventional questions and answers were insufficiently satisfying. Ultimately I began to think in athletic analogies: I am a competitor. At my modest athletic ability I have competed in tennis and in downhill racing. I didn't always win. I realized for the most part, those who were superior to me were better trained.

The thought pattern was readily transferable to business. How could our business be truly competitive if the Chief Executive Officer of any company with whom we competed was smarter than I was? How could we compete if the President of another competitor was more talented than ours? As I reviewed the responsibility of our people, it became obvious that in order to be competitive, we had to be superior counterpart to counterpart.

When I took this thesis to my senior associates, they readily agreed that it would be difficult if I wasn't as capable as our brightest competitive chief executive officer and as a matter of fact they readily agreed I was not. So, yes, I was going to need a mentor. It was a little less appealing for them to imagine that they too would need a mentor to measure up to. They could see that this might evolve to where there would be major considerations of extensive training costs and time. Early on, they established their position that if there is to be an education program, we must find a way of doing it at no impact on budget and no demand on people's time. Obviously, an impossibility.

When we had discussed the subject sufficiently, I made the decision; we would have an extensive education and training program. I was convinced that we could train in sequences and on subjects of timely utility that wouldn't actually cost us because our improved talents would save us other operating expenses and gain us other business benefits virtually contemporaneous to the training. Thus was born the intention and ultimately the execution of an expansive worldwide education program to impart knowledge by Motorola University. The managing of knowledge inescapably involves the process of adding to knowledge in order to employ it.

## CREATIVITY: A VOCATIONAL SKILL

Business knowledge is used frequently to make decisions. Most managers presume that their major responsibility is to make decisions. Deciding is an act of judgment. Judging is one of two key mental processes. The other is creativity.

Early on, I developed a curiosity about creativity. Others probably have had experience such as I had in school and college where a teacher would assign a creative theme for homework. I recall asking those teachers for an explanation as to how one goes about generating the creative ingredient to give the theme its substance? Universally, I would be finessed by such comments as "just start to work on it, the light will go on, in the middle of the night an idea may pop into your mental processes, note it so you don't forget it by morning. Ideas just come." Such comments were hardly helpful.

I continued to harbor my curiosity. In my middle twenties, I came upon a newspaper advertisement headline. "Buy this book and you can make yourself creative." You can imagine that my initial reaction was that this was a come-on. But when I read further that the book *Your Creative Power* was written by a distinguished professional with an impeccable reputation, Alex Osborn, then the head of one of the more respected American advertising agencies, I knew he could not risk his and his firm's reputation. So I bought the book, devoured its 300 pages because it was entertaining and instructive, and distilled 13 integrated steps of thinking creatively. I memorized them and practiced them with my associates and on my own. I discovered after a short period that I was coming up and people around me were caused to come up with more ideas than was our prior disposition. We were achieving a special mastery of sorts.

I came to understand that creativity, as a vocational skill, can be learned and taught. Specific guides, steps and principles readily generate ideas. I now avow that an institution like ours, when it fully dedicates itself to do so, can train the aggregate of our leader-thinkers, which means more than the majority of our people, to being many times more creative than we are today.

The value of ideas is obvious. The value of ideas—primary intellectual capital—is central to the purpose of this publication of knowledge related papers.

There is an inherent relationship between the creativity process and the judgment process. A demonstrative anecdote occurred when a distinguished senior-age, faculty member, inventor-scientist willingly assumed an Active President role of the university whose board I chaired. He took on an interim assignment as acting president between the unanticipatable resignation of a prior president and the recruiting of a full-time president.

Henry would visit with me about once a month. On one of those occasions he had an extensive agenda. He premised the seventh item on the agenda by saying, "Bob, I'm going to need your direct support on the decision that must flow from this issue. As just the acting president and continuing faculty member, I will need the support of the board chairman in authorizing the choice between our two unappealing options."

As Henry introduced the matter, I realized what my job was going to have to be. I was going to have to have at least a third idea. I immediately went into a multiplexing mode, meaning I listened thoughtfully to what he was saying but simultaneously began to have ideas about the university. I didn't know yet what his topic was going to be. I just started to have university related ideas. I was using an Osborn approach of tuning up my mind, seeking quantity of ideas.

As he spoke further, his area of concern became evident. So, I shifted my focus. When he finished his review, I had to agree that the two offerings that were presumed to be self-limiting were objectionable. Then I said, "Henry, let's put those aside. Let's engage in a purposeful creative process between us here and now as you have done so often in the laboratory and elsewhere. Let me start by launching into an idea." I realized as I uttered the first two or three sentences that I was talking my way into a veritable intellectual *cul de sac*. But I wasn't concerned about judging that. I simply finished that thought in order to have started the process of mutual creative thinking.

While that first thought was being expressed, a second idea was brewing (which now becomes our fourth idea). It wasn't very good either. But that led me to a fifth idea. I could tell as I finished expressing that one—which wasn't half bad—that Henry was becoming impatient with my monologue. New thoughts were beginning to click with him as he said "Well, then we could probably consider this," and his became the sixth idea. We traded thoughts back and forth well beyond 10 or 11 ideas between us. At that point he interrupted the process and said, "Thank you. I'll take the issue back to my office. I now know that I will come up with other better and defendable options. I'll let you know what my decision is and I'm sure it will be more than tolerable to the university community."

Notice that without having the availability of all of the potentially useful ideas it is not possible to make the best decision. Decision making is not simply making a choice between a few static suggestions that others may have conjured. The decision making function must include first creating the options worthy of consideration.

## GOING AGAINST THE CROWD: THE ROLE OF COUNTERINTUITIVENESS

Creativity has a bearing on counterintuitiveness. Another book that has had a profound influence on me was the autobiography of Bernard Baruch. Baruch was a Wall Street investment banker in the United States early in the century. But, he was more than that. He was an advisor, even to Presidents of the U.S. In fact, on some occasions he would schedule to sit on certain park benches in New York or Washington, DC. People would seek him out as he would "hold court" responding to their questions or requests for advice. One of his principles was, *if the crowd was going one way he should seriously consider going a very different way.* To begin with, isn't that natural for someone in the stock and bond business? If everyone else is selling, maybe he should be buying. If everyone else is buying, maybe he should be selling. But his thesis was much more pervasive. He applied it to virtually everything.

He was a role model for thinking to me. I began to apply the same thinking methodology. Whenever I saw an industry move or a collective set of thinking on the part of any group of people, I challenged myself that the more likely way that could add value would be quite different than other collective intuitions. This was not intended to be contrarian. Rather, the practice was and is intended to search for alternatives and opposites that may as a consequence of their lack of apparentness be overlooked as the more valuable directions in which to go.

In fact, the intuition of my associates was that we couldn't afford the time and the money for education. The counterintuitive was that it wouldn't cost either net time or money because we would save both by timely usable instruction and we would be the better for it. In fact, within two years after our training and education program was well launched, people who were unaware of the initial discussions would meet me in the halls, speak of how immediately valuable training was and express their hope that I would not fail to support it liberally.

When one searches for the counterintuitive, one is—in a way—searching for the essence. Most subjects are encumbered with all manner of facts and factors. In fact, we can overwhelm ourselves with too much knowledge on most subjects. So there must be a synthesis and a distillation process as we search for the more significant elements, the heart of the matter, the pivot point, the essence. With the distillation and discernment of the essence of the subject at hand, most if not all of the other related "knowledge" may be deemphasized. Choice and action then can be engaged most confidently.

## THE PRACTICE OF RECOMMENDING

How do we practice the application of knowledge so as to ultimately manage it and use it better? There are ways. One that is particularly useful is to make recommendations. Early in our careers, we typically are in the presence of those with more experience and authority. If they are able leaders they will probably provide us with opportunities to be heard, to make recommendations, to allow us to stand for our choice. If we are not privileged to articulate our position, we can at least make a commitment to ourselves as to what our recommendation is on the issue at hand, including how creative we are being. Either way we can test ourselves. What do we learn as we see the events that play themselves out? Do we see that the recommendation of another was really the right answer? Do we see that the one we made which may or may not have been similar to the ultimate decision was more favorable? This practice adds to our confidence and talent in ultimately assuming more responsibility.

## THE QUALITY OF LEADERSHIP AND THE LEADERSHIP OF QUALITY

A consequence of our recommendations and decisions can, to a significant degree, be measured in the manner they help take our institution elsewhere. In our company, the most demanding part of the definition of leadership is "a leader is someone who takes us elsewhere or causes us to do otherwise." This calls for people to have achieved a confidence level that gives them backbone—a willingness to be bold. Boldness is essential. It is one of the ultimate tests of whether or not we have processed and *used* knowledge wisely.

Quality in all of its meanings is important. The quality processes that we conceive from the knowledge we possess are critical to achievements. In business for the most part, we seem to first apply quality techniques to operations activities. But the future of quality as a *bigger* factor in business is going to be the measure of the quality of thought applied.

Operating quality processes and quality management are essential competences in all institutions—certainly business. It takes solid, objective thinking to position the high expectation practices and measurable results that achieve businesses' operational goal of total customer satisfaction, *re* its product and service.

But the thinking that goes into envisioning, strategizing, teaching, inspiring, etc. and leading the institution "elsewhere" is less definitively and less demandingly measured. It should be! Its mastery or insufficiency should be the subject of instructive metrics beyond the other general business consequences.

---

Boldness is essential. It is one of the ultimate tests of whether or not we have processed and *used* knowledge wisely.

---

The measure of the quality of the thought applied will be interpreted through the role modelship we show in teaching, in proving our competence at anticipating and committing to go elsewhere versus our counterpart, the manner in which creatively we have added to the options from which we make good judgments, the counterintuitiveness and the ability to synthesize to essence, etc. These demonstrate that knowledge is more than our possession of facts and data and information as essential as these are in the excellence of management.

## THE HARDNESS OF SOFT VALUES

We must also have a true understanding of values like trust and hope and integrity and respect. These we must know how to apply to our native circumstances and now more than ever to serve the collegial interest of those from many other native cultures.

Some time ago, I was to have the privilege of having my first extended visit with one of our Asiatic executives who was about to become the President of one of our large far east country operations. I spoke to an anthropologist who consulted on matters having to do with that nation. I put the question to him, "Can I talk to our new country president about trust?" His response was direct and useful. "No, you cannot. At this stage of your acquaintanceship, you will confuse him because in his culture trust does not mean the same that it has meant to you and the manner in which you have been imparting it and applying it at Motorola. In his culture, trust first comes from an explicit understanding of all of the factors that are expected. Once he knows what all those detailed factors are with virtually no ambiguity, then he can convey to you in his own way that you can trust him to achieve what have been the defined objectives. But in the culture you come from, Bob, you are willing to deal with more ambiguities and still trust that between you, you will work out a solution truly effective but not necessarily matching consequences to particulars." Knowing how to apply what we know in varying cultures, is essential to our management of that knowledge. As we increase our disciplined appreciation of these intellectual-cultural factors we can additionally enhance the intellectual capital of our broadening institutions.

## CONCLUSION

Thus, the thrust of my message is that the greater value to be achieved under the rubric of managing knowledge and intellectual capital is to be found within us and our peers personally versus otherwise significant institutional policies and practices.

We should *personally embrace:*

- timely mastery, again and again
- teach to learn better
- be best *vis-à-vis counterparts*
- appreciate that knowledge saves time and money
- creative thinking can be taught and learned
- creativity is the differentiator in making judgments
- counterintuitive thinking is more often right
- search for the essence within relevant knowledge
- practice our use of knowledge through recommendations
- strive for leadership through bold activation of what we know
- understand values as well as *facts,* including cultural variances
- strive for highest quality, particularly the quality of thinking

These and similar personal dedications offer promise of moving knowledge toward wisdom.

1996

# ROBERT A. LUTZ
## 1932–

Robert Lutz is the product development genius who brought the world the sleek Dodge Viper, and who, as president and vice chairman of Chrysler, played a pivotal role in turning the company around when it hit hard times in the early 1990s and flirted with bankruptcy for the second time in as many decades. His childhood was less auspicious, however. Between being a poor student and moving so many times between Europe and the United States, he didn't graduate from high school until he was 22 years old. Having received American citizenship back when he was eleven, Lutz joined the Marine Corps. and became a fighter pilot, serving from 1954 to 1959. Afterward, he enrolled at University of California, Berkeley, where he eventually earned an MBA.

Early in his career Lutz worked for General Motors in Europe and for BMW in Germany, then settled down at Ford, where he rose to chairman of Ford of Europe and then vice president for all international operations. Only after feeling stale did he jump ship to Chrysler in 1986. He reflected, "There was one thing, however, that I quickly discovered on joining Chrysler: that the company, despite its bold demeanor and strong profits, was basically following a *defeatist* strategy in its core car and truck business." Between being susceptible to economic swings and aggressive competition, Chrysler managers thought they could never win.

Lutz, who would retire from Chrysler in 1998 at age 67 only to take the CEO job at Exide Corporation, the worlds largest maker of car batteries, went on what he called a crusade to promote "right-brained thinking," or reliance on intuition to make inspirational cars such as the Viper. Part of relying on intuition means not listening to the customer. In *Lutz's Immutable Laws,* a speech delivered at the University of Michigan, he divulges his principles for succeeding in business, which include: "The Customer Is *Not* Always Right," "The Primary Purpose of Business Is *Not* 'To Make Money,' " and "When Everyone Else Is Doing It, DON'T." The primary quality he looks for in managers is right-brain thinking; in other words, thinking that relies on creativity and intuition.

# Lutz's Immutable Laws
## *Robert A. Lutz*

Ibelieve it was the great English poet Alexander Pope who first observed that "a little knowledge can be a dangerous thing." I'd certainly agree with that sentiment. But, somewhat conversely, I'd also argue that even a lot of knowledge, if it's the wrong kind of knowledge or if it's knowledge unwisely applied, can be a very dangerous thing as well. Indeed, the longer I'm in this business, the more I become convinced that this very issue is the key difference between companies that continue to enjoy success, and those that don't.

Over the past few years, in fact, I've been on sort of a personal crusade at Chrysler to legitimize what, for lack of a better term, I'll refer to as "right-brained thinking." Our industry, of course, has a long and glorious history of intuitive, right-brained thinkers—even geniuses—starting with people like Henry Ford the First, Billy Durant, and Walter P. Chrysler. And, of course, a lot of that intuitive genius unfortunately "devolved" into failure—because intuition simply got taken too far. In modern times, however, I think we've gone too far the other way. We've put so much faith in analysis and "quantification" and other areas of left-brained thinking that we've often missed the forest for all the well-examined trees!

To the left-brained thinker, the car business is a science—which, of course, it is. But, I would argue, it's not just a science. And that's because buying a car or truck is not—and never will be—a purely rational decision. Perhaps buying a farm tractor is a purely rational decision. But even that, I suspect, involves a whole jumble of emotions and feelings and other intangible—but very powerful—psychological factors, just as with automobiles.

The automobile business, I submit, really is unlike any other business on the face of the earth. Certainly, we're a business that's highly reliant on technology—and, therefore, also highly reliant on things like logic and predictability and, yes, rationality. But the analogy that I like to use is that we actually have a lot more in common with the movie business than we do with, say, the computer business or the electronics business.

The "technology" side of making a movie is certainly important: the film stock, the location, the sets, the authenticity of the props, and so forth. But what is much more important is the creative spark and the inspiration that goes into the film—that intangible "something" that may be hard to quantify or even to explain, but you definitely know it when you see it. That's what makes the difference between a film like George Lucas's *Star Wars*—done, by the way, at a time when conventional wisdom said that the science fiction genre was passé—and all those movies we see that just sort of blend into the woodwork (even though they had big stars and big budgets, and were "audience-researched" to death).

About a year ago I came across an interview from George Lucas himself that I think pretty accurately describes what I'm saying. He was discussing how distressed he was about the current state of mainstream Hollywood. But, as I read this, just substitute the words "the system" or "Detroit" for the phrase "the studio," and the word "car" for the word "movie," and I think you'll see that his analysis could also easily be applied to where our industry has often gone wrong in the past.

"When I began," Lucas says in the interview, "you'd go to a studio and there'd be three or four people and they'd say, 'Okay, do the movie,' or, 'Don't do the movie.' That was the '70s. But once corporations and Wall Street took over, their way of operating was to create a huge middle-management structure. These are people more interested in stock options than in making good movies, people earning large amounts of money and pretending that they were experts in making movies—and they weren't. And they began to look on the people who made movies as sort of assembly-line workers. They fostered the idea that the talent doesn't know anything, that the talent are idiots, or idiots savants. I mean it's crazy. And you end up with bland and uninteresting movies."

Now, along these same lines, I also came across an interview recently with management expert Tom Peters, of *In Search of Excellence* fame. Peters was asked if he thought the rise of modern, highly-sophisticated market-research tools meant that, in the future, consumers would basically be designing their own products—and that, therefore, the need for creativity on the part of business itself would actually decline.

"No," he said. "I think that's a 50 percent lousy idea. The truth of the matter is that whether we're talking about art, science, or Apple computers, the signature products and services of our time will continue to come from some kinky mind somewhere."

"There is," he continued, "far too much listening to the consumer. This is not saying that when you don't listen at all you turn out better things . . . but the biggest breakthroughs come from people with an egocentric personal vision. The greatest products are the tools and toys that the inventor invents for himself . . . [F]or some business people there's this funny, almost mystical connection with the desires of the consumer—which actually has absolutely nothing to do with watching videotapes of focus groups."

Well, call me "mystical" or call me "kinky" or call me whatever you want, but to me, that's just another way of say-

ing that the business world in general—and the auto industry, in particular—might want to think about paying a little
more attention to things like "intuition" and "instinct" and
"feel" and all those other intangible, yet very powerful,
forces that can't always be shown on a balance sheet.

At Chrysler these last few years, we've done our best to
"destigmatize" right-brained thinking in our company. In
fact, we've gone so far with this concept that you might say
that the inmates are now more or less running the asylum!

But the results, I think, prove that maybe that's not such
a bad idea. We've revolutionized our lineup with products
that in my opinion, haven't just replaced their predecessors,
but have gone a long way toward truly redefining their
respective segment almost every single time. And, by the
way, we've just gotten started: Chrysler will introduce, on
average, one new car or truck model every three months
between now and the year 2000!

But it's not just products. It was also "breakthrough"
thinking—throughout our company, but especially in Tom
Stallkamp's procurement and supply organization—that has
led to our "Extended Enterprise" concept with our suppliers.
A scholarly article in the most recent issue of the *Harvard
Business Review* calls what we have "an American keiretsu,"
but actually, I like to think that it's even more than that. I
think it proves that there really is a place for honest-to-
goodness trust in modern American business—trust that is
built upon clear-headed, "win-win" thinking, as opposed to
the kind of mutual paranoia that has so often characterized
OEM-supplier relationships in the past.

But my favorite example of unbridled creativity at
Chrysler is this one: While attending an annual banquet this
past spring for employees who had recently received U.S.
patents, I was introduced to a retired Chrysler engineer, Mr.
Jose Regueiro. He had been awarded a patent for a diesel
engine "prechamber" that he'd designed. Now, as a retiree,
Mr. Regueiro is under no obligation to continue assigning
his patents to Chrysler, yet he does so because he feels he

owes the company a debt of gratitude for having given him a job after he fled Castro's Cuba some 30 years ago.

---

To the left-brained thinker, the car business is a science . . . But, . . . it's not just a science. And that's because buying a car or truck is not— and never will be—a purely rational decision.

---

But what's really inspirational about Mr. Regueiro's story is this: The idea for his diesel prechamber—a tornado-like whirlwind spinning before his eyes—came to him as part of an hallucinatory vision he had while lying near death in a hospital bed, pumped full of pain-killers, recovering from his second liver transplant (and third major surgery) within just 53 hours! As Mr. Regueiro put it in an interview in our company newspaper, "I kid people that if they want to be really creative, have a couple of liver transplants."

Well, there are, I believe, a lot less painful ways to tap the power of creative, right-brained thinking within our organizations! And, while I certainly don't pretend to have all the answers, I do have a few thoughts about how that might be done. In fact, after three-plus decades in this industry, I've now codified these thoughts into what I call—perhaps intemperately, but what the hell!—"Lutz's Immutable Laws of the Auto Business." I'll share four of these laws with you here today. (And, as I do so, please keep in mind that throughout my career my motto has always been, "Often wrong, but never in doubt!")

*Lutz's Immutable Law Number One:* "The customer is not always right."

In fact, let's face it, the customer—in this business and, I suspect, in many others—is usually, at best, just a rear-view mirror. He can tell you what he likes among the choices that are already out there. But when it comes to the future, why, I ask, should we expect the customer to be the expert in clairvoyance or in creativity? After all, isn't that really what he expects us to be? And, isn't it basically shirking one of our core responsibilities as "car people" to foist this kind of critical, value-added responsibility onto the customer himself?

At the end of the day, being "customer-driven" is certainly a good thing. But if you're so customer-driven that you're merely following yesterday's trends, then ultimately, customers won't be driving your supposedly "customer-driven" products!

*Immutable Law Number Two:* "Teamwork is not always a good thing."

Now, everyone's for teamwork, of course; it's "motherhood and apple pie." We're certainly for it at Chrysler. In fact, in our evolving corporate culture, we're striving to take teamwork to all-new levels. But teamwork can get taken too far, too. In fact, sometimes it's actually a hindrance to true creativity.

---

In fact, let's face it, the customer—in this business and, I suspect, in many others—is usually, at best, just a rear-view mirror.

---

There was a fascinating piece in the Sunday *New York Times* a couple of months ago called "Longing for a New Lone Genius." It argued that the same kind of thinking that has led to today's "P.C." movement has also led to such a "leveling climate" in this country that we've all somehow come to the conclusion that good ideas can only be the products of collective, rather than individual, thought—when, in fact, that's hardly the case at all.

The truth is, while teamwork is indeed a wondrous thing, the genesis of truly breakthrough ideas cannot always be "democratized." Truly new and different ideas actually require, as the article pointed out, a kind of defiance. The person generating them must, as the piece noted, "have a faith that the new paradigm will succeed with the many large problems that confront it, knowing only that the older paradigm has failed with a few."

That, I would argue, is the exact opposite of the "groupthink" phenomenon that, unfortunately, permeates misdirected (or undirected) exercises in teamwork. And if you've got groupthink, you may all "love one another," but it's usually not long before the amorous lemmings all run off the cliff together!

*Immutable Law Number Three:* "The goal of business in general, and of the auto business in particular, is not to make money—or at least it's not just about making money."

Now, before I get myself in big trouble on this one, let me explain. Making a profit is, of course, the first and most fundamental responsibility of any business, both to its shareholders and to society at large. But if your view of business is that it is merely just a sort of big, complex money-laundering scheme—i.e., you put money into one end with the expectation that a greater amount of money will come out the other end, and who cares exactly what it is, in between, that actually makes the money grow—then I can guarantee that you're going to absolutely smother all but the most esoteric, financially-oriented creativity in your organization.

Back to Hollywood again, the great film producer Sam Goldwyn once said, "There's nothing wrong with Hollywood that good movies wouldn't fix." Likewise, I have long held that there wasn't much wrong with Detroit that good, creative cars and trucks couldn't fix. And I would argue that if we don't confuse the ends of success (making money) with the means of getting there (producing truly great products), success will, in fact, be much to maintain.

Finally, *Lutz's Immutable Law Number Four:* "Creativity itself—or, rather, creativity all by itself is not always a good thing, either."

It is, in fact, possible to get so carried away with things like right-brained thinking and "empowerment" and "doing one's own thing" that we shirk our responsibilities to the customer in a different way: by letting costs get out of control. The fact is, being creative is no excuse for being irresponsible! And, even though I believe we could use a whole lot more right-brained thinking in this industry, what we really need is a lot more holistic thinking—the kind of thinking that utilizes both sides of the brain: the logical left as well as the creative right.

The trick is finding the right balance: the right balance between control and creativity, between teamwork and individual initiative, between listening to the customer and listening to that "little voice" that each of us has inside ourselves.

---

The truth is, while teamwork is indeed a wondrous thing, the genesis of truly breakthrough ideas cannot always be "democratized."

---

The Senior Vice President of Human Resources and Quality at McDonnell Douglas, Laurie Broedling, articulated a terrific insight about finding the right balance in a speech recently reprinted in the publication *Vital Speeches of the Day.* She talked about the need to manage on "the edge of chaos," which she defined as that "constantly shifting battle zone between stagnation and anarchy [where] one set of forces (the need for order and control) pulls every business toward stagnation, while another set of forces (the need for growth and creativity) drives it toward disintegration."

The trick, of course, is to stay right on that edge, without slipping into either stagnation or anarchy. And there is, unfortunately, no formula explaining exactly how to do that. And that's because, when all is said and done, it really isn't about the science of management, it's about the art of management.

Years ago, in an article entitled "Management as a Liberal Art," Peter Drucker argued that management is no more a science than is medicine a science. Both, he said, are practices—practices that certainly employ various sciences, but which are both separate disciplines in their own right.

I think it's time that we in this industry rediscovered that fact—and, in the process, rediscovered the kind of knowledge that's really worth having. We should do so for the sake of our customers . . . for the sake of our shareholders . . . and, as an extra bonus, for our own sake.

After all, the kind of knowledge I'm talking about really is the "fun" side of this business, the stuff, as they say, "as dreams are made on"—the stuff that makes this business so special and so different from so many other businesses.

In closing, let me come back to the man whose name is on my company's door, Walter P. Chrysler. "There is," Chrysler said in his autobiography, "a creative joy in manufacturing that only poets are supposed to know."

By helping our organizations unlock that creative joy, we can, I submit, all be poets!

1996

# ANDREW W. ROBERTSON

Regarded as one of the shrewdest managers of his time, Andrew W. Robertson was recruited to become chairman of Westinghouse just as the Great Depression hit. Westinghouse had been founded by George Westinghouse in Pittsburgh in 1886. At the age of 22 he invented the air brake, and then pioneered work in electrical plants. The founder stepped aside in 1910 and died four years later, but the company continued to expand, entering the radio and appliance fields. At about the time that George Westinghouse was in the twilight of his career, Robertson was a school teacher, then a door-to-door salesman of aluminum pots and pans, after which he became an attorney for and then head of a utility holding company. When Westinghouse's chairman died unexpectedly, its directors sought outside help to revive the sluggish company; thus Robertson entered the scene.

According to business analysts back then, Robertson inherited a stubborn company that was as "bulky as a hippopotamus." To liven things up, he organized an advertising department (a first for the company) and decentralized operations. Recognizing the opportunity that World War II presented, he guided the company into the military electronics business. In fact, Westinghouse radar equipment on Oahu warned of planes approaching Pearl Harbor on December 7, 1941; unfortunately the powers-that-be assumed they were American planes.

For Robertson, who reigned from 1930 to 1946, management was to be glorified as it makes all things possible—whether it be selling a Fuller brush or running a railroad—and his deification of management is obvious in *Management's Responsibility*. While he covers a good deal of *highbrow* ground, his essay also includes humorous anecdotes and provocative thoughts. Robertson admitted that management must be strong and even dictatorial: "It is anti-democratic, although private organizations flourish best in democratic countries. However, the democratic rule of the majority will frustrate and defeat any management." In other words, he said, the majority is not always right.

# Management's Responsibility
## *Andrew W. Robertson*

Management is to be found everywhere, in our homes, in our personal affairs, in our factories and generally throughout all social functions, economical, political or otherwise. If a thing is thought to be devoid of management, someone is always popping up to inject a little management into it, such as making a managed currency or a wheat crop or managing the supply of cotton, the number of pigs and everything in general. Unfortunately, the various efforts of management do not always harmonize. In fact, more often than not the efforts of different managements are in conflict with one another so that if one management succeeds, the other must necessarily fail. The hunter of seals is directing all his managerial ability to kill seals. Government may be devoting all its managerial ability to keep the seals alive.

Management has been in existence as long as civilization. But in the present age management controls larger groups than in any other age. It is only during the last fifty years that we have seen organizations of national and international scope. Today we think of management as the organizing force in the world of affairs. It is the *know how* of business and industry. It is concerned with order, discipline and accomplishment, and is against disorder and inertia.

Management uses the intelligence, labor and wealth of man with the materials and forces of nature to produce things or services which other men want. It is absurd, in a sense, to define management to you, but in another sense it is a wise precaution to [ensure] our common approach to the subject. Management is the last and best means by which man, the builder and creator, takes the manifold riches of nature which, in their raw or natural state, are useless to him, and molds them to his needs. The distinction between the work of management and the work of an individual is that the results of management's activities are always for others. To survive, management must produce what others want, whereas the individual, more often than not, is concerned with producing what he alone wants. The multifarious activities of management are beyond description, and some of the activities might be called mismanagement.

---

### Management has been in existence as long as civilization.

---

Management is necessary to sell a steamboat or a Fuller brush; to run a hat-checking concession or an automobile factory; to operate the Pennsylvania Railroad or a beauty parlor; to give a picnic or conduct a funeral.

Management will function in Europe or Africa; but the higher the standard of living, the better management functions. Or restated, the better management functions, the higher the standard of living.

Our attention is directed to that part of management which has to do with private enterprise.

Management enables man to advance through the helpful cooperation of other men. Alone he is pitiful. At best he is little more than an animal and no matter how brilliant he may be he cannot rise far without the help of others. He is born naked and helpless. He travels but a short distance and is tired. His strength wanes unless he is fed. He may know much, but the wisest man has explored only a little bay on the shores of the great ocean of knowledge. Only in the union of minds under capable management does he become supreme. Management unites individuals in effective cooperation. The corporation is the modern vehicle for this purpose. Through it the widow's mite aids the laborer to produce what the consumer wants. Management acts as steward and trustee for all—investor, laborer, and consumer. The results are astonishing. The laborer has received the highest wages for the shortest hours. He has at last found leisure and has become a consumer. He now knows comfort and has luxury. He is unable to appraise his condition as there is nothing in all history with which to compare it. . . .

The world is founded on faith and integrity of others. The goods and services of management are accepted generally upon their face value. I trust the men who make the automobile I buy, and I do not know any of the thousands who have contributed to the finished product. When I step into an airplane I trust my life to the organization which built it and to the pilot who operates it. When I receive a telegram I do not question the integrity of the message.

Management must be honest, capable and wise, even as you and I, and its goods and services must be worthy of highest trust; but it must also accept the task of leadership in the conquest of our natural world. Man must combine his forces to win. Nature is relentless. It will reclaim every secret and recapture every stronghold our age has won unless we are alert to hold it and press on to new victories. It is pleasant to be complacent, but other civilizations as proud as our own have gone down, leaving only broken fragments to tell the story of their glory. Through wise management of our abilities and resources we have advanced far beyond any previous frontier, but what we have gained can be lost. And it will be lost, and retreat will be inevitable, if the attack against business succeeds in curbing management and killing initiative.

Management has served best in free countries. The United States has been ideal for its development. Here the best talent is drafted from 50,000,000 workers. The managerial type of person is rare. It is not enough to be intelligent, industrious and trustworthy. The management of a great modern enterprise must have special courage, unusual foresight and a knowledge of psychology and human conduct beyond mere book knowledge. The necessary coordination and cooperation of thousands of different individuals, all alien of end and of aim, so that their diversified talents and knowledge are harmoniously directed to accomplish a definite thing, is no small task. Teamwork is what does it.

It is easy to get cooperation, but more difficult to get coordination. August Bruski had a wife and a bright boy of 14 and an older daughter. The peace of the little family was almost wrecked over their willingness to cooperate and their failure to coordinate their efforts. The son won a place on the commencement program of his school. He knew his speech perfectly. The family was proud and happy until the night before the great day when the family decided the boy had no suitable clothes unless he could wear his father's trousers, which were six inches too long. The father wasn't willing to have the six inches cut off and the son was in tears at the thought of wearing them rolled up. However, it was decided, after long debate, that that was the best thing to do and the family retired—but not to sleep. The mother shared the horror of her son at the thought of those rolled up trousers and at last decided to get up and cut off the extra six inches, which she did. Meanwhile, the sister tossed and fretted in sympathy with her brother and finally she, too, decided to cut off the extra six inches in an effort to cooperate. So she got up and cut another six inches off the trousers. Cooperation without coordination will not make our pants fit.

Good management is the rule of the best minds. Organizations controlled by management follow the rules laid down by Plato for the perfect society; namely, "the wisest have the most authority." It is anti-democratic, although private organizations flourish best in democratic countries. However, the democratic rule of the majority will frustrate and defeat any management. The crew cannot run the ship. It is popular to think that the majority is always right, but there is as much difference in feeling right and being right as there is in feeling good and being good.

## Management is impersonal. It must travel a narrow road.

A friend was crossing one of the many bridges which span the Allegheny River in downtown Pittsburgh, when he was stopped by two robbers who demanded his pocketbook. My friend protested. The robbers replied that they wanted only what was right and fair and would be willing to submit the matter to a vote of the three of them and let the majority decide. With all solemnity the vote was taken and the majority won and my friend lost his pocketbook.

Decisions in organizations under management are never made by weight of numbers. Every decision is made by those persons best qualified by knowledge to make it. Finally, all decisions of each qualified group or division are coordinated into the activity of the organization as a whole.

Management is impersonal. It must travel a narrow road. The twilight zone of human frailties and error, which bounds all our acts as individuals, is denied it. Management may be kind, but not sentimental; liberal, not extravagant; frugal, not stingy. Higher things are demanded of management than we require of ourselves. . . .

The modern world is complicated beyond belief. No one, not even the simplest citizen, lives what might be called the simple life. None of us can truly take care of himself. We depend entirely upon other people for the necessities and luxuries of our lives. Light comes to us over a wire. Heat through a pipe. Water through another pipe. We are carried to and from our work in public conveyances. Food is to be found around the corner if we can get the necessary nickels to purchase it, and, if we cannot, government has to furnish it or we perish. In such a world, the need of management is imperative. The minute the mob takes over the power plant the city is in darkness. Order and system, which are possible only through management, must prevail throughout the modern world. The managers of today, imperfect men as they are, are still the pick of all the candidates available and it is their responsibility to maintain the proper functioning of the vital necessities of our life. Management may not quit under criticism. It is not enough to stand up under criticism when one merits it; it is necessary to stand up and take it on the chin when one does not merit it. This is the law of good sportsmanship. It is the law of good society, and management must measure up to it. If anyone is the captain of our modern ship, management is. And it cannot desert its post.

The collateral responsibilities of management are many. Large factories and mass production lead to congested living conditions and the inevitable lowering of health and morals. Management is not directly responsible for the social conditions which are the indirect result of its factories and production methods, but it must nevertheless accept a fair share of the responsibility for these indirect results. The rise of material well-being, which is everywhere apparent, was attained only at a price. The innocent victims of these conditions are helpless. They are the weak and the unfortunate and in every age have suffered ill health and have been poorly fed and poorly clad. But their condition, by proper attention, may be ameliorated and management must accept the responsibility for the amelioration. Just as it has long since accepted the responsibility of securing safe and healthful surroundings in which men work, it must now accept the responsibility of helping employees secure safe and healthful surroundings in which to live. Anything short of this is a neglect of clear responsibility.

Since we live in an almost wholly artificial world, there would seem to be no escape from providing artificial or man-made aids to health. Parks and playgrounds must be furnished and a reasonable amount of outdoor life provided. The comfort and health of every community must receive constant attention.

Finally, since management can exist only in an environment suitable to its needs, it must recognize its obligation to the society of which it is a part. In many cases society has decreed regulations and restrictions which hamper management and private enterprise, but society is the sole arbitrator of what it considers right, and management must conform. It has no choice. It is as helpless in the face of social restrictions as it is in the face of economic conditions. All management of private enterprise realizes that changing times affect business and may in time render it useless. The canal has gone. The horse and buggy have gone. The street railway and steam railroads are suffering from changed conditions, but management must accept these things and it must also accept proper governmental regulations.

---

It is not enough to stand up under criticism when one merits it; it is necessary to stand up and take it on the chin when one does not merit it. This is the law of good sportsmanship.

---

And inasmuch as government is forced by the very nature of things to assume a larger and larger role in our everyday life, regulating more and more what we do and how we live, it needs the assistance of management more than the government of any other age. Management should willingly offer its talents and services to government because management is the only source from which government can get the necessary talent to operate its many activities efficiently. It now ignores management, and management scowls at government. They are both wrong. Meanwhile the people suffer. Modern government cannot exist without better management. Management must accept its responsibilities and offer its services to any good government that asks for them. Government has a proper field of regulation which management recognizes and accepts. It is equally true that management has a field of accomplishment which government now lacks and would do well to recognize.

The affairs of man move along with surprising speed and power. We see trade and commerce going on uninterruptedly between individuals and between groups of individuals, with ships crossing every sea and stopping at every port. It is obvious that a well ordered world is necessary for the growth of prosperity and that anything which interferes with the exchange of raw materials or the products of human labor tends to lower the standard of living, but it is not obvious that private enterprise is the mainspring of all our activities. The demagogue ignores private enterprise and considers it of no importance. The situation reminds me of my experience the other day in an airplane. I was sitting forward and looked out the window from time to time. Nothing but the wing obstructed my view. I could see the whole horizon and the ground below at an angle. I repeat, nothing obstructed my view; I could see clearly. I was alarmed when I realized that my view was directly across the end of the motor where there should be a propeller. But there was none. I mean I couldn't *see* one and as far as my eyes were concerned there was no propeller. If I had not known that I couldn't see a fastmoving propeller, I might have assumed that airplanes move through the air by virtue of government regulations, or some mysterious power, without propellers. Sometimes I think we judge our civilization just as faultily. We see things moving along, goods being made, wages being paid, taxes being collected, human beings living and dying with a more or less steady rhythm, and we haven't any idea of what keeps things moving. We can't see the propellers of our civilization. The greater the speed of living, or the higher the standard of living, the less people comprehend it. Almost anyone can understand a horsepower civilization and the simple transactions which constitute its life. Grain is planted, harvested and sold; simple goods are manufactured and purchased. The complete round of life is clearly visible. But who among us can get a glimpse of the mechanism of this Kilowatt Hour Age, which is propelled through space almost as fast as the electric current which symbolizes it? Propellers we cannot see may be overlooked and neglected.

Under such circumstances, when the wisest are at a loss, and it seems easier to be wrong than to be right, management must stand by its colors, struggling to maintain the cause of free enterprise in a world threatened with unwise regulation. Free enterprise may confidently hold up its head as representative of one of the most vital functions in our national economy today. It is the one thing which stands between us and a stale, flat, unhappy world of universal regimentation and individual conformity to a single pattern.

1940

# PART II

# Productivity, Empowerment, and Conflict Management

To achieve management goals, a variety of tools and techniques come into play, which the managers of Part II discuss. For example, Sam Walton, founder of Wal-Mart, pulled goofy stunts like leading hog-calling cheers to motivate the troops. But managers must also deal with conflict as they solve problems, make decisions, and delegate responsibility. The key, according to Andrew Grove, chairman of Intel, is to harness that conflict and turn it into what he calls *constructive confrontation*. A little head-butting goes a long way to problem solving, he writes. Arthur Blank and Bernie Marcus, cofounders of Home Depot, also don't mind a little conflict; they empower their managers and send them on journeys of job discovery that inevitably lead to stepping on other peoples' toes, a natural part of the learning process.

# ANDREW S. GROVE
## 1936–

When Andrew Grove, who was named *Time* magazine's "Man of the Year" in 1997, stepped down as Intel's CEO in 1998, he could take great pride in knowing that Intel chips were in about 85 percent of the world's personal computers. Not a bad success story; and yet, this is a man who lives by the motto, "Only the paranoid survive." Then again, consider his past. During World War II, life for Jewish families in Hungary, where he was born and raised, was not easy. His father disappeared, taken to a labor camp, and his mother and he survived the Nazi occupation by obtaining false papers. When the Soviets invaded Hungary during the popular uprising in 1956, Grove chose to escape to the United States. After a friend and he took a train close to the Austrian border, they hired a hunchback smuggler to sneak them past the Russians.

Grove earned a Ph.D. in chemical engineering from the University of California, Berkeley, and then went to work for Fairchild Semiconductor. There, he befriended Gordon Moore and Robert Noyce, who went on to cofound Intel in 1968. Grove joined them and became president in 1979—that was the year he beat Motorola out to supply the microprocessors for IBM's landmark personal computer. In 1985 he guided Intel's exit from the memory-chip business, firing 6,000 employees in the process, and two years later was named CEO. One of the biggest tests of his tenure was the 1994 flawed chip debacle, in which Intel first balked, then offered to replace the chips, at a cost of close to $1 billion.

In terms of managing oneself, Grove makes a unique point, "You have to accept that no matter where you work, you are not an employee; you are in a business with one employee— yourself. You are in competition with millions of similar businesses . . . capable of doing the same work that you can do and perhaps more eager." As for others, he drives them as hard as himself; *Fortune* named him toughest boss in 1984. Part of his tough guy image arises from tackling problems head-on. In *How to Make Confrontation Work for You,* Grove explains how to harness people's aggressive energy to solve problems in a more efficient manner.

# How to Make Confrontation Work for You
## Andrew S. Grove

"I just don't understand how your new way of measuring things around here will help us at all," the plant manager said, grimacing. Others at the meeting merely looked puzzled. The vice president of manufacturing, the plant manager's direct superior, had just finished vigorously urging the use of a particular statistical indicator to determine whether the company's plants were delivering products on time. Faced with the plant manager's incredulity, the vice president redoubled his efforts, trying again to win over everyone in the room.

The plant manager remained unconvinced. His colleagues then jumped into the fray. Arguments generated rebuttals, numbers collided with other numbers. New ideas began to surface, most of them to be immediately rejected, until eventually the heated exchanges dissipated. The still-animated group of people in the room suddenly realized, with considerable satisfaction, that they had now come up with the right statistical measure.

As the meeting ended, the vice president shook his head in mock dismay. "It's too bad," he said, "that you people are so reticent." He put away his papers somewhat ruefully— his hours of preparation for the meeting had not resulted in his proposal being adopted. But he also knew that what had finally been agreed upon was better than his original idea.

That meeting, which actually took place, exemplifies a direct approach to problem solving that we at Intel have developed over the company's 15 years in business. As we struggled to establish Intel's place in the sun, people focused almost completely on the task at hand, with no one too concerned about protocol and formality in dealing with coworkers. We kept this style as the company grew. Years later when a consultant watched a number of our managers work through problems in small groups, he remarked that we seemed to approach every problem in the same unusual way. In searching for a phrase to describe it, he came up with "constructive confrontation."

What we had stumbled on was a method for putting aggressive energies to work *for* the organization. Too often, in my observation, the failure to face up to these energies, to acknowledge that they exist and have to find expression, ends up bedeviling an organization. This failure is, for example, why most managers don't conduct meaningful performance appraisals—they are afraid to let go enough to tell subordinates what they really think, and also afraid of the angry response that may come back at them.

Why have constructive confrontations? Everybody knows that problems are inevitable in business. Machines stop working properly, orders are lost to the competition, coworkers don't perform their tasks the way we think they should. Such problems often produce conflicts.

---

What we had stumbled on was a method for putting aggressive energies to work *for* the organization.

---

If an order was lost, was it because the salesmen goofed or because product quality has slipped? Members of the sales force and quality-control people will probably disagree.

But if the company is to get the customer back, we have to find the right answer to the question and solve the problem.

Dealing with conflicts lies at the heart of managing any business. As a result, confrontation—facing issues about which there is disagreement—can be avoided only at the manager's peril. The issue can be put off, it can be allowed to fester for a long time, it can be smoothed over or swept under some rug. But it is not going to disappear. Conflicts must be resolved if the organization is to go forward.

Constructive confrontation accelerates problem solving. It requires that participants be direct, that they deal face to face. It pushes people to deal with a problem as soon as possible, keeping it from festering. It encourages all concerned to concentrate on the problem, not on the people caught up in it.

---

## Dealing with conflicts lies at the heart of managing any business.

---

Many managers seem to think it is impolite to tackle anything or anyone head on, even in business. By contrast, we at Intel believe that it is the essence of corporate health to bring a problem out into the open as soon as possible, even if this entails a confrontation. Workplace politicking grows quietly in the dark, like mushrooms; neither can stand the light of day.

I learned this as a relatively young and inexperienced manager, when I let myself get sucked into the middle of some unproductive political infighting. Two of my subordinates, one in charge of manufacturing and the other of quality assurance, came to dislike each other. The manufacturing manager would walk into my office and complain to me that the quality manager didn't know what he was doing. Ten minutes later the quality manager would tell me that his counterpart disregarded procedures, that he didn't give a hoot about quality.

I found myself investigating first one claim and then another, getting more and more anxious and angry. Finally I decided I would not tolerate it anymore. The next time one of them began the routine, I raised my hand and stopped him. "Hold it," I said. "Let's get the other person in here." When he appeared, I said to the manager in my office: "Now tell me what you were going to say." The confrontation between the two was tense and embarrassed—anything but constructive. But after a few such sessions, both managers discovered that dealing directly with each other was a lot less awkward and more productive than a scene in my office.

Constructive confrontation does *not* mean being loud, unpleasant, or rude, and it is not designed to affix blame. The essence of it is to attack a problem by speaking up in a businesslike way. Say that you are in a meeting. The man across the table is droning on with a clearly unworkable idea. When you are sure you understand his point, interrupt him politely: "I disagree with your proposed solution. It won't work because . . ." Attack the problem, not the individual.

---

Constructive confrontation . . . pushes people to deal with a problem as soon as possible, keeping it from festering.

---

If you find yourself saying, "You're out of your mind to even suggest such a thing," you're doing it wrong. Indeed, as long as the focus of what you say is the individual, even the most delicate phrasing won't help much. A remark like "With all due respect, I can't help but wonder what you might have been thinking of when you came up with this plan," while exquisite in its politeness, still misses the target. When you do focus correctly—on the problem—never be rude. Saying "The solution you propose is absurd" isn't constructive confrontation either.

A case in point, about which I still feel bad: A seasoned Intel manager was delivering a report on a key project. I was unhappy with the presentation. Though the project was clearly important, the man was unprepared. As I sat there seething, one of my associates started to criticize the manager, who responded with lame excuses. I then jumped in. My temper got the best of me, and what I said turned into an attack on him rather than on the poor performance we had all witnessed. After I cooled down, I apologized to him, but by then it was too late. A loyal, experienced, and valuable manager had been so hurt that no apology could get through to him. A few months later he left the company.

---

Workplace politicking grows quietly in the dark, like mushrooms; neither can stand the light of day.

---

Constructive confrontation is admittedly hard to practice. While a few people are natural "black belts" at the technique, most find it somewhat painful, at least initially, because they have been brought up to think that politeness excludes confrontation. People who have trouble picking up the technique should be comforted by the fact that they're in good company. Consider the following, from a column by Joseph Kraft: "Ronald Reagan enjoys a reputation as a fierce tiger in asserting American interests. But foreign leaders repeatedly come away from sessions with the President claiming he is a pussycat, too nice even to mention disagreeable subjects."

In our formal course to teach new Intel employees about constructive confrontation, we explain the reasons for using the technique—the need for conflict resolution and the desirability of speeding this process up. We then practice dealing with problems by role playing in small groups, so that at the end of the seminar every participant has had at least a taste of it under supervised conditions—but only a taste. The best way to learn the technique is by observing others in the company—co-workers, supervisors, subordinates—in real confrontations.

Are some people by nature less adept at constructive confrontation? Women, for instance? Actually, I have found that women seem to have an easier time with it and more often do it right. I don't know why.

Some cultures do seem to better prepare people to use the technique, however. I was once asked to teach constructive confrontation to a group of managers at our subsidiary in Japan. The Japanese readily grasped the reasons for the practice, and we sailed along merrily until we came to the role playing. So that I could follow it, they began by doing this in English. It went well. Gradually their role playing switched into Japanese. While I could not follow the dialogue, I noted growing amusement among the Japanese managers who were watching. When I asked them to explain their mirth, it turned out that while the role players had a fairly easy time practicing their confrontational roles in English, they absolutely froze when they tried to do it in Japanese. The ingrained habits of nonconfrontational behavior so strongly established in Japanese upbringing effectively inhibited them from bringing off a confrontation in their native language.

The practice of constructive confrontation has to be managed, of course, particularly its use with people outside the company. Someone who employs the technique with, say, a job applicant is likely to at least confuse and at worst antagonize. At Intel we have learned not to impose our style of direct problem solving on others unfamiliar with it—customers, for example. Once I paid a sales call on one of our largest customers, a company known for its indirect and nonconfrontational internal style. Accompanied by a group of sales and marketing people, I participated in a fairly large meeting, which included some of the senior management of the other company. We ran into a few problems and went to work on them. The discussion meandered around far too long compared with what I was accustomed to at Intel. Without even realizing what I was doing, I started to take over the meeting—asking questions, directing the discussion. Nobody objected, so I thought nothing of it until we left. Once we were outside the customer's building, the Intel sales people gathered around and almost lynched me for behavior they considered totally inappropriate in the customer's presence. They were correct. The story of that meeting reverberated through the other company. Our sales people had to make a number of follow-up visits to smooth the feathers I had ruffled.

Sometimes, of course, a situation simply runs away from us. Rational arguments give way to a scene in which the participants need to win an argument much more than they need to resolve an issue. When that happens, it's best to adjourn the confrontation. When things aren't getting anywhere, raise your hand and say: "Hold it! Let's take this up later when *everybody* is cooler." When you reconvene, chances are that all present will be thinking more clearly. Then they will be ready for the kind of confrontation that works.

1984

When Robert Townsend, author of the bestselling *Up the Organization,* was working for American Express he was soundly criticized by the older executives for wearing pink shirts. Apparently, the Townsend family was imbued with the rebellious spirit—an ancestor of the same name, who ran a pub frequented by British soldiers, was a Revolutionary War spy. After attending elite prep schools and earning an English literature degree at Princeton University, Townsend served in the military as a gunnery officer during World War II. After the war, he joined a brokerage firm. In 1948 he took a job with American Express, starting with Hertz American Express International, a jointly owned car rental company.

What Townsend discovered at American Express was a company that could literally afford to make mistakes. "During those years, the company was rich enough to do—and did—almost everything wrong," he said. In 1962 he left to become president and chairman of the board of Avis, Inc. Townsend turned around the ailing car rental company with the "We're Only No. 2, We Try Harder" advertising campaign. To create a team environment, he forced all managers to go to rental agency school. At first they protested, but they soon realized how hard it was to work the counter and were more sensitive to the frontline troops. During his tenure, which lasted until 1965 (ITT bought the company), Townsend increased Avis's market share by 28 percent and tripled revenues.

Townsend operated without a personal secretary and answered his own phone as much as possible. He felt executives should do their own share of grunt work and delegate the meaty stuff. "Many give lip service, but few delegate authority in important matters. And that means all they delegate is dogwork," he wrote. He was less concerned with organizational charts than with simply motivating the troops: "Get to know your people. . . . And then try to create an organization around your people, not jam your people into those organizational-chart rectangles." Motivating employees is the dominant theme in *People,* for Townsend is convinced that organizations are too much like Caesar's legions—unbearably authoritative.

# People
## *Robert Townsend*

There's nothing fundamentally wrong with our country except that the leaders of all our major organizations are operating on the wrong assumptions. We're in this mess because for the last two hundred years we've been using the Catholic Church and Caesar's legions as our patterns for creating organizations. And until the last forty or fifty years it made sense. The average churchgoer, soldier, and factory worker was uneducated and dependent on orders from above. And authority carried considerable weight because disobedience brought the death penalty or its equivalent.

From the behavior of people in these early industrial organizations we arrived at the following assumptions, on which all modern organizations are still operating:

1. People hate work.
2. They have to be driven and threatened with punishment to get them to work toward organizational objectives.
3. They like security, aren't ambitious, want to be told what to do, dislike responsibility.

You don't think we are operating on these assumptions? Consider:

1. Office hours nine to five for everybody except the fattest cats at the top. Just a giant cheap time clock. (Are we buying brains or hours?)
2. Unilateral promotions. For more money and a bigger title I'm expected to jump at the chance of moving my family to New York City. I run away from the friends and a life style in Denver that have made me and my family happy and effective. (Organization comes first; individuals must sacrifice themselves to its demands.)
3. Hundreds of millions of dollars are spent annually "communicating" with employees. The message always boils down to: "Work hard, obey orders. We'll take care of you." (That message is obsolete by fifty years and wasn't very promising then.)

Back off a minute. Let's pretend we know everything man knows about human nature and its present condition here, but nothing about man's organizations and the assumptions on which they're based. These things we know about man:

1. He's a wanting animal.
2. His behavior is determined by unsatisfied needs that he wants to satisfy.
3. His needs form a value hierarchy that is internal, not external:
   a. Body (I can't breathe.)
   b. Safety (How can I protect myself from . . . ?)
   c. Social (I want to belong.)
   d. Ego (1. Gee, I'm terrific. 2. Aren't I? Yes.)
   e. Development (Gee, I'm better than I was last year.)

Man is totally motivated by each level of need in order—until that level is satisfied. If he hasn't slept in three days he's totally motivated by a need for sleep. After he has slept, eaten, drunk, is safe, and has acceptance in a group, he is no longer motivated by those three levels of needs. (McGregor's examples: The only time you think of air is when you are deprived of it; man lives by bread alone when there is no bread.)*

We know that these first three need levels are pretty well satisfied in America's work force today. So we would expect man's organizations to be designed to feed the ego and development needs. But there's the whole problem. The result of our outmoded organizations is that we're still acting as if people were uneducated peasants. Much of the work done today would be more suitable for young children or mental defectives.

And look at the rewards we're offering our people today: higher wages, medical benefits, vacations, pensions, profit sharing, bowling and baseball teams. *Not one can be enjoyed on the job.* You've got to leave work, get sick, or retire first. No wonder people aren't having fun on the job.

---

The result of our outmoded organizations is that we're still acting as if people were uneducated peasants. Much of the work done today would be more suitable for young children or mental defectives.

---

So what are the valid assumptions for present-day circumstances? McGregor called them "Theory Y":

1. People don't hate work. It's as natural as rest or play.
2. They don't have to be forced or threatened. If they commit themselves to mutual objectives, they'll drive themselves more effectively than you can drive them.
3. But they'll commit themselves only to the extent they can see ways of satisfying their ego and development needs (remember the others are pretty well satisfied and are no longer prime drives).

* From *The Human Side of Enterprise* by Douglas McGregor, 1960.

All you have to do is look around you to see that modern organizations are only getting people to use about 20 percent—the lower fifth—of their capacities. And the painful part is that God didn't design the human animal to function at 20 percent. At that pace it develops enough malfunctions to cause a permanent shortage of psychoanalysts and hospital beds.

Since 1952 I've been stumbling around building and running primitive "Theory Y" departments, divisions, and finally one whole "Theory Y" company: Avis.

In 1962 after thirteen years Avis had never made a profit.* Three years later the company had grown internally (not by acquisitions) from $30 million sales to $75 million sales, and had made successive annual profits of $1 million, $3 million, and $5 million. If I had anything to do with this, I ascribe it all to my application of Theory Y. And a faltering, stumbling, groping, mistake-ridden application it was.

---

> All you have to do is look around you to see that modern organizations are only getting people to use about 20 percent—the lower fifth—of their capacities.

---

You want proof? I can't give it to you. But let me tell you a story. When I became head of Avis I was assured that no one at headquarters was any good, and that my first job was to start recruiting a whole new team. Three years later, Hal Geneen, the President of ITT (which had just acquired Avis), after meeting everybody and listening to them in action for a day, said, "I've never seen such depth of management; why I've already spotted three chief executive officers!" You guessed it. Same people. I'd brought in only two new people, a lawyer and an accountant.

---

* Except one year when they jiggled their depreciation rates.

Bill Bernbach used to say about advertising effectiveness: "Ninety per cent of the battle is what you say and 10 per cent is what medium you say it in." The same thing is true of people. Why spend all that money and time on the *selection* of people when the people you've got are breaking down from under-use.

1970

Jack Stack has made a reputation for himself by promoting a progressive, open-book management philosophy—his testing ground is the Springfield, Missouri–based Springfield Remanufacturing, where he is president and CEO. An open-book approach is a must, considering that the company is totally employee-owned. Back in 1983, the company was created when the employees of the remanufacturing division of International Harvester spun themselves off by buying the business. Now they remanufacture a host of diesel engine brands, as well as other engine types and parts. Stack enjoys promoting their unique history and track record.

To maintain that track record, Stack is careful to treat his dealers with great appreciation; each year he takes them on an all-expenses-paid five-day fishing extravaganza. Developing bonds between employees is equally important, and everyone gets involved in the management of the company. To teach employees how to think like owners, a committee of frontline people is given $5,000 to spend on employee activities, sports events, and parties, and must decide how to spend it. "In the process they learn a lot about the difficulties of managing—how hard it is to be fair, how unreasonable some people can be, how important it is to communicate," Stack explains.

Employee development is of primary concern; however, Stack doesn't give much credence to formal training. He believes in the importance of on-the-job experience: "I can tell you all there is to know about bass fishing. . . . But it won't mean much until you go out on a lake and start throwing a lure. When you feel that first bite or have that first backlash, then you'll begin to learn about fishing." Mistakes in management and on the front lines are forgiveable as long as people are becoming more seasoned and valuable. Stack, who has written extensively for *Inc.* magazine, displays his dedication to all employees in *Mad About Layoffs.* Why is he mad? Because he believes that "layoffs are a sign of management failure," and the workers shouldn't take the brunt of the consequences.

# Mad about Layoffs
## *Jack Stack*

**B**usiness has been taking a beating lately, and we've been taking it lying down. We've been getting hit from the right, the left, and the center. Pat Buchanan accuses us of promoting trade deals that send American jobs to the Third World. Robert Reich talks about a growing wage gap and the rise of the anxious class. But, above all, there are the stories about layoffs—about companies that do layoffs amid record profits, about a stock market that rewards companies for eliminating jobs, about CEOs who fatten their own portfolios by putting thousands of people out of work.

And we've had nothing to say about all that. We've let politicians and pundits define us as ruthless downsizers, wreckers of communities, greedy monsters who care about nothing except "the bottom line of a balance sheet," as Buchanan likes to say. I know. He says he's talking just about "corporate butchers," but if no one stands up and takes him on, we all get tarred by the same brush.

Frankly, it's mind-boggling that more corporate leaders haven't spoken up for business, that no one has said, "Look, we can solve this. We are the most creative businesspeople in the world. Yes, there are problems with the way we've run companies in the past. We can fix those problems. We are the *only* ones who can fix them. There are no political solutions. There are only business solutions. All the answers lie in the private sector."

---

> I have no patience with CEOs who make excuses for layoffs, who say they're cutting jobs only to make the company more competitive in the future, to protect the interests of shareholders, . . . or whatever.

---

So why do we sit here like rabbits frozen in the headlights of an oncoming truck? Part of it, I suppose, is that we hope all of this . . . will go away. I doubt it. These issues have emerged now because of real anxieties that have been nurtured very deliberately—about the wage gap, about technology, about outsourcing, and so on. The layoffs have become a lightning rod for all those anxieties. Especially layoffs at companies with record-breaking profits. Or layoffs that produce a bonanza for the managers who ordered them.

Now, I don't blame people for getting mad about layoffs. I have no patience with CEOs who make excuses for layoffs, who say they're cutting jobs only to make the company more competitive in the future, to protect the interests of shareholders, to avoid bigger layoffs down the road, or whatever. The implication is that, by downsizing, the CEOs are just doing their job and earning their salaries.

Bullshit.

Layoffs are a sign of management failure. You lay people off when you've screwed up, when you've guessed wrong about the market, when you haven't anticipated some critical development or created adequate contingency plans. Reality comes along, smacks you in the head, and forces you to cut costs. Most managers will look for any other costs they can cut before taking away people's jobs. When downsizing is the only choice, it's a sign of how badly management has failed, and the people who get hurt are invariably those who had nothing to do with creating the problems in the first place.

That is a tragedy. It is a terrible injustice. It may be necessary in some circumstances, but it's something most people would work very hard to avoid. I frankly don't understand how some CEOs can take away the livelihood of thousands of people and then pocket millions in bonuses and stock gains. I don't know how they live with themselves. Of course, I also have a hard time understanding why the stock market would bid up the price of a company's stock after a downsizing. Obviously, investors believe lower costs will translate into future profits, but they underestimate just how devastating a layoff can be.

---

Layoffs are a sign of management failure. You lay people off when you've screwed up, when you've guessed wrong about the market, when you haven't anticipated some critical development or created adequate contingency plans.

---

Layoffs are terrible for businesses. They destroy the mutual trust and respect needed to make a company successful. If you're forced to do one, the message should be, "This stinks, and none of us take any satisfaction in it." You should do everything possible to harness the anger of the organization so that you never, ever have to have another layoff. The CEO needs to come right out and say it: "I hate this, it's painful, I'm not going to let it happen again." Even then, it will take a long time to repair the damage.

Let me add that I realize there are times when a company has no choice but to downsize, regardless of who's to blame or what the consequences may be. What's more, the CEO is the only one who can make that call. We certainly don't want the government involved. If you try to discourage layoffs by regulating the process, as the Europeans have done, you will stifle job generation, weaken the economy, and promote exactly the kind of corporate behavior that is the greatest threat to job security in the long run. You have to let the market work, even if it hurts.

But that doesn't mean we as businesspeople have to buy into the crazy notion that layoffs are all right—a normal, inevitable, maybe even necessary condition of doing business in today's economy. You know the line. Companies *have* to eliminate jobs, even in good times, we're told, just to remain competitive. We hear the same message, over and over. Here's one version from a recent *Wall Street Journal* column by Michael Hammer of reengineering fame, titled, "Who's to Blame for All the Layoffs?": "No company knows what its customers will demand, what its products will be, or even in exactly what business it will be five years hence. How can such a company offer its employees more than interim employment?"

---

Layoffs are terrible for businesses. They destroy the mutual trust and respect needed to make a company successful.

---

There's something seriously out of whack about that whole way of thinking. Forget the theory behind it. Forget the credentials of the people who spout it. Look at it as a CEO. Anyone who runs a business today knows that finding and keeping the right people is more important than ever. We know how critical it is to break down the barriers in a company, eliminate the internal marketing and the corporate politics, and get everybody working together, moving in the same direction. We've tried one thing after another—total quality management, self-directed work teams, participatory management, you name it—in an attempt to achieve a sense of common purpose and focus. Even the accounting profession has had to recognize the market value of a company's internal spirit and to quantify its "intellectual capital." So how can we square all that with the idea that in today's economy every company has to lay people off from time to time, and there's nothing much we can do about it, so we might as well just sit back and accept the inevitable? It's nuts. It's corporate insanity. And it's *wrong.*

Preventing layoffs is management's responsibility. It's management's primary responsibility. In a sense, it's management's only responsibility. Because to prevent layoffs, you have to do a lot of other things right. And you're much more likely to do them when you're constantly reminding yourself that jobs are at stake and that you're responsible for the livelihood of real people who have put their trust in you.

So you try to figure out how to protect those jobs, and pretty soon you realize that you need a process to achieve *sustainable growth.* I'm talking about a rate of growth you can maintain year after year, through good times and bad, despite down markets, wrong projections, fickle customers, devious competitors, nasty surprises, whatever. In my company, that rate is 10 to 15 percent a year. This is not just a goal; it's a *mind-set.* Everyone knows the number, thinks about it, looks for ways to achieve it. When we sit down to do our annual plan, our whole focus is on determining where the growth will come from in the following year—and what contingencies and trapdoors we have in case we're wrong.

---

Preventing layoffs is management's responsibility. It's management's primary responsibility. In a sense, it's management's only responsibility.

---

We call this process "high-involvement planning," and its key ingredient is paranoia. We look for every potential booby trap and figure out what we'll do if we step in one.

Once we have the final plan, we build our compensation program around achieving it. Anything we earn above our targets bounces up to a bonus program. We set our base pay at a level we know we can handle, even in a bad year. So the bonus not only drives the profits of the company but ensures that people take home more money when things go well.

---

We know what it's like to go through layoffs. We know how it feels to manage a workforce filled with fear and uncertainty, anger and mistrust. We never want to be in that position again.

---

And what happens if we run into trouble despite all our planning? The first thing that goes is the bonus program. The second is the increase in profits. Only then are we forced to look at our people costs—and the answer still may not be layoffs, because we have places to put people. We have subsidiaries that are growing. We started them partly to create opportunities for our middle managers and partly to give us another layer of protection against layoffs. We could launch them because we had people already trained to run companies, thanks to the Great Game of Business, the open-book-management system we developed in the 1980s. We didn't want to lose those people, and yet we felt—and still feel—the same pressures to reduce overhead as everyone else. The subsidiaries give us a way to keep our overhead in check without laying anyone off. Of course, they also represent the future of our business, and the means for driving shareholder value.

Why do we do all this? Because we believe we're here to create jobs, not eliminate them. We know what it's like to go through layoffs. We know how it feels to manage a workforce filled with fear and uncertainty, anger and mistrust. We never want to be in that position again. This doesn't guarantee that we won't fail, but if we're ever forced into a layoff, at least people will know that we did everything possible to prevent it.

And our way is certainly not the only way. Far from it. I believe the vast majority of businesspeople have the same goals and values as we do. Business, after all, has always been the engine of opportunity in this country. It's the means by which we create better lives for ourselves, better communities for our families, a better future for our children. We *do* have solutions to the problems the politicians are trying to exploit for their own purposes. It's time to stand up and say so.

1996

When *Forbes* magazine named Sam Walton, founder of Wal-Mart, the "richest man in America" in 1985, it was a testimony to his achievement, but also a nuisance. Later he recalled how everyone started asking him for money, from those representing worthy causes to "just about every harebrained, cockamamy schemer in the world." Meanwhile, Walton just wanted to get his hair cut in peace at the local barber. He never forgot his humble upbringing in a poor farm community in rural Missouri, the heart of the dustbowl of the Depression years, and he eschewed a flashy lifestyle. After attending the University of Missouri, his first job was with J. C. Penney, founded by another thrifty character. His career in merchandising was put on hold while he served in the armed forces during World War II. Afterward, determined to enter into business for himself, he did not return to his old job.

Walton bought his first variety store, a Ben Franklin, with $5,000 of his own savings and $20,000 loaned by his father-in-law. Five years later he sold it and opened Walton's 5 & 10 in Bentonville, Arkansas. Not until 1962 did Walton officially open his first store under the Wal-Mart name. Discount pricing and self-service have played a major role in his success, but more important was Walton's strategy for expansion. To keep distribution costs at a minimum, all new stores had to be within a day's drive of an existing distribution center. That meant building a center and saturating an area, before moving on. For years, Walton handpicked spots, flying his plane around the country to find growth areas.

Keeping his employees motivated in his cost conscious stores was a top priority. Walton had 10 rules for building a successful business. Number 6: "CELEBRATE your successes. Find some humor in your failures. Don't take yourself too seriously. Loosen up, and everybody around you will loosen up. Have fun. Show enthusiasm—always." In *Creating a Culture* Walton explains how he livened up meetings with the University of Arkansas cheer that goes in part, "Whoooooooo Pig. Sooey!" No doubt, he hated a long face.

# Creating a Culture
## *Sam Walton*

Not many companies out there gather several hundred of their executives, managers, and associates together every Saturday morning at seven-thirty to talk about business. Even fewer would begin such a meeting by having their chairman call the Hogs. That's one of my favorite ways to wake everybody up, by doing the University of Arkansas's Razorback cheer, real early on a Saturday. You probably have to be there to appreciate the full effect, but it goes like this:

Whoooooooooooooooooooooo Pig. Sooey!
Whoooooooooooooooooooooooooooo Pig. Sooey!
Whoooooooooooooooooooooooooooooooooo Pig. Sooey!
RAZORBACKS!!!!!

And if I'm leading the cheer, you'd better believe we do it loud. I have another cheer I lead whenever I visit a store: our own Wal-Mart cheer. The associates did it for President and Mrs. Bush when they were here in Bentonville not long ago, and you could see by the look on their faces that they weren't used to this kind of enthusiasm. For those of you who don't know, it goes like this:

Give Me a W!
Give Me an A!
Give Me an L!
Give Me a Squiggly!
(Here, everybody sort of does the twist.)
Give Me an M!
Give Me an A!
Give Me an R!
Give Me a T!
What's that spell?
Wal-Mart!
What's that spell?
Wal-Mart!
Who's number one?
THE CUSTOMER!

I know most companies don't have cheers, and most board chairmen probably wouldn't lead them even if they did. But then most companies don't have folks like Mike "Possum" Johnson, who entertained us one Saturday morning back when he was safety director by taking on challengers in a no-holds-barred persimmon-seed-spitting contest, using Robert Rhoads, our company general counsel, as the official target. Most companies also don't have a gospel group called the Singing Truck Drivers, or a management singing group called Jimmy Walker and the Accountants.

---

We're constantly doing crazy things to capture the attention of our folks and lead them to think up surprises of their own. We like to see them do wild things in the stores.

---

My feeling is that just because we work so hard, we don't have to go around with long faces all the time, taking our-

106

selves seriously, pretending we're lost in thought over weighty problems. At Wal-Mart, if you have some important business problem on your mind, you should be bringing it out in the open at a Friday morning session called the merchandising meeting or at the Saturday morning meeting, so we can all try to solve it together. But while we're doing all this work, we like to have a good time. It's sort of a "whistle while you work" philosophy, and we not only have a heck of a good time with it, we work better because of it. We build spirit and excitement. We capture the attention of our folks and keep them interested, simply because they never know what's coming next. We break down barriers, which helps us communicate better with one another. And we make our people feel part of a family in which no one is too important or too puffed up to lead a cheer or be the butt of a joke—or the target in a persimmon-seed-spitting contest.

> My feeling is that just because we work so hard, we don't have to go around with long faces all the time, taking ourselves seriously, pretending we're lost in thought over weighty problems.

We don't pretend to have invented the idea of a strong corporate culture, and we've been aware of a lot of the others that have come before us. In the early days of IBM, some of the things Tom Watson did with his slogans and group activities weren't all that different from the things we do. And, as I've said, we've certainly borrowed every good idea we've come across. Helen and I picked up several ideas on a trip we took to Korea and Japan in 1975. A lot of the things they do over there are very easy to apply to doing business over here. Culturally, things seem so different—like sitting on the floor eating eels and snails—but people are people, and what motivates one group generally will motivate another.

Back in 1984, people outside the company began to realize just how different we folks at Wal-Mart are. That was the year I lost a bet to David Glass* and had to pay up by wearing a grass skirt and doing the hula on Wall Street. I thought I would slip down there and dance, and David would videotape it so he could prove to everyone back at the Saturday morning meeting that I really did it, but when we got there, it turned out David had hired a truckload of real hula dancers and ukulele players—and he had alerted the newspapers and TV networks. We had all kinds of trouble with the police about permits, and the dancers' union wouldn't let them dance without heaters because it was so cold, and we finally had to get permission from the head of Merrill Lynch to dance on his steps. Eventually, though, I slipped on the grass skirt and the Hawaiian shirt and the leis over my suit and did what I think was a pretty fair hula. It was too good a picture to pass up, I guess—this crazy chairman of the board from Arkansas in this silly costume—and it ran everywhere. It was one of the few times one of our company stunts really embarrassed me. But at Wal-Mart, when you make a bet like I did—that we couldn't possibly produce a pretax profit of more than 8 percent—you always pay up. Doing the hula was nothing compared to wrestling a bear, which is what Bob Schneider, once a warehouse manager in Palestine, Texas, had to do after he lost a bet with his crew that they couldn't beat a production record.

---

We build spirit and excitement. We capture the attention of our folks and keep them interested . . . We break down barriers, which helps us communicate better with one another.

---

Most folks probably thought we just had a wacky chairman who was pulling a pretty primitive publicity stunt.

* CEO of Wal-Mart.

What they didn't realize is that this sort of stuff goes on all the time at Wal-Mart. It's part of our culture, and it runs through everything we do. Whether it's Saturday morning meetings or stockholders' meetings or store openings or just normal days, we always have tried to make life as interesting and as unpredictable as we can, and to make Wal-Mart a fun proposition. We're constantly doing crazy things to capture the attention of our folks and lead them to think up surprises of their own. We like to see them do wild things in the stores that are fun for the customers and fun for the associates. If you're committed to the Wal-Mart partnership and its core values, the culture encourages you to think up all sorts of ideas that break the mold and fight monotony.

1992

When Martha Ingram's husband Bronson died in 1995, most didn't consider his wife as the successor to his empire, which included the largest computer wholesaler in the world, Ingram Micro, with sales reaching $22 billion in 1998. To many, she was simply an attractive Southern belle, born and raised in Charleston, South Carolina. But in her youth Ingram had been instilled with both a business sense and confidence; her father owned a broadcasting company, and he always told her that as the oldest child she was expected to take over if anything happened to him. She reflected, "It seems particularly odd in today's world, because women frequently feel there's a glass ceiling. But my father never said anything to me about being a woman or how odd it would be to be in the business world."

Nowadays, plenty of people seek advice from Ingram, a Vassar graduate who is on the boards of Weyerhauser, First American Bank, and Baxter International. Back in 1979, her husband invited her to become more involved in the business—officially, she was vice president of corporate affairs—and in 1981 she became a board member. "I knew that I was part of a team with Bronson. He was certainly the big decision maker, but he bounced a lot off me. . . . I definitely shared with my husband the sense of wanting to win, of wanting to accomplish whatever it was we set out to do."

Once Ingram took the reins, one of her first tasks was to decide what to do with Micro—its fast growth was eating resources, and management was pushing to take the whole company, Ingram Industries, public. But then there were the family's interests to consider. To solve the problem, she decided to spin off Micro, taking it public in 1996, with the family holding about 60 percent of the stock. However, she takes a hands-off approach to operations, leaving that to the CEO. In the following selection, Ingram explains that when employees "feel they work for an employer that truly recognizes the need for balance in all our personal lives, coupled with a sense of social responsibility," they will be committed to giving the company the edge.

# Community Involvement: Key to Profits, Productivity
## *Martha Ingram*

The demands on corporate executives in today's fast-paced business environment are tremendous. Leading the charge is the PC industry. Our internal and external audiences—including shareholders, analysts, customers, vendors and associates—all expect and demand a profitable return on their investments, as well as first-class service.

Servicing that demand can be all-consuming, especially in a society where we unfortunately have created an expectation of instant gratification. No ifs, ands, or buts about it: We want what we want, and we want it now.

To determine how we are doing in delivering to these expectations, each year companies conduct customer surveys that measure customer satisfaction and service, employee morale and retention, and a myriad of other qualifiers, all of which attempt to ensure that the company is on target to profitable growth, while at the same time, trying to outdistance the competition.

These measurement tools are important—if not crucial—for a business to understand its position in the marketplace. However, as we take stock of all that we have accomplished during the past year, I believe that it also is necessary to measure another aspect of the company's performance. It is the

111

aspect called "social responsibility" in the communities in which we live, work and play. Too often we pay little attention to the immediate community that provides us with our greatest asset—our associates.

Many of us have been fortunate to be able to grow our companies, while others have become a target of the latest merger-and-acquisition frenzy. In both good and bad times, it is associates that can make or break the company.

Think about it. Employees are the single sustainable competitive advantage of every company. Employees interact with our customers—our other key audience—daily. As the ultimate representatives of the company, they are the mirror image of the health and well-being of the entire organization. And that is one of the reasons why it is so critical for companies to give back to the community.

Social responsibility can be measured many ways, such as time investments or financial resources. Whether your company gives back by providing products and services to the community or through a program that gives associates time to be actively involved in a volunteer program, consider that studies have shown that employees who volunteer are more loyal to their employers. Further, companies with reputations for being socially responsive have a significant recruiting advantage. People simply like to work for people who care.

There is still another aspect to this social responsibility phenomenon that we employers must face. It is called balance. With the fast-paced, driving nature of our industry, and with the frenetic competitive landscape characterized by ever increasing shorter product life cycles, more intense pressure on sales, margins and profits, it seems that a proper balance is often forsaken between our work lives and our personal lives.

How often do we walk in the door at night to our spouses and children, preoccupied by the events of the day, tired and irritable, and ready only for a little quiet time. Meanwhile, cries of "Mommy's home" or "Daddy's home" are greeted too often with little enthusiasm because of the day we have had. That is a tragedy. Quality time with our children and spouses should always be a priority.

There is no question that our most sustainable, long-term advantage comes from our associates. When they are happy, when they feel they have time for a life at work and a life at home, when they feel they work for an employer that truly recognizes the need for balance in all our personal lives, coupled with a sense of social responsibility, then we will have what others cannot touch—a dedicated, committed and appreciative workforce. This gives a company a competitive edge.

1997

# BERNIE MARCUS AND ARTHUR BLANK

Believe it or not, the cofounders of the phenomenally success-ful Home Depot were both fired from a home improvement center company. They were also destined to be together. Bernie Marcus's parents emigrated from Russia and settled in the tene-ments of Newark, New Jersey, where his father became a cabi-net maker. While in high school Marcus decided that medicine was his calling, became obsessed with Sigmund Freud, and actually learned to hypnotize people. Marcus enrolled in the Rutgers College premed program, but due to limited finances had to transfer to its pharmacy school, graduating in 1954. But as he later admitted, a wanna-be doctor makes for a bad phar-macist, and he eventually found himself managing discount stores. He landed at Handy Dan Home Improvement Centers, a fateful last stop before Home Depot.

Meanwhile, Arthur Blank was growing up in Queens, New York, where his father was—a pharmacist. Blank attended Bab-son College, where he earned a degree in accounting and then took a job with the accounting firm Arthur Young & Company. After five years there, he decided to join the family business. Several years later his mother sold the business to Daylin Cor-poration, which happened to own—Handy Dan. Blank also joined Daylin, becoming president of their drug and discount store division. When that division was sold, Marcus recruited Blank to join the Handy Dan executive team. There, both men worked for a boss who called himself "Ming the Merciless," after the Flash Gordon villain, and there they were both fired in 1978 after a series of conflicts with Ming.

The next year they opened their first Home Depot store. While the first store was indeed the size of their trademark foot-ball fields, money was tight, and behind the front row of prod-ucts the shelves were filled with empty boxes. Twenty years later, with over 750 stores and more than 150,000 associates, empowerment is key. In *The Invisible Fence* Blank takes over the narration and describes how real empowerment means pushing managers to learn the boundaries of their job just like a dog being zapped by an invisible, electric fence.

# The Invisible Fence
*Bernie Marcus and Arthur Blank*

One of the big advantages that we have over most of our competitors is being decentralized. It allows us to be close to the customers and access the best knowledge in the field. That way we can do not only what is right for the stores, but also respond to the marketplace and support the associates in the stores.

We began decentralizing operations away from Atlanta when our West Coast expansion was in full bloom and we created an autonomous California-based division to handle business in that part of the country. That eventually became the model for the whole company: We now have additional regional divisional headquarters in the Northeast, Midwest, Southeast, Southwest, and Canada. In addition, EXPO Design Center has its own individual management structure.

We entered the Northeast market without regional offices in place, something we wouldn't do today. I [Arthur] tried running the Northeast myself for the first year, but quickly realized we needed someone on the ground there full-time, every day, learning, listening, and responding to the market as a native. I turned over that responsibility to Larry Mercer and went looking for a counterpart to him in the Southeast.

That's when Bruce Berg was asked to fly up to New York for a meeting. He was surprised to find a limousine waiting for him with me inside.

"How would you like to be president of the Southeast division?" I asked.

"Yeah," Berg said nonchalantly, "that would be okay."

"Okay," I said. "You're the president of the Southeast division."

The limo was quiet for a few moments as Berg soaked up what had just transpired.

"Hey, Art," he said, breaking the silence, "what does the president of the Southeast division *do?*"

"We'll talk about that later."

Later was two weeks later.

"Bruce, let me put your new responsibilities this way," I explained. "Think of your new job as being enclosed by an invisible fence and you are wearing a collar. Out there, somewhere, is a fence, and you are going to keep running around in the yard doing your thing. At some point, you will inevitably go beyond the boundaries of what your job responsibilities should be and you will hit that fence. And when you do, you will get buzzed."

"Art," Berg asked, "have you ever hit an invisible fence?"

"No."

"Well, I have, and it really hurts."

And sure enough, he was zapped by the fence quite a few times. That's because the role of a Home Depot regional president is a somewhat amorphous position. If things go right in the division, everyone is rewarded. But if anything goes wrong in the division, there is only one call I will make.

We learned together where that fence is; it is in different places for different people, and it moves all the time. The division presidents have a tremendous amount of autonomy. They should—with multibillion-dollar individual businesses under their management, they are effectively running the largest home improvement businesses around. For each of them, that fence will have a different effect, a different amount of juice. It's not a fixed fence for all of them. What works in Maine might not necessarily click in Atlanta or Seattle. Take Vern Joslyn, for example, the president of our largest division, the Northeast. Vern is always the first one to try anything new and, subsequently, everyone in the division follows his lead as entrepreneurial risk-taker.

---

We don't build a straitjacket around our division presidents, and that is by design. We want them to be flexible; we want them to be entrepreneurial.

---

For new division presidents, I might draw the circle around them a little tighter for a time until they become more comfortable and can run freer; they're not going to run into the street and get hit by a car.

When Hurricane Andrew hit South Florida, the invisible fence moved and Berg got buzzed. Since we didn't have a clue in Atlanta what to do, we pretty much left dealing with the storm and its aftermath up to Berg. The system worked, too, until Berg got a bright idea one day about building a huge blacktop addition on the land where our four-day-old Cutler Ridge store had been flattened by the hurricane; Berg needed a place to store all his incoming lumber and building materials.

It was the right decision, but he forgot to tell me about it. On a rare day when Berg was playing hooky on his boat, I called him. Berg got tangled up in the fence pretty good that day.

"Look at the sign on our stores," I said. "Does it say 'Bruce's Depot'?"

"No, it says The Home Depot."

"Well then, don't you think that you should tell *me* when you decide to pave four or five acres and pour $100,000 into a store?"

"Yeah," Berg said sheepishly, "I should have."

I didn't have a problem with the decision—especially at a store hitting $3 million a week in sales, but Berg should have shared the plan with me *before* it happened. "If we are going to work together," I said, "if you are going to be an officer of mine, I will give you great latitude. But other things, I want you to tell me about."

"I don't know the difference."

"Remember the invisible fence?"

"This sucks, man," Berg said. "I don't know where the boundaries are."

"You will get it; don't worry."

Not long after that, Bernie gave Berg some advice.

"First, build trust with Arthur," he said. "Then the fence will be much more elastic."

The invisible fence is not just for our seven division presidents. It is used and applied throughout the company, up to and especially in the stores. Our store managers and their assistant managers have more operating and decision-making leeway than in any other retail chain in America. We want them to roam and test parameters to see how far they can move out on the fringe of the property.

Those who can deal with the fence experiment more. They bring more unconventional thinking to the table rather than always toeing the line.

We don't build a straitjacket around our division presidents, and that is by design. We want them to be flexible; we want them to be entrepreneurial. We would rather have them push harder in that direction than not, and if we impose our own limits on them, they will stay well within those boundaries all the time. But sometimes they need to go beyond that, and that is another element of our company's culture.

We insist, we *demand* that our people take risks, and then take responsibility for those risks. "It is *your* business, *your* division, *your* market, *your* store, *your* aisle, and *your* customer. It is not a Home Depot customer, it is *your* customer."

We have a policy procedure manual, and in it there is a chapter called "Merchandising." When you open up to that chapter, there are no pages.

---

We insist, we *demand* that our people take risks, and then take responsibility for those risks.

---

That's our way of teaching people to think and to think on their feet. Don't wait for some Home Depot bureaucrat to give you an answer or fix your problem. And don't blame somebody else. If you have something that needs to be fixed, fix it! If there are resources to tap into, tap into them! Like we tell our customers . . . *do it yourself.*

This is a very basic business. We are not trying to put people on the moon. There are still things that require a scalpel; others call for a chain saw.

Bruce Berg still bumps up against the invisible fence because he would rather ask for forgiveness than permission. The difference between then and now, as Bernie intimated, is trust. I tend to be more forgiving when our people are entrepreneurial, particularly if it is in the customer's interest.

Operations may change dramatically from one region to another, but the company's principles stay the same. Nobody tinkers with the principles.

Our managers should never feel our presence over their shoulders. We don't feel compelled to check everything they do. We expect them to make decisions and to make mistakes. We are relentless in our desire for our people to have confidence in themselves. We respect confrontation. And we expect it, too.

1999

# JOHN SCULLEY
## 1939–

The man who went from PepsiCo president to Apple Computer CEO, two diametrically opposed cultures, certainly learned a few management lessons, which he divulges in his aptly named book, *Odyssey.* John Sculley's journey began in the early 1960s when, as a student at Brown University, he married Pepsi icon Donald Kendall's stepdaughter. Sculley then entered a graduate program for architecture, but soon switched to Wharton's MBA program. In 1963 he joined McCann-Erickson, an ad agency, where one of his first jobs was to study the potential of the diet soda market. Two years later he divorced, as did Kendall, who promptly suggested that Sculley interview at PepsiCo since they were no longer associated through marriage.

Sculley subsequently joined PepsiCo in 1967 and ten years later found himself the youngest president in the company's history. "If I was brash or arrogant on my way to the top, it mattered little to me," he writes. "I was an impatient perfectionist. I was willing to work relentlessly to get things exactly right. I was unsympathetic of those who couldn't deliver the results I demanded." That drive paid off in 1978 when Pepsi temporarily dethroned Coke as top soda with their Pepsi Generation ad campaign. "We would not have been able to surpass Coke if not for our tough corporate culture. It put us on a search-and-destroy mission against a Goliath," he reflected.

While Sculley admits that making the move from PepsiCo to Apple made no sense, he couldn't resist Apple cofounder Steve Jobs's challenge: "Do you want to spend the rest of your life selling sugared water or do you want a chance to change the world?" In the beginning all was hunky-dory, with Jobs as chairman and Sculley as CEO, but soon problems surfaced as Sculley attempted to bring some discipline to the growing company and Jobs departed. Sculley, who has had an admittedly checkered experience since retiring from Apple, learned a good deal about managing mavericks, and in *Managing Creativity* he describes the fine art of not giving people goals, but rather directions, so they have plenty of room to operate within a company's mission.

# Managing Creativity
## *John Sculley*

Wanted: Impresario to orchestrate a workshop of wizards.

You're not likely to see an advertisement like that in *The Wall Street Journal*. Yet, when I walked through the Macintosh Building with Steve it became clear that he wasn't just another general manager bringing a visitor along to meet another group of employees. He and many of Apple's leaders weren't managers at all; they were impresarios.

It is an important metaphor for inspiring creativity. Not unlike the director of an opera company, the impresario must cleverly deal with the creative temperaments of artists. At times, he may coach because he knows that creativity is a learning process, not a management process. Other times, he may scold because he knows that creativity requires a demanding commitment of self. The impresario must, in fact, be alternately tough and admiring toward his people.

In art, he ensures that the setting and stage are conducive to the production of a masterpiece. His gift is to merge powerful ideas with the performances of his artists. At Apple, we bring together a company of artists; we build the infrastructure of set designers, stagehands, and a supporting cast; and we applaud the performances of our cast members who oftentimes emerge as stars on their own.

This is the difference between inspiring the growing numbers of "knowledge workers" in our economy and simply motivating people. Virtually all our models of motivation derive from industrial and postindustrial labor. Getting people to reach beyond their best abilities is knowing how to manage creativity itself.

---

The traditional management gospel only thwarts us in trying to understand creativity. Management and creativity might even be considered antithetical states.

---

Business literature reveals almost nothing about how to manage creativity. Nor does any other literature. For example, stories about Harold Ross, founding editor of *The New Yorker* and one of the greatest managers of creativity, go into detail about how much he drank, who he fought with, why he cursed writers—but nothing about how he got even the ordinary people under him to do extraordinary things. The same is true of one of the greatest impresarios of all time, Sir Rudolf Bing, the long-time general manager of the Metropolitan Opera in New York. Relentless in his demand for excellence from his artists, he believed in delegating authority, but he retained final authority and assumed all responsibility. "What goes right is the result of teamwork, and what goes wrong is my fault," he said.

The traditional management gospel only thwarts us in trying to understand creativity. Management and creativity might even be considered antithetical states. While management demands consensus, control, certainty, and the status quo, creativity thrives on the opposite: instinct, uncertainty, freedom, and iconoclasm.

The traditional corporation has largely been left-brained, systematized and quantified. The entrepreneurial model often errs on the other side. It's too loose and iconoclastic, so

122

that when the company meets success, its managers find it difficult to control the accompanying growth without abandoning the very characteristics that led to its success. Yet, to nurture the creative impulse of any organization, there needs to be some reconciliation of the two states.

Apple Computer, obviously, starts with an advantage. It has none of the baggage of a second-wave corporation: no aging plants, no older workforce, and no unions. Many came to Apple precisely because they wanted to work in a different kind of company. So I largely work with people who already are motivated by the company's mission to bring the power of computing to individuals. The task is to get them to work at the highest levels of creativity, not just productivity. The difference is you want people to think, not necessarily work faster. The "Think" signs that Tom Watson scattered all over IBM offices in the 1940s are hardly enough today to get people to do extraordinary work.

The Macintosh team, for example, was a young group of disparate individuals going all-out to accomplish the creation of a product that they believed would change the world. To get each artist to exceed his or her abilities, Steve would go to any length. He wouldn't hesitate to ridicule poor performance publicly within the group, yet he was a master at celebrating milestone accomplishments with his team. A little recognition went a long way toward keeping a worn-out engineer not only working but passionate about his work.

He cared, too, about the environment. The Mac building's theme was great art and great artists. Its rooms were named after Picasso, Matisse, Rembrandt, and other creative luminaries. It transformed a building into a creative incubator because all these differences became symbols that Apple was dramatically different from the second-wave company.

At Apple, management didn't get in the way. In fact, Steve Jobs was less a manager and more an impresario. He knew that the role of management wasn't to stifle creativity through structure and process, but to foster it through unusually innovative means and thinking.

---

The "Think" signs that Tom Watson scattered all over IBM offices in the 1940s are hardly enough today to get people to do extraordinary work.

---

There are no six easy steps to anything in management or art. But there are general principles through which the impresario works to create a higher state of creativity within an organization. These help define the corporation's identity and architecture as well. Consider:

**The safer you can make a situation, the higher you can raise the challenge.** So says Tim Gallwey, author of *The Inner Game of Tennis,* and he's right. Apple impresarios try to remove all hierarchical obstacles, but they ensure that the resources are there when needed and help to build support for the work being done. The impresario makes things safe, which allows artists to do their work without having to deal with the structure of production. And we don't want people to worry about hitting a wrong note in trying to play an extremely difficult piece of music. But the piece has to be difficult. If you reduce the risk without raising the level of effort, you get high arrogance and complacency.

**Don't give people goals; give them directions.** We want to lead people to ideas they haven't dreamed of yet. Unlike most corporations, we don't so much try to define our identity; we try to make it recognizable—not too concrete. So we talk endlessly—and aphoristically—about what we do: "We build people, not computers"; or, "The best way to predict the future is to invent it." I know most culture gurus would have companies memorize their corporate vision. We define our identity as the company that "builds great personal computers," yet we resist hardening our vision to specifically defined goals, believing with Eden Phillpotts that "The universe is full of magical things patiently waiting for our wits to grow sharper." Creative people want to have a strong understanding of the standards of the company, even more than they need to know exactly what it's there to do.

We would rather remind ourselves that our products make a difference in customers' lives; whenever that happens, we can be truly proud. So we would rather say, "We help people grow," which refers to ourselves and our customers. The impresario must ensure that such goals and their nuances are thoroughly understood.

**Encourage contrarian thinking.** While an impresario must provide a sense of discipline, you always need some low level of dissent. There should be a level of tension between discipline and anarchy. I would worry if there wasn't always a little bit of anarchy in the organization. It's like arsenic: a little is medicinal but a lot can kill you. You want to impart medicinal levels of anarchy within an organization so that people feel they are free enough to express opinions without worrying about the implications.

As an impresario, I encourage and elicit contrarian views and contrasts. We want people to be able to see more than they ordinarily might. As psychologist Jerome Bruner has said, contrasting viewpoints are far better than absolute judgments, although many corporate leaders today overly venerate decision making and reward judgments. I find the process of reaching a decision more valuable than the results. It's important to place tension between points of view to extract the best from people. Dissent stimulates discussion, prompting others to make more perceptive observations. And it ultimately influences decision making for the better.

**Build a textured environment to extend not just people's aspirations but their sensibilities.** You can't buy creativity. You have to inspire it. Creative people require the tools and environment which foster their success. Above all, they require an atmosphere conducive to fun and to thinking in non-standard ways. The work environment needs to be informal and relaxed; it needs to remove the symbols of management, which in the traditional company means the uniform of the business suit, the closed-in offices, the overabundance of titles, the executive perks. We try to remove all those symbols, creating an egalitarian environment, because we don't believe there is a difference between the contribution of a single artist or an orchestrator.

But we go beyond this.

---

I would worry if there wasn't always a little bit of anarchy in the organization. It's like arsenic: a little is medicinal but a lot can kill you.

---

Managing creativity has nothing to do with people sitting around a square table "brainstorming." The atmosphere is too rigid. We almost never do anything important in any of our offices—that's where we're constrained into rational, rigid thinking. Apple Fellow Alan Kay talks about stimulating the "body mentality" by creating a tactile environment that jump-starts memory, feeling, emotion. At Xerox PARC, the researchers added showers to their office building as ideal "think tanks." When your consciousness is occupied in relaxation, your unconscious mind—the seat of creativity—is freed to act.

In some Apple buildings, each floor is outfitted with a red-topped popcorn cart, so everyone at Apple can even sniff how different we are. It's another symbol to remind us that Apple is not a traditional corporation, so doesn't think in traditional ways. And at the end of each work week on Friday, the company sponsors beer busts in every building. It's not that employees are into drinking beer; it's a weekly gathering point where people can informally exchange discoveries with each other, a way for a large company to become smaller.

Almost every building has its own theme, so meeting and conference rooms aren't identified by cold, impersonal numbers. Instead, they are named by employees who decide on the theme of their building. In our "Land of Oz" building, the conference rooms are named Dorothy and Toto. Our Management Information Systems Group has meeting rooms with names such as "Greed," "Envy," "Sloth," "Lust," and the remaining deadly sins. It's not accidental that many of these are the symbols of childhood (popcorn included). William Blake believed that in growing up, people move from states of innocence to experience, and then if they're fortunate to "higher innocence"—the most creative state of all.

---

## Defensiveness is the bane of all passion-filled creative work.

---

If a traditional corporation did the same, would it work? Probably not. Because these elements of the new architecture only affirm the vision of the company and how it differs from second-wave corporate models.

**Build emotion into the system.** Defensiveness is the bane of all passion-filled creative work. We keep defenses down in several ways. One way is by thinking about problems differently—not as negatives, for example. We are considering giving people medals for problem finding, not just problem solving. Our world is moving so fast that new problems are being created all the time. The people who find them have tremendous powers of creative observation.

We also deflect defensiveness by our large and public system of rewards, which includes cash and stock option bonuses, individual research budgets, extra time off, even all-expense-paid skiing trips, as part of the reward system. There are special bonuses, separate from merit raises and base salary plans, that put thousands of dollars in individuals' hands within two to three weeks of authorization by their manager/impresarios. As crucial as these incentives are to inspire people to exceed their creative limits, however, they often play less of a role than the public celebration of a person's contributions within Apple. It can start with the simple acknowledgment of all contributors under the heading "Kudos" at the beginning of a company report. It ends, perhaps, with the company's Hero Award, the Apple equivalent of the country's Medal of Honor. It's a large and heavy solid brass medallion with a wide ribbon in Apple's rainbow logo colors.

---

Someday, maybe we'll see more companies searching not for managers and employees, but for impresarios and wizards.

---

**Encourage accountability over responsibility.** We don't give creative people traditional responsibilities, like being at the office every day from eight to five, or check on them for efficiency and punctuality. Instead, they are made accountable for the results of their work. People are given the flexibility to perform a lot of work at home. Indeed, some spend only a day or two a week at the office. Just as academia offers its people the freedom to structure their own time, we do the same, and yet people work incredibly hard. It goes back to our roots in academia.

The impresario must have a clear grasp of what it is we are all here to do. His artists need both the freedom and the discipline to let their creative ideas take us on incredible unexplored journeys. Someday, maybe we'll see more companies searching not for managers and employees, but for impresarios and wizards.

1987

128

# PART III

# Hiring, Firing, and Day-to-Day Management

The managers in Part III offer more practical advice on how to achieve the goals set forth in Part I. David Ogilvy opens with, "I have always tried to hire what J.P. Morgan called 'gentlemen with brains.'" By brains Ogilvy doesn't mean IQ; he desires "curiosity, common sense, wisdom, imagination and literacy." As for who to fire, he targets office politicians with a propensity for backstabbing. How meetings are conducted is important; Lee Iacocca fired questions at subordinates so that they would have to answer from the gut, with no opportunity to massage and distill their answers. Henry Ford went as far as to not bestow titles so information flowed fluidly through his organization, rather than being bogged down in a hierarchy. The daily techniques these managers use to handle people deserve careful consideration as they set the tone within the organization.

# DAVID OGILVY
## 1911–1999

On his way to building one of the world's largest advertising agencies, Scottish-born and -raised David Ogilvy influenced hundreds of thousands of people he never met. "Running an agency," he said, "requires midnight oil, salesmanship of the highest order, a deep keel, guts, thrust, and a genius for sustaining the morale of men and women who work in a continuous state of anxiety." To his father, Ogilvy gives credit for providing the guts and brains: "When I was six, he required that I should drink a glass of raw blood every day. To strengthen my mental faculties, he ordained that I should eat calve's brains three times a week, washed down with a bottle of beer. Blood, brains and beer; a noble experiment." *Blood, Brains and Beer* is also the title of his autobiography.

Before founding his agency, Ogilvy bounced through more than a few jobs, including those of chef and stove salesman. He then decided to immigrate to America in search of adventure, and found work with Dr. George Gallup, creator of the Gallup Poll. When World War II broke out, Ogilvy used his position with Gallup to gather information and advise the British Government on American opinions. He was soon invited to join Britain's Secret Service, and his first mission was to help ruin Latin American businessmen supporting Hitler. It was not until several years after the war, and after a stint as a farmer in Amish country, that Ogilvy finally founded Ogilvy & Mather.

As his fame grew, Ogilvy rubbed shoulders with many captains of industry. One troubling observation: "I seldom came across a top man who showed any ability as a leader. All too many of them, far from inspiring their lieutenants, displayed a genius for emasculating them." To office heads, he advised, "If each of us hires people who are smaller than we are, we shall become a company of dwarfs, but if each of us hires people who are bigger than we are, Ogilvy & Mather will become a company of giants." He opens *Managing Crown Princes* with some suggestions on who to hire—namely those who have "curiosity, common sense, wisdom, imagination and literacy."

# Managing Crown Princes
## *David Ogilvy*

I have always tried to hire what J.P. Morgan called "gentlemen with brains." Did he mean gentlemen in the snobbish sense? I think so. The debt owed by the United States to Roosevelt, Dean Acheson, Averell Harriman, Robert Lovett, John J. McLoy, the Rockefeller brothers and many other aristocrats has not been sufficiently acknowledged. I have been particularly lucky with alumni of St. Paul's and Harvard, notably my partners Esty Stowell and Jock Elliott. But I have also been lucky with gentlemen in the wider sense of the word.

*Brains?* It doesn't necessarily mean a high IQ. It means curiosity, common sense, wisdom, imagination and literacy. Why literacy? Because most communication between agencies and clients is in writing. I don't suggest that you have to be a poet, but you won't climb the ladder very high unless you can write lucid memoranda. I persuaded two of my partners to write a book on the subject. I commend it to you.*

Look for young men and women who can one day *lead* your agency. Is there any way of predicting the capacity to lead? The only way I know is to look at their college records.

---

* *Writing that Works,* by Kenneth Roman and Joel Raphaelson. Harper & Row, 1981

If they were leaders between the ages of 18 and 22, the odds are that they will emerge as leaders in middle life.

Make sure you have a Vice-President in charge of Revolution, to engender ferment among your more conventional colleagues.

## CROWN PRINCES

Spot the corners on your staff, and plan their careers. Royal Dutch Shell has found that the most reliable criteria for selecting what they call Crown Princes are these:

1. The power of analysis.
2. Imagination.
3. A sense of reality.
4. The "helicopter quality"—the ability to look at facts and problems from an overall viewpoint.

John Loudon, the distinguished former head of Shell, believes that when it comes to picking people for senior jobs, *character* is more important than any of these qualities. Dare I confess that I have come to believe in *graphology* as an instrument for assessing character? It is regarded as fakery in the United States, but is widely used in French business. Before accepting my offer of marriage, my wife had my handwriting analysed by *two* graphologists. Their reports were consistent—and accurate.

Promote from within or hire from outside? "Mr. Morgan *buys* his partners," said Andrew Carnegie; "I *grow* mine." In the early days of Ogilvy & Mather, shortage of cash obliged me to pay peanut salaries. Pay peanuts, says Jimmy Goldsmith, and you get monkeys. I chose not to promote my monkeys, but to fill senior openings from outside, with stars like Esty Stowell, Jock Elliott and Andrew Kershaw. Even a mature agency with a pool of potential leaders does well to refresh its blood by occasionally hiring partners from outside.

### Who Not to Hire

Never hire your friends. I have made this mistake three times, and had to fire all three. They are no longer my friends.

Never hire your client's children. If you have to fire them, you may lose the client. This is another mistake I have made.

Never hire your own children, or the children of your partners. However able they may be, ambitious people won't stay in outfits which practice nepotism. This is one mistake I did not make; my son is in the real estate business, secure in the knowledge that he owes nothing of his success to his father.

Think twice before hiring people who have been successful in other fields. I have hired a magazine editor, a lawyer and an economist. None of them developed an interest in advertising.

---

Never hire your friends. I have made this mistake three times, and had to fire all three. They are no longer my friends.

---

And never hire your clients. The qualities which make someone a good client are not the qualities required for success in the agency business. I have made this mistake twice.

### Office Politicians

The hothouse atmosphere in agencies can cause outbreaks of psychological warfare to rival university faculties. The politics became so vicious at Milton Biow's agency that he was forced to close down. I know of seven ways to squelch them:

1. Fire the worst of the politicians. You can identify them by how often they send you blind copies of their poison-pen memos to their rivals.
2. When somebody comes to your office and denounces his rival as an incompetent rascal, summon the rival and make the denouncer repeat what he has just told you.
3. Crusade against paper warfare. Make your people settle their fights face to face.
4. Start a luncheon club within the agency. It turns enemies into friends.
5. Discourage poaching.
6. Don't play favorites.
7. Don't play politics. If you practice the fiendish art of *divide et impera,* your agency will go up in smoke.

*Discipline Works*

Insist that your people arrive on time, even if you have to pay them a bonus to do so. Insist that telephones are answered promptly. Be eternally vigilant about the security of your clients' secrets; indiscretion in elevators and restaurants, the premature use of outside typesetters, and the display of forthcoming advertisements on notice boards can do grave damage to your clients.

Sustain unremitting pressure on the professional standards of your staff. It is suicide to settle for second-rate performance. Above all, insist that due dates are kept, even if it means working all night and over the weekend. Hard work, says the Scottish proverb, never killed a man. People die of boredom and disease. There is nothing like an occasional all-night push to enliven morale—provided you are part of the push. Never leave the bridge in a storm.

St Augustine had this to say about pressure:

To be under pressure is inescapable. Pressure takes place through all the world: war, siege, the worries of state. We all know men who grumble under these pressures, and complain. They are cowards. They lack splendor. But there is another sort of man who is under the same pressure, but does not complain. For it is the friction which polishes him. It is pressure which refines and makes him noble.

I have to admit that I have sometimes found the pressure unbearable; my own fault for frittering away so much time on things which lead nowhere. It is a good idea to start the year by writing down exactly what you want to accomplish,

---

Hard work, says the Scottish proverb, never killed a man.

---

and end the year by measuring how much you have accomplished. McKinsey imposes this discipline on its partners and pays them according to how many of the things on their lists they accomplish.

1983

# MARK McCORMACK
## 1930–

It took only one client to put Mark McCormack on the road to becoming the most powerful person in sports—the great golfer Arnold Palmer, whom he signed in 1959. Today McCormack, who founded the International Management Group (IMG), is considered the father of sports marketing. After earning an undergraduate degree at William & Mary, he attended Yale's law school and then joined a Cleveland, Ohio, law firm. Not long after, Palmer walked through the door looking for help. Recognizing the opportunities that sports marketing, merchandising, and licensing presented, McCormack quit the law firm and founded IMG with $500 in start-up capital.

Over the years, McCormack added a variety of characters to his stables, from the violinist Itzhak Perlman to tennis star Chris Evert to recent golf phenom Tiger Woods. To build a global presence, McCormack targeted well-known athletes in various countries with the hope that signing them would lead to other opportunities. Considering that his firm now has 76 offices in 31 nations, the strategy was a success. Next, he went after the events themselves; for example, beginning in 1968, he handled the television and video rights and licensing deals for Wimbledon. His explanation was pure genius: "Bjorn Borg [tennis legend] can break a leg. Wimbledon cannot." Finally, McCormack went on to create his own lucrative events like the "Skins Game."

Today IMG is the largest non-network producer of sports programming as a result of another McCormack epiphany: Sports, not movies, sells cable and satellite systems. The key, he says, is "being where the consumer is going" because, like an industry, sports is filled with fads. If all that is not enough, McCormack is a prolific writer on business and career issues. He penned the best-selling *What They Don't Teach You at Harvard Business School* and writes a monthly newsletter called *Success Secrets,* from which *How to Make or Break a Hire* is excerpted. His advice: "Parade your thoroughbred in front of top management," because it's one thing to be known as a thoroughbred yourself, but even better if you're known to breed them.

# How to Make or Break a Hire
## *Mark McCormack*

Bosses generally have two courses of action after they hire or promote someone to a new position. Some managers sell the new person's talents and potential within the company. Others take the passive route, letting the new person prove him- or herself on his own. Since circumstances vary with each new hire or promotion, a valid case could be made for either approach. But my preference is to sell the new person to his or her peers aggressively.

I really wasn't aware that a choice existed until a friend pointed out that I always did this. I had just given a young but worthy executive a major bump up in responsibilities at our company and, apparently, was singing his praises every chance I got.

My friend noticed the change of tune and called me on it. "You know, Mark," he said, "this fellow has been working for you for nine years, but I've never heard you mention his name until he got this new promotion."

There's a logical explanation for this. With his new promotion, this executive and I had more contact with each other and, consequently, I had more opportunities to observe him in action. But I'm sure I was also selling his promotion. By advertising my elevated opinion of him, I could elevate other people's opinions of him as well. This, in turn, would make him more effective and would increase the chances that the promotion would be a success.

It's a self-fulfilling approach, which makes it all the more puzzling why so many managers ignore it. Rather than assist their newest hire or promotion, they (consciously or otherwise) resist it. This resistance manifests itself in many subtle ways.

For example, we have one senior executive in our company who insists on personally reporting all his division's activities himself. If I call him up to ask "What's new?" he'll tell me about ongoing deals in five different states and three continents. I'm sure he realizes that I know he cannot physically manage all those transactions alone. And yet he'll never mention his associates who are doing all the work. The implication is that he is doing all those deals himself. I suppose he thinks that crediting his subordinates will somehow diminish him in my eyes. Actually, it would make him seem bigger.

The interesting thing about selling a new employee is how easy it is do, at no expense to your ego, dignity, or reputation. Here are five simple steps:

1. Don't forget the ringing endorsement. This is the most rudimentary advice, yet people still forget it. Instead of citing all the positive reasons they hired or promoted the new person in the first place ("She turned around XYZ company's sales force in a year"), they shrug off her arrival as a non-event ("I hope she works out" or "It may take her some time to learn our ways . . ."). The latter is hardly a ringing endorsement. If I were the newly hired or promoted person, I'd prefer my boss didn't comment on me at all.

2. Urge people to get to know the new person. When a new hire or promotion doesn't work out, it's often because people in the company didn't appreciate the significance of his arrival or what he was capable of. I am constantly cajoling our executives to meet new

people in our company. If I know that Jane Jones is working in an area that the new person, Tom Smith, is familiar with, I will write to Jane Jones to say, "Tom Smith knows more about this area than anyone in our company. Before you proceed any further, you should spend some time going over this with him . . ." That kind of memo sells the new person more effectively than any compliment.

3. Give her high-visibility assignments. As a manager, you can't always wait for your new person to find her special niche within the company. You sometimes have to create the niche by giving her high-profile assignments: e.g., dealing with a major customer, heading up a crucial project, chairing a task force. The more serious the assignment, the more seriously your new person will be taken.

4. Include the new person in your meetings. Quite often, the simple inclusion of the new person in meetings elevates his or her status and credibility. I will often include people in meetings even though their presence is not absolutely necessary. Doing so not only lets me introduce them to a totally new set of characters and contacts, but if, at some point in the meeting, I defer to them and let them demonstrate their expertise, I have enhanced their standing with everyone in the room.

5. Parade your thoroughbred in front of top management. Like the executive mentioned above, a lot of managers are afraid to expose their subordinates to the higher ranks of the company. They reserve that privilege for themselves. Of course, the opposite approach is the smarter move. It's one thing to be known as a thoroughbred executive yourself. It's even better to be known as someone who breeds and attracts other thoroughbreds too.

1997

139

# LOUIS F. SWIFT

Back in 1855, Gustavus Franklin Swift, a *Mayflower* descendent and the 9th of 12 children, started his own meat market business in Cape Cod, Massachusetts—he was only 16 years old. Twenty years later he moved to Chicago to deal in cattle, but there were two major problems: It was expensive shipping the live animals east, and they lost valuable weight on the journey. So Swift experimented with slaughtering the animals in Chicago and then shipping the meat east via refrigerated rail cars. At first he had only 10 cars, but by 1926, with son Louis now running the company, they were operating 5000, and his experiments had revolutionized the meatpacking industry. By then the company was making everything from bacon to soap.

Operations were standardized to both control quality and to avoid scandal. (Their competitor, Armour, was the basis for Upton Sinclair's scathing novel *The Jungle,* in which he details the horrible working conditions of their meatpacking plant.) Mistakes, even relating to such things as cleanliness, could result in food poisoning and death, and were therefore intolerable. The younger Swift recalled, "Father did not consider that any mistakes were allowable in a well-managed business." And Louis concurred: "If any other attitude is taken toward errors, then there is no controlling them."

One of Gustav Swift's favorite tools for communicating displeasure was sarcasm. "He was unquestionably sarcastic," his son wrote. "Sarcasm was his tool for keeping his subordinates alert and free from mistakes which would not be repeated." While the Swifts could be tough bosses, as early as 1900 they were encouraging their employees to buy stock in the company and were quick to give good employees raises, but no verbal praise for fear of spoiling them. The younger Swift certainly portrays his father's dynamic personality in *How G. F. Swift Bossed His Job,* and he also provides some excellent management tips. For example, Swift writes that he received weekly reports that were timely and poignant: "A report which can be treated by the executive as routine is a nonessential routine, and probably should be eliminated."

# How G. F. Swift Bossed His Job
## *Louis F. Swift*

My father doted on weekly reports. Not that he enjoyed going over weary wastes of figures. He did not, for he much preferred action above sitting studiously at a desk for any length of time.

But when the business began to grow beyond the possible supervision of its head, he was forced to become a manager rather than an overseer. And the weekly report was one of his most effective tools of management.

"You've got to know how you stand every week," he used to tell any one who might question the necessity for voluminous reports at such frequent intervals. "If you wait a month, maybe you're broke."

His training had been in a school of business which scarcely knew reports existed. His beginnings had been small, his development through individual enterprises almost microscopic when compared with Swift and Company within five years of its start at Chicago. His inclinations naturally held to spreading his time over just as much as possible of the physical equipment of the business, in the idea that only thus could he hope to know what was going on.

He quickly realized, however, as the business sprang up to unthought of heights, that he must work out other ways to keep a finger on, and in, every activity of Swift and Company. The report, detailed weekly and brought right up to the minute, was his solution of his difficulties in managing so large a property.

---

You've got to know how you stand every week. . . . If you wait a month, maybe you're broke.

---

Every essential fact bearing on the well-being and progress of the business came to him weekly as a matter of routine. It was never disposed of as routine, however. A report which can be treated by the executive as routine is a non-essential routine, and probably should be discontinued!

Better than the regular reports, however, he liked to go over reports of weak departments. Not that a losing part of the business caused him pleasure; rather he enjoyed the sheer difficulty of going into a seat of trouble, digging out the facts, aligning them, and putting things right. So when a department was losing money, he insisted on more frequent and more complete figures than he got from the rest of the business.

The man responsible for the losing department had little rest during the period of loss. My father believed in frequent reminders, and in prompt corrective measures. If correction did not take place, and quickly, then something drastic happened.

Once, for example, all the meat in pickle at the Kansas City plant went sour. This was a serious loss, not only of the money value of the meat, but also of the profits on sales which could not be made because of the curtailed supply.

The reason for the loss was, of course, a faulty cure in use at this plant. And the remedy might have been to reprimand the manager and the man in charge of curing, so that the trouble would not recur through carelessness.

Fundamentally, however, the trouble lay deeper than in the carelessness of the man who had made the error. The weakness was in the management for allowing to continue a condition which at the time was universal in the industry.

The cures for pork were all secret. The head man at each plant had his secret formula. By paying him a large salary, Swift and Company obtained his services, including his general supervision of the curing, and his personal mixing of the pickle. And of course the product of every plant was different. A Swift ham from Omaha was slightly different from a Swift ham from Chicago or St. Joseph or St. Paul or Kansas City.

---

Every essential fact bearing on the well-being and progress of the business came to him weekly as a matter of routine. It was never disposed of as routine, however.

---

The unfortunate happening at Kansas City brought sharply to his mind the fundamental unsoundness of operating this way. So my father called a meeting at Chicago of the head men in the operating end of the business—managers, general superintendents, and so on.

When he had stated the problem, he asked for a vote. The problem was essentially that, if we demanded that the formulas be given to Swift and Company, the men who had the formulas would quit, leaving us in difficulties. Should we demand that they give up their formulas, or should we continue at the old way of doing?

Decidedly the men in that meeting were opposed to taking the bull by the horns. "No," voted each man, as my father asked his opinion. Then the chief spoke.

"You've all voted 'no,' because you're afraid to face a little possible trouble. There's no use dodging trouble, if you've got to do things the wrong way to dodge it. You're wrong on this. I'm going to vote 'yes,' and it will be 'yes.' "

143

The meeting had, so it seemed to many of the men gathered there, been called for no purpose. They thought the new rule might better have been promulgated by a general order from Chicago. But in this, too, they were wrong.

My father wanted to hear at first hand just what they thought about the proposed plan. He wanted them to convince him if right was on their side. Failing that, he decreed that the cure used at each plant should be forwarded to Chicago, the best of the formulas selected, and this standardized formula sent to each plant to be used in future. And by deciding this in the meeting, he let those men who believed sincerely in his judgment see for themselves that he was basing his decision on a principle rather than on caprice.

---

"I vote 'no,' and the noes have it. You men voted 'yes' because you thought I would. I pay you for your real opinions, not to say what you think I think."

---

The change went through without a ripple. The men in charge of curing at each plant sent in their formulas despite the many and lusty threats of quitting which they had previously made. With one or two exceptions, the formulas were almost identical in ingredients and proportions. The standard formula was worked out, after considerable experimenting, almost like these five or six. And, only slightly modified through the experience of the years since it was adopted, this formula is used today as the standard cure in Swift and Company plants everywhere in preparing our pork products for market.

It afterwards developed that the man whose cure was used at Kansas City, one of those who called his cure a secret, was a weak superintendent. In reality he did not know what his own cure was. He trusted the cure to his employees beneath him; they used the hit-or-miss cure, probably no two times alike. This was the reason he would not tell what the cure was. He did not know himself.

The meeting about secret formulas was not the only one which my father ended by voting "yes" when the rest of the meeting had voted unanimously "no." Because he was dominant in the business, because his ideas generally prevailed—of this, more later—his people from time to time fell into the habit of voting on a business question which he brought up as they believed he was going to vote.

---

If the top man makes his decision the moment he has the facts at his disposal, and then dismisses the meeting, it stops the time-wasting before it has a chance to get started.

---

I recall one meeting where every one gathered, from his whole attitude, that G. F. Swift was in favor of the plan which was up for discussion. So, despite some transparent weaknesses in the idea, they voted "yes." After every one had voted—the votes were always polled singly—my father announced:

"I vote 'no,' and the noes have it. You men voted 'yes' because you thought I would. I pay you for your real opinions, not to say what you think I think." It was a good object lesson; it ended the "yessing" for a good many months.

He was not arbitrary when he made these decisions over the stated judgments of his right-hand men. He had the confidence in himself which had been bred by his continuously successful conduct of the business. He knew the right turn of the road to take, where most of his men were guessing in the light of information far less complete than his own. No wonder he generally arrived at the destination while the rest were still wondering what it was all about.

A good deal may be said in favor of this type of conference, after all. It measures up to the ordinary conference as a means of bringing out opinions and information from every one. And then it leaves to the man who is best qualified to decide, the final step, the making of the decision. It puts an automatic stop to buck-passing. No business man of experience will deny that meetings are the champion expedient of the buck-passer and of the time-waster. If the top man makes his decision the moment he has the facts at his disposal, and then dismisses the meeting, it stops the time-wasting before it has a chance to get started. The plan has not been disregarded since my father's time. . . .

He was always known as a pusher of men, but never as an inconsiderate driver by the men who remained with him long enough to get really acquainted with his ways. He worked hard himself, harder than he asked any one else to work. And the men who worked with him liked his pushing.

No business man ever attained greater results from his men than did my father, largely by the simple expedient of expecting of them greater results than other managers looked for. "No dead lines," was a saying he strongly favored—and by it he meant something which had nothing to do with stocks and rates of turnover.

---

No business man of experience will deny that meetings are the champion expedient of the buck-passer and of the time-waster.

---

To my father a dead line was a line which kept some one in the organization from taking an interest in some department or activity with which his daily work did not bring him into contact. The whole business of the company was to be considered the concern of everybody. He would not accept the excuse that "It wasn't in my department" or "I have nothing to do with the sales department." He wanted no tattling; but he wanted every Swift man to think of himself as a Swift man rather than a lard department man, or a hide cellar foreman, or whatever his job.

Because my father was the most important individual in Swift and Company, every Swift man must recognize a duty to him as part of his duty to the company.

How deeply this idea was ingrained in my father's mind, and in his attitude toward making the business, was brought out several times by incidents which in the light of today's attitude toward employees are downright startling. One had to do with a time when his horse, left unhitched before the old Live Stock Exchange Building, took it into his head to run away just as my father was coming out of the door.

Down the crowded street ran the horse, the buggy swaying dangerously through the crowded traffic. Then, out from the sidewalk dashed a workman, seized the horse's head, and after being dragged a few feet brought the rig to a stop.

---

No business man ever attained greater results
from his men than did my father, largely by
the simple expedient of expecting of them
greater results than other managers looked for.

---

My father had been only a few feet behind, on the dead run. He came panting up and addressed the man who had done the risky job:

"What's your name?"

"John Brown, sir."

"Who do you work for?"

With a world of pride in his voice, and the realization that he had done a job for which he would doubtless be praised, the man answered: "I work for you, Mr. Swift."

"All right," declared my father, by now in complete command of the situation. "Be about your business."

Crestfallen, the workman went back to his job—doubtless believing that he worked for a curmudgeon with not an idea of gratitude in his head. Meanwhile father returned to the office, had the man given an increase in pay, called in the superintendent under whom Brown worked and said, "Here's a man worth keeping an eye on. He just did so-and-so. He thinks quickly, and acts quickly. Chances are he'd make a good foreman, first time there's an opening."

---

> He did not believe in bestowing large titles on employees. One of the surest ways to arouse his irritability was by going to him with such a question as, "What shall we call Mr. So-and-so's new assistant?"

---

As for praising the man for bravery, it never entered his chief's mind. The buggy careening down the street belonged to him, and hence was the particular lookout of any Swift employee. Why shouldn't any man have tried to stop it? The point was that by stopping it, Brown had shown himself a better man than the mass and hence deserved his advancement. The raise and the recommendation were not, be it noted, for stopping the horse; they were for having the qualities which he showed when he happened to stop the runaway! . . .

He was in his relations with the people under him, as in all his relationships, absolutely and meticulously fair. But he was never guilty of letting any one believe that he expected from an employee anything less than the utmost. That would not have been good management!

Just as he did not believe in praising a man, so he did not believe in bestowing large titles on employees. One of the surest ways to arouse his irritability was by going to him with such a question as, "What shall we call Mr. So-and-so's new assistant?"

"I've got no use for those titles," he would exclaim in some wrath, waving the interrupter out of the office with gestures of impatience. And very few indeed were the titles bestowed.

The same thing is true in our business today.

Along with his dislike for titles, my father harbored a deep conviction that the business could get along no matter who was in charge. "Swift and Company can get along without any man, myself included," he remarked a few times in my hearing. "This business will be a bigger business after I'm gone—that's what I'm building for."

1927

# AUGUST HECKSCHER
## 1848–1941

Although not an Andrew Carnegie nor a John D. Rockefeller, August Heckscher was one of the more powerful American industrialists of the late 1800s and early 1900s, becoming involved in coal and zinc, among other businesses. Power was bred in his bones; his father had fought against Napoleon Bonaparte and later became prime minister of Germany. Young Heckscher received an excellent education in Germany and Switzerland, but at age nineteen decided to strike out for the United States with $500 in gold that his mother strapped around his waist. Once in the United States, he found work in a Pennsylvania anthracite coal mine. When the manager fell ill, Heckscher took over (both a blessing and a hardship, as unions and gangs were attempting to control the fields).

In 1917, B.C. Forbes, founder of *Forbes* magazine, named Heckscher one of the nation's top industrialists and asked him what it took to succeed. He replied, "Thoroughness and perserverence are cardinal requisites. The trouble with most Americans who fail to succeed is not that they are not brilliant enough, but because they have not laid the proper foundation." The opportunity to be commander arose when he and a cousin purchased a bankrupt zinc plant and later organized the New Jersey Zinc Mines; however, established firms didn't appreciate the upstart Hechscher and fought to void his claims to certain mining lands.

The legal battle lasted 10 years, during which time he lost much of his money to the financial panic of 1890. Hecksher eventually won his legal battle and rebuilt his fortune, as he expanded his operations to include copper mines, real estate development, fire truck manufacturing, and philanthropy. The one question that Heckscher raised in juggling such diverse interests was: "Can good management be reduced to simple rules?" In the following selection he answers himself by describing what managers must be aware of on a day-to-day basis, such as knowing exactly what everyone else in the field is doing. He concludes, "Anyone who knows how to swim can swim in almost any kind of water."

# Can Good Management Be Reduced to Simple Rules?

## *August Heckscher*

In our boarding school in Germany we had a swimming pool. I was 10 years old—this was 64 years ago—and I was afraid to go near the pool lest someone might push me in; I could not swim. One day a couple of the older boys grabbed me by the feet and shoulders and threw me in. Of course I swallowed a lot of water and I thought I was going to drown, but I didn't—I learned to swim. In three days I was swimming well enough, and never since have I been afraid of the water.

Less than a year after coming to this country, I was given a job keeping the books of a coal mine in the Shenandoah region of Pennsylvania. This was just after the close of the Civil War, when the miners' unions were terrorizing the coal fields, the Molly Maguires formulating their policy of murder, and the railroads giving rebates: everything was generally upset. Before I was a fortnight old in my new job, the illness of the owner threw me into the sole management and practical proprietorship of the mine. I learned how to conduct a coal mining business. Since then I have no longer been afraid of any business.

Anyone who knows how to swim can swim in almost any kind of water. Anyone who knows how to conduct one kind of business can learn how to conduct almost any other kind, for certain elemental principles run through business regardless of its size or character. I know this from my own experience, for I have been in about 20 different kinds of business and most of them have been successful.

I went into coal mining, knowing only that coal was black. I went into zinc mining, knowing only that zinc was a metal and was not black, and so on through various other kinds of mining. I went into steel making, knowing nothing of steel. And finally, I went into real estate, knowing nothing of real estate. The failures in this chain have not been expensive, while on the other hand some of the successes have been rather striking, as for instance the Lehigh Zinc and Iron Company, the New Jersey Zinc Company, the Crucible Steel Company, which I joined under first-class leadership, the American La France Fire Engine Company, the Union Bag and Paper Company, and the Anahama Realty Corporation—to mention only the leaders.

---

Anyone who knows how to conduct one kind of business can learn how to conduct almost any other kind. . . .

---

This is in no sense merely a financing or a promoting roster. In the first venture I had no money with which to finance. The money had to be made out of the coal mine. In each subsequent venture I have had an increasingly greater amount of personal funds available, but in many enterprises I was personally the active manager until the danger point had been passed or until it appeared that the business was not worth trying to make successful and had therefore better be killed. I do not believe in letting a business die. I believe in saving it while a shred of hope remains, and killing it when there is not even a shred remaining.

But the interesting thing to me about these various business adventures—and probably it is because I consider business as an adventure that I have been in so many different kinds, for once a business has ceased to be an adventure and becomes comparatively humdrum I want to go on to something else—is that exactly the same set of principles seems to work equally well among all of them.

There is a similarity among all kinds of mining, but there is apparently nothing in common between mining and real estate operations or steel-making. But fundamental principles apply throughout, and since I learned my principles in a great Hamburg exporting house—which dealt in almost everything under the sun—it seems quite safe to say that they are universal in their application. And let me say that I do not claim credit for having discovered these principles. They are as old as business, and as free as the air we breathe.

---

I do not believe in letting a business die. I believe in saving it while a shred of hope remains, and killing it when there is not even a shred remaining.

---

I do not pretend to have worked out the laws of business. I am only offering a few first principles that are to me absolutely basic. From what I have seen of business generally in this past half century, both as an active participant and as a bank director, I am convinced that a great many businesses do not come through simply because the managers refuse to recognize certain elementary principles and to reduce all their problems to the terms of these principles. For what is the use of trying to solve complex problems when those complex problems can as easily be resolved into simple, elementary ones that solve themselves through mere statement?

All of this naturally does not apply to problems of a purely technical nature—to problems which belong primarily in the field of the engineer or of the chemist. For that which is technical, one needs a technical man and, if competent, he is nearly always worth his price—whatever it may be. But the technique and the direction of an enterprise are very different subjects. The technique is essentially of detail—perfection in technique will not of itself make a business successful, although bad technique will most certainly make it a failure.

Indeed, I have never made the slightest effort to master more than the principles of the technical side of any enterprise in which I have been concerned. I have found it necessary to know only enough to grasp what the purely technical men are talking about. One has to keep a perspective on a business in order to direct it, and one of the easiest ways to lose that perspective is to become involved in the scientific niceties of technical processes. This invariably occurs. I doubt if any brain is sufficiently large to permit its owner to be a first-class technician and a first-class business man, and for that reason I should never put a professional man or any specialist at the head of a business. It is not impossible for one man to have both business and professional knowledge—but it is highly improbable.

No individual business is quite like any other individual business, but also they are not wholly unlike, and it has been my experience that the principles of greatest importance are universal. Sticking close to these principles leads one inevitably to judge the importance and to work out the details of any particular business without any great difficulty.

Perhaps these "principles" are not principles. Possibly they are only practises. But I do not see how a man, bearing them in mind, can well go wrong. They are not inclusive. They are only suggestive. Here they are:

154

# I

A thorough acquaintance with general business methods.

This seems so elementary at first glance as not to be worth talking about. It is elementary, but it is, nevertheless, worth talking about and for this reason: A business continues only as its income exceeds its outgo. Every business problem eventually gets down to that. Therefore, we must know through every minute whether income is exceeding outgo and, if not, why not. . . .

# II

If a competitor is selling or producing cheaper than you are, find out why and then shape your policy on the facts.

This again brings us back to fundamentals. Nearly every enterprise is in competition with at least one other enterprise, and it is right and healthful that it should be. But if the other man is consistently underselling you, the only thing to do is find out why. Otherwise your business will be undermined before you know it. The obvious reply to a lower price is a still lower one—a rate war. Rate wars do not pay; like most wars they leave the participants so exhausted at the end that a fresh neutral can step in and take the business. The better course is to discover how the other man makes his price or his quality.

You know your own figures and from them you can judge his; unless he is operating more efficiently than you are, his price may be a result of bad bookkeeping—he may not know that he is selling at a loss. If such proves to be the case it is better to go along on less business for a while than to go out fighting for orders that do not bring profits. There is nothing in striving to see who can lose the most money. Next best to making a profit yourself is to increase the loss of a reckless competitor.

If, on the other hand, you find that he is making his prices through lower costs due to better methods, the only course left to you is to better your own methods so that you will at least be on even terms. . . .

# III

If you cannot pay debts when they are due, fully explain why and preserve your credit.

---

So powerful is a good reputation that a man can actually go through bankruptcy without losing his credit.

---

Following an exact financial schedule will ordinarily bring funds in hand to retire notes or accounts when they fall due. And putting most of the profits into surplus instead of into your pocket will usually provide a sufficient reserve to make good any defaults by other than very large debtors. But a young business will not have a reserve, and an older business may have a succession of losses or postponements which impair the reserve to such a degree that it cannot meet its obligations as they mature. The largest asset in an emergency is reputation.

---

Most men of poor financial reputation are exceedingly good at excuses—a man may be too competent at making excuses.

---

So powerful is a good reputation that a man can actually go through bankruptcy without losing his credit. A financial reputation is built by the man himself rather than by his bank statements. From my membership of bank boards I know that this is now recognized by every intelligently managed financial institution. For even the best of financial statements have a way of shrivelling in bad times. The payments of bills when they become due is the surest way to build a reputation, and when it is not possible to make the payment at the time, a full explanation of why, if you are in the right, will keep your reputation from being impaired.

---

Do not nurse a loss. It is impossible to do business without now and again sustaining a loss. The big losses come from trying to avoid the inevitable. . . .

---

This is something very different from an excuse. Most men of poor financial reputation are exceedingly good at excuses—a man may be too competent at making excuses. The sort of explanation I have in mind comprehends laying before the debtor the facts on which you predicated your ability to pay. If you thereby disclose a fine grasp of business and a careful attention to every detail, showing clearly that the default is not due to any false reasoning, the postponing of the payment may really increase your credit standing.

## IV

Do not nurse a loss. It is impossible to do business without now and again sustaining a loss. The big losses come from trying to avoid the inevitable—from hanging on to hopes rather than facts and thereby bringing on complications which, had the loss been taken at the beginning, could have been avoided. I found that out through the ownership of a copper mine in Vermont, where I persevered despite every obstacle and lost nearly $5,000,000 in the end.

In our first zinc venture we had an example of this, that nearly put us under. Our sales manager thought that he could get a higher price for zinc by waiting until the market grew better. The price was then falling. Our warehouses filled up with zinc and almost before we realized it most of our working capital was in unsold zinc. We could have borrowed money against that zinc and held on, but if the market fell very low, as it promised, we should have trouble in meeting our notes. We were also in a period of destructive competition. We decided, after some stormy sessions, to get rid of our stock at whatever price we could. Events proved that had we not done so—had we borrowed and attempted to hold out against the market—we should have failed utterly. As it was we got by with a loss which, although it strained us, did not break us. Had the zinc been sold right at the beginning instead of being allowed to accumulate, we should have got out with a slight loss.

Nursing a loss is inconsistent with business principles. It is one way of letting the emotions obscure the facts.

# V

When you are managing a business know its every detail and what every one else in your field is doing.

---

A manager who finds himself too busy to know everything about the business he is supposed to be running is not the man for manager.

---

This may seem inconsistent with what I said earlier in this article, but I am again barring technical details. What I mean is that an active manager must know absolutely what is going on. If he finds he cannot attend to details, then he ought to resign and let someone else take active charge. This is perhaps the old-fashioned theory of business, but it is a theory which, to my mind at least, is absolutely correct.

It is not difficult to grasp detail provided one does not have to give any time to learning the rudiments of business. I do not care how large the operations may be, it is always possible to have the details summarized in such form that they can be kept track of. Income, outgo, costs, and the why of every item, have to be continuously before the manager or he will not be able to keep a close rein on the business.

Experience quickly teaches which items are important and which are not and the time consumed in examining them is not nearly so great as might be imagined. An hour a day is enough to keep one fully informed on essential financial items, but the time involved is not important. A manager who finds himself too busy to know everything about the business he is supposed to be running is not the man for manager. Personally I have always retired from a managership the moment I found I did not want to give my entire time to it.

In the New Jersey Zinc Company, with its far-flung ownership of mines, operating plants, railroads, water plants, and townsites in many states of the Union we have a plan of accounting so searching and so perfect that at each weekly executive meeting we can report our total earnings up to the night of the preceding day. At the end of the year we are not 2% out—and always to the good. It is a plan that, 40 years ago when I was young and a fairly good accountant, I worked out. I had been told that "it couldn't be done," but it has never failed us.

Management to me is essentially first knowing the principles of business and then applying them to the particular business in hand.

1923

# LEE IACOCCA
## 1924–

Most remember Lee Iacocca for saving Chrysler from certain extinction back in 1979 and 1980, when he obtained $1.2 billion in federal government loans. But he first gained national recognition in April 1964, when he made the covers of both *Time* and *Newsweek* as father of the revered Ford Mustang. His pioneering effort at Ford eventually carried him to the presidency of the company in 1970. From his experiences, Iacocca has learned to take a somewhat humorous look at management: "If you make believe that 10 guys in pinstriped suits are back in a kindergarten class playing with building blocks, you'll get a rough picture of what life in a corporation is like." In other words, management tends to act with the emotional maturity of children. As a matter of fact, after much ridiculous infighting with Henry Ford II, the legendary Henry's grandson and chairman of Ford, Iacocca was canned in 1978.

Recruited immediately for Chrysler's top post, Iacocca soon found himself negotiating with the government, overseeing massive layoffs, and demanding concessions from the unions, all to save the nearly bankrupt company. He recalled telling the union officials, "I've got a shotgun at your head. I've got thousands of jobs available at $17 an hour. I've got none at $20. So you better come to your senses." Ultimately, the company's financial woes were turned around by the antithesis of the Mustang; it was the minivan that came to the rescue.

One criticism of the now-retired Iacocca was that he did not share power well. He conceded, "If I've got a fault, it's probably that I manage hands-on too much. You shouldn't get so antsy that your people don't even have time to find where the bathroom is." Faults and all, he had America's ear, penning his autobiography in 1984 and *Talking Straight* in 1988. In the following selection from the latter book, Iacocca discusses the importance of "skip meetings" (meaning skipping levels, not missing meetings) to deinsulate himself. He had found that formal meetings with top executives were "so highly structured you could almost smell that the system had already filtered or homogenized what they could say."

# Skip Meetings
## *Lee Iacocca*

Ibegan skip meetings many years ago, because the system had gotten so big that I was talking only to my top two or three people. Oh, I heard from plenty of people in endless committee meetings. But those meetings were so highly structured you could almost smell that the system had already filtered or homogenized what they could say. I didn't want to wreck the system or go around the organization, but I wanted to stop being insulated at the top of the pyramid.

So every few weeks I call in a department manager or a top engineer or a plant manager and meet with him one-on-one. These people are known as the high-po's—or high potentials—who, unless they mess up, will be running the company five or ten years from now. When they come in, they're usually a little reticent, praying they don't spill coffee on me or knock over a vase. I relax them by telling them this is not a performance review and everything's off the record and strictly confidential. Otherwise, they'd all run for cover. My questions are always simple. How do you get along with the rest of the system? Does it work? Do you know what's coming up and going down? Once I start firing away, I find that they loosen up pretty quickly.

If you handle things right, the idea takes hold. I'd been

doing skip meetings for many years when suddenly I noticed some of my other top people doing them too. Now members of our executive committee have picked up the habit.

After a year's worth of skip meetings, I may not remember who told me what, but I manage to get a feel for whether things are going right and whether the engine's hitting on all cylinders. I also get to know, close up, a lot of our best middle managers, whom otherwise I would never even meet.

I'll give you an example. I had been trying to put in a system of brand management under which every brand of car would have one person accountable for giving that brand an identity to the public. The manager would have control of the Plymouth car line and its marketing, for example, a full three years before the product was due to come to market.

---

My questions are always simple. How do you get along with the rest of the system? Does it work? Do you know what's coming up and going down?

---

At first we only put our toe in the water. We appointed a brand manager for product and a brand manager for marketing, and we told them: You two are going to be like Siamese twins. Live with each other. Get together day and night.

Turned out, the idea was a fiasco. How did I find out? Because in a lot of the skip meetings, people told me it wasn't working. I heard the same things over and over again. There should be one guy, not two. Also, the current two weren't able to get access to the company's resources early enough to have real responsibility. They were stuck on the outside like cheerleaders. That's how I discovered that we had to take the system apart and give the brand managers genuine power.

Whether it's through skip meetings or other means, it's absolutely essential to let your people express themselves. And that means letting them make mistakes. You've got to allow them to walk into your office and say, "Boss, I blew it." That's called growing.

I'm reminded of the guy who says to the football player, "Geez, your team won the Super Bowl—how do you feel about it?"

"Terrific," the player says. "A dream come true."

Then the first guy says, "Yeah, but you didn't play. You were on the bench the whole sixty minutes."

"Well, that's true," the player says, "but I was suited up and felt like part of the team."

That's not my approach. My feeling is that there's nothing like playing. Being active is the key. I like to get my people into the game.

---

Whether it's through skip meetings or other means, it's absolutely essential to let your people express themselves.

---

Last year I decided to reorganize Chrysler for that reason alone. I came to the conclusion that I wasn't using all my people to their fullest potential. I was deep in talent, but it was arranged in such a monolithic way that I couldn't get some of the second-level people into the flow of things.

That's when I said to myself: *I've got so much on my plate. Why don't I use some of these guys more? Why am I standing on the ceremony of an organizational chart?*

I decided to make a number of my second-tier people more accountable. At the same time, I also wanted to deploy them so that they'd be closer to the marketplace. I didn't need them to talk among themselves but to talk to the people who buy from us.

And so I divvied up the company into manageable pieces and told these executives to go play the game to the hilt. It's now their show. Make it or break it.

---

Once you've given a guy turf in a hierarchy, the minute you openly take away any of it, even if it's one lousy blade of crab grass, he gets miffed.

---

When you try something like that, you have to be cautious or you'll bruise some mighty big egos. In reorganizing things, I had to switch some areas of responsibility. One lesson I learned a long time ago is that once you've given a guy turf in a hierarchy, the minute you openly take away any of it, even if it's one lousy blade of crab grass, he gets miffed.

---

I know right away when someone's mad, because he'll use the standard ploy to tip me off: You go to see the head of personnel and ask what your benefits are and what you would get if you retired tomorrow.

---

I suppose I can't blame anyone who reacts like that, because I was the same way in my career. When Henry Ford named me head of the Ford Division, I was given everything but the assembly plants. Now I didn't know a damn thing about assembly plants, but I did know that the guy I was replacing used to have them. So even though I was being given the opportunity of a lifetime, I was ticked off that Henry didn't have the confidence in me to give me the assembly operations. I needed those plants like a hole in the head, but I was offended anyway.

In my own company I've had situations where a guy's plate was so full that the food was spilling onto the floor, but if I lightened his load, he saw it as a threat to his power and forgot completely what the objectives of the company were.

I know right away when someone's mad, because he'll use the standard ploy to tip me off: You go to see the head of personnel and ask what your benefits are and what you would get if you retired tomorrow. Naturally word gets back to the boss. I have to confess it's a maneuver that I once used myself. The tricky part if you're the boss is that you can never be sure whether the guy's trying to deliver a message or whether he's just playing chicken with you.

1988

Even as a boy growing up on a farm, Henry Ford could read machines like others read books. As far back as 1885, he repaired an early gas engine and then built one himself just to see if he understood how it worked. His father, however, discouraged Henry's bent toward machines. "My father offered me forty acres of timber land, provided I gave up being a machinist," he reflected. Ford took the land, but the promise didn't last long; he couldn't resist a machinist job at the Detroit Electric Company, and he later became a chief engineer for Thomas Edison's Light Company. Ford left Edison in 1899 to pursue his dreams, and founded the Ford Motor Company in 1903, almost 20 years after first tinkering with an engine.

Ford's fundamental business decision to make "a car for the great multitude" drove his success. Early going was tough: "There was no 'demand' for automobiles—there never is for a new article. . . . At first the 'horseless carriage' was considered a freak notion and many wise people explained with particularity why it could never be more than a toy." Then in 1908 he presented to the world the economical and durable Model T, a phenomenal hit. In 1913 the introduction of the conveyor belt assembly line truly vaulted Ford onto the world's stage, and within a few years the Ford Motor Company was producing half of the cars in the world. Ultimately, the assembly line cut production time down from over 12 hours to just over 1½ hours.

Intertwined with assembly line production was Ford's philosophy on management: "Industry is management, and management is leadership, and leadership is perfect when it so simplifies operations that orders are not necessary." His rigid, factory-oriented mentality led to the famous quote, "A customer can have any color of car they want as long as it is black," and no doubt he was a bit of an autocrat. Still, Ford understood that service should come before profit, and in *Machines and Men* he outlines some of his other principles that made him the greatest car manufacturer ever. Consider that he fears anyone called a "genius for organization." To Ford, that implies a great family tree overburdened with berries.

# Machines and Men
## *Henry Ford*

That which one has to fight hardest against in bringing together a large number of people to do work is excess organization and consequent red tape. To my mind there is no bent of mind more dangerous than that which is sometimes described as the "genius for organization." This usually results in the birth of a great big chart showing, after the fashion of a family tree, how authority ramifies. The tree is heavy with nice round berries, each of which bears the name of a man or of an office. Every man has a title and certain duties which are strictly limited by the circumference of his berry.

If a straw boss wants to say something to the general superintendent, his message has to go through the subforeman, the foreman, the department head, and all the assistant superintendents, before, in the course of time, it reaches the general superintendent. Probably by that time what he wanted to talk about is already history. It takes about six weeks for the message of a man living in a berry on the lower left-hand corner of the chart to reach the president or chairman of the board, and if it ever does reach one of these august officials, it has by that time gathered to itself about a pound of criticisms, suggestions, and comments. Very few things are ever taken under "official consideration" until long after the time when they actually ought to have been done. The buck is passed to and fro and all responsibility is dodged by individuals—following the lazy notion that two heads are better than one.

Now a business, in my way of thinking, is not a machine. It is a collection of people who are brought together to do work and not to write letters to one another. It is not necessary for any one department to know what any other department is doing. If a man is doing his work he will not have time to take up any other work. It is the business of those who plan the entire work to see that all of the departments are working properly toward the same end. It is not necessary to have meetings to establish good feeling between individuals or departments. It is not necessary for people to love each other in order to work together. Too much good fellowship may indeed be a very bad thing, for it may lead to one man trying to cover up the faults of another. That is bad for both men.

---

Very few things are ever taken under "official consideration" until long after the time when they actually ought to have been done.

---

When we are at work we ought to be at work. When we are at play we ought to be at play. There is no use trying to mix the two. The sole object ought to be to get the work done and to get paid for it. When the work is done, then the play can come, but not before. And so the Ford factories and enterprises have no organization, no specific duties attaching to any position, no line of succession or of authority, very few titles, and no conferences. We have only the clerical help that is absolutely required; we have no elaborate records of any kind, and consequently no red tape.

We make the individual responsibility complete. The workman is absolutely responsible for his work. The straw boss is responsible for the workmen under him. The foreman is responsible for his group. The department head is responsible for the department. The general superintendent is responsible for the whole factory. Every man has to know what is going on in his sphere. I say "general superintendent." There is no such formal title. One man is in charge of the factory and has been for years. He has two men with him, who, without in any way having their duties defined, have taken particular sections of the work to themselves. With them are about half a dozen other men in the nature of assistants, but without specific duties. They have all made jobs for themselves—but there are no limits to their jobs. They just work in where they best fit. One man chases stock and shortages. Another has grabbed inspection, and so on.

This may seem haphazard, but it is not. A group of men, wholly intent upon getting work done, have no difficulty in seeing that the work is done. They do not get into trouble about the limits of authority, because they are not thinking of titles. If they had offices and all that, they would shortly be giving up their time to office work and to wondering why did they not have a better office than some other fellow.

Because there are no titles and no limits of authority, there is no question of red tape or going over a man's head. Any workman can go to anybody, and so established has become this custom, that a foreman does not get sore if a workman goes over him and directly to the head of the factory. The workman rarely ever does so, because a foreman knows as well as he knows his own name that if he has been unjust it will be very quickly found out, and he shall no longer be a foreman. One of the things that we will not tolerate is injustice of any kind. The moment a man starts to swell with authority he is discovered, and he goes out, or goes back to a machine. A large amount of labour unrest comes from the unjust exercise of authority by those in subordinate positions, and I am afraid that in far too many manufacturing institutions it is really not possible for a workman to get a square deal.

The work and the work alone controls us. That is one of the reasons why we have no titles. Most men can swing a job, but they are floored by a title. The effect of a title is very peculiar. It has been used too much as a sign of emancipation from work. It is almost equivalent to a badge bearing the legend:

"This man has nothing to do but regard himself as important and all others as inferior."

Not only is a title often injurious to the wearer, but it has its effect on others as well. There is perhaps no greater single source of personal dissatisfaction among men than the fact that the title-bearers are not always the real leaders. Everybody acknowledges a real leader—a man who is fit to plan and command. And when you find a real leader who bears a title, you will have to inquire of someone else what his title is. He doesn't boast about it.

---

The work and the work alone controls us. That is one of the reasons why we have no titles. Most men can swing a job, but they are floored by a title.

---

Titles in business have been greatly overdone and business has suffered. One of the bad features is the division of responsibility according to titles, which goes so far as to amount to a removal altogether of responsibility. Where responsibility is broken up into many small bits and divided among many departments, each department under its own titular head, who in turn is surrounded by a group bearing their nice sub-titles, it is difficult to find any one who really feels responsible. Everyone knows what "passing the buck" means. The game must have originated in industrial organizations where the departments simply shove responsibility along. The health of every organization depends on every member—whatever his place—feeling that everything that

170

happens to come to his notice relating to the welfare of the business is his own job. Railroads have gone to the devil under the eyes of departments that say:

"Oh, that doesn't come under our department. Department X, 100 miles away, has that in charge."

There used to be a lot of advice given to officials not to hide behind their titles. The very necessity for the advice showed a condition that needed more than advice to correct it. And the correction is just this—abolish the titles. A few may be legally necessary; a few may be useful in directing the public how to do business with the concern, but for the rest the best rule is simple: "Get rid of them."

As a matter of fact, the record of business in general just now is such as to detract very much from the value of titles. No one would boast of being president of a bankrupt bank. Business on the whole has not been so skillfully steered as to leave much margin for pride in the steersmen. The men who bear titles now and are worth anything are forgetting their titles and are down in the foundation of business looking for the weak spots. They are back again in the places from which they rose—trying to reconstruct from the bottom up. And when a man is really at work, he needs no title. His work honours him.

All of our people come into the factory or the offices through the employment departments. As I have said, we do not hire experts—neither do we hire men on past experiences or for any position other than the lowest. Since we do not take a man on his past history, we do not refuse him because of his past history. I never met a man who was thoroughly bad. There is always some good in him—if he gets a chance. That is the reason we do not care in the least about a man's antecedents—we do not hire a man's history, we hire the man. If he has been in jail, that is no reason to say that he will be in jail again. I think, on the contrary, he is, if given a chance, very likely to make a special effort to keep out of jail. Our employment office does not bar a man for anything he has previously done—he is equally acceptable whether he has been in Sing Sing or at Harvard and we do not even inquire from which place he has graduated. All that he needs is the desire to work. If he does not desire to work, it is very unlikely that he will apply for a position, for it is pretty well understood that a man in the Ford plant works.

We do not, to repeat, care what a man has been. If he has gone to college he ought to be able to go ahead faster, but he has to start at the bottom and prove his ability. Every man's future rests solely with himself. There is far too much loose talk about men being unable to obtain recognition. With us every man is fairly certain to get the exact recognition he deserves.

Of course, there are certain factors in the desire for recognition which must be reckoned with. The whole modern industrial system has warped the desire so out of shape that it is now almost an obsession. There was a time when a man's personal advancement depended entirely and immediately upon his work, and not upon any one's favour; but nowadays it often depends far too much upon the individual's good fortune in catching some influential eye. That is what we have successfully fought against. Men will work with the idea of catching somebody's eye; they will work with the idea that if they fail to get credit for what they have done, they might as well have done it badly or not have done it at all. Thus the work sometimes becomes a secondary consideration. The job in hand—the article in hand, the special kind of service in hand—turns out to be not the principal job. The main work becomes personal advancement—a platform from which to catch somebody's eye. This habit of making the work secondary and the recognition primary is unfair to the work. It makes recognition and credit the real job. And this also has an unfortunate effect on the worker. It encourages a peculiar kind of ambition which is neither lovely nor productive. It produces the kind of man who imagines that by "standing in with the boss" he will get ahead. Every shop knows this kind of man. And the worst of it is there are some things in the present industrial system which make it appear that the game really pays. Foremen are only human. It is natural that they should be flattered by being made to believe that they hold the weal or woe of workmen in their hands. It is natural, also, that being open to flattery, their self-seeking subordinates should flatter them still more to obtain and profit by their favour. That is why I want as little as possible of the personal element.

---

> Our employment office does not bar a man for anything he has previously done—he is equally acceptable whether he has been in Sing Sing or at Harvard and we do not even inquire from which place he has graduated.

---

It is particularly easy for any man who never knows it all to go forward to a higher position with us. Some men will work hard but they do not possess the capacity to think and especially to think quickly. Such men get as far as their ability deserves. A man may, by his industry, deserve advancement, but it cannot be possibly given him unless he also has a certain element of leadership. This is not a dream world we are living in. I think that every man in the shaking-down process of our factory eventually lands about where he belongs.

We are never satisfied with the way that everything is done in any part of the organization; we always think it ought to be done better and that eventually it will be done better. The spirit of crowding forces the man who has the qualities for a higher place eventually to get it. He perhaps would not get the place if at any time the organization—which is a word I do not like to use—became fixed, so that there would be routine steps and dead men's shoes. But we have so few titles that a man who ought to be doing something better than he is doing, very soon gets to doing it—he is not restrained by the fact that there is no position ahead of him "open"—for there are no "positions." We have no cut-and-dried places—our best men make their places. This is easy enough to do, for there is always work, and when you think of getting the work done instead of finding a title to fit a man who wants to be promoted, then there is no difficulty about promotion. The promotion itself is not formal; the man simply finds himself doing something other than what he was doing and getting more money.

All of our people have thus come up from the bottom. The head of the factory started as a machinist. The man in charge of the big River Rouge plant began as a pattern-maker. Another man overseeing one of the principal departments started as a sweeper. There is not a single man anywhere in the factory who did not simply come in off the street. Everything that we have developed has been done by men who have qualified themselves with us. We fortunately did not inherit any traditions and we are not founding any. If we have a tradition it is this:

Everything can always be done better than it is being done.

That pressing always to do work better and faster solves nearly every factory problem. A department gets its standing on its rate of production. The rate of production and the cost of production are distinct elements. The foremen and superintendents would only be wasting time were they to keep a check on the costs in their departments. There are certain costs—such as the rate of wages, the overhead, the price of materials, and the like, which they could not in any way control, so they do not bother about them. What they can control is the rate of production in their own departments. The rating of a department is gained by dividing the number of parts produced by the number of hands working. Every foreman checks his own department daily—he carries the figures always with him. The superintendent has a tabulation of all the scores; if there is something wrong in a department the output score shows it at once, the superintendent makes inquiries and the foreman looks alive. A considerable part of the incentive to better methods is directly traceable to this simple rule-of-thumb method of rating production. The foreman need not be a cost accountant — he is no better a foreman for being one. His charges are the machines and the human beings in his department. When they are working at their best he has performed his service. The rate of his production is his guide. There is no reason for him to scatter his energies over collateral subjects.

This rating system simply forces a foreman to forget personalities — to forget everything other than the work in hand. If he should select the people he likes instead of the people who can best do the work, his department record will quickly show up that fact.

---

If we have a tradition it is this: Everything can always be done better than it is being done.

---

There is no difficulty in picking out men. They pick themselves out because — although one hears a great deal about the lack of opportunity for advancement — the average workman is more interested in a steady job than he is in advancement. Scarcely more than five percent of those who work for wages, while they have the desire to receive more money, have also the willingness to accept the additional responsibility and the additional work which goes with the higher places. Only about twenty-five per cent are even willing to be straw bosses, and most of them take that position because it carries with it more pay than working on a machine. Men of a more mechanical turn of mind, but with no desire for responsibility, go into the tool-making departments where they receive considerably more pay than in production proper. But the vast majority of men want to stay put. They want to be led. They want to have everything done for them and to have no responsibility. Therefore, in spite of the great mass of men, the difficulty is not to discover men to advance, but men who are willing to be advanced.

The accepted theory is that all people are anxious for advancement, and a great many pretty plans have been built up from that. I can only say that we do not find that to be the case. The Americans in our employ do want to go ahead, but they by no means do always want to go clear through to the top. The foreigners, generally speaking, are content to stay as straw bosses. Why all of this is, I do not know. I am giving the facts.

As I have said, everyone in the place reserves an open mind as to the way in which every job is being done. If there is any fixed theory—any fixed rule—it is that no job is being done well enough. The whole factory management is always open to suggestion, and we have an informal suggestion system by which any workman can communicate any idea that comes to him and get action on it.

The saving of a cent per piece may be distinctly worth while. A saving of one cent on a part at our present rate of production represents twelve thousand dollars a year. One cent saved on each part would amount to millions a year. Therefore, in comparing savings, the calculations are carried out to the thousandth part of a cent. If the new way suggested shows a saving and the cost of making the change will pay for itself within a reasonable time—say within three months— the change is made practically as of course. These changes are by no means limited to improvements which will increase production or decrease cost. A great many—perhaps most of them—are in the line of making the work easier. We do not want any hard, man-killing work about the place, and there is now very little of it. And usually it so works out that adopting the way which is easier on the men also decreases the cost. There is a most intimate connection between decency and good business. We also investigate down to the last decimal whether it is cheaper to make or to buy a part.

The suggestions come from everywhere. The Polish workmen seem to be the cleverest of all of the foreigners in

176

making them. One, who could not speak English, indicated that if the tool in his machine were set at a different angle it might wear longer. As it was it lasted only four or five cuts. He was right, and a lot of money was saved in grinding. Another Pole, running a drill press, rigged up a little fixture to save handling the part after drilling. That was adopted generally and a considerable saving resulted. The men often try out little attachments of their own because, concentrating on one thing, they can, if they have a mind that way, usually devise some improvement. The cleanliness of a man's machine also — although cleaning a machine is no part of his duty — is usually an indication of his intelligence.

Here are some of the suggestions: A proposal that castings be taken from the foundry to the machine shop on an overhead conveyor saved seventy men in the transport division. There used to be seventeen men — and this was when production was smaller — taking the burrs off gears, and it was a hard, nasty job. A man roughly sketched a special machine. His idea was worked out and the machine built. Now four men have several times the output of the seventeen men — and have no hard work at all to do. Changing from a solid to a welded rod in one part of the chassis effected an immediate saving of about one half million a year on a smaller than the present-day production. Making certain tubes out of flat sheets instead of drawing them in the usual way effected another enormous saving.

The old method of making a certain gear comprised four operations, and 12 per cent of the steel went into scrap. We use most of our scrap and eventually we will use it all, but that is no reason for not cutting down on scrap — the mere fact that all waste is not a dead loss is no excuse for permitting waste. One of the workmen devised a very simple new method for making this gear in which the scrap was only one per cent. Again, the cam shaft has to have heat treatment in order to make the surface hard; the cam shafts always came out of the heat-treat oven somewhat warped, and even back in 1918, we employed 37 men just to straighten the shafts.

Several of our men experimented for about a year and finally worked out a new form of oven in which the shafts could not warp. In 1921, with the production much larger than in 1918, we employed only eight men in the whole operation.

And then there is the pressing need to take away the necessity for skill in any job done by any one. The old-time tool hardener was an expert. He had to judge the heating temperatures. It was a hit-or-miss operation. The wonder is that he hit so often. The heat treatment in the hardening of steel is highly important—providing one knows exactly the right heat to apply. That cannot be known by rule-of-thumb. It has to be measured. We introduced a system by which the man at the furnace has nothing at all to do with the heat. He does not see the pyrometer—the instrument which registers the temperature. Coloured electric lights give him his signals.

None of our machines is ever built haphazardly. The idea is investigated in detail before a move is made. Sometimes wooden models are constructed or again the parts are drawn to full size on a blackboard. We are not bound by precedent but we leave nothing to luck, and we have yet to build a machine that will not do the work for which it was designed. About ninety per cent of all experiments have been successful.

Whatever expertness in fabrication that has developed has been due to men. I think that if men are unhampered and they know that they are serving, they will always put all of mind and will into even the most trivial of tasks.

1926

# PART IV

## The Power of Technology

Technology can make a manager's life easier or more complicated; it can be used to control people or to enable them. Michael Dell exemplifies the manager who has used technology rather than abusing it. He warns that "if you're preoccupied with the ways in which your staff might abuse technology, you're going to miss out on the benefits while your competitors run away with the future." As Jim Barksdale, retired CEO of Netscape, points out, technology is no longer just part of backroom operations; today, information technology departments are "expected to produce new products and services to reach customers." On the marketing and sales side, Esther Dyson and J. Willard Marriott both make it clear that modern technology has changed the nature of pricing a product and its demand. The message is clear: You must use technology *throughout* the organization, but be wary of its dehumanizing downside.

Michael Dell has obsessively pursued every interest he has ever had. As a kid, he sold subscriptions for *The Houston Post* with such enthusiasm that one year he made more money than his history and economics teacher. (The somewhat disappointed teacher discovered the accomplishment during a school project in which the students filled out tax returns.) In 1980, at age 15, Dell bought an Apple II with his hard-earned money, and then, to his parents' dismay, took it apart. In 1983 he entered the University of Texas as a premed student, where he started selling upgraded personal computers from his dorm room. The summer after his freshman year Dell sold $180,000 worth of upgraded PCs—and never looked back.

Dell quit school in May of 1984 to pursue his business full time. Two years later he was doing $60 million in revenues and in early 1999, Dell was selling $14 million *a day* over the Internet. Another testimony to his success: At one point in the 1990s Dell stock was up 36,000 percent. Even the competition can't deny Dell's organizational and marketing genius, and other firms are quickly emulating the computer manufacturer's business model, which involves selling direct to the consumer. One of the advantages, according to Dell, is the proximity to the customer and subsequent feedback. "In a business based on a direct model, you get the facts immediately, whether you like them or not," he explains.

The direct model not only eliminates the reseller, but focuses on keeping inventory to a minimum. Dell seeks what he calls *inventory velocity,* which means "squeezing time out of every step in the process." By building efficient supply lines, Dell's inventory levels are below eight days, so the company doesn't have money tied up and won't be caught with obsolete products, which is easy enough in the rapidly changing computer industry. To remain incredibly efficient, Dell has waged what he calls a campaign of internal evangelism, which he describes in the following selection. One of his techniques is to plaster posters around the offices of himself in the classic Uncle Sam pose, declaring, "Michael Wants YOU to Know the Net!"

# Waging a Campaign of Internal Evangelism
## *Michael Dell*

One of the sayings around Dell is that if you want to get people to think big, you need to act big. We were certainly thinking big when we set about constructing a successful Internet model. We didn't want to just set up an online store as an appendage to our business. A lot of businesses who look at the Internet simply as a way to launch electronic sales are missing the point. The real potential of the Internet is its ability to speed information flow, and that affects all kinds of transactions.

---

One of the sayings around Dell is that if you want to get people to think big, you need to act big.

---

We wanted the Internet to become a key part of our entire business system. We wanted to make the Internet the first point of contact for every customer and prospect, and we planned for 50 percent of all customer transactions to be online within a few years.

To execute these objectives, we had to act big. We provided enthusiastic executive sponsorship of the initiative to integrate the Internet into every part of our business model. Rather than just using the Internet in our sales and configuration systems, we decided to employ Internet technology throughout all of our information systems, in order to connect more quickly and efficiently with customers and suppliers. Our information technology perspective was—and still is—to reduce obstacles to the origin and flow of information, and to simplify the systems in an effort to really maximize our business processes.

I had said, "Look, anything that we produce, whether it's a business card or a box or a piece of direct mail or a letter or a ROM-BIOS, anything that has our name on it should have *www.dell.com* on it." There was no part of the company that was exempt. I'd rather overkill a great idea than underexploit it.

Before I visit a customer, I always log on to their website to see how much I can learn about their company. I can get a real flavor of the company and its culture from its website.

Thanks to an intense marketing campaign, *www.dell.com* was showing up everywhere: in advertisements, on company business cards, on every box coming out of the factory, even on a sign pointing to the men's rest room at a European management team meeting in Germany.

Inside the company, however, there were people who didn't understand how the Internet would change our business. To make sure everyone in the company was Internet-literate, we conducted a campaign of internal evangelism. We went into the cubes and high traffic points and plastered them with posters showing me in an Uncle Sam pose with the caption, "Michael wants YOU to know the Net!" I sent out a company-wide e-mail describing Dell's Internet strategy and how easy it is to place an order through *www.dell.com,* then asked all our managers to buy a book through Amazon.com so that they could familiarize themselves with Internet commerce. We sponsored a scavenger hunt for people to find information on the Web. We set up an online literacy quiz called "Know The Net" and challenged all our people to take it. We also gave every employee throughout the company globally access to the Internet and our own Intranet and encouraged their use.

A surprising percentage of our people also weren't aware of how the Internet could help our business. Sales and service departments didn't understand its implications and were fearful, at first, that the Net would automate their jobs away. We invested a lot in educating our sales representatives, especially the field-based account executives who own customer relationships. We showed them how the Internet made them more effective while also providing a value-added service for the customer. The reps soon saw that *www.dell.com* was a source of highly qualified leads. They could close sales with fewer calls and have greater reach within existing accounts. With our growth rates, there was more than enough business for everybody.

---

To make sure everyone in the company was Internet-literate, we conducted a campaign of internal evangelism.

---

Some might argue that if you give employees access to the World Wide Web, they will spend all their time surfing the Net. But that's like saying, "We don't want to teach our people how to read because they might spend all their time reading." That's the wrong way to approach it. As a resource, the Internet enables and enhances so many business functions—if you're preoccupied with the ways in which your staff might abuse the technology, you're going to miss out on the benefits while your competitors run away with the future.

I remember talking with one of our customers about this. They actually did a measurement to see how much nonbusiness time their employees spent on the Internet. It came out to six minutes a day. That's less time than most people spend on one personal phone call. My feeling is, if you're an employee at Dell and you occasionally go online to order a book, you're saving thirty minutes that you otherwise would have spent going to the bookstore!

For us, the issue wasn't whether people would waste time on the Internet but whether they would use the Internet enough. Not to become completely familiar with a transformative business tool like the Internet is just foolish—especially when it's an integral part of your company's strategy and competitive advantage.

We faced a similar crossroads years ago, around 1986, when we first started using e-mail. People would ask me, "How do you get your employees to use e-mail?" My response was, "That's easy. You just ask them if they got that note you sent them on e-mail." No one likes to be uninformed, right?

---

For us, the issue wasn't whether people would waste time on the Internet but whether they would use the Internet enough.

---

One of the things that makes the Internet so exciting is that it brings the outside in. In today's marketplace, you can't afford to become insulated in your own activities. Our industry changes so quickly that if we don't constantly refresh our knowledge and stay in front of new technologies and concepts, we'll quickly become obsolete. The Internet allows us to bring in an outside point of view, whether it's a customer perspective or news about our competitors or developments in other areas of the world.

Before I visit a customer, I always log on to their website to see how much I can learn about their company. I can get a real flavor of the company and its culture from its website. Certainly I'll be more fluent as a result of looking at their website than I would be from reading a static annual report with a bunch of pretty pictures. We want everyone in our company to be doing that, so that we better understand our customers, our competitors, our suppliers, our market, and the world around us.

1999

Born and raised in Jackson Mississippi, Jim Barksdale knows more than a few good Southern aphorisms, such as, "It's not the size of the dog in the fight, it's the size of the fight in the dog." After graduating from the University of Mississippi with a business degree, he joined IBM as a marketing and sales trainee. Eventually, Barksdale moved on to Federal Express, where he led the company's charge into a sophisticated computerized tracking and delivery system. It proved such a success for Federal Express that in 1983, after only six years there, he was named CEO. In 1991 Barksdale was recruited to become president and COO of McCaw Cellular Communications, which was later bought out by AT&T Wireless Services.

In 1995 Barksdale left AT&T to become president and CEO of Netscape, which provides Internet browser and network software, along with other products and services. Many questioned the risky venture, but he explained, "I was at that stage of my career where I was free to retire or take one more bite at the apple. I took one more bite at the apple, and I have been pleased." One of his primary missions was, he said, "to provide adult supervision" for the young techies, such as cofounder Marc Andreesen. It's been some babysitting job. Two months into his tenure, he helped take the company public; in 1997 the stock dropped about 69 percent, so he took a pay cut—rewarding himself one dollar; and in January 1998, he announced that Netscape would give its browser away free to maintain its market share.

Then came the battle with Bill Gates during the Microsoft antitrust trial of the late 1990s, in which Barksdale showed plenty of fight as top dog of Netscape and as a witness for the government. In a semifinal round, America Online bought Netscape in 1999, so Barksdale struck off on his own, organizing a venture capital firm. The one common theme through his varied experiences is technology. As he explains in the following selection, information technology is no longer merely a support center, it is the business. And beware of the power of Metcalfe's law, Barksdale writes, which states that "the value of a network grows exponentially."

# IT Departments:
## Getting Down to Business
### *Jim Barksdale*

Until very recently, Information Technology (IT) departments used to act as cost centers, and their main activities were purchasing, deploying, and maintaining hardware and software systems. Today, though, IT departments are increasingly facing line-of-business pressures. They're now expected to produce new products and services to reach customers.

Why has this change come about? It's because, in the Net Economy, business issues and technology issues go hand in hand. In a globally networked business environment, understanding how technology can help your company grow new revenue streams and reduce expenses is a critical part of making your company successful.

## IT: A STRATEGIC ASSET

Look at E*Trade, for example. It's a new company launched solely as an online service for selling mutual funds and stocks. Even though it's a relative newcomer, E*Trade has the second-highest market share of all financial services firms that are online. The company's entire business revolves around its IT infrastructure. E*Trade was able to get on the

187

Internet quicker than anybody else and provide a great service, even though it had never been in the business before. That, of course, drives bigger companies like Charles Schwab, Merrill Lynch, and others to follow suit. They're forced into action by the small, innovative companies that set the trends and try out new ways of doing things.

As a result, no IT department today is being looked at as a cost center. Instead, everyone's asking "How do I do what Michael Dell does?" He sells five to six million dollars' worth of products a day over the Internet. The IT systems he uses to do this are all automated, and they tie into his back-end legacy systems. We all know the Dell story, right? A billion-dollar market created in 18 months. I don't care if you're in the railroad business, people notice that. Businesspeople look at that and they say, "How does that either affect my business, or how do I take advantage of that opportunity?" All you need are a few of those kinds of successes, and pretty soon everybody wants to jump on the bandwagon.

IT departments have traditionally worried about how to maximize efficiency inside their organizations. The Net Economy has forced them to think about how to build an infrastructure that lets them easily communicate with a network of business partners and customers outside the organization.

## METCALFE'S LAW SUPERSEDES MOORE'S LAW

For more than 30 years now, we've all been excited about Moore's Law, which states that every 18 months or so the speed of microprocessors doubles and the cost decreases proportionally. Today, however, companies like Citibank or Ford Motor Company or Federal Express, all good customers of Netscape's, are no longer constrained by processor speed. Moore's Law is not going to do a whole lot more for these companies.

The important law to pay attention to now is Metcalfe's Law. This is named after Bob Metcalfe, the inventor of Ethernet and the founder of 3Com. Metcalfe's Law, which was the law we built Federal Express on without knowing it, and was the law we built the cellular telephone industry on without knowing it, says that the value of a network grows exponentially. Every endpoint that's added can then be connected to all the other endpoints. In other words, the number of endpoints squared is an indicator of the value of a network. The network that doesn't reach everywhere is of little value. Think about what a tough job the first telephone salesman had. Who was the first customer going to talk to?

Companies today are driven more by the networking truths of Metcalfe's Law than by the hardware truths of Moore's Law. That's one of the features of the Net Economy. And to make sure they can take full advantage of Metcalfe's Law, companies are looking to their IT departments to build networks that are reliable and that interconnect all facets of the business.

## VIRTUAL SPACE VERSUS BRICKS AND MORTAR

It used to be that to build your business, you needed to think about bricks and mortar—in other words, physical retail space. In the new world of the Net Economy, however, your showroom can exist solely in virtual space. Amazon.com, a relative newcomer to the book business (and a business whose "store" is solely online), now has a higher market cap than Barnes & Noble. Yet Barnes & Noble has been in the business much longer and has about $1 billion in hard assets in retail stores. How did this happen, and what does it mean?

The secret to many great opportunities on the Internet is that there are things that you can do in virtual space that you can't do in real space. Amazon.com can pretend to have 2.5 million volumes on the shelves when you go to its bookstore, even though everybody knows those are not all on one shelf. Amazon.com can give the appearance that no bookstore in the world can give in real space—they can look like a virtual Library of Congress.

Obviously not everything is going to be disintermediated, but I do think we're going to find more ways to have customers intermediate. We're going to find new values for our assets and our core competencies in the Net Economy.

A few years ago, Citibank was going through a major transformation that led the company to a long-term strategy session that culminated last summer when John Reed, the chairman and CEO of Citicorp, announced that the company wanted to reach a billion customers by the year 2010. That is an enormous goal. After the merger is complete of Travelers Group and Citicorp, one of the biggest announcements of mergers we've seen in a long time, the combined company will have 100 million customers. So Citibank is only off now by about one order of magnitude, and we wish them luck.

A company can't get to a billion customers — or 100 million customers — in the conventional way, using bricks-and-mortar real estate. Citibank realized that for them to get to that level of scalability and opportunity, they'd have to do things in a different way, a more economical way, and not be dependent on the ways of the past. Citibank has to provide access points to its services that are very, very easy for its customers to get to. It has to develop and retain a relationship with each customer that's broad and deep yet costs less to maintain then ever before. To accomplish this, the company's IT department is building a high-performance, scalable, centrally managed, open standards-based infrastructure so Citibank can not only easily connect with new customers but also interconnect all of its legacy systems with its business partners and *their* legacy systems.

## END-TO-END COMMERCE

This kind of end-to-end commerce is a critical aspect of the Net Economy. In this interconnected world, companies are running their IT departments as if they were ISPs, or Internet Service Providers. They're providing large-scale Internet applications to their customers, partners, and suppliers. At Netscape, we call IT departments that are doing this Enterprise Service Providers, or ESPs.

As ESPs, IT departments have a whole new set of requirements. Their systems have to be up 24 hours a day, 7 days a week. To ensure consistency of access and service across the Net—and to cut administration costs—the systems should be centrally managed. They must also be able to scale extremely well. IT groups never know how many customers or partners they're going to have to connect with—it could be 100, 1,000, 10,000, or 10 million. They just need to be ready. And they need to be able to easily connect to partners' legacy systems.

In addition, a company's time to market is quicker on the Net. Products a company can bring online today, it tries out today; if customers don't show an interest, the company just calls it market research and tries out another one.

It's not like running a TV ad, which is the old way of marketing to millions of people. Because in the new way of marketing to millions, via the Internet, customers can answer back. You have to process the transaction. So the old broadcast model for media doesn't work. That's why the Internet really is a new form of media. It creates new kinds of interaction and transaction opportunities.

The ESP concept is an evolving trend that we see when we call on customers and prospects. Their IT departments are no longer cost centers. Instead, they're working to reach out to customers and partners, and many of them are behind the power curve. As they ramp up to participate in the Net Economy, IT departments have an unprecedented opportunity to make major contributions to the bottom line as they develop new applications and services. It's a whole new business role for IT. And it's a whole new way for technology to get down to business.

1998

# CHARLES B. WANG
## 1944–

Close on the heels of Microsoft and Oracle is the world's third-largest software maker, Computer Associates International (CA), cofounded in 1975 by Charles Wang and Russell Artzt. Recently, Wang has been making deals in China, his homeland, bringing his story full circle. After the Communist revolution in 1949, the family fled their Shanghai home and emigrated to the United States, where they landed in a Queens, New York, housing project. After earning degrees in mathematics and physics from Queens College, Wang settled on becoming a computer programmer because there were so many help-wanted ads for them and he figured it was a growing industry.

When the company he was working for decided to sell its software division, he and Artzt went for it. Artzt handled research and development while Wang was the consummate salesman. Artzt recalled, "He'd [Wang] pick 20 pages out of the yellow pages, drink three cups of coffee, and not go to the bathroom until he'd cold-called every potential customer." No doubt Wang, author of two books, believes in the power of information technology. He writes, "I cannot be clearer than this: Give up any idea you may have about how information technology can support your business. Your business is information and information is your business."

Wang took CA public in 1981, and they have used the proceeds to gobble up some 60 other companies. CA even has merger/acquisition software that evaluates and ranks employees. Within seven days they are either brought onboard or fired. "We tell them the truth, so they can get on with their lives," Wang explains. Truth is important to Wang, who has come under fire for what some call ruthless merger tactics and for selling so much of his own CA stock. In *Repairing the CEO/CIO Disconnect* he bluntly explains that there's more to bleeding-edge technology than just bleeding. Rather than just expecting to pay the price for the best technology, everyone, including CEOs, should understand it to a degree, according to Wang. He aptly points out that if you're transferred to Paris, you try to learn the basics of French—the same should be done for technology.

# Repairing the
# CEO/CIO Disconnect
## *Charles B. Wang*

**A**re you on the bleeding edge, or just bleeding? Costly technology investments stand a better chance of success when coordinated by the CEO and CIO—two executives who often find themselves speaking separate languages. Here's how to translate.

Computing may be the key factor in corporate success, but as often as not it is the key factor in corporate failure. Using official figures and assessments by hundreds of chief executives, I calculate that as much as $1 trillion spent in the U.S. over the decade on information technology has been wasted. That approaches a third of the total amount spent, meaning $1 of every $3 the average business invested in IT has been lost.

Why the waste? The answer may be an ineffective relationship between yourself and your chief information officer. Do you recognize yourself in the following scenarios?

- When your chief information officer—regardless of title, CIO describes the job—comes to see you, you wish it were your CFO, your COO, or your human-resources vice president.
- Your CIO doesn't ask you what you want technology to do—it's simply a given that your company is going

to get the latest and greatest, so there's nothing to discuss.

- Or perhaps your CIO doesn't speak to you at all, but—as is more than likely—reports to your CFO.

If any of these scenarios looks familiar, you should be seriously concerned. You may have sidestepped all that unintelligible talk of UNIX (which does not refer to neutered slaves in old gladiator movies), but at a price you should be unwilling to pay. If information technology is not a major part of your responsibility as the corporate leader, why is your company paying so much for it?

---

## Are you on the bleeding edge, or just bleeding?

---

Computing is now a major cost of doing business. At a growing number of companies, it is the largest cost after personnel. The ostensible rationale: Information technology is not only as central to business as the wheel was to early transport, but it is also the engine driving that wheel. The computer is a decision-making tool, but it also creates the data upon which decisions are made.

Almost everyone subscribes to this holy writ today. However, many chief executives don't really believe it. They regularly turn their backs on the subject while spouting the common objections to a hands-on approach to IT, including:

- *Information technology is complicated.* Yes, and so are finance, marketing, and long-range planning. Yet all of us can sit through highly detailed meetings rife with numbers. Why? Because we are convinced that understanding the numbers is key to understanding our businesses. Understanding information technology isn't?
- *Information technology demands expertise.* So do finance and marketing, but only to a point. Most chief execu-

194

tives are hardly as expert in federal taxation as their CFOs are, nor should they be. We designate experts in diverse areas precisely to free us to lead our companies. Emulating their expertise would waste valuable time. We simply must be able to communicate with them.

- *CIOs speak technobabble, making communication virtually impossible.* Maybe (and as the head of a major software company, I may be guilty of contributing to this problem), but chief executives who are promoted to run a subsidiary in Paris somehow immediately try to learn at least rudimentary French. And when a CEO moves from running a hotel chain to an airline, he or she always starts by learning airline nomenclature. Why is learning the language of information technology so different?

   It isn't, but like it or not, we've been taught otherwise. Peter Drucker believes the problem will be solved when a new generation of business leaders takes charge—people who have grown up with computers. Whether or not this problem will resolve itself in the future, our dilemma is not 20 years from now. It is now, and it is serious.

The chief executive's disconnect from technology and hence from his or her own top technologist has critical ramifications. Technology-shy leaders tend to depend totally on their CIOs. "Here's money," they say. "Get us the best."

---

If information technology is not a major part of your responsibility as the corporate leader, why is your company paying so much for it?

---

Few CIOs are technology-shy—that's why we hire them—and by nature, they love technology, especially that which some people call leading-edge. Often, this is what I

195

term "bleeding-edge" technology, innovations so new and unproven they have not been widely used. This technology frequently doesn't connect to what's already installed, what your people already are trained to use, and what already has cost your company more than you might know from looking at the invoices, which leave out a lot.

Bleeding-edge technology is super-expensive. Not only have you lost the investment in training on the previous technology (multiply the hardware and software invoice costs by four), but you are looking at lots of what technology people call "downtime." This is like calling death a long nap.

---

## Take direct responsibility for your company's investment in information technology.

---

Downtime can be fatal to any corporation. Think of your reaction when you finally get through to an airline phone rep, who tells you, "Our computer is down." A couple of doses of this, and you're bound to choose another carrier — and to wonder if the computer is ever down when it comes to scheduled maintenance of the air-safety systems. Downtime costs your company money or clients or both.

Even worse, your bleeding-edge technology may not work at all. That's not downtime, that's a direct hit at your bottom line.

Aren't these problems inevitable? No. They are caused by a disconnect that can be fixed, and with surprising ease. Here are 10 steps to repairing the problem so that information technology can work for your company, not against it:

1. Take direct responsibility for your company's investment in information technology.
2. Make sure your CIO reports to you.
3. Learn enough about computing so you are at least familiar with most of the terminology.

4. Sit down with your CIO and review his or her latest plans as you would plans for finance or marketing.
5. Ask how the fulfillment of these plans will affect your bottom line.
6. Inquire about downside risk: Does this new stuff work with your old stuff (in computing, ancient can be 18 months)? Does it require massive training, and has the training been factored into the price, or conveniently dissolved into someone else's budget? Is it tried-and-true or something just developed by some guru who never had to meet a payroll? How long will it take to get it up and running? Is it 100 percent reliable or just 99.4 percent—which is unacceptable if your computing is mission-critical.

---

Remember, either your company will use IT, or IT will use your company. You are responsible to make the call.

---

7. Bring your CIO into your company's business. For example, if your company makes its money from producing shoes, talk shoes, shoes, and more shoes.
8. Then instruct your CIO to learn the shoe business from top to bottom, and to come back with a new plan that projects measurable advantages from any new technology. "Measurable" is the key word.
9. Keep reading about information technology; it changes fast. Stay on top of it.
10. Buy yourself a laptop as a reward: You've certainly come a long way.

Remember, either your company will use IT, or IT will use your company. You are responsible to make the call.

1994

To manage his hotel chain and more than 200,000 employees, Bill Marriott has racked up as many as 150,000 air miles a year. The family business has come a long way since his father bought an A & W Root Beer stand in 1927. It wasn't until 1957 that the first Marriott hotel was opened. On the day of the grand opening, father and son were found putting the final touches to the hotel. Marriott is the first to say, "No grunt work = no growth. No growth = no future." In 1964 he took the reins from his father and for the next 15 years they continued to focus on food. As of 1980 they owned only 75 hotels, but then Marriott made the decision to build them at a much faster rate and immediately sell them while keeping the lucrative management contracts.

Changing the focus of the company was not easy. "The ability to maintain order and embrace change simultaneously is no small feat," wrote Marriott. "It's a little like ballet. Executed well, it looks effortless." One of the problems the company faced was finding an army of housekeepers who earn low wages. To limit turnover and absenteeism, Marriott instituted several programs, including stock options for everyone, and childcare. Management is also hands-on. "If I had to pick one facet of our corporate order that I maintain is absolutely vital to our future well-being, it would be hands-on management," he has said. In other words, upper-level managers must inspect the hotels to ensure quality.

Marriott also encourages creativity to stay ahead of the competition. "Companies that don't risk anything will inevitably find themselves falling behind those that do. . . . The trick is to manage risk productively." Risk is the operative word when dealing with the sometimes unpredictable real estate market. To eliminate unnecessary risk, computer systems are crucial, whether it be checking on franchise applicants or handling reservations. In the following selection Marriott provides a case study for how technology aids revenue management and forecasting product demand. "Simple assumptions about consumer behavior that may have been adequate in the past no longer assure optimal decisions," he writes, so put technology to work.

# Room at the Revenue Inn
## *J. Willard Marriott, Jr. and Robert G. Cross*

It's an age-old retail maxim: When demand falters, lower prices and take the hit in your margins. But in an environment characterized by fickle consumers and vicious competitors, gauging demand by intuition alone can be a risky business. Revenue management can help you play the supply curve—and maximize revenue from each and every sale.

Traditionally, companies have achieved growth through a wide variety of strategies: capital outlays such as expansion; mergers and acquisitions; product development that taps new market segments; and aggressive sales positioning. While effective, these well-known growth strategies incur substantial cost and are associated with substantial risk.

With demanding investors pressuring management to produce more from less, the emphasis in recent years has been on cutting costs and squeezing more from the workplace. But real growth comes from the marketplace, not the workplace. While the potential productivity gains derived from improving internal processes have a ceiling, the growth potential of the marketplace does not. Yet many companies overlook a growth strategy that hones in on generating more revenue from current assets through better management of supply and demand—Revenue Management (RM).

Defined as the application of disciplined tactics that predict consumer behavior and optimize product availability and price to maximize profitable revenue growth, revenue management helps companies capture revenues they have been leaving on the table. In essence, the strategy lets companies use their knowledge of consumers' wants and needs to sell the right product to the right customer at the right time for the right price.

---

Real growth comes from the marketplace, not the workplace. While the potential productivity gains derived from improving internal processes have a ceiling, the growth potential of the marketplace does not.

---

Companies that adopt sophisticated RM report top-line revenue increases of between 3 percent and 7 percent. Since RM doesn't require proportionate capital outlays, this growth translates into hefty bottom-line profit increases of between 50 percent and 100 percent.

## IN THE BEGINNING . . .

While today's sophisticated RM is supported by redesigned business processes and large computer systems that analyze massive databases, some of the strategy's core concepts are simple to apply. Marriott International actually pioneered a rudimentary form of RM at its first hotel, the Twin Bridges Marriott in Arlington, Virginia, back in 1957.

The hotel charged different rates for its rooms according to how many people occupied them — $9 for one person, $10 for two, $11 for three, and $12 for four people — and an extra $1 for use of a rollaway cot or crib. Accordingly, a fully occupied room could bring in a maximum of $13.

When a slacking off of demand prompted creative means of improving revenues, the hotel, which had a drive-up registration window, began to evaluate the revenue potential of each carload by counting the number of people in each car. When it looked as if a particular night would be sold out, cars with fewer than four occupants were turned away to maximize the revenue brought in by the remaining rooms—a strategy that generated up to 44 percent more revenue at no additional cost.

Today's RM is just a much more sophisticated application of this fundamental business practice—saving inventory for high-value customers. This concept was developed into a highly evolved science by the airline industry when post-deregulation fare wars produced record numbers of passengers and, with them, record losses. The intense competition following deregulation spurred the airlines to discount many seats unnecessarily. As a result, they began to differentiate between customers according to willingness to pay and save the scarce seats on high-demand flights for full-fare passengers—a strategy known as "yield management."

By capturing passenger booking data and analyzing the demand patterns on flights, the airlines would decide how many seats to sell on each future flight at restricted discount fares, how many seats to allocate to groups, and how many seats to save for late-booking business travelers who are more time sensitive than price sensitive. Without sophisticated decision systems, the risk of getting the passenger mix wrong would be high. If the airline held back too many seats for last-minute business customers, it would kill the opportunity to sell those seats earlier at advance-purchase discounted fares. If the anticipated last-minute bookers didn't materialize or if they booked seats and then didn't show up, airplanes would take off with empty seats, resulting in lost revenue.

Marriott had many of the same problems balancing room demand. Just as empty seats on an airplane represent lost revenue opportunity, so do empty room nights. After talking to various airlines about their practices, Marriott was sure that once significant differences in its business were addressed, these advanced concepts would work in the hotel business.

Marriott now uses automated RM systems that provide daily forecasts of future guest demand for each Marriott, Courtyard, and Residence Inn around the world. By analyzing historical seasonality and trends to forecast future demand by customer segment, the systems enable Marriott to better manage both the occupancy and rate of more than 160,000 rooms. Predictions of peak occupancy days, cancellations, no-shows, and stay-throughs enable managers to adjust room rates and manage both lengths of stay and discount business.

The result? A substantial increase in Marriott's primary revenue productivity measurement—revenue per available room. Marriott pioneered innovative "weekend products" in the hotel business—a low-tech form of revenue management that uses price rather than capital to balance supply and demand. To bolster weekend revenues at locations that serve primarily business travelers and tend to be emptier on weekends, the chain offered discount package programs designed to attract customers from the local market.

When a senior executive theorized that accepting a guest who planned a one-night stay on the hotel's peak night— Wednesday—often meant turning away guests who might have stayed longer, the company ran a simulation study that showed it was possible to forecast guest demand by both price and length of stay with a fair degree of accuracy. The demand forecasting system (DFS) concept was met with skepticism, especially from "old-timers" who felt that either guest behavior could not be predicted or, if it could be, that they could do it better than a machine. But testing proved them wrong. In an early test phase, conventional wisdom held that no discount rates whatsoever be given at the Munich Marriott during Oktoberfest because of the tremendous demand. Yet, the DFS recommended that the hotels offer some rooms at a discount, but only for those guests who would stay for an extended period either before or after the peak celebration days. Although counter to what the general manager felt was common sense, he applied the DFS recommendation and was pleasantly surprised with the results at the end of Oktoberfest. Although the average daily rate was down 11.7 percent for the period, occupancy was up more than 20 percent and overall revenues were up 12.3 percent.

---

By analyzing historical seasonality and trends to forecast future demand by customer segment, the systems enable Marriott to better manage both the occupancy and rate of more than 160,000 rooms.

---

RM has since enabled Marriott International to use technology to manage its business more effectively and become a pricing leader in its industry. Successful execution adds between $150 million and $200 million in annual revenue to Marriott's $10 billion-plus top-line. The company continues to refine its RM techniques and is now implementing RM at the Marriott-owned Ritz-Carlton hotels and plans to make it available to the company's recently acquired Renaissance hotels as well.

Applicable by virtually all companies, an RM concept such as that implemented by Marriott goes beyond installing a computer system. It is an integrated set of business processes that brings together people and systems with the goal of understanding the market, anticipating customer behavior at the micromarket level, and responding quickly to exploit opportunities.

Installing RM processes and systems requires a relatively small investment, but the return on the investment can be astronomical. Generally, the average gross return on information systems is around 81 percent, according to a study conducted by Erik Brynjolfsson of MIT. By giving companies specific knowledge about future customer behavior, RM systems routinely generate annual returns in excess of 200 percent. In many companies, the systems pay for themselves within months.

Originally conceived as an inventory management tool, the process is now used by RM professionals in decisions involving product mix, capacity expansion plans, operational efficiency, and resource allocation. An emerging growth strategy *The Wall Street Journal* says is "poised to explode," RM may well be the most effective key to profitable growth for many companies. Alfred Kahn, former chairman of the Civil Aeronautics Board and the father of airline deregulation, seconds the endorsement, terming RM a "devastatingly effective competitive weapon."

---

Installing RM processes and systems requires a relatively small investment, but the return on the investment can be astronomical.

---

Furthermore, recent studies by Mercer Management have demonstrated that the market value of growth companies can increase twice as fast as the value of companies focused on cost-cutting. In fact, each $1 of profit generated through revenue growth can be worth three times as much to shareholders as $1 of profit generated by cost reduction.

There is no doubt that to be successful in business today, companies must grow. And top-line growth that drives bottomline profits is what RM is all about.

## THE CORE CONCEPTS OF REVENUE MANAGEMENT

While RM systems can be complex, many of the core concepts can be expressed in simple terms:

## *Focus on Price Rather than Costs When Balancing Supply and Demand*

Virtually every company has to deal with supply/demand imbalances, and the natural tendency is to remedy such imbalances by using capital. Manufacturers expand production capabilities when demand increases and close plants when demand is down and profit pressure intensifies. RM principles suggest adjusting prices, not necessarily costs, as a first response to changes in demand. After all, the issue is typically market-related; therefore, the first response should be market-related, as well. Discounts can be used to stimulate certain submarkets to consume excess capacity or production. Marriott, for example, often provides a rate incentive for business guests who have booked rooms for peak Monday and Tuesday nights to check into the hotels on Sunday nights, providing business for one of Marriott's slowest nights and generating increased revenue.

## *Replace Cost-Based Pricing with Market-Based Pricing*

Most companies price products based on the cost of producing, selling, and delivering them. But consumers aren't concerned with costs—they place a value on goods and services based on their own needs and desires. A company's job is to find the market's acceptable price. While the perceived value may be enhanced by improving the product or repositioning it, the consumer will either buy or not buy at the price placed on the product. Intimate knowledge of the market helps determine the prices that are acceptable to consumers and which will give you a suitable return.

## *Sell to Segmented Micromarkets, Not Mass Markets*

Most companies strive to deliver what the consumer wants faster, better, and cheaper than anyone else. But unfortunately, not all consumers want the same thing. In today's increasingly chaotic marketplace, the consumer's buying decision is often dictated by particular circumstances at a specific moment of time. Effective market segmentation is now determined by a customer's willingness to pay at a specific moment in time, not by the traditional demographics and psychographics. For example, someone on a business trip is more likely to pay a higher price for a convenient downtown location than someone with the same demographic and psychographic profile who is on vacation. The vacationer is willing to shift venues to save money. Both market segments must be addressed simultaneously.

---

Consumers aren't concerned with costs—they place a value on goods and services based on their own needs and desires. A company's job is to find the market's acceptable price.

---

*Save Your Products for Your Most Valuable Customers*
In many cases, different market segments will compete for the same product, which may be in short supply. As a general rule, people least likely to pay the highest price often seek to purchase early, shutting out later customers who would have paid more. This results in a consumer surplus for the customer who bought the product at a below-market price, and creates poor customer service when you cannot produce for those who are willing to pay more, but cannot or have not planned in advance. Predicting which segments will pay the most is critical in order to save those products for them. This is how airlines serve late-booking business travelers willing to pay full fare in order to have seats available to them at the last minute.

*Make Decisions Based on Knowledge, Not Supposition*
As markets become more complex, decisions about product availability and price are more difficult. Simple assumptions about consumer behavior that may have been adequate in the past no longer assure optimal decisions. The larger a company is and the more complex its markets, the more crit-

ical it is to ensure that decisions are based on actual market knowledge, not supposition. RM's sophisticated forecasting tools convert uncertainty about customer demand into probability, enabling better business decisions. Computer systems review every day's sales activity, the consumer response to changes in product or price, and other relevant data. Forecasts are run overnight to give decision makers fresh knowledge about the market each morning. Companies that experience tremendous market activity during the course of a day may require reforecasting hourly, or even more frequently. Some may even reforecast after every transaction—and for good reason. Studies indicate the improvements in decision-making from such dynamic reforecasting can increase revenues from 1 percent to 2 percent. For a $1 billion company, that translates to $10 million to $20 million annually.

*Exploit Each Product's Value Cycle*
Once customer behavior is forecasted, how do you maximize the value of your product in the market over time? RM systems use mathematical models to optimize the revenue stream from a given product. After forecasting demand in the various micromarkets, the system calculates the timing and price point combinations that will result in the optimal revenue. While no computer model can completely account for all the variances of consumer reactions in a complex marketplace, tests of this type of computer model achieve increases of 5 percent to 10 percent.

1997

# ESTHER DYSON

Esther Dyson has been called the most famous woman in the computer business today—and oddly enough she's not a billionaire. She does hold the title of president of Edventure Holdings, her New York–based company that invests in start-ups; organizes high-powered conferences; and publishes *Release 1.0,* an influential newsletter on the digital frontier. She graduated from Radcliffe with a degree in economics, and while there, she was a copy editor and reporter for the *Harvard Crimson,* an interest she pursued by taking a job with *Forbes* in 1974. After three years as a fact checker and reporter, she moved on to Wall Street as an analyst.

Dyson's territory involved covering some unproven companies such as Microsoft and Apple Computer. She reflected, "At the time, Silicon Valley was called the Bay Area, and nobody really cared about these companies." The opportunity to network was exceptional, and she rubbed elbows with the likes of Bill Gates. Smitten with computers, in 1982 she started editing the *Rosen Electronics Letter* and then bought Ben Rosen out two years later for $400,000. Dyson subsequently renamed the publication *Release 1.0.* Her clarity of vision and canny predictions made her letter a must-read. When asked about her rise to prominence, she answered humbly, "I was a girl, and there weren't many of them around in this business. So maybe I became better known than I should be."

Dyson took an active role in the future of the Internet by becoming chairwoman of the Internet Corporation for Assigned Names and Numbers (ICANN), which handles issues related to domain names and addresses. For many technologists, the Internet provides boundless opportunity, but it also throws some new twists into the business management formula, and in *Friction Freedom* Dyson describes how it is changing the way we view not only the flow of goods, of course, but time and fixed assets. She writes, "So instead of thinking of a good as something tangible, we can now think of it as a stretch of time on the assembly line." Only by using technology to better manage inventories and to compress time, will profits be had.

# Friction Freedom
## *Esther Dyson*

W e're moving toward a
culture where everything moves faster, where no one has
any time, where we measure out our days not in coffee
spoons but in e-mails, beeper buzzes, timed phone calls, children's scheduled play dates, and vacations with cell phone
and laptop at hand.

This obsession with time and our ability to measure it
will ultimately affect our perception and pricing of tangible
goods. We already speak of "disintermediation," where we
eliminate the retail sector, thus stretching back into the manufacturing sector and forward into pricing. We also will take
out the friction of time, which kept pricing relatively static.

"Friction-free"—Bill Gates's cute word for "profitless"—
means that pricing becomes increasingly efficient. In
response, vendors will have to figure out how to collect
money *before* the fact. The challenge: How do you reduce the
fungibility of fungible goods in such a friction-free, timeless
world? Branding is one solution. But how can manufacturers maximize the reach of their brands? The answer:
through the artificial segmentation of time.

We used to see objects as more or less fixed things, without a time element. Yes, there were disposable or perishable
items, such as razor blades or food, but people tended to buy

*things*, not the rights to use them. Even when we rented things, such as land, we saw them as permanent—"fixed assets."

Now we have started to look at goods as a *flow* of services or usage rights over time: not just housing rentals but also video rentals, condo time-shares, executive jet partnerships, even so-called serial monogamy.

But let's go back one step further in time, before the good is even created. I believe we will soon look at goods as the embodiment of time on a production line. Pricing will no longer be fixed but will reactively shift up and down over time.

---

"Friction-free"—Bill Gates's cute word for "profitless"—means that pricing becomes increasingly efficient.

---

Consider the airline seat. You used to pay a fixed price for, say, a flight from New York to San Francisco, whatever the time of day, whatever the airline, whenever you bought the ticket. Certain flights would sell out early, but that was just life. Of course, rich people could buy first-class seats, but that's about all the flexibility there was. Once the plane took off, a vacant seat had no value for the airline. (But it did add value for the people in the seats nearby: An empty seat let them have a more comfortable flight.) Then, as everyone knows, we got deregulation on one side and yield management on the other. In the airlines, and later in the hotel and car rental businesses, canny businesspeople began to understand how demand varied over time and place right up to the moment of departure. However, the genius of yield management is not just to predict demand and adjust prices accordingly but to segment the market into different levels of price sensitivity. This is hard to do because if you advertise a cheap price, even people who are willing to pay more are likely to take you up on your offer. It's no cheaper for the airlines to serve you if you stay over on Saturday night, but that arbitrary restriction, along with time windows for ticket purchases, keeps many less price-conscious people paying higher fares.

Two well-known results of yield management have been special sales and last-minute, seat-bumping auctions. Many college students, retirees, and people with flexible schedules now buy tickets hoping to get bumped and win a free travel voucher or even cash. The airlines, for their part, use these people to manage the inevitable variations in no-show rates.

Such practices, aided and abetted by the Internet, which collapse the time once allocated for distribution and marketing, are about to spread to physical goods. Vendors have to ask: How can we put market segmentation into products when anyone can compare prices over the Net? While vendors can't let consumers use a CD player, for instance, on Sundays only, they can, for a 25 percent discount, give customers the option of downloading content at midnight when bandwidth is more plentiful.

---

The genius of yield management is not just to predict demand and adjust prices accordingly but to segment the market into different levels of price sensitivity.

---

It used to be that convenience was at least one factor in pricing. Buy the CD player at a nice neighborhood store for list price or go to the crowded discount outlet for a better deal. But the Internet is scotching that approach even as it's creating more of a market (as in Priceline.com) for cheap airline seats that would otherwise go unused (and reducing the bumping market). In a world where distribution becomes increasingly efficient and competitive, everyone has access to the same deals.

So instead of thinking of a good as something tangible, we can now think of it as a stretch of time on the assembly line. If a product is produced without being ordered, it begins to lose value. As margins get squeezed by Net-based competition, every producer will be trying to maximize use of production facilities and charge the highest amount possible while minimizing inventories. Most manufacturers simply won't produce without orders in advance since they'll be losing money from the moment they acquire the raw materials or parts until they finally deliver the goods. As more and more manufacturers build primarily to order, not only will there be less inventory in general but also fewer goods available at the customer's convenience.

It will simply be too expensive for a manufacturer to make things that may or may not be demanded in the market—just as a plane wouldn't fly without advance bookings and a resort wouldn't open without advance reservations. There still will be some goods available on demand from manufacturers that produce goods on spec. But those companies will be competing with firms that will offer consumers early sign-up prices (that is, discounts for ordering a product before it's manufactured)—just as the seat auctions compete with the airlines' own restricted advance-purchase fares. And at the other end of the scale, there will also be very expensive items, kept in stock for the customers willing to pay a premium to get them immediately, with the cost of inventory included in the price.

---

**Instead of thinking of a good as something tangible, we can now think of it as a stretch of time on the assembly line.**

---

Currently, goods are priced cheaper after they fail to sell, as in most retail stores where, complain managers, shoppers have now become conditioned to wait for sales. Goods are most valuable when they are wanted. But in the future, it probably won't pay to keep any inventory at all in retail stores, except possibly in fancy showrooms for the rich or bargain stores for the less prosperous. Manufacturers trying to maintain prices won't want their brand names on unordered surplus merchandise, and they won't put their brand names on production made for spec.

---

As the Net makes shopping for the best prices convenient for everyone, manufacturers will need to find some way to create artificial market segmentation.

---

So how *can* manufacturers keep prices up among people who are willing to pay more? One way is to post high prices to begin with and have the odd unannounced sale to catch people who didn't bite at the regular price. Another way might be to limit the low prices to the equivalent of a Saturday-night stayover, i.e., all goods ordered between 2 A.M. and 6 A.M., in the time zone to which they are to be shipped, get a 25 percent discount. Yes, some people will hire their teenage kids to stay up late or get a friend in France to place the order. Others will program software agents to catch such specials and order for them. The manufacturers will counter with clever tricks such as simple questions to which an agent, or the average French person, would not know the answer, such as "What is Monica's mother's first name?" And if your teenage kid can't answer, well, those are the breaks. And from the vendor's point of view, it wouldn't have been a very profitable sale anyway, but it keeps the assembly line running.

As the Net makes shopping for the best prices convenient for everyone, manufacturers will need to find some way to create artificial market segmentation. The only inconvenience left in a friction-free world is time.

1998

American Express legend James Robinson is descended from old-money Atlanta bankers; green runs through his veins. After attending Georgia Tech and earning an MBA from Harvard in 1961, he immediately walked into the hallowed halls of business by becoming the assistant to the chairman of Morgan Guaranty Trust. In 1968 he became a partner in White Weld & Co., an investment banking firm. A family friend and American Express board member recruited Robinson to head up American Express's international banking arm. Twelve- and 14-hour days were the norm, and while he encouraged creative thinking, he also demanded zealous analysis and forecasting that led to some complaints of bureaucracy. Robinson took over as CEO in 1977, at the tender age of 41.

To fuel growth, he went in search of a "fourth leg" for the company and set out to build a financial services supermarket. Robinson's first takeover attempt, which involved McGraw-Hill in 1979, turned into an embarrassing spectacle when the media giant rejected American Express's bid and a public relations battle ensued. Two years later he found that "fourth leg" when the company bought Shearson Loeb Rhoades. By the late 1980s he was regarded as one of America's top CEOs and was an adviser to the Bush administration. Still, Robinson, who remains on Coca-Cola's board and active in investment banking, is best known for his "flawed flamboyance" and for the intrigue behind his ouster, which involved a boardroom battle.

Robinson finally bowed out in 1993. One legacy he left is how important it is to track customer behavior and to leverage technology (American Express continues to excel at it), which he describes in the following selection. While some of his references are dated, his core messages, such as the importance of providing personalized and humanistic support in a high-tech age, are as applicable today as they were in 1981. There's also the opportunity for the reader to answer some of his general concerns, such as will technology "enhance our freedom of choice" or will it bring about "dehumanized work and more authoritarian control?"

# Managing Technology
# through People
## *James D. Robinson III*

In a recent interview, novelist and poet Robert Penn Warren asked, "Will man ride technology or will technology ride man?"

Businessmen know that this is not an abstract, philosophical question. It is a practical one that affects hundreds of daily business decisions. In fact, the multiple effects of technology on people is already one of the major issues facing society.

Will we use technology to enhance our freedom of choice, decision making and quality of life or will we allow it to bring about less freedom, fewer choices, dehumanized work and more authoritarian control? Will we become the tool of our tools?

Even an engineering school graduate such as myself has mixed feelings about technology's increasing presence in our lives. During my venture capital days in investment banking, I worked with several technology-related companies. As I watched them grow I began to appreciate how rapidly computer-based innovations were changing the business environment, and how such watershed events as the development of the transistor and the microprocessor were affecting society.

An example is the new electronic techniques for transferring money—the so-called Electronic Funds Transfer

(EFT) systems. Will they totally or partially replace paper and people in the financial services industry? It depends in part on whether customers believe that EFT systems expand or limit their choices, their privacy and economic freedom. This dilemma compels us to think through the cashless society question more carefully. We should not prematurely commit ourselves to systems unless they provide a meaningful service to those who use them. Blindly striving for market position or profit margins by embracing new technology for its own sake is not, in the long run, in anyone's best interest.

In the financial services industry, the concerns of the public are well known. The issues are the potential of fraud, invasion of privacy and the dehumanization of business relationships. More broadly, individuals are concerned about who has access to computer information and the right to correct misinformation. They are concerned about the potential misuse of computerized records, whether by the IRS, the health-care industry or credit-card companies. They want to be assured that the individual is still heard and guaranteed an equal voice with the computer.

---

It . . . makes good management sense to introduce new technologies into the workplace with sensitivity to the individual worker.

---

Businesses that ignore these fears do so at their peril. In fact, many corporations that collect, retain and disseminate substantial amounts of personal information about the individuals to whom they provide services are taking steps to reassure customers that the privacy and security of the information gathered is being maintained.

A.T.&T., for example, has taken steps to limit the amount of information it normally collects from customers and has redesigned employee personnel forms. American Express also has a strict, company-wide privacy code which restricts the use of personal information and third-party access to customer files. Since 1976, card members have had the option of removing their names from mailing lists sold to other companies, and we have endorsed EFT legislation which protects consumers.

Indeed, the issue of privacy is a global one. International transmission of information of citizens of one country across its borders (so-called "trans-border data flow") is a subject of increasing international discussion. In September 1980, both the Council of Europe and the Organization for Economic Cooperation and Development (OECD) approved documents on privacy suggesting minimum standards for protection of data moving across national boundaries.

Just as it makes good business sense to support personalized service and humanistic values in a high-technology age, it also makes good management sense to introduce new technologies into the workplace with sensitivity to the individual worker.

The advent of rapid technological change poses a variety of managerial problems which top executives must resolve. Most people are suspicious of change and particularly fear "technological unemployment." Blue collar workers worry about their jobs being taken over by machines. Clerical workers fear that computers will render their jobs even more routine and mechanical or worry that their status in the company will be affected adversely. When middle managers' compensation is tied to the number of people supervised, they are undeniably afraid of new staff-reducing technologies. They wonder whether their title, salary and importance within the organization will decrease as well.

Chief executives can no longer ignore these considerations or assume that they will be adequately handled by senior management. The morale and productivity of companies in the next decade may very well hinge on how well organizations ease employees' fears about new technologies and the dislocations they will bring to the workplace.

There are a number of steps that CEOs can take to minimize adverse effects:

First, it is essential to involve employees in the design of new systems which will affect them. When employees' concerns are not taken into account, the results can be costly and counterproductive. Companies like Dana Corporation and Continental Bank long ago began involving their employees in major work area changes, thereby substantially lessening problems such as the one—a classic example—that befell an airline a few years ago. The airline had installed automated ticket dispensers at its counters in a number of airports. From the first day, however, the machines repeatedly malfunctioned. Repairmen tried to ferret out the problem but failed. It took several months and a substantial amount of money for them to discover that it was a design problem that could have been avoided by having those who were going to use the equipment test it first. The machines had been designed and tested by men who were substantially taller than most of the women who used the machine. Because of the height difference women were unable to tear the paper from the dispenser at the correct angle, causing the device to jam. Obviously, many of the snags which later developed, as well as the frustration generated by the breakdown of the machinery, could have been prevented.

Second, thought must be given to the way in which new technologies are presented to employees. Mismanagement at this stage can undermine ultimate acceptance. For example, companies which introduce word processors as vehicles for job enhancement and new career opportunities find that the new equipment is more quickly and positively accepted by employees than when the machinery is introduced as just another clerical machine. Of course, new career paths and upgraded incentives must be offered to reinforce the new image of word processing. It is not enough merely to tell one's staff that word processing, for example, is an estimable career. The company must reward its operators with appropriate pay and advancement opportunities.

Another example of a poorly presented technological change took place at an east coast university. A highly automated calendar system was used to aid the administration in scheduling. Faculty and staff effectively sabotaged the system, because, to them, it limited their professional freedom and over-regimented their work life. The concerns of those affected had not been considered in planning for the new system.

> It is essential to involve employees in the design of new systems which will affect them.

There is another reason why management should be more thoroughly acquainted with these systems. Future productivity increases will come about, in large part, through office automation at the non-clerical level. Today, for example, on-line records, electronic mail, schedule planning and text editing are already available to some managers. Soon they will become economically attractive to many more businesses. Educating managers about the advantages of these technology-based work processes may prove costly, but cannot be overlooked.

> It should be a personal goal of all CEOs, especially in service businesses, to make certain that *people* ride technology both in the marketplace and workplace.

Third, training programs can be arranged for those whose jobs may be affected by technological change. That includes programs for those who wish to improve themselves by acquiring new skills. Training should be practical and to the point, aimed directly at the work to be performed.

In addition, those who will actually be displaced by new technology must be given training to enable their successful transfer to other job designations. New technology should not appear to be an insurmountable barrier to anyone, nor as a symbol of anyone's diminished status in the organization.

---

## Technology can solve many of the productivity and resource problems that now face us, but we must be alert to its potential hazards.

---

American Express, for example, is offering a variety of training programs in its travelers cheque division. Employees who cannot or do not wish to move from New York to the more highly computerized operating center, soon to be built in Salt Lake City, have been given the opportunity through a variety of courses and field work programs to retrain and upgrade themselves.

Finally, employees must be convinced of the benefits of new technologies to both themselves and the company. Only when employees agree that working smarter and finding ways to do existing jobs more efficiently is better for them and society, will American business improve its competitive edge and flexibility in world markets.

It should be a personal goal of all CEOs, especially in service businesses, to make certain that *people* ride technology both in the marketplace and workplace. Technology can solve many of the productivity and resource problems that now face us, but we must be alert to its potential hazards. Only if business addresses itself to the impact of technological change on the individual will technology work for society as a whole.

1981

# PART V

# Lessons from around the World

Advances in technology have made the world a smaller place; therefore, global and cultural issues have become another important concern for managers to contend with. Part V offers management lessons from both American executives with global experience and insightful international executives, such as Akio Morita, who cofounded Sony. Morita criticizes American managers for becoming entranced with shuffling around paper assets rather than building real assets. He also presents a case for a new paradigm of competitiveness. Roberto Goizueta, the late chairman and CEO of Coca-Cola, had to contend with those who criticized his company for what they viewed as "Coca-Colanization." His answer: The only way to succeed internationally is by building an extremely strong brand. Our *smaller* world offers too many sales opportunities and too much knowledge-sharing to ignore the lessons offered by these authors.

# ROBERTO C. GOIZUETA
## 1931–1997

Roberto Goizueta served as Coca-Cola's CEO and chairman from 1981 until his death. Along with Jack Welch, chairman of General Electric, he was recognized as the greatest builder of shareholder wealth in the first half of the 1990s. One major reason for his success: He thought like an owner, a basic right that he and his family had lost in Cuba. Growing up in Cuba, Goizueta lived a privileged life due to his family's thriving sugar refinery and property holdings. To learn English, he attended a private school in Connecticut for one year, which paved his way to Yale University, where he majored in chemical engineering. But instead of joining the family business, Goizueta applied to Coca-Cola and took an entry-level job as a chemist at the company's Havana plant in 1954. Five years later Castro took over and seized much of the family's property.

Goizueta, with $40 in his pocket and 100 shares of Coke, escaped to Miami. "It was a shocker," he reflected. "All of a sudden you don't own anything, except the stock. . . . It brings a sense of humility." Later that experience motivated him to deliver to Coke's shareholders, and his mission became: Create value over time for the owners. Realizing that Coca-Cola was a conservative company, Goizueta spoke out against employees wrapping themselves in the corporate flag and preventing change. To the contrary, Goizueta welcomed it, championing the introduction of diet and caffeine-free versions of Coke in the early 1980s and the notorious new coke formula in 1985.

In the early days of his tenure, Goizueta surrounded himself with business wizards from Egypt, Argentina, and Brazil, among other countries, and said, "We're a kind of United Nations." The importance of Coke's global opportunities was not lost on him. In *Globalization: A Soft Drink Perspective,* Goizueta explores the issues involved in managing a product and a trademark around the world. One piece of advice: To connect with the customer, search for common cultural themes such as sports and music. Goizueta also warns the reader that meanings in English can become twisted in translation. For example, in Chinese characters, Coca-Cola literally means "bite the wax tadpole."

# Globalization:
# A Soft Drink Perspective
## *Roberto C. Goizueta*

A few years back, some clever person—not on our payroll I can assure you—coined the phrase "Coca-Colanization" to criticize what he saw as the imposition of American consumer goods and tastes on the rest of the world.

But that is not what has happened. Rather, as the world has shrunk, consumers have gained the freedom to pick and choose the products they find most appealing, regardless of their origin, and in so doing, consumers themselves have internationalized certain products.

The range of products consumers have chosen for internationalization runs from French Hermes ties and Italian Gucci shoes to American blue jeans and t-shirts . . . from Japanese Walkmen to Korean running shoes . . . from sushi to pizza to rock and roll. And I hope you won't consider me immodest if I add that Coca-Cola is the most internationalized product of all.

Another way of making this point is to say that people around the world are today connected to each other by brand-name consumer products as much as by anything else. Tokyo, London, New York and Los Angeles resemble each other today far more than they did 25 years ago, in large part because their residents' tastes in consumer products have converged.

This trend, incidentally, has not gone unnoticed on Wall Street. Buying consumer product companies for their international brand names is perceived by many as a cost-effective shortcut to the global marketplace.

And it has been said that every corner of the free world now gets increasingly subjected to the same intense and similar communications — commercial, cultural, social and hard news.

The move toward globalization has also prompted a curiously academic debate in marketing circles as to what global marketing is, whether it is even possible, and if so, for what companies. *The Wall Street Journal,* for example, ran a piece last May on the "demise" of global marketing. In it, the chairman of an international advertising agency, not ours by the way, was quoted as saying that Coca-Cola was about the only product he could think of that lends itself to global marketing.

In the other corner, we have Ted Levitt, the Harvard Business School professor who first popularized the concept of global marketing in the early '80s. In a *Harvard Business Review* article last spring, he clearly and cogently answered his critics by theorizing that, "consciousness converges towards global commonality and modernity, cosmopolizing preferences and homogenizing consumption."

---

People around the world are today connected to each other by brand-name consumer products as much as by anything else.

---

Well . . . later in the article, he made the same point in English: "Everywhere," he said, "people want the same variety . . . success becomes a matter of combining global reach with local vigor." Professor Levitt's piece did not mention our Company, but it was illustrated exclusively with photos of our products.

We, at our Company, live by a simple code "Think globally but act locally."

Whether you look at Coca-Cola as merely the most-successful example of global marketing . . . or as the only successful example . . . the recognition given our Company is well deserved. We are a truly global company and in many ways the world's only truly global soft drink company. Nearly half of all soft drinks sold around the world are our products. 560 million times a day, consumers in more than 160 countries refresh themselves with Coca-Cola, diet Coke, Fanta, Sprite and our other soft drinks. No other company sells even half as much.

So, while it is not for me to say to what extent our experience is universally applicable, I can tell you what I see as the cornerstones of successful global marketing.

First, a company wanting to go global must have, or build, or buy, a powerful trademark. Of course, the best example is . . . Coca-Cola. Long considered the world's most ubiquitous trademark, it is today more valuable than ever, expanded in recent years to new products and without peer in its appeal and relevance to consumers. Last year, the San Francisco based consulting firm of Landor and Associates independently conducted three separate surveys of consumers around the world, testing their reactions to more than 600 brand names.

The results showed Coca-Cola to be not only the best-known and most respected brand name in the United States, but the most powerful in the world. In this country, the point spread between Coca-Cola and the second place trademark, Campbell's, as in soup, was greater than the spread between Campbell's and the 50th place finisher, Dole, as in pineapple. As *Fortune* magazine noted in reporting the results, "the name Coca-Cola is so powerful it's practically off the charts."

And internationally, the spread between Coca-Cola and second place finisher IBM was larger than between IBM and tenth place BMW.

When I read those results, I sat up nights trying to figure out how our management could take credit for them . . . but

I couldn't do it. No company can build that kind of world-wide prominence by itself. You have to have help around the world—you have to have a global business system. In our case, the help comes from a worldwide network of employees, business partners, vendors and customers. But whatever form it takes, a worldwide system is the second prerequisite for successful globalization.

---

A company wanting to go global must have, or build, or buy, a powerful trademark.

---

No one who works for The Coca-Cola Company sells our products directly to consumers. Our prosperity is tied to the efforts of our more than 1,000 bottling partners and millions of customers—the worldwide Coca-Cola system.

More than anything, this system is dedicated people working long and hard to sell products they believe in. It is the father-son team of Ray and Colin Mazza who each week drive 7,000 kilometers through the Australian outback, delivering Coca-Cola to isolated pockets of consumers. It is Pops Valentine, a 73-year-old Philippino, who sells cold Coca-Cola for at least twelve hours every day, refusing to leave the marketplace until he has sold fifty cases. It is Moroccan salesmen like Larbi Lahgui, loading donkeys with Coca-Cola for transport through the steep, narrow streets of Fez.

Of course, the system must do much more than just deliver cases. In order to appeal to cultures as diverse as those of Switzerland and Swaziland, it must also tailor products and messages to local markets.

For example, we are currently rolling out a global advertising campaign based on our very successful U.S. campaign, "You Can't Beat the Feeling." Our research showed us that the basic elements of that theme had wide universal appeal, but the message will be adapted and localized in many of the countries in which it will appear.

In the Caribbean, Africa and the South Pacific, for example, the music will feature a distinctive reggae beat. In Japan our theme will translate as "I Feel Coke," in Italy, "Unique Sensation," and in Chile, "The Feeling of Life."

---

A worldwide system is the second prerequisite for successful globalization. . . . Our prosperity is tied to the efforts of our more than 1,000 bottling partners and millions of customers.

---

No discussion of translations would be complete without an illustration of the pitfalls that await the unwary marketer . . . When we re-entered China in 1979, we discovered that the literal representation of Coca-Cola in Chinese characters meant "bite the wax tadpole." We knew right away we had a problem, so we engaged an Oriental language specialist to experiment with alternatives. After looking into several dialects, he finally came up with four Mandarin characters sounding very similar to Coca-Cola and meaning "Can Happy, Mouth Happy," and we were happy with that.

Cultural differences affect more than just advertising and promotion. They affect our product line. Some people would say: An orange is an orange is an orange. In fact, that just isn't the case. In Germany, a tart orange taste is preferred, while in Italy, it is sweet. So to create a beverage that refreshes and appeals to people in every culture, we frequently use available local fruit to make our Fanta orange soft drink.

Powerful brands and a flexible worldwide system are fairly obvious prerequisites to global marketing. But my formula for international success also contains a third, less obvious, less tangible ingredient. That ingredient is a central theme, idea or symbol that binds together the business system, the brands and the consumers.

The link between our products, bottlers, customers and consumers is an image that began to take shape in 1886, when a man named Frank Robinson first wrote the words "Coca-Cola" in his beautiful, flowing Spencerian script. In the 103 years since then, that image has grown into more than the simple moment of refreshment it originally stood for . . . In more ways than one, it has become a symbol of many other good things.

---

Cultural differences affect more than just advertising and promotion. They affect our product line.

---

Through our advertising and marketing, we have encouraged consumers to associate Coca-Cola with their best feelings and memories . . . friends and family . . . joy and laughter . . . sports and music. Through our insistence on product integrity, we have made sure that, whenever and wherever they drink a Coke, the product will live up to their expectations. Through our worldwide system, we have ensured that Coca-Cola is there, so that wherever consumers travel, they can always find a point of reference, a friendly reminder of home, no matter where their home is. And through our efforts to serve our customers and consumers with a passion, they, in turn, have come to feel passionate about Coca-Cola.

Over time, the image . . . this idea . . . of Coca-Cola has attracted people who have worked hard to enhance and perpetuate its relevance. And throughout the system, business relationships have been strengthened and made personal by a shared commitment to this central Coca-Cola theme.

And, of course, consumers have also embraced this idea. As an example of what I mean, let me close by sharing with you a letter I recently received from a young woman in New York City.

Dear Mr. Goizueta:

This letter has been in my thoughts for about ten years. Now that I too, am a professional, it's an idea that all makes sense. Years ago, when I had the opportunity to travel to Israel, one memory stood out then and continues to do so now. Whatever boundaries or dividing lines are placed throughout this world, Coca-Cola transcends all of them. I camped out on a beach in Dahab (part of Egypt now) and Coca-Cola was well known to all the inhabitants. What a wonderful company you chair, one that can reach all people, no matter where they live or their economic status. Rich, poor, at war or at peace, Coke is there. Maybe Coca-Cola should be served at all world summits, just to prove there are some things even man can't come between.

Now . . . such a letter would sound phony or, at best, sheer hyperbole if written about any other product. And yet, it rings so true when written about Coke.

---

Through our insistence on product integrity, we have made sure that, whenever and wherever they drink a Coke, the product will live up to their expectations.

---

The feeling this letter expresses is more than product loyalty. It's the kind of deep heartfelt bond shared by Coca-Cola consumers and the members of the Coca-Cola system around the world. And, ladies and gentlemen, that bond is what we cherish and value above all else. It is also the true measure of success in the global marketplace.

1989

# SHELLY LAZARUS
## 1947–

Very few jobs could be more difficult than overseeing a stable of creative advertising types while catering to suited clients of the corporate world; however, as CEO and chairwoman of the advertising firm Ogilvy & Mather, Shelly Lazarus has excelled. Back when she was a psychology major at Smith College, she was more interested in marrying her sweetheart than anything else. Then, in her senior year, she attended a career conference on advertising—and she was hooked. "They were talking about positioning products and had all the leaders of different agencies there. I was amazed you could do something that fun and make a living," she said. Before entering the advertising world, she earned an MBA from Columbia University in 1970 and then went to work for Clairol as an assistant product manager.

The next year Lazarus joined Ogilvy & Mather as a junior account executive. "When I started out, 25 years ago, I was often the only woman at the table. We'd be talking about what women would buy, and then suddenly everyone would look at me—it was amazing, there I was, suddenly representing all women, everywhere." She became head of the New York office in 1991 and president of North America in 1994. In her march to the top, she was never bothered by sexism: "In advertising, success is measured by ideas, creativity is rewarded. . . . Those who perform well are rewarded with more responsibility—it is a meritocracy."

After almost 25 years with the company, Lazarus was named CEO in 1996 and then chairwoman in 1997. One of her keys to success in an intense industry is befriending instead of just networking. For example, for years she had coffee with an IBM marketing vice president, and then one day in 1994, presto, she won the entire account, worth $500 million at the time. Another key is her focus on a strategy of "global branding," which involves more than just marketing, as she has learned from overseeing a company with almost 400 offices in over 90 countries. Lazarus writes, "For some marketers, global branding has become a management tool. It is a way of controlling and policing a business without dictatorship."

# Global Branding
## *Shelly Lazarus*

We now recognize that the traditional approaches to global marketing weren't really global at all. There was the classic global formula of "make it in New York and just ship it around the world." Alternatively, one would simply take a global brand and manage it locally: same name, 50 different executions. Today the world is too small and the media too vast for these simplistic approaches. As we face increasingly sophisticated consumers and competitors, we need new solutions that are truly global—relevant and potent to any consumer anywhere in the world.

I believe the need for new solutions will drive us all to focus even more on brands. The brand must be at the center of everything the agencies and clients do to promote their products around the world.

Regardless of scale, brands are the single most important asset a company can have—and in the global marketplace, they are even more important.

We know a brand is the relationship between a product and its user. Understanding that relationship and using it to shape everything that touches the consumer is the marketing challenge today.

Delivering on that promise on a global scale can be daunting, especially when there are so many ways to go about it.

There are global brands like IBM and American Express that have global customers, a user base that transcends local markets. These customers travel and see the brand all over the globe. Building that brand means the brand must be the same everywhere.

---

The traditional approaches to global marketing weren't really global at all. There was the classic global formula of "make it in New York and just ship it around the world."

---

Some global brands are global because their appeal transcends borders. For all our cultural, political, economic and language differences, people are more alike than not. Huggies diapers are marketed the same way around the world, as are Dove Beauty Bar and Pond's. These brands tap into universal truths and are then made to live locally. They aren't foreign. These brands are familiar and friendly.

This is where the leverage of global branding pays off. It's hard enough to have one really good idea; it's even harder to have 60 good ideas and to execute those ideas well in 60 different ways. If you get it right, one idea becomes the only idea—and it works everywhere.

---

Brands are the single most important asset a company can have—and in the global marketplace, they are even more important.

---

For some marketers, global branding has become a management tool. It is a way of controlling and policing a business without dictatorship. If the brand is the shared idea, and if the brand values are clearly understood across geographies, if there is buy-in everywhere on what the content of that brand is all about, then management can allow geographies greater freedom to manage their local businesses.

---

> The real trick to global branding is good local people. You can't manage a successful global brand by shipping ex-pats all over the globe.

---

The management of global brands has also taken the client-agency relationship to a higher level of sophistication. Where we work in partnership in every geography around the globe for the sake of the brand, these relationships must be deep. They must be long term. The commitment required to create these global alignments should breed magnificent partnership between client and agency.

Three final thoughts on global brands:

No amount of strategic insight can replace good work. The same standard of quality needs to be brought against global work as local. Without this no partnership will be viable. It's all about the work.

Second, the real trick to global branding is good local people. You can't manage a successful global brand by shipping ex-pats all over the globe. Local people who understand the bigger brand and can make it live locally are invaluable.

Finally, you'll notice I haven't used the word advertising once yet. For good reason. Advertising is not the same as branding. It's an important tool, it does a unique service, but increasingly, branding is about bringing the brand truth through all the points of contact with the consumer.

The brand must inform everything—from the ads to the sales call to the showroom to the packaging to the Web site—and anything that touches the consumer. If clients and their agencies truly understand this, and execute this, then they will build powerful global brands.

1998

In war-devastated 1946 Japan, Akio Morita and his friend, Masaru Ibuka, set about building "a clever company that would make new high-technology products in ingenious ways" and help rebuild Japan's economy. That company is Sony. Morita's father, however, had hoped that his eldest son would follow him into the sake business, a family tradition for 14 generations. But Morita had been obsessed with electronics since his youth and credits his unwitting mother for his interest: "My mother was very fond of Western classical music, and she bought many phonograph records for our old Victrola. . . . and I believe my interest in electronics and sound reproduction began because of her." In middle school he spent a whole year trying to build a voice recorder—all he had to show for it was poor grades and a good scolding.

Morita went on to study physics at the Osaka Imperial University just as World War II was breaking out. During the war, the lab in which he worked became a naval research facility and Morita himself became a lieutenant. After the war, he went into business with his friend, and their first innovative product was the tape recorder—Morita finally conquered voice recording—only postwar Japan was not interested in toys. Both fortunately and unfortunately, the courts were overwhelmed at the time, so he marketed the recorder as a replacement for scarce stenographers.

Morita took a global view in building Sony. "He saw long before his contemporaries that a shrinking world could represent enormous opportunities for a company that could think beyond its own borders, both physically and psychologically," Kenichi Ohmae, management consultant extraordinaire (see pages 243–249), wrote of Morita. To pursue these opportunities, Morita moved his entire family to the United States in 1963. He took many learned lessons back to Japan, which are, in part, described in *Morita Shock*. Morita calls for Japan, which has suffered economically in the 1990s, "to stop viewing business as a strictly a 'burden sharing' enterprise," and to "incorporate the idea of 'reward sharing' "—a concept all companies must be vigilant in implementing.

# Morita Shock: A New Paradigm for True Partnership
## Akio Morita

I have often spoken in the past of my firm belief that America has been shifting too much emphasis from "value-added" manufacturing to financial money games; of my concern that more people are interested in trying to shuffle paper assets around than building lasting assets by producing real goods. I have also spoken about the tendency I have seen towards a short-term focus on quarterly results rather than the vital long-term vision needed to sustain and promote a healthy industrial base. As well, some of you may already know of my conviction that a society which values MBAs, lawyers, and financial wizards over engineers and product planners is moving in the wrong direction.

And though I remain convinced of these views, and am encouraged by the recent moves in the United States to reverse these trends, there is another side to the coin. What I have come to believe is that the crucial burden of change in these final years of the twentieth century lies not west of here but east: in Japan.

Japan is in desperate need of a new philosophy of management; a new paradigm for competitiveness; a new sense of self. For the past 45 years Japan has thought of itself as a rebuilding nation with a duty to focus solely on its own self interests in molding a newly democratic, free-market society.

The end of the war gave birth to a new Japan, and the policies of government, the practices of business, and the assistance of the United States were all aimed at nurturing this new infant member of the global community. But those days are over, and the old ways of doing things can no longer apply.

---

A society which values MBAs, lawyers, and financial wizards over engineers and product planners is moving in the wrong direction.

---

Unfortunately, however, as Japan has grown to become the second largest economy in the world, it has not outgrown its reliance on several — if I may borrow a golf term — "handicaps" which have helped it become a player on the professional level of the free trade game.

These "handicaps" have allowed Japan to play its own version of the free trade game, to obviously successful results. But it is now these same "handicaps" or, if you will, old fashioned practices which prevent Japan from being able to join the leading economies of Europe and North America in true global partnership.

## TIME FOR SACRIFICE

A few months ago I visited Europe as a member of a Keidanren — Japanese Federation of Economic Organizations — study mission. I was very impressed to see first hand how European countries — many of which have had difficult relations, or were even enemies in the past — are now making serious efforts towards economic and monetary union. Each European Community member is faithfully acting on the principle of self-sacrifice for the greater good of Europe.

This willingness to pursue common over self interest is both amazing and admirable.

But the only sacrifice Japan has known is that which it asks of its working people, the sacrifice which the people have given to lay the foundation and stoke the engine of our industrial economy. As a member of the global community, this is not true self-sacrifice, only sacrifice for the selfish pursuit of domestic interests. This is why many people have said that Japan is unfair. They believe that the way Japanese corporations compete in the marketplace does not fit in with the approach taken by other countries.

---

And though from an objective, economic standpoint, arguments can be made for and against the Japanese way of doing business, I learned in Europe that . . . the Japanese way is simply not accepted.

---

On a comparative scale, Japanese companies pay their employees less for longer hours worked, take slimmer profit margins, and pay stockholders smaller dividends. This allows them to compete viciously on price, a practice that is found in the extreme in the Japanese domestic market. For example, since the introduction of television to Japan in 1953, over 30 different companies have at one time or another been in this market. Today, less than a dozen remain.

This competitive approach, fully accepted as necessary by society, made Japanese industry strong. But it does not translate well overseas. For it is precisely this philosophy of competitiveness which also leads to multilateral trade friction.

And though from an objective, economic standpoint, arguments can be made for and against the Japanese way of doing business, I learned in Europe that from a political and social perspective there is no debate. The Japanese way is simply not accepted. The European position on "transplants" is a good example. The European leaders I met with generally felt that they could not accept Japanese cars made in Europe as European. The reasons for this, I believe, must go beyond the issues of local content and location of home headquarters because companies like Ford do not seem to have similar problems. So I conclude that it must be due to Japan's peculiar business philosophy. And rather than argue the pros and cons, I feel that if Japan is to contribute to and be a part of the global economy, it must re-invent itself to blend with prevailing attitudes and practices of international business.

> Japan is in desperate need of a new philosophy
> of management; a new paradigm for competi-
> tiveness; a new sense of self.

Now, I am not saying that Japan should abandon its solid manufacturing fundamentals, long-term business vision, or its commitment to employee welfare. These are indeed several aspects of Japanese corporate culture which should not only be kept, but fostered elsewhere as well. But in order for Japan to build partnerships with the leading — and I must say "Western" — economies, there are key areas where Japan must shed its ties to the past.

## QUALITY OF LIFE

Japan needs a new philosophy of management. The success of today's business and industry owes much to the sacrifices employees have made for their companies. Of course, in return, corporations have provided the security of a "lifetime employment" system for workers, but we must do more. It can be said that the standard of living has improved, but we cannot claim the same for the overall "quality of life." Americans and Europeans know very well how important "quality of life" truly is. And on this score there is much Japan can learn.

---

If Japan is to contribute to and be a part of the global economy, it must re-invent itself to blend with prevailing attitudes and practices of international business.

---

It is time for management and employees to stop viewing business as strictly a "burden sharing" enterprise. We must also incorporate the idea of "reward sharing." If we can bring the salary, benefit, and vacation packages our employees receive in line with so-called "Western" standards, we can help boost the quality of life. Additionally, if employees of Japanese companies have more free time and disposable income, I believe it could help stimulate the domestic marketplace to become more open and thus more profitable for foreign companies doing business in Japan.

At the same time, Japanese corporations must re-evaluate their practice of paying small dividends to shareholders. Rather than building vast reserves of cash, Japanese companies should show a greater willingness to share the fruits of their profits with worldwide stockholders and employees. By doing so, Japanese companies can help to reinvigorate the domestic and international economy, and thereby become full-time contributing members of the global community.

But this is still not enough. Perhaps even more importantly, Japan needs a new paradigm for competitiveness. Though it is true that Japan's competitive practices were born from the historically severe competition found in the domestic market, we cannot assume that the same practices will be welcome elsewhere.

I will not go so far as to say, as some have, that Japan pursues "adversarial trade," but Japanese preoccupation with market share is very strong. Japan's corporations have, in many cases, sacrificed potential and legitimate profits in an effort to secure a strong place in the market; taking razor-thin profit margins which no Western company would be able to tolerate.

## GLOBAL RESPONSIBILITY

Now, by and large, this does not violate the rules of competition, but it surely fails to embrace the spirit of competition in the United States and Europe. And often it is not only the employees and stockholders who must bear the brunt of this strategy, but smaller suppliers and sub-contractors are also forced to face severe hardships.

---

Japanese companies should show a greater willingness to share the fruits of their profits with worldwide stockholders and employees.

---

It comes as no surprise, then, that foreign competitors sometimes feel threatened by what they find to be a different Japanese approach to competition. This is because they do not have the luxury of a sacrificing labor force and low dividend outlays. Without this sort of "handicap" it is difficult to compete in the marketplace without curtailing investment for the future.

Thus I believe Japanese corporations—each in their own way, but with a sense of urgency—must develop a new philosophy for management. One which looks to increase not simply sales and cash reserves, but "quality of life" for its employees. And we need a new paradigm for competitiveness. One which conforms to the standard, accepted practices of the international community. And on a broader scale, Japan must learn from the grand example of "EC 1992" that sacrificing certain self interests, if it serves the greater good of bringing all nations together—in equality—is certainly a worthwhile and important effort.

Global responsibility and leadership does not come without first making a commitment to being a contributing, global team player.

Though I firmly believe Japan must change, I harbor no illusions that the transition will come swiftly or easily. That is why I feel it is important for me to give voice to these ideas now. Because until Japan is ready to redefine itself, it cannot hope to be accepted on the same stage as Europe and North America. And thus true Global Partnership—the only real hope for tackling the challenges of a borderless world—cannot be achieved. And without true Partnership, the vexing global problems of today will remain with all of us tomorrow, and well into the century yet to come.

I would like to emphasize that this is the time for both of us, Americans and Japanese, to stop blaming each other. Instead, we must do our best to examine and improve ourselves.

1992

# KENICHI OHMAE
## 1943–

Crowned "Japan's only successful management guru" by *Financial Times*, Kenichi Ohmae has a few things to say about management. He certainly didn't start out as a guru; he earned a Ph.D. in nuclear physics at the Massachusetts Institute of Technology, then went to work as an engineer at Hitachi. Within a few years he jumped ship to the world of international consulting by joining the venerable consulting firm McKinsey & Company, where he rose to director of the Tokyo office. Besides bringing an analytical mind to the discipline, he also views the world holistically—his hobbies include sailing and scuba diving, and he is an accomplished clarinetist.

To focus on national issues in his economically troubled homeland, Ohmae took early retirement from McKinsey in 1994, organized a movement calling for reforms, and ran for the governor of Tokyo in 1995. Although he lost, he remains a strong voice for change. In 1998 he colaunched Business Breakthrough, a satellite channel that offers programming on business and management issues. For those who can't afford Ohmae's $50,000 fee for an hour-long talk, it's a good option. There are also his numerous best-selling books, including the 1982 *The Mind of the Strategist,* in which Ohmae wrote, "Everyone thinks the Japanese possess some special magic that enables them to run rings around their competitors in world markets." That image has been erased, of course, and while Ohmae never believed in magic, he does have faith in intuition.

One of the secrets of good management, Ohmae believes, is viewing the company, customers, and competition as one big comprehensive picture. Seeing the big picture requires intuitive elements, according to Ohmae: "That spark of insight is essential. Without it, strategies disintegrate into stereotypes." In the following selection, Ohmae elaborates on the role intuition plays in strategy, which includes being attuned to the three "R"s: reality, ripeness, and resources. While there is no formula for success, Ohmae believes that "there are habits of mind and modes of thinking that can be acquired through practice to . . . improve your odds of coming up with winning strategic concepts."

# The Mind of the Strategist
## *Kenichi Ohmae*

In my experience, there are at least three major constraints to which the business strategist needs to be sensitive. I think of them as the essential R's: reality, ripeness, and resources.

Let's begin with *reality*. Unlike scientific conceptualizers or creative artists, business strategists—as we have asserted repeatedly—must always be aware of the customer, the competition, and the company's field of competence.

Suppose you were a strategist for a light bulb manufacturer. You decided to address the challenge of product improvement solely from the perspective of customer needs, and eventually you came up with a very elegant proposal for an everlasting light bulb. Would your employer be very receptive to a formula that made the company's product line obsolete? I doubt it. Again, what would Gillette or Wilkinson do with a strategy that killed its aftermarket in blades? How could a panty hose manufacturer win with a product that did not snag or run?

In their race for preeminence in the world color TV (CTV) market, I believe that Japanese manufacturers ignored the realities of their domestic distribution structure, to their current peril. In their zeal to produce better, more reliable products, they developed color sets that last an average of seven years—nearly half again as long as previous models. Domestically, each of the three leading Japanese CTV makers—Matsushita, Hitachi, and Toshiba—relies heavily on franchised retailer outlets. These retailers are now hurting badly because customer demands for replacement and need for repair are at a low ebb.

Conversely, the Japanese dental industry, acutely aware of the long-term implications of new technology, rejected a plastic tooth coating developed in Switzerland and currently in use there. The reason is quite obvious. The coating, which reputedly can retard tooth decay dramatically, could affect employment as well as revenues among Japanese dentists and manufacturers of dental products.

*Ripeness,* or timing, is the second key consideration that the business strategist must address. Unless the time is ripe for the proposed strategy, it is virtually certain to fail.

---

## More strategies fail because they are overripe than because they are premature.

---

The introduction of dishwashers in Japan a decade ago is an example of premature strategy. Not only was the average Japanese kitchen too small to accommodate a new appliance, the average homemaker was not ready for it. The attitude prevailing among homemakers, who took inordinate pride in their household chores, was that dishwashers were for the lazy or the idle rich. Today, after a decade of consciousness raising with respect to women's role, the concomitant rise in the number of working women, and the spurt of new home construction with more kitchen space, the time may be ripe for dishwashers.

Ten years ago, garbage disposal units for kitchen sinks likewise flopped on the Japanese market, but for a different reason. At that time, the sewage system in Japan's major

244

cities was not capable of handling the additional load. This is another product for which the time may now be ripe.

Again, the makers of pneumatic shock absorbers came a cropper in the mid-1960s when they tried to repeat their success in selling to bus makers by introducing shock absorbers on trucks. The bus industry was oriented to people; truck makers cared less about driver comfort than efficient transport of goods. Today the story may well be different.

In my experience, however, more strategies fail because they are overripe than because they are premature. Think how many American and European manufacturers lost their competitive edge in international markets because they resisted automation and robotics until it was too late. Watches, autos, and cameras are a few examples that come to mind.

Word processor manufacturers who have dragged their feet in developing and marketing a unique, cost-effective product may likewise discover that time has passed them by. In my opinion, the personal computer, which can easily incorporate the same functions at little incremental cost, is well placed to usurp the word processor's role in the home market and at the low end of the office automation segment.

Video disks could prove another example of an overripe product introduction strategy, simply because too many households have already invested in videotape recorders (VTRs). In Japan, close to 10 percent of homes, representing a major share of the market for high-pricetag consumer electronic products, are already equipped with VTRs; few of these are likely to be early customers for the new alternative technology.

*Resources,* my third R, constitute such an obvious constraint that it is amazing that they should be ignored or neglected by strategists. Yet examples abound of strategies that failed because their authors were not sensitive to their own resource limitations. Take diversification as a case in point. Few food companies trying to move into pharmaceuticals, chemical companies moving into foods, or electronic component manufacturers moving into final assembly have succeeded. The basic reason in most cases has been that the companies involved were not sensitive to the limitations of their own internal resources and skills.

Toyota, for example, made the quantum jump from loom machines to automobiles successfully because the latter business was started and organized as a separate entity, able to build its own resources and develop its own core strengths. So far, however, the same company's efforts to diversity into housing have not succeeded. The reason may very well be that Toyota, instead of applying the same principle and setting up housing as a separate entity, chose instead to rely on drawing the necessary resources from its automobile organization. This has not worked so far for Toyota, because a mind-set and organization oriented toward mass production were ill-suited to respond to market needs in the eclectic housing arena.

Suntory's unimpressive performance in the beer business is another example of inadequate attention to internal resources. Despite its financial clout and an extensive distribution network, Suntory has not been able to erode Kirin's leading position in Japan's beer market by exploiting its dominant whiskey image. As a whiskey maker, Suntory's strengths are inherently oriented to the long term and thus not geared to the economics of beer distribution (e.g., multiple distribution centers and a relatively short delivery radius) or to the beer customer's buying preferences and habits.

Or consider the recent plight of EMI, the English firm which developed and launched the first X-ray computer tomography (CT) scanner. Lacking the resources to fund additional R&D and market its product aggressively, the fledgling developer was soon swamped by Siemens, GE, and Philips, who applied their ample R&D resources to extending the original CT concept rapidly to other beams and rays including ultrasonic and nuclear magnetic resonances.

Or take another example. Right now, a number of companies from different industries are jockeying for position in Japan's burgeoning office automation (OA) market. Among the entrants are general manufacturers, consumer electronic companies, telecommunications organizations, and semiconductor producers. I believe their growth in OA will be limited until they extend their current hardware orientation to include the one critical resource they now lack: software engineers. In order to gain a 1 percent share of Japan's minicomputer market, a company needs as many as 150 sales engineers.

## CONDITIONS OF CREATIVITY

Being attuned to the three R's is a necessary precondition of creative insight, but in itself it will not fan the spark of creative power within us. For that, other elements are needed. Obviously, there is no single approach that will dependably turn anyone into a superstrategist, but there are certain things we can consciously do to stretch or stimulate our creative prowess. Most important, I believe, we need to cultivate three interrelated conditions: an initial charge, directional antennae, and a capacity to tolerate static.

Call it what you will — vision, focus, inner drive — the initial charge must be there. It is the mainspring of intuitive creativity. We have seen how Yamaha, originally a wood-based furniture company, was transformed into a major force in the leisure industry by just such a vision, born of one man's desire to bring positive enrichment into the lives of the work-oriented Japanese. From this vision he developed a totally new thrust for Yamaha.

An entire family of musical instruments and accessories — organs, trumpets, cornets, trombones, guitars, and so on — was developed to complement Yamaha's pianos. These were followed by stereo equipment, sporting goods, motorcycles, and pleasure boats. Music schools were established. Then came the Yamaha Music Camp, complete with a resort lodge complex, a game preserve, an archery range, and other leisure-oriented pursuits. Today, Yamaha plans concerts and is involved with concert hall management as well, reaping profits while enriching the lives of millions of Japanese.

If the initial charge provides the creative impetus, directional antennae are required to recognize phenomena which, as the saying goes, are in the air. These antennae are the component in the creative process that uncovers and selects, among a welter of facts and existing conditions, potentially profitable ideas that were always there but were visible only to eyes not blinded by habit.

---

Creative concepts often have a disruptive as well as a constructive aspect.

---

Consider how these directional antennae work for Dr. Kazuma Tateishi, founder and chairman of Omron Tateishi Electronics. Tateishi has an uncanny flair for sensing phenomena to which the concept of flow can be applied. He perceived the banking business as a flow of cash, traffic jams and congested train stations as blocked flows of cars and people, and production lines as a physical flow of parts. From these perceptions evolved the development of Japan's first automated banking system, the introduction of sequence controllers that automatically regulate traffic according to road conditions and volume, and the evolution of the world's first unmanned railroad station based on a completely automatic system that can exchange bills for coins, issue tickets and season passes, and adjust fares and operate turnstiles. Today, Omron's automated systems are used in many industrial operations from production to distribution. Dr. Tateishi is a remarkable example of a man whose directional antennae have enabled him to implement his youthful creed: "Man should do only what only man can do."

Creative concepts often have a disruptive as well as a constructive aspect. They can shatter set patterns of thinking, threaten the status quo, or at the very least stir up people's anxieties. Often when people set out to sell or implement a creative idea, they are taking a big risk of failing, losing money, or simply making fools of themselves. That is why the will to cope with criticism, hostility, and even derision, while not necessarily a condition of creative thinking, does seem to be an important characteristic of successful innovative strategists. To squeeze the last drop out of my original metaphor, I call this the static-tolerance component of creativity.

Witness the static that Soichiro Honda had to tolerate in order to bring his clean-engine car to market. Only corporate insiders can tell how much intracompany interference he had to cope with. That the government vainly brought severe pressure on him to stay out of the auto market is no secret, however. Neither is the public ridicule he bore when industry experts scoffed at his concept.

Dr. Koji Kobayashi of NEC tolerated static of a rather different kind. Despite prevailing industry trends, he clung fast to his intuitive belief (some twenty years ahead of its time) that computers and telecommunications would one day be linked. To do so, he had to bear heavy financial burdens, internal dissension, and scorn.

All this leads me to a final observation. Strategic success cannot be reduced to a formula, nor can anyone become a strategic thinker merely by reading a book. Nevertheless, there are habits of mind and modes of thinking that can be acquired through practice to help you free the creative power of your subconscious and improve your odds of coming up with winning strategic concepts.

1982

# ANITA RODDICK
## 1942–

Anita Roddick, founder of The Body Shop, is the daughter of Italian parents who immigrated to Britain. She has traveled the world many times over for pleasure and business, while building a cosmetics firm with over 1,000 outlets in more than 40 countries. Growing up, Roddick imagined herself becoming an actress, but when it came time for college, her mother convinced her that being a teacher was a more "suitable" profession. After teaching stints in Israel and England, Roddick embarked on a voyage that included Switzerland, Tahiti, and South Africa, among other countries. "Everywhere I went I did my best to get to know the local people, to talk to them and eat with them and learn about their lives," she wrote in her autobiography.

Roddick married in 1971, opened a hotel/restaurant, and had two children. After a few years her husband, also a vagabond of sorts, decided to pursue his dream of riding a horse from Buenos Aires to New York City. To support herself and her children, Roddick started making shampoos, lotions, and creams from natural ingredients that were packaged in environmentally friendly containers. The first Body Shop opened in 1976, next door to a funeral parlor, which created a stir and won her free publicity. She is quick to point out that "in my view the cosmetics industry should be promoting health and well-being; instead it hypes an outdated notion of glamour and sells false hopes and fantasy."

Managing her highly successful business does present problems. "We're having to grow up," Roddick said. "We have to get methods and processes in, and the result of that is a hierarchy that comes in, and I think it's antiproductive." Although she came under fire a few years ago for not always measuring up to her proclaimed high standards, it's clear she wants idealism on the agenda when it comes to measuring success. "We need to measure progress by human development, not gross product," she writes in *It's All Our Business*. Part of management's responsibility, especially in the arena of world trade, "is just saying no to dealing with torturers and despots."

# It's All Our Business
## *Anita Roddick*

One of the economic establishment's most sacred cows is the unshakable belief in the omnipotence of unfettered free trade. There is growing global acceptance of this dogma; many celebrate its spread. Listening to much of the debate, I wonder if we come from the same world. I've heard much about increased rates of growth in trade, but little about stronger communities of healthier children, much about the march of progress, but little about the people and cultures who are being trampled underfoot.

I am no loony do-gooder, traipsing the world hugging trees and staring into crystals. I'm a trader. I love buying and selling. In the past 17 years, I have established England's most successful international retailing company, with 1,000 shops in 45 countries. But I am concerned about quality in trade, not just quantity.

Now, it is true that my thinking was forged in the 1960s and, in those days, I would have slit my wrists rather than work in an institution of corporate Britain or America—or even see myself as an astute business person. But over the past decade, while many businesses have pursued what I called business as usual, I have been part of a different, smaller business movement—one that has tried to put ideal-ism back on the agenda. We want a new paradigm, a whole new framework, which sees how business can and must be a force for positive social change. It must not only avoid hideous evil—it must actively do good.

---

I am no loony do-gooder, traipsing the world hugging trees and staring into crystals. I'm a trader. I love buying and selling.

---

This movement is everywhere and is growing. We are forming our own networks, creating new markets of informed and morally motivated consumers. We are thriving as businesses and as moral forces.

Business is now entering center-stage. It is faster, more creative and more wealthy than governments. It has to come with moral sympathy and an honourable code of behaviour. According to the theory some call free trade, but I call licen-tious trade, we should all be happy that the globe is quickly becoming a playground for those of us who can move our cap-ital and our projects quickly from place to place. We business people, according to this theory, will make everyone better off if we can roam from country to country with no restrictions— in search of the lowest wages, the loosest environmental regu-lations, the most docile and desperate workers.

---

While many businesses have pursued what I called business as usual, I have been part of a different, smaller business movement—one that has tried to put idealism back on the agenda.

---

There is always some place in the world that is worse off, where the living conditions are more wretched. Just look at industry after industry in search of even lower wages and looser standards, from Europe or the United States to Taiwan to Malaysia. Each country is just another pit stop in the race to the bottom. The new frontier is China, where wages and environmental standards are still low and human rights even more sordidly suppressed. The new nomadic capital never sets down roots, never builds communities; it leaves behind toxic wastes and embittered workers.

---

If we do not build an economic growth that helps to sustain communities, cultures, and families, the consequences will be severe.

---

This is not hyperbole. Go out and check. Visit the cities that capital flight has left behind in the United States and Britain. Go to the places I have been around the world where capital has newly—and temporarily—alighted. Hold the mutated babies, genetically handicapped by toxic wastes dumped in local streams. Meet the indigenous communities being driven out of existence. Look at the environmental destruction. The pure free-trade dogmatists are entirely unabashed by these so-called "externalities," arguing that all we need is even more free trade to produce more revenue to clean up the damage. It is hard to know whether to laugh or cry.

Now if this blind pursuit of licentious trade continues, political instability will return in a big way. The rise of fascism, racism and brutal nationalism we see on continent after continent is no accident. Demagogues prey on insecurity and fear; they breed in the darkness of poverty and desolation. If we do not build an economic growth that helps to sustain communities, cultures, and families, the consequences will be severe. Even if our politics survives, our globe will not.

Ah yes, the argument goes—but free trade brings growth and jobs. That's the rub. I don't believe that unfettered free trade inevitably brings growth in anything except short-term transnational profits and long-term environmental destruction. We need a broader model. I call it fair trade. I call it sustainable trade. The label doesn't matter—the content does.

We need trade that respects and supports communities and families, that safeguards the environment, that encourages countries to educate their children, heal their sick, value the work of women and respect human rights. We need to measure progress by human development not gross product.

Political leaders in struggling countries are faced with a choice—lower your standards or lose our capital. This must stop. So what's my alternative?

---

The new corporate responsibility is as simple as just saying no to dealing with torturers and despots.

---

Corporate responsibility—plain and simple. We have to rethink our approach to these issues. And then we have to act—in ways big and small—to bring sustainable and healthy growth across the globe. Political postures must change—businesses have to stop endlessly whining for easier rules, lower costs, and fewer restrictions. And our business practices must change. We have to take longer-term views, invest in communities and build long-lasting markets.

The new corporate responsibility is as simple as just saying no to dealing with torturers and despots. This is what Levi-Strauss decided when it closed operations in China. That one action, by the way, has enamoured them to the hearts of the young. Consumers are expecting moral decisions. The world applauded when the Olympics chose not to go to Beijing—we should listen to that message.

The new corporate responsibility is as complex as changing our basic notions of what motivates us as business people, of what our basic corporate goals should be. This shocks many people; they think it is a radical idea to consider anything other than financial profits. But corporations are invented. They are human institutions, not species found in nature. We, as business people, can and must change our views and our values.

Less than a century ago, visionary business leaders were hooted out of business associations for saying that businesses had a responsibility to support charity; they were told that the concept of "good corporate citizenship" was radical pap. Indeed, any and all corporate contributions to charity were often illegal. Depressions and world wars changed us then; global poverty and environmental destruction must change us now.

---

People understand that their purchases are moral choices as well. In the 1990s, people want to like not only the product, but they want to like the company.

---

Let me tell you about some experiences at my company. We sell millions of bars of soap a year. We originally bought them from a German supplier. They were effective and they were cheap. And they were cheap because our supplier was using exploited immigrant labour. We decided this made no sense — for any community. So we built our own soap factory.

Soap Works, our factory, is the result of a moral decision. I could have set this up in a safe suburban industrial park. Investing in Glasgow, one of the worst examples of unemployment and housing in western Europe, was a moral choice. I would rather employ the unemployable than the already employed. The soaps are up to 30 per cent more expensive, and we are putting 25 per cent of the profits back into the community. But it is better for my company. It is an example of what keeps the soul of the company alive.

Why do these moral business decisions work? Because people understand that their purchases are moral choices as well. In the 1990s, people want to like not only the product, but they want to like the company. Customers crave knowledge; they yearn for information that informs radical choice.

You ask whether a broad change in business ethics can happen voluntarily, or whether we'll need to face more regulation. We at the Body Shop believe that businesses should be held environmentally and socially accountable. But we also believe we should go beyond the law, and exercise exemplary behavior. We know we aren't perfect—but we are trying each and every day to improve.

We in our company couldn't wait for the EC to ratify environmental auditing; we did it ourselves. We measured our waste and our energy use. We are building a wind farm to put the energy back into the national grid. We clean up our mess, and we strive consistently towards sustainability.

You ask about business's broader responsibility. Let me be very practical about one of the ways we approach this question in our work. We are always looking for fair trading schemes with local communities. We believe small is beautiful, and are committed to making this a growing part of our sourcing policy.

By themselves, these Body Shop projects won't transform the global economy, but they do transform my company's thinking about our responsibility as a business. And I would rather be measured by how I treat weaker and frailer communities I trade with than by my profits. And if all of us in business committed ourselves to such an attitude and such undertakings, big things would indeed happen.

A three-hour drive north from Mexico City is a project we started in 1992 with the Nanhu Indians in the Mesquital Valley. Living in an unforgiving environment, the Indians are using their own resources, the maguey cactus, in order to survive. The Nanhu make body scrubs from the fibres of these cacti. The women have banded together into five coop-eratives in order to keep their communities together. Many of the men have left, sending very little money back from Mexico City or the United States, where they try to find work as laborers. Faced with virtual abandonment, these women found a way to survive.

Thanks to the efforts by the Body Shop, non-governmental organizations and, now, the Mexican govern-ment's Solidaridad Programme, the women are making a sustainable, if still very tough, living. They are replanting. We are working with them to find new products for the cacti and new products to diversify their economic base.

In Nepal, the Bansbari paper-making factory has been operating since 1987, when it started with 20 employees. When I was last there, it had 68 employees; pay is equal for both sexes. We had nearly £250,000 worth of business with them last year.

The Community Fund—funded from the 10 per cent premium we pay on products, had reached more than £25,000 by last Christmas. This fund is being used for a tremendous variety of products, all at the request of the com-munity itself. A medical fund; tree planting; scholarships for girls; a revolving loan fund to help new small businesses.

---

I would rather be measured by how I treat weaker and frailer communities I trade with than by my profits.

---

These projects help to expand opportunities, sustain communities, and generate income. These are just some of my attempts; I urge each of you to go out and develop your own. When you do this sort of work, it absolutely brings a spiritual dimension to the workplace.

For me, fair trade is not just about creating another prod-uct or market for the Body Shop. It's about exchange and value, trade and respect, friendship and trust, about which we have a lot to learn from the Kayapo in Brazil. They provide a lesson for us all in establishing the true value of the rainforest—the single greatest biological resource on earth. The Kayapo themselves know a great deal, and that brings me to my first proposal, the need to protect indigenous intellectual property rights.

Under the Gatt now being negotiated, there is a strong chance that multinational food, chemical, and pharmaceutical companies will tighten their control over genetic resources derived from the biodiversity of the rainforest. These companies are gathering information and genetic materials, manipulating them using new biotechnology, and then parenting the result.

Corporate botanists turn to local farmers and herbalists for knowledge and ideas. These local experts point the industrial researchers to valuable plants and potential applications that have been developed over centuries. There's nothing in Gatt that requires these species-skimming corporations to compensate these people in any way.

This isn't fair—the third world will end up not getting paid for what it has, and then paying for what it gave away, when it ends up importing the patented, first-world product.

Genetic information processed in corporate laboratories shouldn't be protected, if similar information developed by third-world farmers or indigenous people is not.

Earlier this year, the Body Shop announced its intention to become the first company to sign an intellectual property rights agreement with an indigenous people—the Kayapo Indians. So we must press for this change in the Gatt process as a sign of willingness to look anew at simple issues of fairness in trade and respect for indigenous peoples.

Next, we must aggressively expand efforts to develop a corporate code of conduct—a formal, articulated, and well-defined set of principles that all business members of the International Chamber of Commerce agree to live up to. A broadly adhered-to code of conduct would shut down the excuse about competition making ethical behavior impossible once and for all—we could all agree not to compete in ways destructive to communities or the environment.

What I hope I have done is to humanize the issue, stand up for the voices of unrepresented people, grassroots organizations, and the thousands of workers who are abused in the race for ever-cheaper consumer products. I hope I have spoken on behalf of all the citizens of this planet who believe that we are all in the middle of the greatest suspense story ever told—whether we will survive as a species.

1993

# GIOVANNI AGNELLI

Giovanni Agnelli ruled Fiat, one of the world's largest car makers, like a noble king and was a hero to his Italian countrymen. The company, which has also made steel, machine tools, jet fighters, locomotives, nuclear plants, and electronic equipment, among other products, was founded in 1899. One of the founders was Agnelli's grandfather, Giovanni Agnelli, his namesake. Agnelli the younger was trained as a lawyer at the University of Turin, Italy; however, he was an intermittent student as World War II was raging and he ended up serving with the Italian cavalry on the Russian front, with an armored-car unit in Africa, and as a liaison officer with the American armed forces. Once the war ended, it was 20 years before he was named chairman and CEO.

Agnelli was characterized as a speed demon always in a hurry, who exercised daily and found time to take a 45-minute nap after lunch. It was not always smooth going in Italy, especially in the late 1960s and early 1970s which were marked by labor disruption. Line workers assaulted foremen; general slowdowns killed production targets; and absenteeism cost the company millions of dollars. In 1969, a general strike across the country even led to the resignation of the Italian premier and his cabinet. It solved little, for the next year Agnelli reported, "On certain days one man in five—indeed one in four—failed to report for work. The number of hours lost through absenteeism alone exceeds 33 million."

Regardless, Agnelli was able to grow revenues from $1.6 billion in 1966 to $2.7 billion in 1970. Part of his success formula was to develop alliances with other manufacturers such as Citroen and Deere & Co. Another piece of the formula he felt was crucial is the quality of management. "For instance, I believe that the worker will accept the managers' authority only if managers obtain profit through efficiency, and if efficiency, in its turn, is obtained through a process of organization giving new dignity to the worker's imagination and responsibility," he writes in *Closing the Management Gap*. Management, he fears, cannot keep pace with scientific and technical developments; thus, the gap.

# Closing the Management Gap
## *Giovanni Agnelli*

U p to the present time, the management gap has generally been regarded as an imbalance between managerial resources and the demands created by special circumstances, such as expansion, the diversification of production, the conversion of production, the conversion of production facilities and changes in the nature and structure of a firm. In this sense, "closing the management gap" has been viewed as an occasional and technical problem to be solved within the walls of the firm.

Today, however, the management gap is an endless, worldwide process. To close it is a task which faces all industries all the time. The technical problems of management can be analyzed scientifically, but it is difficult to define the dividing line between science and art, and between specialization and general knowledge of the manager's job. The further we push the boundaries of science and technology in management, the more complex become the problems that can be solved only by art, that is by individual or group inventiveness—a blend of intuition and culture. Scientific elaborations continually rationalize our experiences; but everyday experiences show us how much art is needed to overcome new, exciting challenges. These challenges can be met if more men become managers and if more managers appeal to inventiveness.

We live in an era of astonishing scientific achievement and technological development, an era in which every goal seems to be within our reach. Society expects that the new technology will eliminate disease, hunger, poverty, ignorance, and other age-old physical, social and economic problems.

---

**The pace of innovation does not allow us to consider any stage that we have reached as permanent.**

---

Societies react in different ways and degrees to scientific achievement and to technological development, since diversity arises from values and beliefs unique to each of them. But the failure to make technical innovations and their fruits available to society is blamed on the economic choices of the business community.

New technology extends the area of economic opportunities to include almost all of man's social and cultural activities (for instance, information, education and leisure). Thus, the manager becomes an agent of social change. Through technological innovation new opportunities and new courses of action are made available to all men. But this very fact catalyzes the quest for change in the existing social system. Therefore, everywhere, the manager's responsibilities towards society and community increase, and he cannot refuse them.

The pace of innovation does not allow us to consider any stage that we have reached as permanent. Development tends to become a mandatory and permanent process. First of all, in any society economic development is identified with the growth and expansion of the industrial system. Public opinion urges businessmen and managers to plan and achieve increasingly ambitious undertakings. However, any development program must result from the cooperation of

change shown by the industrial structure. It is necessary, I think, to promote better understanding of this reality.

We managers are responsible for our own environment. Our enterprises, I would suspect, do not take all those steps that might help in creating and spreading what I would like to call an open-to-the-world managerial mind. For the corporation is not a world apart; it lives in the mainstream of society, and it must maintain a permanent exchange of ideas and experiences with society. The corporation belongs to, and is an expression of, the culture of its own society. Today, in particular, the corporation is the most dynamic of social institutions; as such, the ideas and experiences worked out within its framework should come out and interact with those of the rest of society.

The corporation cannot be a mere enclave in the society in which it operates. In fact, there is a great danger of being successful in terms of production, while ignoring the changes we have brought about outside the factory. We cannot ignore the problems of housing, education, transportation, urban development, social and political change, which are more and more the consequence of our entrepreneurial decisions.

## THE MANAGEMENT GAP

In this perspective, we cannot deny that there is a gap between the vast opportunities offered by technology and science, and the scarce managerial resources available to meet the demands of community and society. To quote from a recent document of the Italian business community: "We must consider managers as potential entrepreneurs, and both white and blue collar workers must be considered as potential managers." In fact, a large number of entrepreneurs are required to promote the development of every society; a large number of managers are required to sustain the process of development. Management, therefore, is the most essential and also the scarcest resource in all societies, at all stages of economic development. Scarcity is not just a question of the number of managers. In addition the manager's technical, cultural and human profile is too often out of tune with his new, enlarged and expanded responsibilities within and outside of the corporation.

The expression "management gap" now takes on a new meaning: a meaning full of social, economic and cultural implications. It becomes a problem common to all countries, assuming various forms depending upon their differing social and cultural conditions.

In the advanced industrial countries the management gap is primarily evident when corporations must cope with such issues as the assimilation of sophisticated techniques, the improvement of basic and applied research, the conversion of obsolete industrial sectors, the establishment of new industrial plants in backward areas, and the merging of industries to make them more competitive.

In less advanced countries, where the industrial process is becoming widespread, the management gap is felt primarily when coping with the basic issue of industrial rationalization. The list of needs is impressive indeed; it is enough to consider the enormous management problems in the area of public services.

In the least developed countries the management gap is evidenced by the difficulty in initiating activities capable of breaking through economic inertia, or in promoting the success of the new existent modern corporations.

The management gap is a permanent feature of our society. It may be invisible for a short period of time, but it becomes evident as soon as scientific progress opens new opportunities, thereby creating new expectations and demands. The international business community cannot delay in identifying it, understanding its implications, and taking steps to overcome it. Our future depends on our ability to solve this issue.

# A COMPLEX ROLE

A job tends to become a sterile routine when codified within the rigid schemes of technical procedures. Management is not only a technique; the goal of developing management as an art must be an intimate of our approach, if we want to attract men capable of global and thorough understanding. The recruitment, training, and career of the manager, as well as the optimal conditions which allow him to perform his duties, must be inspired by a wider vision, cultural as well as technical.

An ancient Greek philosopher described the qualities indispensable to a good general. I think these words also apply today to the case of the manager:

> I believe . . . that we must choose a general, not because
> of noble birth as priests are chosen, nor because of
> wealth as the superintendents of gymnasia, but because
> he is temperate, self-restrained, vigilant, frugal, hard-
> ened to labor, alert, free from avarice, neither too young
> nor too old, indeed a father of children if possible, a
> ready speaker, and a man with a good reputation . . .
> he must be tested by the standard of character.*

To bring this description up to date, let me contribute to the profile of the manager in the '70s. The professional function of the manager should be the integration of men on the job, so as to obtain from each and all of them the maximum of creativity and responsibility. For this reason the manager must be credible when he indicates the goals to be achieved and when he evaluates his staff.

The responsibility of the manager is the exercise of leadership within the firm, in choosing and deciding between innovation and continuity, in organizing and programming response to the demands of the market and the community.

---

* Onasander, *The General*, Loeb Classical Library, pp. 357–383.

To fulfill these responsibilities, the manager must have understanding, flexibility, and imagination. These are personal characteristics, and they are of basic importance.

The appreciation of his role compels the manager to be open to innovation and to anticipate future developments, opportunities and resources by utilizing his present assets in the most effective way.

The social role of the manager is performed in the relations between the firm and the community, by overcoming tensions and emphasizing cooperation. Within the firm, the manager performs this role when dealing with his staff and with the unions, to improve working conditions and labor relations. Outside the firm the manager must cooperate with political leaders and public officials to harmonize goals, means, and timing of development programs; the manager, in this connection, should help to develop a thorough and efficient utilization of all resources. His standing in the community should reflect his personal qualities rather than his role as head of the firm.

The power of the manager is derived, in every case, from his ability to control the processes that eliminate waste and maximize profit, thus increasing the potential for investment.

At the same time, I believe that managers must also be guaranteed prestige, credit, and autonomy in the conduct of their work. They must be given a well-trained staff, adequate means, reliable information, and opportunities for updating their knowledge and skill. They must be assured of responsible and intelligent cooperation in the strategy decisions and in the evaluation of the results by the stockholders. Their democratic dialogue with labor and staff, and political leaders and public officials must also be encouraged; adequate economic and social rewards must be provided, as well as security and support in times of tension and conflict. Last, but not least, we cannot forget the importance of managerial mobility for the business community and the society at large.

1969

In an electronic world dominated by the likes of IBM and Microsoft, few have heard of Nixdorf Computer AG, once West Germany's high-flying computer and software manufacturer. Fewer still have heard of Klaus Luft, the wunderkind who was handpicked by founder Heinz Nixdorf to take over the company. Nixdorf had dropped out of college, where he was studying physics and economics, to start his company in 1952. Thirteen years later Nixdorf Computer AG started building minicomputers and evolved into a full-service hardware/software company that tailored its products to individual companies, much like competitor IBM. As early as 1968 it established a foothold in the United States, with a branch office in California to keep an eye on the Silicon Valley wizards.

When Nixdorf died in 1986, the 19-year-veteran Luft stepped into his shoes. He had high standards to live up to; since 1977 the company had enjoyed annual growth of 20 to 25 percent. Luft, who rose up through marketing, finance, and production groups, brought vitality to the company, driving a Porsche to work and playing floor hockey with employees once a week. The founder's death, however, was distracting as rumors of a takeover or merger immediately circulated. Luft said his first task was "to get people away from merger and acquisition talk and show that we are ready to go our own way."

With the industry's growth stalling and competitors such as IBM attacking its market share, the company experienced its first downturn in 1988, but Luft hesitated when it came to cutting costs. "What we are not doing is taking a razor and cutting everything by 10 percent," he said. "We are a marketing-driven company. The investment in our work force is critical for future growth." Luft has since retired and Nixdorf did indeed merge with Siemens AG, a fellow European firm, but his lessons are not lost. In *What American CEOs Can Learn from German Management,* he compares American business to American football, which he believes to involve too much planning to gain only a few yards. He espouses big changes that go straight for the goal.

# What American CEOs Can Learn from German Management
## *Klaus Luft*

I n the computer industry, things are moving so fast that success depends not only on keeping pace with technological development, but being ahead of the game. It is a process of constant re-appraisal and never more so than during a recession. This is a time when everyone tries to get their business in shape by reducing stocks, or calling in debts to improve liquidity. Competition is much more fierce and a concern has to think on its feet. Most important of all is the need for flexibility and the ability to react more quickly than your rivals. A computer manufacturer, however, if he is clever enough, will survive the storm better than most. His business is rationalization. The unfavorable economic situation has prompted many companies, for instance, to shelve investment decisions and this has greatly influenced demand at home and abroad. However, the majority has opted for improved productivity by installing computer systems, thus meeting economic difficulties head-on in an effort to retain its competitive edge.

Productivity is the key and it is essential that a company does not slip back to a negative growth rate. It is the chief executive's role to ensure that his employees work intensively to avoid this. *Business Week* recently published an inflation scoreboard where it subtracted the rate of inflation from the growth rate of individual concerns during 1980. For many the results were not that impressive and they recorded negative scores. Companies have to create a strong awareness of productivity among its employees. At Nixdorf we have done this by creating decentralized units or profit centers, employing 40 to 200 people and using a comprehensive management information system to educate them.

Two years ago, we restructured our company to improve the flow of research and development information to our top management. It was not just a matter of keeping track of technological progress, although that was important. The aim was to generate an inner dynamism within the company and involve our managers more deeply in all aspects of innovation. We actively wanted to encourage the exchange of ideas at all levels, not only within Nixdorf. At the Hanover Trade Fair, for example, it is our policy to invite customers, competitors and suppliers to talk to us. We get hundreds of different impressions. Representatives from other companies visit us here in Paderborn and one of the board members usually confers with them. We also send our people around the world so they can get a first-hand view of what is happening elsewhere. They become more receptive to ideas and see for themselves what new product might be developed and then marketed. I listen closely to what they have to say because we must keep our finger on the pulse of new technology. Without it, we can't survive.

In many big companies, good ideas can be killed with scarcely a hearing. There are companies in Germany that aim to create innovative technology, but in my opinion this is not enough. A company has to gear its products to the market if it wants to be financially viable. One must work closely with one's important customers.

In the past, the industry has been guilty of constructing a citadel around computer technology which to outsiders seemed alien and impenetrable. Innovation has helped us break through these barriers, and shaping our technology around our clients' requirements has given us contact with the market we seek.

Keeping abreast of computer developments on a world-wide basis is clearly crucial, but it is also essential to have access to this technology, even if developed outside the company. Basically, no single concern, no matter how big, can glean enough from its own research and development people. Even the largest are forced to buy technology. As it is, we allocate about 120 million DM ($48 million) to R & D which represents about 10 percent of income from sales. But, in real terms, the money available for this sector at IBM or UNIVAC far exceeds what we can spend. So it is important for us — as it is for any medium-size company — to get our strategy right.

Essentially, there are three different approaches. One is to develop the product, or part of it, from one's own R & D department. But with technological advances so rapid nowadays, it is impossible to be self-sufficient, as even the computer giants have discovered. The second method is to carry out joint R & D with other companies, which we do in the United States. The third approach is to buy products, or develop this technology under license, which allows you to tap the know-how of other concerns. So far, this has worked well because in the competitive computer world it has not been difficult to find companies ready to cooperate.

---

No single concern, no matter how big, can glean enough from its own research and development people.

---

In the United States, in particular, there are a lot of small, flexible companies which specialize in developing part of a system. We are able to acquire their expertise and employ it in our own products. Balancing our overall strategy allows us to establish investment priorities, improve know-how and thereby accelerate innovation.

For example, Nixdorf development centers, in Boston, Richmond, Virginia, and in California's Silicon Valley, are a key to the American R & D, which generates much of the progress in the industry. As computer manufacturers, we could not do without them. But this has been just one of the benefits of operating in America. We started out there in 1969, acutely aware of the need to penetrate this huge market and now we are the largest foreign supplier of computers in America. Last year, we increased our sales by 38 percent to a total of $140 million and this represents around 20 percent of overall turnover. Having done battle in their homeland, we reckon we are better equipped to take on our American competitors in Europe. Nixdorf has learned a lot from operating there, but meanwhile the Americans could benefit from studying our methods.

Recently, I went to a football game in the United States and was struck by the similarity between the style of play and the American overall approach to business. When the home team gained five yards, the crowd's enthusiasm was incredible. When they penetrated 10 yards into the opposition's territory, the stadium was in an uproar. In European football, spectators scream when a player takes a shot at the goal, not when their team is in mid-field. Many Americans have told me that their game is an expression of their basic philosophy: the plan is all-important. They divide everything into small steps and this almost becomes more important than reaching the final objective. To me a company has to be more direct in its approach. The reward comes when the ball is in the back of the net, not before.

The best approach is to be more responsive to changing circumstances. For instance, today I might decide on three steps which the company has to take. By tomorrow I might have reassessed the situation. Maybe step number two has to be radically altered. This could also apply to the budget. American concerns are usually rigid in this respect. They work out the budget and everyone has to make do with it. Again, our system is more dynamic. A general plan is agreed upon, but this can be exceeded if one of our units decides more people are needed. If it can increase its turnover, its expenditure can go up. It can also work in the reverse direction. Such decisions involve millions of dollars.

---

I went to a football game in the United States and was struck by the similarity between the style of play and the American overall approach to business.

---

The differing approaches can be well illustrated in military terms. I would prefer a unit to operate according to an *Auftragstaktik* (target-oriented tactics). In other words, the soldiers are told to show up at a particular destination at such and such a time. In America, it is the *Befehlstaktik* (command tactics) that count. The unit is told to arrive at a certain time but to take a well-defined route—to go along this street, cross that river, traverse that wood and negotiate this field. There are many variants on this and there are many well-managed firms in the States, but the comparison is nevertheless an apt one.

---

In a world that is continuously changing, management has to remain flexible and a chief executive has to ensure that his staff thinks dynamically.

---

The Americans have many strong points. They are very good at innovating and when something is successful they follow it up with great drive and determination. Managers are open to ideas and more accessible than their European counterparts. But they operate within a much more rigid hierarchy. By contrast we make great efforts to understand what is happening at shop-floor level. I am a firm believer in the entrepreneurial spirit, and our small business units are empowered to make up their own minds about the development of product ideas and which segment of the market they should approach. The unit leader reviews the general framework with us and then acts independently. In America managers discuss problems with fellow managers and supervisors before making important decisions.

An efficient business depends on good performance and Nixdorf employees—to use my company as an example—are geared to think in terms of productivity. Success has to be earned anew each day and a chief executive should remind himself of this each morning. In a huge company there is a latent danger not to drive home this point forcefully enough. The larger the company the bigger the danger. In a world that is continuously changing, management has to remain flexible and a chief executive has to ensure that his staff thinks dynamically. This does not mean that he is involved in every R & D issue that arises. But he has to know enough to be able to gauge the future impact of these technologies and then guide the company in the appropriate direction. His job is to motivate his managers, push them toward innovative thinking and innovative products.

1981

# PART VI

# Evolution of the Organization

Like all creatures, the nature of the business organization has evolved from a relatively simple to a complex species. The pioneers learned by trial and error, and along the way discovered more than a few basic principles worth ruminating over—some of which are presented here. This part begins with Charles Babbage, mathematician, inventor, and would-be manufacturer, who researched many manufacturing firms and provided a basic template for the division of labor. He also reminds us that "when the human hand, or the human head, has been for some time occupied in any kind of work, it cannot instantly change its employment with full effect." A century later comes Alfred Sloan, who experimented with a complicated decentralized organizational structure while at the helm of General Motors and set the modern standard. The section concludes with Royal Little, who's considered the father of the conglomerate. He exemplifies the corporate executive dominating the second half of the twentieth century, who believes in building a multinational conglomerate to diversify risk. Each of these managers presents the crucial management issues of his day that pushed the evolution of the organization forward.

In the early 1900s, the work of Frederick Winslow Taylor, who promoted scientific management, and Henry Ford, who built the first successful conveyor belt assembly line, were based on Charles Babbage's vision of industrial organization—his role was crucial in creating a template for modern management practices. Babbage's research work led to his development of a calculating or Difference Machine that anticipated the computer. While trying to build the prototype, he studied the manufacturing methods of many different factories, and that experience inspired his seminal 1832 book, *On the Economy of Machinery and Manufactures.*

The great-grandfather of the computer was the son of a banker and studied mathematics at Cambridge, where in 1812 he founded the Analytical Society, which helped revive mathematics as a cherished discipline in England. However, he was thrown out of Cambridge for writing what was judged by the Church as a blasphemous thesis. He would later return to Cambridge University as a mathematics professor from 1828 to 1839.

Beginning in 1815 Babbage lived in London and was devoted to scientific studies, which included working out the first actuarial tables. He started work on his Difference Machine in 1823 and struggled with it for some 20 years, although he ultimately failed, due mostly to scant finances. On a side note, to celebrate the bicentennial of Babbage's birth in 1992, the Science Museum in London built Difference Engine No. 2 per his original drawings. It was made from 4,000 parts, had a cast-iron frame seven feet tall and eleven feet long—and it worked. Ultimately, Babbage's greatest contribution to industry was his partnering with a brilliant machine-tool builder, Joseph Clement, and pushing manufacturing technology forward to meet his needs for complicated and refined parts. That partnership and his study of workshops and factories across Europe in 1827 and 1828 eventually led to *On the Economy of Machinery and Manufactures,* from which *On the Division of Labor* is excerpted.

# On the Division of Labour
## *Charles Babbage*

P erhaps the most important
principle on which the economy of a manufacture depends,
is the *division of labour* amongst the persons who perform the
work. The first application of this principle must have been
made in a very early stage of society; for it must soon have
been apparent, that more comforts and conveniences could
be acquired by one man restricting his occupation to the art
of making bows, another to that of building houses, a third
boats, and so on. This division of labour into trades was not,
however, the result of an opinion that the general riches of
the community would be increased by such an arrangement:
but it must have arisen from the circumstance, of each individual so employed discovering that he himself could thus
make a greater profit of his labour than by pursuing more
varied occupations. Society must have made considerable
advances before this principle could have been carried into
the workshop; for it is only in countries which have attained
a high degree of civilization, and in articles in which there is
a great competition amongst the producers, that the most
perfect system of the division of labour is to be observed.
The principles on which the advantages of this system
depend, have been much the subject of discussion amongst

writers on Political Economy; but the relative importance of their influence does not appear, in all cases, to have been estimated with sufficient precision. It is my intention, in the first instance, to state shortly those principles, and then to point out what appears to me to have been omitted by those who have previously treated the subject.

1. *Of the time required for learning.* It will readily be admitted, that the portion of time occupied in the acquisition of any art will depend on the difficulty of its execution; and that the greater the number of distinct processes, the longer will be the time which the apprentice must employ in acquiring it. Five or seven years have been adopted, in a great many trades, as the time considered requisite for a lad to acquire a sufficient knowledge of his art, and to repay by his labour, during the latter portion of his time, the expense incurred by his master at its commencement. If, however, instead of learning all the different processes for making a needle, for instance, his attention be confined to one operation, a very small portion of his time will be consumed unprofitably at the commencement, and the whole of the rest of it will be beneficial to his master: and if there be any competition amongst the masters, the apprentice will be able to make better terms, and diminish the period of his servitude. Again; the facility of acquiring skill in a single process, and the early period of life at which it can be made a source of profit, will induce a greater number of parents to bring up their children to it; and from this circumstance also, the number of workmen being increased, the wages will soon fall.

A certain quantity of material will be consumed unprofitably, or spoiled by every person who learns an art; and, as he applies himself to each new process, he will waste a certain quantity of the raw material, or of the partly manufactured commodity. But whether one man commits this waste in acquiring successively each process, or many persons separately learn the several processes, the quantity of waste will remain the same: in this view of the subject, therefore, the division of labour will neither increase nor diminish the price of production.

---

> The portion of time occupied in the acquisition of any art will depend on the difficulty of its execution; and that the greater the number of distinct processes, the longer will be the time which the apprentice must employ in acquiring it.

---

2. Another source of the advantage resulting from the division of labour is, that *time is always lost from changing from one occupation to another.* When the human hand, or the human head, has been for some time occupied in any kind of work, it cannot instantly change its employment with full effect. The muscles of the limbs employed have acquired a flexibility during their exertion, and those to be put in action a stiffness during rest, which renders every change slow and unequal in the commencement. A similar result seems to take place in any change of mental exertion; the attention bestowed on the new subject is not so perfect at the first commencement as it becomes after some exercise. Long habit also produces in the muscles exercised a capacity for enduring fatigue to a much greater degree than they could support under other circumstances.

Another cause of the loss of time in changing from one operation to another, arises from the employment of different tools in the two processes. If these tools are simple in their nature, and the change is not frequently repeated, the loss of time is not considerable; but in many processes of the arts the tools are of great delicacy, requiring accurate adjustment whenever they are used. In many cases the time employed in adjusting, bears a large proportion to that employed in using the tool. The sliding-rest, the dividing and the drilling-engine, are of this kind; and hence in manufactories of sufficient extent, it is found to be good economy to keep one machine constantly employed in one kind of work: one lathe, for example, having a screw motion to its sliding-rest along the whole length of its bed, is kept constantly making cylinders; another, having a motion for rendering uniform the velocity of the work at the point at which it passes the tool, is kept for facing surfaces; whilst a third is constantly employed in cutting wheels.

---

Another source of the advantage resulting from the division of labour is, that *time is always lost from changing from one occupation to another.*

---

3. *Skill acquired by frequent repetition of the same processes.* The constant repetition of the same process necessarily produces in the workman a degree of excellence and rapidity in his particular department, which is never possessed by one person who is obliged to execute many different processes. This rapidity is still farther increased from the circumstance that most of the operations in factories, where the division of labour is carried to a considerable extent, are paid for as piece work. It is difficult to estimate in numbers the effect of this cause upon production. In nail-making, Adam Smith has stated, that it is almost three to one; for, he observes, that a smith accustomed to make nails, but whose whole business has not been that of a nailer, can make only from eight hundred to a thousand per day; whilst a lad who had never exercised any other trade, can make upwards of two thousand three hundred a day.

Upon an occasion when a large issue of bank-notes was required, a clerk at the Bank of England signed his name, consisting of seven letters, including the initial of his Christian name, five thousand three hundred times during eleven working hours; and he also arranged the notes he had signed in parcels of fifty each. In different trades the economy of production arising from this cause, will necessarily be different. The case of nail-making is perhaps, rather an extreme one. It must, however, be observed that, in one sense, this is not a permanent source of advantage; for, although it acts at the commencement of an establishment, yet every month adds to the skill of the workmen; and at the end of three or four years they will not be very far behind those who have practised only the particular branch of their art.

---

The constant repetition of the same process necessarily produces in the workman a degree of excellence and rapidity in his particular department, which is never possessed by one person who is obliged to execute many different processes.

---

4. *The division of labour suggests the contrivance of tools and machinery to execute its processes.* When each process, by which any article is produced, is the sole occupation of one individual, his whole attention being devoted to a very limited and simple operation, any improvement in the form of his tools, or in the mode of using them, is much more likely to occur to his mind, than if it were distracted by a greater variety of circumstances. Such an improvement in the tool is generally the first step towards a machine. If a piece of metal is to be cut in a lathe, for example, there is one angle at which the cutting-tool must be held to ensure the cleanest cut; and it is quite natural that the idea of fixing the tool at that angle should present itself to an intelligent workman. The necessity of moving the tool slowly, and in a direction parallel to itself, would suggest the use of a screw, and thus arises the sliding-rest. It was probably the idea of mounting a chisel in

a frame, to prevent its cutting too deeply, which gave rise to the common carpenter's plane. In cases where a blow from a hammer is employed, experience teaches the proper force required. The transition from the hammer held in the hand to one mounted upon an axis, and lifted regularly to a certain height by some mechanical contrivance, requires perhaps a greater degree of invention. Yet it is not difficult to perceive, that, if the hammer always falls from the same height, its effect must be always the same.

When each process has been reduced to the use of some simple tool, the union of all these tools, actuated by one moving power, constitutes a machine. In contriving tools and simplifying processes, the operative workmen are, perhaps, most successful; but it requires far other habits to combine into one machine these scattered arts. A previous education as a workman in the peculiar trade, is undoubtedly a valuable preliminary; but in order to make such combinations with any reasonable expectation of success, an extensive knowledge of machinery, and the power of making mechanical drawings, are essentially requisite. These accomplishments are now much more common than they were formerly; and their absence was, perhaps, one of the causes of the multitude of failures in the early history of many of our manufactures.

Such are the principles usually assigned as the causes of the advantage resulting from the division of labour. As in the view I have taken of the question, the most important and influential cause has been altogether unnoticed, I shall restate those principles in the words of Adam Smith: "The great increase in the quantity of work, which, in consequence of the division of labour, the same number of people are capable of performing, is owing to three different circumstances: first, to the increase of dexterity in every particular workman; secondly, to the saving of time, which is commonly lost in passing from one species of work to another; and, lastly, to the invention of a great number of machines which facilitate and abridge labour, and enable one man to do the work of many." Now, although all these are important causes, and each has its influence on the result; yet it appears to me, that any explanation of the cheapness of manufactured articles, as consequent upon the division of labour, would be incomplete if the following principle were omitted to be stated.

*That the master manufacturer, by dividing the work to be executed into different processes, each requiring different degrees of skill and force, can purchase exactly that precise quantity of both which is necessary for each process; whereas, if the whole work were executed by one workman, that person must possess sufficient skill to perform the most difficult, and sufficient strength to execute the most laborious, of the operations into which the art is divided.*

1832

# Andrew Carnegie
## 1835–1919

When Andrew Carnegie was a boy growing up in Scotland, his hero was William Wallace, the commoner who rose up to lead the fight for independence from England. Throughout his life Carnegie remained a rebellious individual who devoutly believed in the survival of the fittest. Even as a child, he was able to manipulate those around him; the neighborhood kids gathered food for his rabbits, and in return, he would name a rabbit after each helper. (He used the same trick when he named his first steel mill after the man he knew would be his most important customer, Edgar Thomson, head of the Pennsylvania Railroad.) The Carnegie family immigrated to Pittsburgh in 1848 when Andrew's father, a craftsman loom operator, was driven out of business by the Industrial Revolution—the same revolution his son would take advantage of.

Once in the United States, Carnegie's first job was as a bobbin boy, earning $1.20 a week. At 16 he became a telegraph operator for the Pennsylvania Railroad. After 12 years, which included a long stint as a superintendent, Carnegie left the railroad and started the Keystone Bridge Works, envisioning the need for steel bridges. Carnegie then concentrated on steel production in the early 1870s, building the most efficient plant in the world. He could undercut the competition with lower prices and crush any trusts that formed against him.

Carnegie attributed much of his success to the men around him, and he wrote an epithet that read, "Here lies one who knew how to get around him men cleverer than himself." He also claimed to be a liberally minded employer and that mindset is certainly on display in the following selection from 1886. At the time, this essay raised the ire of fellow capitalists because Carnegie was espousing that employees should be given some ownership in the company and that trade unions were beneficial. But then came the Homestead Steel Works strike of 1892, which ended in a bloody battle and strongly suggested that Carnegie wasn't so liberal after all. Nevertheless, his essay remains of historical importance as it attempts to reconcile differences between capital and labor.

# An Employer's View of the Labor Question
## *Andrew Carnegie*

The struggle in which labor has been engaged during the past three hundred years, first against authority and then against capital, has been a triumphal march. Victory after victory has been achieved. Even so late as in Shakespeare's time, remains of villeinage or serfdom still existed in England. Before that, not only the labor but the person of the laborer belonged to the chief. The workers were either slaves or serfs; men and women were sold with the estate upon which they worked, and became the property of the new lord, just as did the timber which grew on the land. In those days we hear nothing of strikes or of trades-unions, or differences of opinion between employer and employed. The fact is, labor had then no right which the chief, or employer, was bound to respect. Even as late as the beginning of this century, the position of the laborer in some departments was such as can scarcely be credited. What do our laboring friends think of this, that down to 1779 the miners of Britain were in a state of serfdom. They "were compelled by law to remain in the pits as long as the owner chose to keep them at work there, and were actually sold as part of the capital invested in the works. If they accepted an engagement elsewhere, their master could always have them fetched back and flogged as thieves for having attempted to rob him of their labor. This law was modified in 1779, but was not repealed till after the acts passed in 1797 and 1799."* This was only ninety-seven years ago. Men are still living who were living then. Again, in France, as late as 1806, every workman had to procure a license; and in Russia, down to our own days, agricultural laborers were sold with the soil they tilled.

Consider the change, nay, the revolution! Now the poorest laborer in America or in England, or indeed throughout the civilized world, who can handle a pick or a shovel, stands upon equal terms with the purchaser of his labor. He sells or withholds it as may seem best to him. He negotiates, and thus rises to the dignity of an independent contractor. When he has performed the work he bargained to do, he owes his employer nothing, and is under no obligation to him. Not only has the laborer conquered his political and personal freedom: he has achieved industrial freedom as well, as far as the law can give it, and he now fronts his master, proclaiming himself his equal under the law.

But, notwithstanding this complete revolution, it is evident that the permanent relations to each other of labor and capital have not yet evolved. The present adjustment does not work without friction, and changes must be made before we can have industrial peace. Today we find collisions between these forces, capital and labor, when there should be combination. The mill hands of an industrial village in France have just risen against their employers, attacked the manager's home and killed him. The streets of another French village are barricaded against the expected forces of order. The ship-builders of Sunderland, in England, are at the verge of starvation, owing to a quarrel with their employers; and Leicester has just been the scene of industrial riots. In our country, labor disputes and strikes were never so numerous as now. East and West, North and South, every-

* *The Trades-Unions of England* by Louis Philippe Albert d'Orleans, Comte de Paris (1830–1894). His *Les Associations ouvrières en Angleterre* was translated and published in England in 1869 (Thomas Hughes, ed.).

where, there is unrest, showing that an equilibrium has not yet been reached between employers and employed.

A strike or lockout is, in itself, a ridiculous affair. Whether a failure or a success, it gives no direct proof of its justice or injustice. In this it resembles war between two nations. It is simply a question of strength and endurance between the contestants. The gage of battle, or the duel, is not more senseless, as a means of establishing what is just and fair, than an industrial strike or lockout. It would be folly to conclude that we have reached any permanent adjustment between capital and labor until strikes and lockouts are as much things of the past as the gage of battle or the duel have become in the most advanced communities.

Taking for granted, then, that some further modifications must be made between capital and labor, I propose to consider the various plans that have been suggested by which labor can advance another stage in its development in relation to capital. And, as a preliminary, let it be noted that it is only labor and capital in their greatest masses which it is necessary to consider. It is only in large establishments that the industrial unrest of which I have spoken ominously manifests itself. The farmer who hires a man to assist him, or the gentleman who engages a groom or a butler, is not affected

---

A strike or lockout is, in itself, a ridiculous affair. Whether a failure or a success, it gives no direct proof of its justice or injustice. In this it resembles war between two nations.

---

by strikes. The innumerable cases in which a few men only are directly concerned, which comprise in the aggregate the most of labor, present upon the whole a tolerably satisfactory condition of affairs. This clears the ground of much, and leaves us to deal only with the immense mining and manufacturing concerns of recent growth, in which capital and labor often array themselves in alarming antagonism.

Among expedients suggested for their better reconciliation, the first place must be assigned to the idea of cooperation, or the plan by which the workers are to become partowners in enterprises, and share their fortunes. There is no doubt that if this could be effected it would have the same beneficial effect upon the workman which the ownership of land has upon the man who has hitherto tilled the land for another. The sense of ownership would make of him more of a man as regards himself, and hence more of a citizen as regards the commonwealth. But we are here met by a difficulty which I confess I have not yet been able to overcome, and which renders me less sanguine than I should like to be in regard to cooperation. The difficulty is this, and it seems to me inherent in all gigantic manufacturing, mining, and commercial operations. Two men or two combinations of men will erect blast-furnaces, iron-mills, cotton-mills, or piano manufactories adjoining each other, or engage in shipping or commercial business. They will start with equal capital and credit; and to those only superficially acquainted with the personnel of these concerns, success will seem as likely to attend the one as the other. Nevertheless, one will fail after dragging along a lifeless existence, and pass into the hands of its creditors; while the neighboring mill or business will make a fortune for its owners. Now, the successful manufacturer, dividing every month or every year a proportion of his profits among his workmen, either as a bonus or as dividends upon shares owned by them, will not only have a happy and contented body of operatives, but he will inevitably attract from his rival the very best workmen in every department. His rival, having no profits to divide among his workmen, and paying them only a small assured minimum to enable them to live, finds himself despoiled of foremen and of workmen necessary to carry on his business successfully. His workmen are discontented and, in their own opinion, defrauded of the proper fruits of their skill, through incapacity or inattention of their employers. Thus, unequal business capacity in the management produces unequal results.

It will be precisely the same if one of these manufactories belongs to the workmen themselves; but in this case, in the present stage of development of the workmen, the chances of failure will be enormously increased. It is, indeed, greatly to be doubted whether any body of working-men in the world could today organize and successfully carry on a mining or manufacturing or commercial business in competition with concerns owned by men trained to affairs. If any such cooperative organization succeeds, it may be taken for granted that it is principally owing to the exceptional business ability of one of the managers, and only in a very small degree to the efforts of the mass of workmen-owners. This business ability is excessively rare, as is proved by the incredibly large proportion of those who enter upon the stormy sea of business only to fail. I should say that twenty cooperative concerns would fail to every one that would succeed. There are, of course, a few successful establishments, notably two in France and one in England, which are organized upon the cooperative plan, in which the workmen participate in the profits. But these were all created by the present owners, who now generously share the profits with their workmen, and are making the success of their manufactories upon the cooperative plan the proud work of their lives. What these concerns will become when the genius for affairs is no longer with them to guide, is a matter of grave doubt and, to me, of foreboding. I can, of course, picture in my mind a state of civilization in which the most talented business men shall find their most cherished work in carrying on immense concerns, not primarily for their own personal aggrandizement, but for the good of the masses of workers engaged therein, and their families; but this is only a foreshadowing of a dim and distant future. When a class of such men has evolved, the problem of capital and labor will be permanently solved to the entire satisfaction of both. But as this manifestly belongs to a future generation, I cannot consider coöperation, or common ownership, as the next immediate step in advance which it is possible for labor to make in its upward path.

The next suggestion is that peaceful settlement of differences should be reached through arbitration. Here we are upon firmer ground. I would lay it down as a maxim that there is no excuse for a strike or a lockout until arbitration of differences has been offered by one party and refused by the other. No doubt serious trouble attends even arbitration at present, from the difficulty of procuring suitable men to judge intelligently between the disputants. There is a natural disinclination among business men to expose their business to men in whom they have not entire confidence. We lack, so far, in America a retired class of men of affairs. Our vile practice is to keep on accumulating more dollars until we die. If it were the custom here, as it is in England, for men to withdraw from active business after acquiring a fortune, this class would furnish the proper arbitrators. On the other hand, the ex-presidents of trades-unions, such as Mr. Jarrett or Mr. Wihle,* after they have retired from active control, would commend themselves to the manufacturers and to the men as possessed of the necessary technical knowledge, and educated to a point where commercial reasons would not be without their proper weight upon them. I consider that of all the agencies immediately available to prevent wasteful and embittering contests between capital and labor, arbitration is the most powerful and most beneficial.

The influence of trades-unions upon the relations between the employer and employed has been much discussed. Some establishments in America have refused to recognize the right of the men to form themselves into these unions, although I am not aware that any concern in England would dare to take this position. This policy, how-

---

* John Jarret and William Wihle (correct spelling is Weihe) were presidents of the Amalgamated Association of Iron and Steel Workers.

all social forces, and in any case the final decision falls, rightfully, upon the political class.

Secondly, in our industrial society culture places the work of man above any other factor in the productive process. The worker, as a man, claims a new status. For instance, I believe that the worker will accept the manager's authority only if managers obtain profit through efficiency, and if efficiency, in its turn, is obtained through a process of organization giving new dignity to the worker's imagination and responsibility. On the one hand, society rightly demands ever greater economic growth and faster social change, but on the other, the revolution of rising expectations spurs on both the developed and the developing world.

## A Crucial Crossroad

There is a close relationship between the social tensions of our time and the awareness that higher stages of development may be attained only through a new sense of identity. This concern is common to all groups and societies; social unrest, or even social disruption, has this very same root. Lack of a strong and diffused sense of identity is likely to produce decay, which in some circumstances may lead to a loss of independence. But this is a price that very few people are willing to pay. A thorough understanding of the development process in all its aspects is required; at the same time it is also necessary to perceive their distinctive traits.

Innovation is an issue which is not limited to the industrial process. Innovation must be global, balanced, systematic, and applied to all facets of society. Lacking such an attitude, the industrial system runs into bottlenecks that, curtailing the benefits of innovation, might eventually jeopardize society's development. In fact, our political and administrative bodies do not seem to be characterized by great dynamism, nor do they have the same disposition to ever, may be regarded as only a temporary phase of the situation. The right of the working-men to combine and to form trades-unions is no less sacred than the right of the manufacturer to enter into associations and conferences with his fellows, and it must sooner or later be conceded. Indeed, it gives one but a poor opinion of the American workman if he permits himself to be deprived of a right which his fellow in England long since conquered for himself. My experience has been that trades-unions, upon the whole, are beneficial

---

There is no excuse for a strike or a lockout until arbitration of differences has been offered by one party and refused by the other.

---

both to labor and to capital. They certainly educate the working-men, and give them a truer conception of the relations of capital and labor than they could otherwise form. The ablest and best workmen eventually come to the front in these organizations; and it may be laid down as a rule that the more intelligent the workman the fewer the contests with employers. It is not the intelligent workman, who knows that labor without his brother capital is helpless, but the blatant ignorant man, who regards capital as the natural enemy of labor, who does so much to embitter the relations between employer and employed; and the power of this ignorant demagogue arises chiefly from the lack of proper organization among the men through which their real voice can be expressed. This voice will always be found in favor of the judicious and intelligent representative. Of course, as men become intelligent more deference must be paid to them personally and to their rights, and even to their opinions and prejudices; and, upon the whole, a greater share of profits must be paid in the day of prosperity to the intelligent than to the ignorant workman. He cannot be imposed upon so readily. On the other hand, he will be found much readier to accept reduced compensation when business is depressed; and it is better in the long run for capital to be served by the highest intelligence, and to be made well aware of the fact that it is dealing with men who know what is due to them, both as to treatment and compensation.

---

Bitter strikes seldom occur in small establishments where the owner comes into direct contact with his men, and knows their qualities, their struggles, and their aspirations.

---

One great source of the trouble between employers and employed arises from the fact that the immense establishments of today, in which alone we find serious conflicts between capital and labor, are not managed by their owners, but by salaried officers, who cannot possibly have any permanent interest in the welfare of the working-men. These officials are chiefly anxious to present a satisfactory balance-sheet at the end of the year, that their hundreds of shareholders may receive the usual dividends, and that they may therefore be secure in their positions, and be allowed to manage the business without unpleasant interference either by directors or shareholders. It is notable that bitter strikes seldom occur in small establishments where the owner comes into direct contact with his men, and knows their qualities, their struggles, and their aspirations. It is the chairman, situated hundreds of miles away from his men, who only pays a flying visit to the works and perhaps finds time to walk through the mill or mine once or twice a year, that is chiefly responsible for the disputes which break out at intervals. I have noticed that the manager who confers oftenest with a committee of his leading men has the least trouble with his workmen. Although it may be impracticable for the presidents of these large corporations to know the working-men personally, the manager at the mills, having a committee of his best men to present their suggestions and wishes from time to time, can do much to maintain and strengthen amicable relations, if not interfered with from headquarters. I, therefore, recognize in trades-unions, or, better still, in organizations of the men of each establishment, who select representatives to speak for them, a means, not of further embittering the relations between employer and employed, but of improving them.

It is astonishing how small a sacrifice upon the part of the employer will sometimes greatly benefit the men. I remember that at one of our meetings with a committee, it was incidentally remarked by one speaker that the necessity for obtaining credit at the stores in the neighborhood was a grave tax upon the men. An ordinary workman, he said, could not afford to maintain himself and family for a month, and as he only received his pay monthly, he was compelled to obtain credit and to pay exorbitantly for everything, whereas, if he had the cash, he could buy at twenty-five per cent less. "Well," I said, "why cannot we overcome that by paying every two weeks?" The reply was: "We did not like to ask it, because we have always understood that it would cause much trouble; but if you do that it will be worth an advance of five percent in our wages." We have paid semi-monthly since. Another speaker happened to say that although they were in the midst of coal, the price charged for small lots delivered at their houses was a certain sum per bushel. The price named was double what our best coal was costing us. How easy for us to deliver to our men such coal as they required, and charge them cost! This was done without a cent's loss to us, but with much gain to the men. Several other points similar to these have arisen by which their labors might be lightened or products increased, and others suggesting changes in machinery or facilities which, but for the conferences referred to, would have been unthought of by the employer and probably never asked for by the men. For these and other reasons I attribute the greatest importance to an organization of the men, through whose duly elected representatives the managers may be kept informed from time to time of their grievances and suggestions. No matter how able the manager, the clever workman can often show him how beneficial changes can be made in the special branch in which that workman labors. Unless the relations between manager and workmen are not only amicable but friendly, the owners miss much; nor is any man a first-class manager who has not the confidence and respect, and even the admiration, of his workmen. No man is a true gentleman who does not inspire the affection and devotion of his servants.

---

The manager who confers oftenest with a committee of his leading men has the least trouble with his workmen.

---

Dismissing, therefore, for the present all consideration of cooperation as not being within measurable distance, I believe that the next steps in the advance toward permanent, peaceful relations between capital and labor are:

*First.* That compensation be paid the men based upon a sliding scale in proportion to the prices received for product.

*Second.* A proper organization of the men of every works to be made, by which the natural leaders, the best men, will eventually come to the front and confer freely with the employers.

*Third.* Peaceful arbitration to be in all cases resorted to for the settlement of differences which the owners and the mill committee cannot themselves adjust in friendly conference.

*Fourth.* No interruption ever to occur to the operations of the establishment, since the decision of the arbitrators shall be made to take effect from the date of reference.

If these measures were adopted by an establishment, several important advantages would be gained:

*First.* The employer and employed would simultaneously share their prosperity or adversity with each other. The scale once settled, the feeling of antagonism would be gone, and a feeling of mutuality would ensue. Capital and labor would be shoulder to shoulder, supporting each other.

*Second.* There could be neither strike nor lockout, since both parties had agreed to abide by a forthcoming decision of disputed points. Knowing that in the last resort strangers were to be called in to decide what should be a family affair, the cases would, indeed, be few which would not be amicably adjusted by the original parties without calling in others to judge between them.

---

It is astonishing how small a sacrifice upon the part of the employer will sometimes greatly benefit the men.

---

Whatever the future may have in store for labor, the evolutionist, who sees nothing but certain and steady progress for the race, will never attempt to set bounds to its triumphs, even to its final form of complete and universal industrial cooperation, which I hope is some day to be reached. But I am persuaded that the next step forward is to be in the direction I have here ventured to point out; and as one who is now most anxious to contribute his part toward helping forward the day of amicable relations between the two forces of capital and labor, which are not enemies, but are really auxiliaries who stand or fall together, I ask at the hands of both capital and labor a careful consideration of these views.

1886

Charles R. Flint, who was operating in one of the more tumultuous times of American business, was and is recognized as "The Father of the Trusts." His own ancestors arrived on American shores in 1642, and fought in the Revolutionary War, before moving north to Maine, where Flint's father was born and raised and became a shipbuilder. The family moved to Brooklyn, New York, and after graduating high school in 1868, Flint went into business for himself as a dock clerk, making a decent $4 a day. A year later he went to work for an international exporter/importer and by 1872 he was a full partner in the firm—W. R. Grace & Co.

In the subsequent years, Flint discovered that wild fluctuations in market prices for goods made him more of a speculator than a merchant, and that's when he decided combining a series of companies to create a trust made sense to control the market. His first foray involved a crude rubber trust in 1880, and he went on to pull together different industrial combinations that made a variety of products from starch to office machines. One of the more notable firms was the Computing-Tabulating-Recording Company, a maker of computing-scale and time-recording machines, that he organized in 1911. Three years later he hired Thomas Watson to head the company, from which Watson created IBM (see Thomas Watson, Jr., on pages 462–469).

According to Flint, the Chicago newspapers gave him the title "The Father of Trusts." It was 1900, and he had been asked to give a speech defending industrial consolidation. The speech began, "A combination of labor is a trades union, a combination of intelligence a university, a combination of money a bank—a combination of labor, intelligence and money is an industrial combination—Work, Brains, and Money." Pro-business U.S. President William McKinley supposedly ordered 500,000 copies of the speech, to be distributed across the country. The essence of that speech echoes in *Industrial Consolidation,* in which Flint declares trusts give the manager and the customer the best of everything.

# Industrial Consolidation
## *Charles R. Flint*

Thomas great advantages to be derived from coöperation became apparent when manufacturing companies were consolidated to reduce the costs of production and distribution; but in the 1880s Industrial Consolidation was still a theory, not a condition.

Now, in the light of thirty years' experience, during which time I have acted as organizer or industrial expert in the formation of twenty-four consolidations, let me review the general advantages of this form of industrial economy.

The most important benefit to be derived from it is the attainment of high-speed-automatic-machine-low-cost-standardized-quantity production, which makes possible the manufacture and maintenance of products of superior quality.

Because of the magnitude of their affairs, industrial consolidations are able to offer, in salaries and a percentage of net profits generally over and above a previous maximum, a sufficient inducement to secure men of the first order of ability—men who are not tempted by a fixed salary, but by the incentive of making a record and profiting by it.

The consolidated corporation, under a system of comparative accounting and comparative administration, subdivides its business so that each of its various departments is headed by a man who, through long experience and concentration, operates at the highest efficiency. Furthermore, industrial consolidations are able not only to secure the best men as executives, administrators and employees, but also to retain men of the highest standing in the consultative professions, — lawyers, engineers, architects, chemists and other advisers and technicians. Thus better service is assured, with an overhead cost less than the aggregate amount which was paid to men of lesser capacity by the various constituent companies.

The consolidation not only adopts the best methods to be found in any of its various plants, but it improves them through continual experimentation by the ablest experts.

It reduces stocks of merchandise, thereby saving interest and carrying charges, and minimizing loss from depreciation.

It centralizes sales and advertising, and eliminates duplicate trade catalogues.

It centralizes purchases, and secures important benefits through quantity and time contracts.

It greatly reduces the volume of fixed and circulating capital per unit of output.

It retains lawyers and experts of experience and demonstrated ability for patent and trademark protection. By consolidation, inventive genius is less hampered by conflicting patents, and expensive litigation is largely eliminated.

---

The consolidation not only adopts the best methods to be found in any of its various plants, but it improves them through continual experimentation by the ablest experts.

---

It utilizes the advantages of a central traffic control, eliminating duplicate routes in the transportation of products sold and received, and locates factories with relation to labor, raw material and markets.

Throughout the country there are many examples of manufacturers who haul their raw material and fuel hundreds of miles to a factory, and then ship back to centers of consumption which are near the source of the raw material. Many factory locations have become obsolete as a result of changed conditions; they are often relics of ancient happenings. . . .

The natural evolution of industrial methods and processes has not only been fully demonstrated, but it is as certain to continue as the operation of the law of gravitation.

But are those advantages fairly distributed? Rockefeller, Ford, Carnegie, Frick, Schwab loom up like first power lighthouses. The public generally is dazzled by their great fortunes, instead of fully appreciating the great service they have rendered in lighting the way to industrial progress. There is no reason to envy their great fortunes; they can spend but comparatively little on themselves. I was a guest in 1875 of Frederick Barreda who was living more extravagantly than any man in this country. His residence on Madison Avenue was of the best. He owned a place in Newport, now owned and occupied by the Astors, the finest estate in Maryland, and a magnificent residence in Paris. In my youthful inexperience I said: "Mr. Barreda, you have magnificent facilities for enjoyment."

"Magnificent discomfort!" he replied. "I have worked up the most elaborate system for irritation and trouble that could be devised. In business you excite the earnest industry and loyalty of young men by picturing attractive prospects. I can inspire but little interest and loyalty in a large retinue of servants—my property is neglected, many of my belongings have been stolen, more are misused, and most of the entertaining is done by servants in my absence at my expense."

While I do not wish to detract from the glory of the multimillionaire philanthropists, the fact is that the only way they can get any real satisfaction out of their surplus wealth is by devoting it to beneficence. It is to their credit that they have generally shown in the disposition of their fortunes for the public weal the ability that they displayed in acquiring them. They have certainly blazed the way to a prosperity that has resulted in the well-being of the people at large. On the coast north of Cape Hatteras, the old time wreekers, to secure plunder, used to display false lights which caused merchant ships to run on the reefs to death and destruction. Lenin has displayed in industry the false lights of communism that have led to industrial chaos and the starvation of millions.

Before the formation of "Industrials," I could have named many firms that flourished by being expert in the manufacture of deceptive goods, in many cases counterfeit goods; but such concerns now find it almost impossible to compete with standardized productions whose trademark brands are internationally advertised and known to be reliable. I know of no industrial consolidation today that does not realize the importance of improving and standardizing its products.

The amount received by promoters—generally in junior securities—has been greatly overestimated: except in cases where the principal objective has been a large flotation of speculative securities, the promoter's share has been but a small percentage of the increased profits realized through consolidation.

---

I know of no industrial consolidation today
that does not realize the importance of
improving and standardizing its products.

---

The boards of directors of industrial consolidations have had the opportunity to observe so many object lessons of success and failure that most of them, I am glad to record, have arrived at the age of wisdom; they have, to a large extent, availed themselves of the advantages of consolidation stated above; so that the industrials of the present day are generally administered with good judgment.

Even in the past when business management had not the experience that it has today, the common shares sometimes called capitalized hopes—have been converted into thousands of millions of dollars in dividends and increased tangible assets.

Industrial consolidation has proved itself, with the result that the number of consolidations in America and the industrial countries of Europe is steadily increasing.

1923

# ALEXANDER GRAHAM BELL
## 1847–1922

From Alexander Graham Bell's invention of the telephone sprang the greatest monopoly ever, AT&T. The need to communicate was in his genes; his father was a world-renowned voice researcher and inventor of the Visible Speech System, a method for educating the deaf. Bell was born in Scotland, but his family decided to immigrate to Canada in 1870 after two of his siblings died from tuberculosis. Although Aleck, as Alexander was known, wanted to be a musician, he followed in his father's footsteps and started teaching his father's system to deaf students in New England, later opening a training school in Boston in 1872 and teaching speech at Boston University from 1873 to 1877.

In the early 1870s he also started to experiment with transmitting sound via electricity, and soon he was in a neck and neck race to be the first to patent the telephone. At the time, Bell wrote, "He [competitor Elisha Gray] has the advantage over me in being a practical electrician—but I have reason to believe that I am better acquainted with the phenomena of sound than he is—so that I have an advantage there." At his home, Bell strung wire out one window and in another and would spend nights talking to himself via his telephone to perfect it. He first demonstrated his invention in 1876 and founded Bell Telephone in 1877, with financial backing from his father-in-law, who was pivotal in the management of the company. Bell's wife, in fact, was the largest stockholder.

Inventing the telephone and establishing a profitable business were two very different accomplishments—the invention would prove the easier. Bell took no role in the management of the company, preferring to work on new projects such as a respirator, prompted by the death of a prematurely born son who could not breath properly. However, as one of the founders of what became AT&T, Bell was quite interested in monopolies and their effects, and he discusses them in *When Does Profit Become Usury?*—a hot topic in the early 1900s. Bigger organizations certainly provided for greater efficiencies, but they also scared the public. The question he must answer: Should monopolies be stamped out as we would the plague?

# When Does Profit Become Usury?
## Alexander Graham Bell

We have arrived at a critical point in our history. Competition as an element in business is going out, and monopolies, which are opposed to competition, are coming in.

Individual producers no longer count. The nineteenth century saw them largely replaced by associations of individuals known as "corporations" or "companies," which did business upon such a scale that individual producers were unable to compete. In process of time, the large fish ate the smaller; until now, in the twentieth century, we find the companies themselves being gobbled up by still larger aggregations of capital and labor in the form of "trusts," or "combines," which threaten to monopolize the sources of our wealth, and to extinguish competition altogether.

Competition tends to bring down prices to the lowest point at which producers are willing to sell. Monopoly tends to raise them to the highest point at which people are able to buy. The few are obtaining a power of extortion over the many, and the possibilities of evil are very great. What to do with the trusts has become the great problem of the age.

While local companies are subject to state governments, the trusts extend their field of operations beyond their jurisdiction, and only the National Government can reach them.

Congress, however, has jurisdiction only over inter-state commerce, and trade and commerce with foreign countries, so that it requires the cooperation of the National and state governments fully to cope with the situation.

The attitude of Congress, as shown by the Anti-Trust Act of July 2, 1890, and the Wilson Tariff Act of August 27, 1894, seems to be in harmony with the attitude of the state legislatures in dealing with combines that are within their jurisdiction—they seek to get rid of monopolies altogether by declaring illegal all combinations that tend to destroy competition; and the courts have sustained them in this attitude.

Now the thought occurs in this connection: Have these combinations no good points about them that should give us pause? Are they so wholly bad that capital punishment is necessary, and reformation quite out of the question? Are we wise in seeking to stamp them out as we would the plague? Do they constitute a diseased product of our time, or are they the result of a natural and healthy growth?

The history of the past is strongly suggestive of a natural process of evolution, and man cannot combat a law of nature. The whole history of the nineteenth century reveals a gradual and steady change in our methods of conducting business, whereby large aggregates of capital and an organized army of individuals under a single control take the place of multitudes of small capitalists at war with one another, each competing with the others in his own interests, and in opposition to the interests of the others, and all at war with the public to make the most out of the people in their own selfish interests.

Now it is noteworthy that, so far as the producers are concerned, combination means peace; competition, warfare. Competition means a mob, without organization, and weak for effective work; combination, an organized force, powerful and efficient. It is only necessary that this force should be controlled in the interests of the people as a whole in order to be beneficial in every way.

May it not be possible that we are making a great mistake in deciding that all combinations in restraint of competition are necessarily injurious and should be declared illegal? Is not the remedy control rather than destruction?

Let us look at the matter from a theoretical point of view, by considering a hypothetical case:

Certain companies, in competition with one another, sell their products to the public at a certain price, and make a certain profit.

After a while they find that, by combining themselves into one company, or "trust," the expenses of production and distribution would be so much reduced that it would be possible for them to sell their products to the public at less price than before, and yet derive a greater profit themselves.

Let them do so, and combine. Now who is injured by this destruction of competition? Not the public, who receive the goods at less price than formerly. Not the companies, who make a greater profit. And yet this is a combination in restraint of competition. By this very restraint of competition, both parties are benefited. Why, then, should such a combination be made unlawful? A combination that reduces the cost of production and distribution is certainly beneficial in its essence. It constitutes a labor-saving device.

---

A limit should be set to the amount of profit that can be made. Everything beyond an equitable return upon the capital invested should be treated as usury, and be forbidden by law.

---

Such a combination can hardly be considered as hurtful to the public even though it does not lower prices, but simply leaves them as before, for the increased profits that arise to the combines represent a natural reward for the introduction of improved machinery of production and distribution.

It is not, then, until the prices are raised above the level produced by competition that injury to the public begins to be the result. The evil arises when the public is forced to pay higher prices, in spite of the fact that the cost of production and distribution has been reduced.

The combination in itself is a good thing, even though it tends to destroy competition and to create a monopoly, because it has reduced the cost of production and distribution. It only becomes hurtful when it becomes a monopoly and raises the price to the public. It is potentially hurtful if it has the power to raise prices, even though it does not actually do so.

The hurtful thing is not the combination itself, but its abuse of power to control the price paid by the public. The remedy, then, should be sought, not in the destruction of the combination, by declaring it unlawful, but in limiting the power of the combination to control prices.

There should be some recognized relation between the cost of production and the amount of profit. A limit should be set to the amount of profit that can be made. Everything beyond an equitable return upon the capital invested should be treated as usury, and be forbidden by law.

The exactions of money-lenders having been limited by law, why not the usury of the trusts and combines?

---

**The hurtful thing is not the combination itself, but its abuse of power to control the price paid by the public.**

---

Of course, difficult questions immediately arise: When does profit become usury? Where is the boundary line between legitimate profit and usury? If we make it too high, the public will suffer. If we make it too low, capital will be driven out of business. It is just here, however, that the efforts of Congress and the state legislatures can be most hopefully applied. That usury in business does exist is undoubted; and it is just this feature connected with business combinations that makes them harmful to the public. The remedy at present adopted is to kill the usurer. Would it not be better to limit his exaction?

In the brief for the United States prepared by Mr. J. C. McReynolds and Mr. Edwin P. Grosvenor, special assistants to the Attorney-General, in the case of the United States against the American Tobacco Company, this sentence occurred: "Congress was striking at an existing evil, the destruction of competition by powerful organizations, and the resulting oppression of the public."

Now, "the destruction of competition by powerful organizations" seems to be inevitable. It is probably the most characteristic feature of the age in which we live; and it seems to represent an advanced position in our civilization reached by a gradual process of evolution with which man cannot cope. From the earliest dawn of the nineteenth century up to the present time, there has been a continual advance toward this position in spite of strenuous opposition at every stage. However we may deplore the result, in our ignorance of the objects of nature in bringing it about, why should it not be wise in us to accept the situation, rather than wage a hopeless battle against nature itself? We may yet find ourselves in the position of the buffalo that tried to stop the advance of a moving railroad train by butting against it with his horns. Railroading advanced over the prairies, and where are the buffalo to-day? We cannot prevent the destruction of competition by powerful organizations.

"The resulting oppression of the public," however, is another matter, and we may hopefully seek to remedy it by legislative enactment. Congress must control these powerful organizations so as to limit their extortions; or else the Government will be obliged to take possession of them and run them in the interests of the public. There appears to be no half way. It is impracticable to kill them; and, even were it permitted, it would not be to the interests of the community to do so at the expense of returning to the old wasteful system of competitive warfare.

To the producers, the combines have brought peace instead of war, by establishing among them a union of interests instead of opposition to one another. In the present stage of the evolution, however, the war continues to be waged by the producers in more efficient form on account of their organization against the consumers, who constitute the bulk of the population of the United States.

A glance backward over the history of the struggle will assure us that these great and powerful organizations have come to stay. Why, then, should not Congress and the state legislatures recognize the situation, arbitrate between the opposing forces, and disarm the aggressors by regulating and controlling the exactions of the trusts, and thus bring peace by a peaceful method? This surely would be a much safer policy than to attempt to pacify the country by the wholesale execution of the disturbers of the public peace.

---

Congress must control these powerful organizations so as to limit their extortions; or else the Government will be obliged to take possession of them and run them in the interests of the public.

---

In conclusion, the following appear to be the only practicable methods of dealing with trusts:

(1) Control, by suitable legislation, the amount of profit they can legally receive from the public; or

(2) Buy them out, and have the Government run their business in the interests of the people so that the profits shall be reduced to the minimum consistent with running expenses. This has been the plan adopted with the Post Office business, and it means socialism to a greater or less extent.

The former plan is in every way preferable; but, if we long neglect the opportunity we now have of establishing legislative control over their exactions, the continued advance in power and influence possessed by these great corporations may ultimately compel the people, in self-defense, to adopt the alternative plan.

The immediate problem is the problem of control. Destruction is out of the question; and Government ownership is a very doubtful remedy, to which there are many objections.

1909

Alfred Sloan revolutionized management with his ingenious plan of "decentralization with coordinated control," a philosophy he imposed upon General Motors when he took the helm in 1923. The company had been founded in 1908 by William C. Durant, who over the next few years focused on building a vertical organization that included all facets of automobile manufacturing. In 1916 Durant bought the Hyatt Roller Bearing Company for $13.5 million, and with the company came Sloan, who had graduated from MIT in 1895 with a degree in electrical engineering and became a partner in Hyatt with a $5,000 investment. Sloan soon discovered that Durant could create but he could not administer, and by 1920 the company was on the verge of financial collapse, with Sloan about to resign.

Instead, the du Pont family, who had become major shareholders, forced Durant out, and three years later Sloan was made president. His organizational blueprint, he said, was modeled partly after the Constitution of the United States. The corporate divisions (the states) were allowed to operate independently; however, they had to abide by the policies ordained by committees (the laws passed by Congress), and Sloan (the executive branch) provided leadership for the policy making. The actual policy committees were made up of the men on the frontlines, for as Sloan explained, "Policies should be performed by the men who make them. . . . A group of men who have invented a policy together understand the policy."

After 30 years at the head of GM, Sloan wrote *My Years with General Motors,* which was an instant best-seller and became a manifesto for management practices. In it he describes how most of his time was spent on organization and governing groups. "This was required," he wrote, "because of the paramount importance, in an organization like General Motors, of providing the right framework for decisions." As early as 1926 Sloan had synthesized his ideas on management in the following essay, *Modern Ideals for Big Business.* He called for a more open management style, for no longer could businesses afford to operate by "the public be damned" method of yesterday's tycoons.

# Modern Ideals of Big Business
## *Alfred P. Sloan, Jr.*

T he enormous scale upon which business is now done has not only changed the methods of industrial management, but it has also brought about an entirely new conception of the relation of business to the public. There was a time when corporations of large size were so new that it was natural for the men who created them to feel that they owned them in the old sense of private ownership of a purely personal business. They resented the idea that the public should be told anything about their internal condition, just as much as they would have resented the idea that the public should be told anything about their intimate family life. "The public be damned" was a natural enough reaction of these pioneers in corporation management.

Of course, this attitude has altogether changed. There may be, here and there, a corporation executive who still feels resentful of public curiosity about his company's affairs; but I cannot recall such a one among my acquaintance. The men I know belong to a generation deeply conscious of the public interest that is implicit in the operations of a great corporation. An industry that numbers its stockholders by the thousands among the mass of the citizenry of the country cannot ignore the right of these thousands, or of the millions from whom they are drawn, to know all that there is to know about the business in which they have invested their money.

---

There was a time when corporations of large size were so new that it was natural for the men who created them to feel that they owned them.

---

Investment by the public in the securities of a great corporation is an act of faith as well as an act of judgment. That faith must be justified, not only by the good faith of the management, but also by the management's making accessible to the public all the facts that are necessary for the formation of that judgment. And as the facts about the business change, the public must be informed of the changes, for these alter the conditions of their investment, and they are entitled to know about them.

For this reason, as President of General Motors Corporation, I frequently send out a general letter to all our stockholders, informing them of the operations of the company. These letters are also given to the press, so that they may be accessible to the general public. For example, in one of these letters, I explained briefly, but with exact figures, the plants and products of General Motors. I had discovered that many of our stockholders had only the vaguest ideas about the companies comprised in the parent organization. I therefore told them exactly what these companies are, where their plants are located, what each one manufactures, how much of their stock or of their assets is owned by General Motors, and gave a chart showing the relationship of each to the scheme of rounded production to which all are essential. In another letter, I gave facts and figures about General Motors—its corporate structure, its economic function, its assets, its liabilities, its sales records, its managerial structure, its records of earnings, its special methods of stimulating operating efficiency. Other letters have explained why we encourage legitimate installment purchases of cars and how we manage this type of business, the origin and development and management of our Canadian organization, why we bought and how we use what we call the "proving grounds" where new models are tested and new ideas developed. One letter discussed in great detail the financial control policies of the corporation, and explained our system of forecasting future business prospects. Some of these letters are simply called "current developments."

---

Investment by the public in the securities of a great corporation is an act of faith as well as an act of judgment.

---

The favorable reaction of the stockholders to this policy of personal communication with them is evidenced by the numerous letters I receive from them expressing appreciation of it. These letters sometimes come from people who own only two or three shares of stock, and they are men and women of every occupation, from steel worker to banker. Some write to show their gratification on receipt of a dividend check, some ask for further information on some point covered in one of my letters, while others simply express their cordial approval of the policy itself. I recall especially a letter from a steel worker in Pittsburgh, who told how he had invested his savings in one share of stock, and, as his dividends and later savings had accumulated, he had bought additional shares. It was especially pleasant to feel that words of mine had had some influence in the evolution of this wage-earner into a modest capitalist. His letter, like all that I receive from stockholders, I answered personally, for there is no stronger asset of a corporation than the good-will made possible by such direct contacts as these.

I have enlarged on this habit of constantly telling our stockholders and the public about things they have a right to know, because it goes to the heart of the modern ideal of business. That ideal demands frankness as one of the first characteristics of management. And of course that implies things even more important. It requires that the corporation shall be of such a character that frankness cannot injure it—that it must be in a legitimate business, that it shall manage that business honorably in every detail, that its structure and purposes and methods shall be so economically sound that general knowledge of them shall have no power to alter their character or to injure their operation. It implies that their human relations, with their employees, shall be above criticism. The great modern corporations live, as it were, in glass houses, open to the public gaze, and of course no one who lives and works in such a situation can afford to be other than honorable, humane, and strictly obedient to economic law.

## "THOSE WHO MAKE NO MISTAKES ARE THOSE WHO MAKE NOTHING"

There is, of course, no way to be sure that honest mistakes will not be made. Life itself is a process of trial and error, and those people who make no mistakes are those who make nothing. But a mistake is very different from an intentional wrong.

It is obvious, too, that there are limits to what the public should be told—even to what the stockholder should be told. If the management is dealing with a serious problem of personnel, for example, such as the question of which of two men should be chosen for a desirable vacancy, no conceivable good could be attained by discussing the matter in public, and serious harm might be done. In general, the current details of management are not matters that are of legitimate public interest. Even general policies sometimes depend for their success upon the assurance that they shall not be prematurely made public, and in such cases clearly the stock-holder's own interest is best protected by the management refraining from any announcement. But all fundamental facts ought always to be available—and not merely available, but voluntarily passed on to the public.

---

### The great modern corporations live . . . in glass houses, open to the public gaze.

---

It seems to me that large corporations have an especial duty to the public in the scrupulous observance of economic law. A one-man business can violate fundamental economics without doing general harm. The owner himself will eventually be ruined, and his creditors will suffer. But when the large corporation engages in an uneconomic policy, its power for evil is enormous. In the first place, its prestige makes its acts a public example, that may lead hundreds into error and disaster. And if it follows such a policy to its own destruction, thousands suffer in its fall. These facts place upon corporate management a heavy responsibility to avoid everything that in any degree trespasses upon the known principles of economics. And it further places upon corporate management the duty of using its greater resources of men and means to make investigations of economic phenomena that will enlarge our knowledge of these economic principles.

There are two fields in which the modern corporation realizes it has no business to be active. One is religion. The other is politics. By politics, I mean the partisan struggle for preferment and the general run of legislation. If our fundamental economic structure were threatened by political action—if, for example, an attack were made on the gold standard—I should say that then it would not only be proper for corporations to take a stand, but that it would be their duty, as being specially qualified to speak and as having a special responsibility to guard. But no corporation has a right to concern itself with the political faith of its employees, or with the ordinary political activities of the community.

## CAN A CORPORATION HAVE TOO MANY STOCKHOLDERS?

There is one tendency in the development of modern corporations that should receive serious public consideration. This is the tendency to diffuse stock ownership to a point where there ceases to be a responsible and consistent control of ownership and management. Just how far this process can go with safety to the public, on the one hand, and with efficiency of management, on the other, is worth thoughtful study. Considerable diffusion is inevitable, because, as corporations grow in size, they must more and more appeal to the general public for the enormous sums necessary to finance the needed additions to capital investment in new plant and new equipment. But it seems to me that there is a point beyond which diffusion of stock ownership must enfeeble the corporation by depriving it of virile interest in management upon the part of some one man or group of men to whom its success is a matter of personal and vital interest. And conversely, at that same point, the public interest becomes involved when the public can no longer locate some tangible personality within the ownership which it may hold responsible for the corporation's conduct.

My personal ideal in this matter is represented by the situation in General Motors. It might seem natural that I should say this because I happen at the moment to be president of that particular corporation, but the fact is that I am with that corporation because I like its lay-out, and not that I like it just because I am with it. In General Motors, there is a very wide diffusion of stock ownership, as the corporation has 40 percent of its stock in the hands of seventy thousand stockholders. On the other hand, the remaining 60 percent is in the

316

hands of a small group of men, of identical business interests. They definitely control the corporation. They regard the seventy thousand small stockholders as full partners in the enterprise, entitled to full knowledge of its condition and operations — partners just as truly as if each one were personally known to them and as if each had been invited to share in its capital by personal solicitation. But this small, controlling group has an especial public responsibility, by virtue of that control; and an especial personal interest in the corporation's success, by virtue of their larger personal investment. If it is badly managed, they must take the public blame for it. If it does wrong, they are personally the wrongdoers. From the point of view of the public, this is the ideal situation. It is the strongest possible safeguard of the public interest.

## How Personal Initiative Is Stimulated

On the other hand, this situation profoundly influences the effectiveness of the corporation's management as a sheer business enterprise. This small group has risked in it a considerable share of their private fortunes. It must succeed, or they will lose their money. And they have the controlling power to select and direct its management. Obviously, they will lose no opportunity to see that the management is sound, industrious, and progressive. The business will receive all that a personal business would receive in the way of initiative, encouragement, caution, provision for future needs — all that makes for growth and success. By this arrangement, all the virtues of private enterprise are carried over into the large corporation, without loss of the special advantages of the corporate form and of its possibilities for wider development.

In the actual management of the business itself, this effective control expresses itself in the form of an executive committee, which is the heart of the management. In it, all questions of corporate policy, and all major problems of management, are discussed and decided. In these discussions, every man is expected to take the fullest share. After they are finished and a vote taken, the decisions then become law to all, and are loyally executed with unanimous support.

But at this point, centralized authority ceases. Our ideal is centralization of policy and decentralization of management. The president of each of our constituent companies (the man who would be called the general manager of a factory branch in most corporations) is allowed an altogether free hand in his company. He is expected to carry out the general policies of the executive committee, but the methods by which he does this are as personal to himself and as free from our interference as if he were the head of an independent corporation. Only by this freedom can we hope that men of the caliber required will be retained. Men capable of getting the results we want will not work under orders. They have too much independence, too much imagination. Their methods of getting things done are too personal to themselves to be brought under rules and regulations. We would not think of reversing a decision of theirs—except in a contingency so unusual that an occasion to do so has never once arisen in all the years of our operation. Of course, we occasionally suggest things, but we do not go further than that.

---

Our ideal is centralization of policy and decentralization of management.

---

By this plan, we get all the advantages of personal, independent management—its initiative, its ability quickly to adapt its methods to changing conditions, its close personal contact with its working force. We avoid some of the dangers that confront corporations as they grow beyond certain limits—such dangers as arise when the size becomes so great that no one man can possibly be wise enough, or wide-visioned enough, or versatile enough, or have time enough really to be effective as its chief executive. Another danger we avoid is the tendency of corporations to become impersonal bureaucracies, in which the management degenerates almost into an automaton, mechanically performing duties that have lost their imagination and vitality and have become mere routine.

---

Men capable of getting the results we want will not work under orders. They have too much independence, too much imagination.

---

Necessarily, to make our theory work, our executives must have a definite financial interest in the success of the business as a whole. The equivalent of the rewards of private enterprise must be offered to men of this type; and it must be offered in the contingent form that would obtain if they were actually in private business, for it is exactly the sporting element of uncertainty as to the size of the reward that is a chief fascination of private enterprise. By apportioning a certain small percentage of the profits of the parent corporation to a special fund, with corresponding apportionments of blocks of its common stock to the same fund, General Motors has provided a special body of assets which will be distributed in about four years, or at the end of the seventh year of its existence, and which will make each one of the eighty executives in it independently wealthy, if the combined efforts of all continue to make the corporation as successful as it has been thus far.

Broadly speaking, I should say that the big corporation has justified itself, not only as an economic and efficient instrument for the production of goods, but also as a social force. It has corrected the evils that seemed years ago to be inherent in it; and, as today conducted, it is a good employer, a good neighbor, and a good citizen.

1926

# WALTER B. WRISTON
## 1919–

Walter Wriston, who commanded Citibank for 17 years, has been called the third most important banker of the century, after J. P. Morgan and A. P. Giannini. From his parents, he inherited the brainpower for the job; his father was first a history professor and later the president of Brown University, and his mother was a graduate of Vassar. During a family vacation to Europe in 1939, Wriston witnessed the blind madness of the Nazi Youth marching and singing. "I saw what happens with total regulation of people's lives, which starts with economic regulation and leaps over into politics and abolition of free speech," he recalled. He, of course, would always fight regulation.

Wriston earned a history and foreign affairs degree from Connecticut Wesleyan in 1941 and a masters in diplomacy in 1942, after which he joined the State Department. The lessons learned in diplomacy would pay off later as Wriston built a global powerhouse. The next year he was drafted and eventually found himself in the Philippines operating an encoding device for the Signals Corps, another experience that molded his future, as he became obsessed with technology. After the war, he joined National City Bank of New York (Citibank). "I didn't have any set of goals and perspectives," he later recalled. "I came in looking for a job so I could eat."

As Wriston moved up the ladder, he realized that "you can't do good business with bad people and you can't get hurt with good people." So when he became president and CEO in 1967 and then chairman in 1970, he emphasized recruiting the brightest available minds. He also fought laws that prevented banks from operating across state lines, called for deregulation, and pioneered lending in Third World countries. For him, the multinational companies that dominated the post–World War II landscape involved a natural evolution of the business organization, and he provides a poignant history of world trade in the following selection. One insight: Merely building a factory on foreign soil does little to "arouse the passions of the populace," unless the company explains how jobs provide upward mobility on merit.

# The Multinational Company: New Weight in an Old Balance
## *Walter B. Wriston*

Someone once remarked that at the very beginning of the world, when Adam and Eve were driven from the Garden of Eden and told that henceforth they must earn their bread by the sweat of their brows, Adam consoled Eve by saying: "We live in an age of transition." For them change was both rapid and drastic. Moreover, the physical change was accompanied by an equally great alteration in their value systems; they had learned to distinguish good from evil.

All history has been dominated by change — or the lack of it. Today, as at the beginning, change is swift and startling in the scientific and technological world. But it is the changes in our value systems which cause us the most agony. Despite protestations that innovation is welcome, mankind in general and sovereign authority and bureaucracies in particular resist it to the bitter end. Nothing upsets us more than to be told, as Abraham Lincoln put it, "that our purposes differ from those of the Almighty." Everywhere change is popular in concept but uncomfortable in practice. The canny bureaucrat never opposes the idea of change; instead he throws up a smokescreen of plausible reasons to abort change "now." Each new invention and innovation in thought is resisted in order to protect whatever status quo is regarded as normal in its specific environment.

Today, as always, we are in an age of transition, and, as always, various segments of society are moving at different speeds. For example, the value systems of the young generally change faster than those of the aged. The scientist who split the atom finds that his disciplines have moved at a faster gait than have those in international law. The economies of the developed countries surely move at a different pace from those of developing lands.

---

All history has been dominated by change—or the lack of it. Today, as at the beginning, change is swift and startling in the scientific and technological world.

---

A few years ago, Thomas Hughes wrote, at least half seriously: "One can say that the twentieth century is currently made up of fourteenth-century farmers, fifteenth-century theologians, sixteenth-century politicians, seventeenth-century economists, eighteenth-century bureaucrats, nineteenth-century generals, and twenty-first-century scientists." It is not a bad analysis save for the American farmer, who belongs to the twentieth century.

The discontinuities in world society are partly responsible for the current concern about world corporations. Those multinational companies have been blamed for everything from interfering in the political affairs of host countries to causing the revaluation of currencies by speculating on the international markets. One enterprising publisher, presumably in an effort to sell more books, titled a scholarly work on the multinational company *Sovereignty at Bay*. Recently Chile persuaded the United Nations to conduct an inquiry into the affairs of world corporations. For whatever reasons or whatever motives, all would agree that the world corporation is now being examined intensively and extensively, but not always competently or without bias.

In order to draw any useful conclusions about the place of the world corporation, it is necessary to set today's multinational enterprise in historical perspective. It may then be possible to advance some ideas as to why our world corporations are so profoundly upsetting to so many people in and out of governments around the world.

Despite the enormous advances in the sciences of communication and the remarkable technology for instant transfer of visual images via satellite, we are still surprised and amazed when other people in different parts of the world espouse value systems radically at variance with our own. For example, it surprises many Americans to find that some of the ideas of Colbert, Finance Minister of Louis XIV, still appear to dominate a section of European thinking about trade and investment. The highly restrictive purchasing regulations which obtain in many European countries stem from Colbert's dictum, "All purchases must be made in France rather than in foreign countries, even if the goods should be a little poorer and a little more expensive, because if the money does not go out of the realm, the advantage to the state is double. . . ." In my own country, some of our Buy American laws were passed, unwittingly, under the influence of Colbert's dead hand.

To a European or to a Japanese, it is elemental that foreign trade is a country's lifeblood; it generates the revenue that sustains their governments. It appears obvious to them that foreign trade should inevitably be part of their foreign policy. It comes as a shock to Americans, however, to discover foreign ambassadors in the United States helping to sell airplane engines, machine tools, or whatever their nationals need help in selling. At the same time, it is equally incomprehensible to Europeans, to Japanese, to Latin Americans and Africans that the United States government takes a basically adversary position toward business. Activities of American companies in foreign lands have long been regarded with great suspicion here at home. To Americans, foreign trade has, until recently, been a peripheral activity engaged in only in the event that the domestic market did not absorb our entire production. All these attitudes are deeply rooted in history and so will change slowly. The consequence is the inherent unpopularity of the world corporation.

There are other roots of this hostility, however, which date back to Medieval times. The first merchants, traders, and money lenders were motivated largely by profit considerations. Feudal barons, on the other hand, looked to military power for survival and expansion. As competition between feudal rulers increased, the merchants and traders began to associate themselves with the sovereign authorities in order to gain commercial advantage. In return for commercial favors, they financed the wars of competing sovereigns. Merchants bankrolled the Crusades; in return they got monopoly powers in trade in large areas of the known world. The fusion of trade and the royal sovereign in the fifteenth to the seventeenth centuries eventually became known as mercantilism, and all external business was conducted by the chosen instruments of the state. It is not surprising, therefore, if today the developing countries believe that the navy always follows the traders, if indeed it does not precede them. In the mercantilist world, total commerce and industry was viewed as a zero-sum game; profit for one side inevitably meant equal loss for the other. The trick was to maximize gains at the expense of others. The reality that buyer and seller could both profit from the same transaction defied mercantilist logic, and its truth was perceived over many years with painful slowness.

In the mercantilist world, nations vied for overseas territories in order to control their markets. Many countries set up monopolistic trading corporations to manage trade and supply all commodities to the colonists, whether natives or settlers. There were the Dutch East India Company, the English East India Company, the French East India Company, the Hudson Bay Company, and the Virginia Company.

Since these companies made a profit, mercantilist dogma made it clear that exploitation of the colonists must be involved. Therefore, this practice of picking a commercial enterprise as a chosen instrument served to intensify the hostility against both the monopolistic companies and against the metropolitan country which chartered it. In the American case, enmity generated by this commercial device was one of the precipitating causes of the Revolution. An excerpt from a Boston newspaper printed in 1765 summed up the colonial sentiment: "A colonist cannot make a button, a horseshoe, nor a hobnail but some sooty ironmonger or respectable buttonmaker of England shall bawl and squall that his honor's worship is most egregiously maltreated, injured, cheated, and robbed by the rascally Americans."

On the other side of the world, trade as exploitation also left its imprint. The Meiji restoration, dating from 1868, marked the beginning of the modern Japanese state. But even that enlightened restoration was based broadly on the concept that Japan could not withstand hated foreign encroachments unless its society was totally reorganized as an industrial power with great military strength. Japanese hatred of foreigners was not new; it dated back three centuries to the edict of 1636 which closed Japan to all foreigners, particularly Christians. The edict forbade Japanese ships from sailing to foreign countries, it prohibited Japanese from going abroad on penalty of death, and prescribed death to any Japanese who had lived abroad and tried to return to his homeland. While much of this changed following the restoration, the concept of strong, centralized power endured.

While many peoples of the world were building centralized government structures, America's economic and political impulses developed along contrary lines. Colonial experience led Americans to be opposed to centralization of economic power in chartered companies and to centralization of political power. The separation of powers, written into our constitution as a guarantee of political freedom, also affected economic thought. The proof of this hostility to the centralization of power is evident from the fact that our basic antitrust law bears the name of a senator whose credentials as a conservative were impeccable.

Moreover, the existence of the frontier tended for many years to dominate our thinking. It was not a totally alien frontier such as existed in the older settled parts of the world, but was merely the edge of untapped resources and an enormous land mass. Our huge continent furnished an outlet for all our goods and services. The development of those seemingly illimitable resources demanded both practical and technical innovation. Because of this heritage, many Americans even today fail to understand that the American market is only a subsection of the world market and that our value system is not shared by many others. Thus, the Japanese and the Europeans are hard put to comprehend what often seems the strange behavior of my fellow countrymen. The arrogance of the American government's desire to export its complicated antitrust concepts around the world is properly viewed by our friends abroad with both amazement and hostility. Governments in Japan and in Europe regard their business establishments as great national assets which furnish the revenue to support the increasing standards of living of their people and the world's people as well. It is difficult for them to understand, let alone credit, the basically adversary position taken by the American government toward United States business.

In this country, we are acutely conscious of the mercantilist tradition in Europe and the enormous concentration of power in the zaibatsu complexes of Japan. Many former colonial countries see the chartered monopolies of the imperial nations as the forerunners of today's world corporations. To them, our global corporations seem to be merely thinly disguised government-directed chosen instruments dedicated to the pursuit of governmental foreign policy under the guise of a commercial establishment. Bitter experience with government-chartered monopolies throughout history did little to create a welcome environment in many of the developing countries for the new worldwide economic structures which began to grow during the great postwar international expansion. Even today, the Sunday supplements love to hint darkly that the modern world corporation is really an instrument of today's nation state. The suspicion of a modern mercantilism hangs in the air. The days of gunboat diplomacy are indeed gone. We have now come full circle in the Western world to what appears to many as the successor of the chosen instrument of imperialism. Thus, the world corporation is now under attack, not only by the host governments but, in many cases, by its own government wherever the head office is located.

---

The arrogance of the American government's desire to export its complicated antitrust concepts around the world is properly viewed by our friends abroad with both amazement and hostility.

---

Part of this attack stems from the clash of historic value systems. As new philosophers, thinkers, and traders appeared on the world stage at the time of the industrial revolution, the idea began to dawn that man by his own efforts could improve his lot in the world. Economic growth and improvement and the betterment of social conditions seemed attainable dreams. The enunciation of the principles of free trade and the doctrines of comparative advantage by Smith, Ricardo, and others can be seen as a decisive break with the mercantilist tradition. What flowed from these new ideas was a concept of dynamic economic growth, as opposed to the old notion that profit to one was loss to the other—the zero-sum game. With this new concept came a recognition of the growing interdependence of economic units. The new emerging entrepreneurial class showed an aversion to war, and began to develop more of an adversary relationship with government. In short, the hostility was mutual. The momentum of this new trend continued despite efforts by some governments to control it.

It was against this background of changing values that the prototype world corporations first began to appear in the latter half of the nineteenth century. As far back as 1865 Frederick Bayer put a plant in Albany, New York; the next year Alfred Nobel established a factory in Hamburg; and the year after that, Singer operated his first overseas plant in Glasgow.

In widest historical perspective, commercial and political history exhibited an interplay between two basically competing value systems. The first stems from the Medieval Age and developed through the mercantilism of the sixteenth and seventeenth centuries into nineteenth-century imperialism, then twentieth-century totalitarianism. This was accompanied by the business tradition of the chosen instrument of governmental policy. The second value system arose from the earliest merchant and financier classes of the precapitalistic era and grew through the industrial revolution. The entrepreneurial tradition of the capitalist, independent of government, eventuated in an adversary relationship between business and the state.

Of course, as in all living things, neither system developed in a pure form. But through the period of the Second World War, there is no question that the mercantilist-imperialist tradition was dominant. The latter entrepreneurial tradition, when it gained preeminence from time to time and from place to place, was responsible for much of the progress in general welfare that has taken place among the world's peoples.

Viewed against this background, the modern world corporation is the extension to global proportions of the business tradition that grew out of capitalism and the industrial revolution. It is now learning how to operate in the global marketplace. The motivating factors which drive the world corporations today are basically the same as those which drove earlier entrepreneurs. Like their predecessors, the world corporations are a new expression of the entrepreneurial thrust that thrives on the free exchange of goods, services, factors of production, technology, capital, and ideas. The engine that drives the growth of nations gives humanity the wherewithal to deal with the wretchedness of the human condition. Most important of all, it can function amid diverse value systems, though, like all instruments of progress, it must move in a resisting medium. The principal reason the world corporations are so profoundly disturbing to so many governments and to the citizens of so many countries is that they represent today's visible agents of change.

Woodrow Wilson proclaimed a league of free nations, but the League of Nations did not survive. Wendell Willkie argued, correctly, that we have one world, a fact which the astronauts vividly described. Nevertheless, the politicians of the world will not act. The political problems of the United Nations are a stark manifestation. The disorder, almost paralysis, of the political aspect of the European Economic Community is further evidence. Despite all our advances, the world is still socially fragmented and the incompatibility of the world's value systems has always been and still remains a cause of potential conflict. History is replete with the tragedies wrought by efforts of one society to impose its concepts upon others.

Agents of change involve new ideas and values. They have never been welcome in any society. This is especially true when the carrier of new or strange values is, or is thought to be, alien to the society that is affected. Often the most effective way to resist change is by identifying the carrier of the new values as foreign. The word for "foreigner" from the Golden Age of Greece right up to the Middle Ages was "barbarian." Anyone who spoke a foreign language, dressed differently, adhered to different customs and mores was automatically considered a barbarian. "Stranger" and "foreigner" have thus from time immemorial been pejorative terms, and often synonymous with "enemy."

It should not surprise us, therefore, that the world corporation is sometimes unwelcome even though it is the carrier of technology which is the best hope of closing the gap between the very rich and the very poor. It is often unwelcome because it is perhaps the most effective instrument by which value systems are transferred from one part of the world to another.

---

### History is replete with the tragedies wrought by efforts of one society to impose its concepts upon others.

---

Mere physical change, manifested by a new factory, a new building, or a piece of complex machinery, generally does not arouse the passions of the populace. But when the change moves into the realm of ideas, a wholly different and more massive impact upon society follows. If, for example, a world corporation introduces the idea of upward mobility based only on merit and not on status, this may well offend an establishment fighting to preserve its privileges.

The nature of the value systems which are carried by world corporations as agents of change run the gamut from simple improvements, like better lighting in manufacturing plants, to renovating whole neighborhoods. For example, Park Avenue in New York City north of Grand Central Station used to be lined on both sides with old apartment houses. It was not until a multinational corporation, Unilever, saw the potential of putting a modern office building in this area that a whole new development was sparked in the city.

In the ancient struggle between those who believe in an open society where men, money, and ideas can move freely across national borders and those who would return to the jungle of economic nationalism, the men and women of the world corporations may furnish a new weight in the balance.

The world corporation specifically challenges the validity of the old tradition of the corporation as the chosen instrument of political domination. Because the world corporation confronts that ancient concept, we stand in danger on our planet of reverting to bankrupt atavistic ideas. The acceleration of change brought to a community by a world corporation unfortunately tends to make the old values look even better to many people.

Since time has proved that it is more effective to attack the carrier of an alien idea than the idea itself, the agents of change come under sustained intensified attack. The emergence in the United States of the Burke-Hartke Bill as the most retrogressive piece of legislation since the Smoot-Hawley tariff is only one national manifestation of this political device. Expropriation by developing countries is another.

At this moment, with currencies changing in value more often and in wider swings than we have recently been accustomed to, some governments resort to the ancient primitive device of finding a devil to divert attention from unpleasant facts. One such fact is that only governments create inflation because they alone can print money. If it is true that the "gnomes of Zurich" were invented by a British prime minister to divert attention from the real reason he had to devalue sterling, it is equally true that the world corporation now furnishes a convenient scapegoat to explain away the fact that we in America have printed too many dollars too fast and that the American government has balanced the federal budget only 7 times in the last 25 years and shows little inclination to improve on that record in the future.

The development of the world corporation into a truly multinational organization has produced a group of managers of many nationalities whose perception of the needs and wants of the human race knows no boundaries. They really believe in one world. They understand with great clarity that the payrolls and jobs furnished by the world corporation exceed profit by a factor of 20 to 1. They know that there can be no truly profitable markets where poverty is the rule of life. They are a group which recognizes no distinction because of color or sex, since they understand with the clarity born of experience that talent is the commodity in shortest supply in the world. They are managers who are against the partitioning of the world, not only on a political or theoretical basis, but on the pragmatic ground that the planet has become too small, that our fate has become too interwoven one with the other to engage in the old nationalistic games which have so long diluted the talent, misused the resources, and dissipated the energy of mankind.

The international managers in the great world corporations are exposed daily to a bewildering variety of value systems and a steadily rising tempo of nationalism in many of the nation-states of the world. Out of this experience is emerging the perception that the relationship of the world corporation to the various governments around the world is worthy of reexamination. It is clear to those managing American-based multinational enterprises that a pure adversary relationship between business and government has become an anachronism in the twentieth century. We have even permitted, without effective contradiction, the concept to be floated that a businessman who talks to his elected representative is somehow evil and that his voice should not be heard on matters of public policy.

---

All the great issues of our time, and most of the small ones, are settled in the untidy atmosphere of give and take, of compromise and of negotiation.

---

On the other side of the oceans, the perception is growing that a new age of mercantilism is not the answer to the problems of the twentieth century. Neither the pure adversary relationship nor the chosen instrument approach is responsive to today's world. Old ideas die hard; yesterday's liberal, who feels that central, national control is the answer to everything, is still in control of many intellectual circles. They all labor under an old illusion which John Gardner once put as follows: "Those who seek to bring societies down always dream that after the blood bath they will be calling the tune." Their outworn doctrine of a controlled economy is becoming more and more a manifestation of the persistence of illusion over reality.

All the great issues of our time, and most of the small ones, are settled in the untidy atmosphere of give and take, of compromise and of negotiation. This is fortunate because the distributive judgment of the people, in the marketplace as well as at the polls, has always been superior to the fiat of a dictator.

In this dialogue, the role of the world corporation as an agent of change may well be even more important than its demonstrated capacity to raise living standards. The pressure to develop the economy of the world into a real community must come, in part, from an increasing number of multinational firms which see the world as a whole. "Today's world economy . . . ," Peter Drucker has said, "owes almost nothing to political imagination. It is coming into being despite political fragmentation." The world corporation has become a new weight in an old balance. It must play a constructive role in moving the world toward the freer exchange of both ideas and the means of production so that the people of our planet may one day enjoy the fruits of a truly global society. This is a goal worthy of us all.

1973

Royal Little is considered the father of the conglomerate, and he pioneered the management philosophy with great success a decade before it became the rage in the 1960s. He learned how *not* to run a business from his stepfather. Little reflected, "Every printing business he started went broke, so we had to move to the next state to keep one jump ahead of the sheriff." Consequently, he attended 17 different schools before college. Fortunately, his prominent uncle, Arthur D. Little, who founded the consulting firm of the same name, invited him to return to Massachusetts to finish high school and then go to college. Little entered Harvard, class of 1919, but dropped out to join the army and fight in World War I.

After receiving six months of infantry training and 90 days of officer's training, he shipped out as a first lieutenant. Upon return, he finished his work at Harvard and, although his uncle wanted him to study chemical engineering at MIT, Little went into business for himself. Until the next world war, he struggled as an entrepreneur in the textile industry. But during World War II he organized Textron, made parachutes and jungle hammocks, and suddenly found himself with enough cash to buy out other textile companies. He expanded into other industries—such as making radar antennas and helicopters in the 1950s—to build his cutting-edge conglomerate.

As Little searched for companies and industries to balance his conglomerate, he came to hate waste. He said, "An inefficient operation really bugged me. . . . Flying over New York, I always look down and see miles of cemeteries and say, Why can't we cremate them and save the land?" So Little would institute strict financial controls and set parameters for operation. Although the conglomerate is closely related to the multinational as companies seek various means of diversification, Little and his kindred peers will always come under fire for trying to manage too many businesses. In response, Little wrote *Conglomerates Are Doing Better than You Think* in 1984. He declares that the conglomerate concept remains foolproof, and the key to running one effectively is to give division managers free reign.

# Conglomerates Are Doing Better than You Think
## *Royal Little*

As the founder of the first conglomerate, Textron, I am particularly interested in dispelling the myths that surround these companies. They are reputed to be less profitable than nondiversified companies and to trade at a discount on the stock market. The surprising truth is that, measured by return on shareholders' equity, the conglomerates are outperforming the rest of industry and their shares recently sold at higher price-earnings multiples.

To get at the facts about conglomerates, I have—with the help of *Fortune*'s staff—compared the performance of 39 conglomerates and 226 nondiversified industrial companies on the *Fortune* 500 list that had more than $1 billion in sales in 1983. We took the comparison back to 1978, the year the Securities and Exchange Commission required companies to begin reporting on the performance of their divisions. Before then it was hard to tell how many lines of business a company was in. How many businesses must a company be in to qualify as a conglomerate? There's no universal definition. For this article, I used *Fortune*'s rule: A conglomerate must have at least four unrelated businesses, none accounting for more than 50 percent of its sales.

The nondiversified companies did produce a higher median return on shareholders' equity in 1978 and 1979. But in 1980 the performance of the two types of companies tied, and during the next three years conglomerates came out ahead. Moreover, the conglomerates achieved a greater margin of superiority than the nondiversified companies did in their good years.

---

Conglomerates are outperforming the rest of industry and their shares recently sold at higher price-earnings multiples.

---

The recession year of 1982 shows emphatically how diversity protects a company from business cycles. The conglomerates scored a median return of 12.5 percent vs. 10.8 percent for the others. Only three conglomerates on our list lost money that year. And two, Colt Industries and Crane Co., hit the skids because they had got too involved in a single business—steel. Many nondiversified companies had terrible losses in 1982. Bethlehem Steel and International Harvester lost more than $1 billion each. Nine other companies among the *Fortune* 500 dropped between $50 million and $100 million, and 18 dropped between $100 million and $1 billion. Total deficits among nondiversified industrials amounted to $8.2 billion. Service companies were badly hurt too. Federally insured savings and loan institutions lost $4.3 billion and the airlines $916 million.

Judging by median price-earnings multiples, the so-called conglomerate discount no longer exists—and I'm not sure it ever was significant. Wall Street may have just found the companies hard to analyze. At the end of 1978, 1979, and 1982 the nondiversified companies sold at a slightly higher multiple than the conglomerates. The two kinds of companies were tied for 1981, and the conglomerates had a higher multiple for 1982 and 1983. Conglomerates are better understood now—though Wall Street still hasn't put enough well-trained specialists on the job of following them. They sold for a median price-earnings multiple of 12 in 1983, compared with 11 for the nondiversified companies, which reflects the growing appreciation of the advantage they have in bad years.

The advantage is becoming more significant because the return on net worth of the *Fortune* 500 has been falling for the past four years. Even in 1983, a good year, 60 of the 500 industrials lost money. With severe foreign competition, heavy industry faces a difficult future in this country. But if you are diversified it won't kill you if you have a business that's not doing too well, and you can even get right out of an industry that looks bad. Of the 60 *Fortune* 500 money losers last year, only four were conglomerates. As things get tougher the conglomerates will look better.

Safety in recession years is only one reason for diversifying. Others include getting out of a low-growth or low-return industry, or expanding without violating the antitrust laws. Most manufacturing companies are diversified to some extent, even if they can't be classified as conglomerates. Only a few top high-technology companies—IBM, Wang, Hewlett-Packard—have not diversified. They have all the growth they need and their return on capital is excellent.

The key to running a conglomerate well is to give the division managers the authority to run their own shows—but to make sure they are motivated. You must have people who are competent in their businesses, and you don't want to restrict them too much, except for approval from the board of directors for things like capital expenditures. In Textron we gave the division managers tremendous latitude, but we put some pressure on them every month by ranking them in order of performance. So a division manager was No. 1, No. 2, or No. 10. That was a clear incentive. We also gave them a carrot. The managers could earn cash bonuses of up to 100 percent of their salaries, depending on the return on capital they achieved.

My reason for diversifying was to break out of a low-return industry. I had been carrying around the idea of creating a diversified company for a long, long time. In 1923 I had set up my own company in South Boston, Special Yarns Corp., which eventually became Textron. A couple of years later Eliot Farley, who was my former boss and had helped me set up the company, said to me, "Royal, some day you ought to consider getting diversified and I've even got the name. You should call it Disassociated Industries." I though he was crazy. Thirty years later, when I was 57, I finally got smart.

---

If you are diversified it won't kill you if you have a business that's not doing too well, and you can even get right out of an industry that looks bad. Of the 60 *Fortune* 500 money losers last year, only four were conglomerates.

---

Textron remained very small until World War II. During the 1930s we just battled to keep from going broke all the time. After the war we found ourselves in a highly cyclical business with a low return on capital. Most Southern textile mills were controlled by families and were producing greige goods—unfinished, undyed fabric—in a highly competitive market. When profits were high, the last thing the owners wanted was to pay out a lot of dividends on which they would pay 70 percent taxes, which was the top bracket then. But any accumulation of surplus earnings deemed by the government "unreasonable" made the companies subject to a 38.5 percent penalty tax. So what did the mass producers do? They poured money into new mills that weren't needed and turned out cotton fabrics the market couldn't absorb except at much lower prices. That's how the tax laws helped make the textile industry unattractive to the investor. And it's typical of single-industry companies to overexpand in boom times.

Suspicion about conglomerates is nothing new—I ran into it when I started diversifying. We held a special stockholders' meeting on June 30, 1952, to change the articles of association so we could buy businesses outside textiles. The stockholders approved and the board was enthusiastic. Unfortunately no one else was. The entire financial community thought I was crazy.

I found that out when we tried to finance our first deal in 1953. We wanted to buy the Burkart Manufacturing Co. It had started out making horse blankets in St. Louis and graduated to auto seat stuffing. I needed several million dollars to buy the company. When I approached Roger Damon, president of the First National Bank of Boston, he said. "Roy, your idea of unrelated diversification just won't work. No one person can possibly run 30 different businesses. However, we are going to support you on this one acquisition, hoping you will abandon the whole concept in the future." We raised the working capital by borrowing on all of Textron's receivables, and our profit-sharing plan bought the fixed assets and leased them to us.

---

The key to running a conglomerate well is to give the division managers the authority to run their own shows—but to make sure they are motivated.

---

We acquired two other companies early in 1954, Dalmo Victor and MB Manufacturing, and then we ran out of money. At that point we could have remained a struggling textile company with three small nontextile divisions. But we were able to secure loans to buy a position in American Woolen Co., and after a year-long court battle—during which we proved that American Woolen's management had used 75,000 forged proxies—we won control. That gave us $75 million in working capital and a $30-million tax loss carry-forward. By the time I retired in 1961 we had bought around 100 companies, mostly small and often family-owned.

You had to find companies that had the potential, even if they were very small, to increase earnings either by growing or by reducing costs. When we bought a chainsaw company called Homelite Corp. in 1955, it was tiny compared with its competitor, McCulloch Corp. But we knew McCulloch had a high-cost operation beside the Los Angeles airport. So we moved Homelite out of unionized New England and built beautiful new plants down South, and we beat McCulloch with lower costs. Since I am interested in golf, we bought the E-Z-Go Golf Cart Co. in 1960 when it was doing about $1 million in sales. We expanded its low-cost operation in Augusta, Georgia, and we put Cushman Co. right out of the golf-cart business. Homelite and E-Z-Go's sales, along with those of two small metal fastener companies we acquired in the 1950s, Townsend Co. and Camcar Manufacturing Co., are now more than ten times what they were when we bought them.

To get into defense contracting, we acquired three divisions of the Bell Aircraft Corp. in 1960, when their sales were only $100 million a year. Now their sales are way over $1 billion a year. Of course, we had a lot of disasters too, but none big enough to hurt us seriously. I wrote a book about them, *How to Lose $100 Million and Other Valuable Advice*, adapted for *Fortune* in the August 27, 1979, issue. It was the first book by a businessman pointing out all his mistakes.

My goal at Textron was to increase the return on average common stockholders' equity from 5 percent or 6 percent annually, the usual rate when it was just a textile company, to 20 percent. The company met that goal in 1967. Unfortunately the return at Textron has slipped back down to 7.1 percent. It has bought no large manufacturing business in the last ten years. Sales grew only from $1.9 billion to $3 billion in the last ten years, while other conglomerates that used to be smaller than Textron have left it behind. United Technologies, which was about the same size as Textron ten years ago, is up to nearly $15 billion in sales.

While Textron diversified to escape the low returns, other companies did so to break out of businesses with limited growth potential. The Emerson Electric Co. is an outstanding example. When Wallace "Buck" Persons took over in 1956, Emerson was a little company making small electric motors. Persons made unusually astute acquisitions and monitored the divisions closely. He would have the top managers in to a meeting once a month and go over things in detail to put pressure on them. But his greatest feat was to establish good relations with the financial community. Unlike other executives, he spent a lot of time talking to people in the investment business and he got their confidence. As a result, Emerson's price-earnings multiple was around 30 for many years.

---

> You had to find companies that had the potential, even if they were very small, to increase earnings either by growing or by reducing costs.

---

The unusually high ratio permitted Persons to buy some fine companies using stock instead of cash, while most of Textron's acquisitions had to be made with cash because we had a lower multiple. He could afford to pay 15 times earnings for a company. Charles F. Knight took over from Persons in 1974 and has maintained a record I don't think any other conglomerate can match: Emerson has raised its total earnings and earnings per share every year since Persons took over 26 years ago.

Minnesota Mining & Manufacturing started out mining fluorspar and using it to make sandpaper. You couldn't get much less scope than that. I'm told there was a time in the taverns of northern Minnesota when you could buy two shares of 3M for a shot of whiskey. William McKnight, who led the company from 1929 to 1966, believed in research and development, and much of 3M's diversification was achieved by creating new products instead of acquiring other companies. The company has never paid a big dividend, but the dividends have increased for 26 consecutive years and have always kept ahead of inflation. For a decade sales have grown faster than the *Fortune* 500's sales. Even in 1982 3M's sales gained.

At Textron we took advantage of tax loss carry-forwards, but for some companies these were the main reason for conglomerating. The railroads built up tax losses they couldn't use unless they diversified. Ben Heineman, who became chief executive of the Chicago & North Western Railroad in 1956, diversified successfully during the 1970s after changing the name to Northwest Industries, and used up the railroad's huge carry-forwards. He got rid of the railroad by selling it to the employees. The Illinois Central diversified as IC Industries but hung on to the railroad, so its median return on net worth in the last six years was only 8.8 percent, compared with 19.2 percent for Northwest Industries. But if IC had remained just a railroad, it would still probably be making nothing but tax loss carry-forwards.

Some companies diversify to get into lucrative defense businesses—Textron, fortunitously, bought the Bell units just before the Army decided to equip all its divisions with helicopters—but other companies worry when too much of their profit comes from defense contracts, which can be unreliable. United Technologies got to be too dependent on Pentagon contracts. Harry Gray has done a terrific job of diversifying the company, especially with the purchase of Otis Elevator and Carrier Corp. in the late 1970s. He was the first businessman to make unfriendly tender offers relatively respectable among lenders. Many banks wouldn't touch an unfriendly offer before he started making them in 1976, but Gray was a pretty important customer.

The idea of diversifying is so appealing that some companies were created just to be conglomerates. Teledyne is one of those, and from the point of view of the stockholder, it is probably the best of the diversified companies. Like many successful conglomerates, Teledyne is the creation of one strong man. Henry Singleton left Litton Industries in 1960 to start it, and he remains the chief executive to this day. He made many unrelated acquisitions, just as I did, but he made fewer mistakes.

---

Minnesota Mining & Manufacturing started out mining fluorspar and using it to make sandpaper. You couldn't get much less scope than that. . . . [yet] much of 3M's diversification was achieved by creating new products instead of acquiring other companies.

---

Some of Singleton's policies were considered pretty unorthodox in the investment community. Teledyne has never paid a cash dividend, for example. Singleton purchased large positions in several major corporations. A $49.1-million write-down of its International Harvester shares hurt Teledyne's stock in 1982, but other investments paid off, especially Singleton's purchase of a 25 percent interest in Litton Industries at an average price of $12.50 between 1975 and 1978. Litton shares traded for $68 late in April.

No other company I know of has ever bought in such a large percentage of its own shares and stayed public. The company has reduced its outstanding shares to 20.4 million from a peak of 89 million in 1971 (adjusted for subsequent splits and stock dividends). Anyone who has held Teledyne stock since the initial $1.9-million offering in 1960 has seen the investment increase by over 14,000 percent. That's better than 24 percent compounded annually.

Conglomerates were so successful in the 1960s that inevitably the whole thing got out of hand. Their managers found they could increase earnings per share just by making acquisitions, so long as their companies had higher multiples than the companies they acquired. An acquiring company would be buying earnings cheap and adding them to its own, and the market would almost invariably bid up its shares to reflect those added earnings. While Emerson Electric used this ploy wisely, other conglomerates started buying anything that came along. The break came in 1968, when investors began to understand how poor the quality of those earnings was.

Litton has symbolized the rise, fall, and revival of the conglomerate. When I bought Dalmo Victor in San Carlos, California, in 1954, I was told I should also buy a little company across the street called Electro-Dynamics Corp., which subsequently became Litton Industries. It was very limited in scope but highly profitable. Roy Ash and Tex Thornton took the company over and diversified into at least 20 different businesses. Litton's multiple got as high as 47. In the early 1960s it made the mistake of taking on two big companies that really had problems, Ingalls Shipbuilding in Pascagoula, Mississippi, and Royal McBee, the typewriter company. The problems finally caught up with the company in 1968, and Litton announced a decline in quarterly earnings for the first time in its 14 years. The shares went into a long decline, from $120.375 in 1968 to $2.875 in 1974. It took a long time to straighten out those companies but today Litton is once again a top performer in median return on stockholders' equity, ranking fourth among conglomerates over the past six years.

Jimmy Ling built LTV up from nothing, but he got into real trouble when he sold the public 20 percent of his subsidiaries and then borrowed heavily on the remaining 80 percent of the overpriced shares. He bought the Jones & Laughlin Steel Co. with that money. But in 1969 LTV's earnings declined, and the price of the subsidiaries' stock came tumbling down. He was caught with too much debt, and that was the end of Jimmy Ling at LTV.

344

The spinoff trend started in 1972. The conglomerates had bought too many small companies, and they began selling the ones with the least growth potential to put more capital into the most promising divisions. That trend has slowed down now. By 1972, of course, I was out of Textron, but I was running Narragansett Capital Corp., a Small Business Investment Company, and we were able to pick up dozens of divested cash cows that weren't growing. We used leveraged buyouts, which enabled us to give the managers a piece of the action. So in a way I had the best of both conglomerate cycles—when they were diversifying in the 1950s and 1960s and when they were selling off in the 1970s.

---

Conglomerates were so successful in the 1960s that inevitably the whole thing got out of hand. Their managers found they could increase earnings per share just by making acquisitions, so long as their companies had higher multiples than the companies they acquired.

---

Diversifying is as desirable today as ever, but a lot harder. When I was building up Textron 30 years ago, you could buy a company at eight times its annual earnings. Today you may have to pay 15 times earnings. I couldn't create a Textron today and make a decent return, nor could anybody else.

But for those who have already created a conglomerate, or anyone who can figure out how to do it without acquisitions today—say, by creating new products through research and development—my basic concept of unrelated diversification is as sound as ever. The bad reputation the conglomerates acquired in the late 1960s and early 1970s just doesn't square with the facts today. I would like to see *Fortune* start comparing the performance of conglomerates and nondiversified companies every year. A well-run diversified company shouldn't ever lose money. I may be sticking my neck out, but I think very few of the 39 examined for this article will lose money in the future.

1984

# PART VII

# Bashing Bureaucracy

Two of the prominent rallying cries of the 1990s have been "Flatten the Organization" and "Break Down Walls." Within every company, managers are searching for ways to become more fluid, to invigorate their people, and to act like entrepreneurs—and ultimately to be more productive. Part VII offers a host of red-tape-cutting, bureaucracy-bashing ideas (knives and sledge hammers not needed). Jan Carlzon, who made airline SAS synonymous with service, declares, "If you can flatten your own pyramids you will be creating a far more powerful and resilient organization that not only serves customers better but also unleashes the hidden energy within your employees." General Electric CEO Jack Welch concurs with Carlzon; he wants all 200,000 GE employees to "come to work every day intent on finding a better way." To do so, he espouses demolishing walls between divisions, departments, and even suppliers and customers.

Jan Carlzon made his name as president and CEO of Scandinavian Airline System (SAS), world renowned for its service. After earning an MBA from the Stockholm School of Economics in 1967, he joined Vingresor, a package vacation subsidiary of SAS, where he started as a product manager and worked his way up to the head of marketing. Top brass was impressed, and although he had only six years of experience in the workforce, they made the 32-year-old Carlzon managing director of Vingresor. It was trial by fire, and he found himself trying to solve too many problems for too many people. He learned to step back and "keep the big picture in mind."

Four years later Carlzon became the world's youngest airline president when he was appointed managing director of Linjeflyg, Sweden's domestic airline and another SAS subsidiary. Although the company was bleeding money, he was amazed to discover the biggest concern was the flight attendants' uniforms. While Carlzon was making Linjeflyg profitable, the parent company suffered losses in 1979 and 1980—after 17 straight years of profit. Again they turned to Carlzon, who took command in 1981. The ownership structure of SAS alone was a manager's nightmare; it was half-owned by private stockholders, and half by the governments of Sweden, Denmark, and Norway.

When it came to improving profits, Carlzon observed, "SAS's top management at the time used the standard weapon: the cheese slicer, which disregards market demands and instead cuts costs equally from all activities and all departments." He went the other route and increased expenses in specific areas to attract customers. Most important, Carlzon involved the employees. "Giving someone the freedom to take responsibility releases resources that would otherwise remain concealed," he said. Frontline troops were empowered; however, in *Flattening the Pyramid* he warns against ignoring middle managers. You must explain how their role changes from being merely administrative to being part of a support team, Carlzon explains, or they'll react with bitterness, and confusion will reign.

# Flattening the Pyramid
## *Jan Carlzon*

Any business organization seeking to establish a customer orientation and create a good impression during its "moments of truth" must flatten the pyramid—that is, eliminate the hierarchical tiers of responsibility in order to respond directly and quickly to customers' needs. The customer-oriented company is organized for change.

"Managing" is thus shifted from the executive suite to the operational level where everyone is now a manager of his own situation. When problems arise, each employee has the authority to analyze the situation, determine the appropriate action, and see to it that the action is carried out, either alone or with the help of others.

It may seem like a mere word game to call everyone a "manager," but I use the term to remind my staff—and perhaps most those at the upper levels of the old pyramid—that their roles have undergone a fundamental change. If the top executives who were once the managers must learn to be leaders, then those people out in the front lines must make all the operational decisions. They are the ones who most directly influence the customer's impression of the company during those "moments of truth."

Consider the following before-and-after scenario of how flattening the pyramids might make an airline staff better able to serve its passengers' needs.

Let's say that you've preordered a special vegetarian meal for your SAS flight from Stockholm to New York. Nervously, you approach the check-in counter to find out whether your meal has been delivered to the plane.

"I don't know," the agent sighs. "I'm sorry, but I'm busy, and I'm not familiar with the food service."

"But what can I do?" you ask.

"You'll have to ask at the gate," she replies. "They'll certainly be able to help you there."

The agent quickly moves on to help the next person in line. Given no alternative, you go to the gate and ask again.

The gate attendant is friendly, but he doesn't know where your meal is either. "I wish I could help, but I don't have anything to do with food service. Just check with the stewardess when you get on board and things should certainly work out."

Reluctantly, you board the plane. When you ask the stewardess about your vegetarian meal, she is bewildered. She hasn't heard anything about special food orders, but the plane is about to take off and nothing can be done now. "You should have contacted us earlier," she reprimands. "There would have been no problem if only we had known in time."

In this situation, the hierarchical organizational structure has caused the airline to ruin three "moments of truth." No one the passenger encountered had the authority to handle the specific problem, and no one dared step out of his normal role to try to solve it.

Let's now suppose that the organization has changed its structure by flattening the pyramid and putting a team of people in charge of the Stockholm-New York flight from start to finish.

The team has 15 members, two of whom function as "coaches," one indoors and one out by the plane. The indoor coach sits in on the flight crew's briefing and consults with them about preflight information such as the appropriate time to begin boarding, whether any infants or disabled people are on the passenger list, and whether anyone has ordered a special meal.

In the morning, the indoor team assembles at the check-in counters to solve passengers' ticketing problems, assign seats, handle fragile baggage, and so forth. When a mother arrives with her baby, she is greeted with a smile and told that a suspended cradle has already been put on board and that the seat beside hers will be kept free if at all possible.

When you arrive at check-in and ask about your vegetarian meal, you won't be hurriedly dismissed by the agent behind the counter. Thanks to the new team arrangement, your meal request becomes that agent's responsibility. She can confirm that it is already on board—or take steps to make sure it's loaded by the time you step into the plane.

As more and more passengers check in, the SAS team gradually moves to the departure gate, where they nod to their passengers in recognition. They are well acquainted with the flight to New York and can answer all the usual questions: how to transfer from JFK to La Guardia, why there is a stopover in Oslo, the actual flight time, and whether the captain will announce when they are flying over Greenland.

Problems are solved on the spot, as soon as they arise. No frontline employee has to wait for a supervisor's permission. No passenger boards the plane while still worried or dissatisfied.

Furthermore, by giving more responsibility to the frontline personnel, we are letting them provide the service that they had wanted to provide all along but couldn't because of an inflexible hierarchical structure.

Take, for example, the announcements made over a plane's public address system. In the old days, the SAS rule book included paragraphs that the crew read verbatim. When we gave the employees more flexibility, we encouraged them to toss out the script and improvise in a conversational matter that suited them, the passengers, and the current situation on the plane.

And did our employees take our advice? At least one of them certainly did. On the morning flight from Stockholm to Copenhagen on September 20, 1982—the day after the Social Democrats were returned to power after a six-year hiatus—the captain picked up the microphone and said, "Good morning, comrades." Then he went on to deliver a brilliant political satire.

> By giving more responsibility to the frontline personnel, we are letting them provide the service that they had wanted to provide all along but couldn't because of an inflexible hierarchical structure.

Now, no instruction manual could have detailed how to address a plane full of businessmen on the morning after a Socialist victory. Allowed to take responsibility for the situation, however, the captain seized a "moment of truth" that the passengers aren't likely to forget.

On another flight, a curious coach passenger peeked into the first-class cabin. Catching his eye, the purser invited him in and showed him around. After a tour of the cockpit too, the purser offered him a drink. "How do you like working for SAS these days?" the passenger asked.

"It's wonderful—like being at an entirely new company."

"How, specifically?"

"Well, I can bring a passenger in here and offer him a drink without having to ask anybody's permission or write a report later accounting for my actions or the missing drinks."

Of course, the organizational transformation at SAS has not always been smooth and painless. In our hurry to find some quick solutions to SAS's financial problems when I first joined the company, we flattened the organizational structure so rapidly that we certainly stumbled occasionally along the way.

At first, so that the effects of our changes would be immediate, we simply circumvented middle managers and went directly to the front line. The front line, too, bypassed middle managers and came straight to the top for assistance. We responded by issuing company-wide memos reaffirming that the front line had the power to make individual decisions.

Initially we met with such fantastic success with the frontline people that we didn't notice anything was wrong elsewhere in the organization.

Yet, the middle managers, who were understandably confused by their new role within the organization, became hostile and counterproductive. We had put them in a completely unfamiliar situation where they were squeezed from both directions. Directives came shooting down from above that conflicted with their expectations and experience. They heard what we said but didn't know how to translate it into practical actions. From below came demands for responsibility and power to make decisions, which they viewed as a threat to their own position.

We had directed middle managers to go out and listen to the people in the front line—to find out what they needed to do their jobs. The managers, however, were not accustomed to thinking of themselves as filling a support function, especially if they are supporting people previously considered subordinates. The word "support" conjurs up an image of attending to needs, not administering. At SAS, like at other companies, support and service had always been relegated to a low status. Every promotion had moved people away from serving the customer and toward administration.

So, even after we reorganized the company, middle managers continued to sit in their offices lined with regulations books, policies, and directives. And when the people on the front lines "broke the rules" to help the customers, naturally the middle managers responded by reining them in. This infuriated the front line.

Although our new strategy of decentralizing responsibility was a big hit with our frontline employees, we had a much tougher time finding the right way to inspire middle managers. For example, upon returning from the United States to Sweden one time I entered the terminal and was met by a chaotic scene. Apparently the monitors matching up flight numbers with the corresponding conveyor belts that carried the baggage were on the blink, and everyone was madly searching for their luggage.

I suggested to the woman at the information counter that she post a few signs—handwritten, if need be—to alleviate the confusion.

"I wish I could," she responded. "The system broke down last Monday and I told the boss then that we should put up some temporary signs so people could find their baggage. But he said that it would be fixed soon enough, so the signs were unnecessary."

"But that was a week ago!"

"I know! But now that an entire week has gone by, he says the monitors are *sure* to be fixed soon."

Back at the head office I phoned the appropriate division head and asked him to give the woman's boss a choice: he could take his handsome desk from his spacious office and move it down to the arrivals terminal, where he could witness the problems personally and continue making decisions about them. Or he could stay right where he was. But if he did, he would have to yield his decision-making power to the frontline people in the arrivals terminal.

The supervisor had not understood that his role had changed under our new organization. In the past he had issued orders and instructions to his staff. Now his job was to serve them by ensuring that they understood their department's objectives and that they had the information and resources required to meet those objectives down in the arrivals terminal. He wasn't supposed to sit in his office and decide whether or not handwritten baggage signs should be posted.

Much of the fault for this was ours. We had let our middle managers down. We had given the front line the right to accept responsibility, yet we hadn't given middle managers viable alternatives to their old role as rule interpreters. We hadn't told middle management how to handle what might, at first glance, look like a demotion.

---

Although our new strategy of decentralizing responsibility was a big hit with our frontline employees, we had a much tougher time finding the right way to inspire middle managers.

---

Let me give you another example of the initial mixed success of our organizational changes at SAS.

One day an SAS flight across Sweden had fallen far behind schedule because of snow. Taking responsibility for the situation, the purser decided on her own to compensate the customers for their inconvenience by offering free coffee and biscuits. She knew from experience that, because she was offering them at no charge, she would need about 40 additional servings. So she went to catering and ordered the extra coffee and biscuits.

The SAS catering supervisor turned her down. It was against regulations to request more than the amount of food allotted to a particular flight, and the supervisor refused to budge. But the purser wasn't thwarted. She noticed a Finnair plane docked at the next gate. Finnair is an external customer of the SAS catering department, and as such is not subject to SAS internal regulations.

Thinking quickly, the SAS purser turned to her colleague in the Finnair plane and asked him to order 40 cups of coffee and 40 biscuits. He placed the order which, according to regulations, the catering supervisor was obligated to fulfill. Then the SAS purser bought the snack from Finnair with SAS petty cash and served the grateful passengers.

In this case, the purser dared to find a way to circumvent regulations in order to meet the customers' needs—something she surely never would have tried under the old system. At the same time, however, the catering supervisor couldn't understand why a lowly purser had the right to make decisions that had always been in his purview and so he became confused and angry.

---

People sometimes equate delegating responsibility with abdicating one's own influence. . . . Actually, the middle manager's role is indispensable in the smooth functioning of a decentralized organization.

---

What he hadn't realized—what we hadn't adequately explained—was that he never should have questioned her authority or in any way have interfered with her attempt to satisfy customers. In that "moment of truth," the purser had to act quickly or forever lose an opportunity to satisfy those customers. She could have taken her request to her supervisor, but that action would have initiated a bureaucratic process that would have remained unresolved long after the late flight had finally departed. The catering supervisor could have questioned the purser's decision later, but no one has the authority to interfere during a moment of truth. Seizing these golden opportunities to serve the customer is the responsibility of the front line. Enabling them to do so is the responsibility of middle managers.

Eventually, we formed a much clearer idea of how the flattened pyramid should operate and were able to communicate the new roles to middle managers as well. The work still begins with something handed down from above— overall objectives for achieving the company goals. Upon receiving these broad objectives, middle management first breaks them down into a set of smaller objectives that the frontline people will be able to accomplish. At that point the role of middle manager is transformed from administration to support.

People sometimes equate delegating responsibility with abdicating one's own influence. But that's hardly the case. Actually, the middle manager's role is indispensable in the smooth functioning of a decentralized organization.

---

If you can flatten your own pyramids you will be creating a far more powerful and resilient organization that not only serves customers better but also unleashes the hidden energy within your employees.

---

To motivate the front line and support their efforts requires skilled and knowledgeable middle managers who are proficient at coaching, informing, criticizing, praising, educating, and so forth. Their authority applies to translating the overall strategies into practical guidelines that the front line can follow and then mobilizing the necessary resources for the front line to achieve its objectives. This requires hard-nosed business planning along with healthy doses of creativity and resourcefulness.

Despite some minor setbacks along the way, the SAS pyramid has truly been flattened, and our employees tell us that they're working with newfound motivation and confidence.

I urge others to take a close, hard look at their own organizations. If you can flatten your own pyramids you will be creating a far more powerful and resilient organization that not only serves customers better but also unleashes the hidden energy within your employees. The results can be absolutely astounding.

1987

Who would have thought that "Neutron Jack," the tough CEO of General Electric (GE), was a high school altar boy, and becomes sentimental when discussing his mom. But it was Welch's mother who helped him to overcome a childhood stutter and pushed him through the University of Massachusetts and then the University of Illinois, where he earned a Ph.D. in chemical engineering. So what about the tough guy image? No doubt, in blue collar Salem, Massachusetts, where Welch grew up, sports was everything and bred in him the will to win. That also helps to explain the direct philosophy he brought to the top post in 1981: Every GE business unit had to be number one or two in their respective industry, or they were gone.

Welch actually refers to the behemoth GE as a "grocery store"—it helps him roll up his sleeves, serve the customer, and think informally. He said, "The story about GE that hasn't been told is the value of an informal place. I think it's a big thought. I don't think people have ever figured out that being informal is a big deal." Welch has always despised bureaucracy. Back in 1961, after being on the job at GE as a junior engineer, he quit because he couldn't stand the bureaucracy. Fortunately, Welch's boss convinced him to return. He was made a divisional vice president in 1973 and that year stated boldly on his employee evaluation that his long-range goal was to become CEO.

One of the keys to his long-term success is not only balancing the needs of the different divisions, but balancing short-term and long-term goals. "You can't grow long-term if you can't eat short-term. Anybody can manage short. Anybody can manage long. Balancing those two things is what management is," he said. A tangible example is the company's Six Sigma program, an initiative to improve quality that involves investing now for the future. To also achieve that balance, Welch espouses "sharing best practices" and "boundaryless behavior," and he develops his three operating principles—Boundaryless Behavior, Speed, and Stretch—in the following selection. He's decidedly not interested in people who are willing to do time in "the bowels of the bureaucracy."

# Removing Walls
## *John F. Welch, Jr.*

We run General Electric on a simple premise: the only way to win, in the brutally competitive global environment in which we operate, is to get more output from less input in all 12 of our businesses and, by doing so, become the lowest-cost producer of high-quality goods and services in the world.

We are betting everything on our people—powering them, giving them the resources, and getting out of their way.

## THREE OPERATING PRINCIPLES

We use three operating principles to define our atmosphere and behavior:

- Boundaryless . . . in all our behavior;
- Speed . . . in everything we do;
- Stretch . . . in every target we set.

1. *Boundaryless behavior* is the soul of today's GE. In large, old institutions like ours, people tend to build layers and walls between themselves and others. These walls cramp

people, inhibit creativity, waste time, restrict vision, smother dreams, and slow things down.

The challenge is to break down these walls and barriers. The progress we've made so far has released a flood of ideas that are improving every operation. We've adapted product introduction techniques from Chrysler and Canon, effective sourcing techniques from GM and Toyota, and approaches to quality from Motorola and Ford. We've moved more effectively into the foreign markets with advice and best practices from pioneers like IBM, Johnson & Johnson, Xerox, and others.

---

Internally, boundaryless behavior means piercing the walls of 100-year-old fiefdoms and empires called finance, engineering, manufacturing, marketing; and gathering teams from all those functions in one room, with one shared vision and one consuming passion—to design the world's best products.

---

Removing walls means we involve suppliers as participants in our design and manufacturing processes. It means having major launch customers like British Airways, Tokyo Electric Power, or CSX in the room and involved in the design of a new jet engine, a revolutionary gas turbine, or a new AC locomotive—or having a panel of doctors helping us develop a new ultrasound system.

Internally, boundaryless behavior means piercing the walls of 100-year-old fiefdoms and empires called finance, engineering, manufacturing, marketing; and gathering teams from all those functions in one room, with one shared vision and one consuming passion—to design the world's best products.

The compulsion to manage, to control, to direct, is a powerful one, reinforced by a century-old tradition at GE of measuring one's self-worth by how many people "work for you" and if the word "manager" appears in your title. The highest compliment you could give GE managers a few years ago was to say they were "on top of things" or had gotten "their arms around them." These techniques are more useful in tackling people than coaching them.

---

In a boundaryless atmosphere, a good idea
sprouts and blossoms and is nurtured by all.
No one cares where the seed came from.

---

What we look for today at GE are leaders who can energize, excite, and coach rather than enervate, depress, and control. And never has this atmosphere been more critical. Today, everyone must be engaged if we are to win. We need people who are unwilling to just "put in their time" in the bowels of the bureaucracy before they get a chance to make decisions. We need people who are willing to try something and be rewarded in their souls as well as their wallets.

In a boundaryless atmosphere, a good idea sprouts and blossoms and is nurtured by all. No one cares where the seed came from. Ideas are judged on the basis of their quality rather than the altitude of their origin. And because informality is warming every corner of our company, today's GE has become both a lot more fun to work at and a lot faster.

2. *Speed* is the second element we are after. The faster the pace of change, the bigger the advantage.

With the drag and nonsense of boundaries, management layers, bureaucracy, and formality cleared, the organization accelerates. Where we once relied on "moonshot" development programs that took years to reach the market, new GE products are now coming out with drumbeat rapidity. There is now a product announcement at Appliances every 90 days—unthinkable years ago. The GE90, the world's most powerful commercial jet engine, was designed and built in one-half the normal time, by a boundaryless team. Another team developed a breakthrough ultrasound innovation in less than a year-and-a-half. We designed and built a new AC locomotive in 18 months. We're developing an absolute cascade of new energy-efficient lighting products, plastics for the construction industry, and revolutionary turbines that extend the limits of thermodynamics and materials.

3. *Stretch* is a concept that would have produced smirks, if not laughter, in GE four years ago, because it means using dreams to set business targets—with no real idea of how to get there. If you know how to get there, it's not a stretch target. We didn't have a clue how we were going to get to 10 inventory turns when we set that target. But we're getting there. As soon as we become sure we can do it, it's time for another stretch. The CEO of Yokogawa, our Japanese partner in the Medical Systems business, calls this concept "bullet-train thinking." If you want a 10-miles-per-hour increase in train speed, you tinker with horsepower; if you want to double its speed, you have to break out of conventional thinking and performance expectations.

---

If you want a 10-miles-per-hour increase in train speed, you tinker with horsepower; if you want to double its speed, you have to break out of conventional thinking and performance expectations.

---

Stretch allows organizations to set the bar higher than they ever dreamed possible. Whether it be a 100-fold improvement in quality, 10-fold reduction in product development time or margin rates never before dreamed of, the openness never before dreamed of, the openness, candor, and trust of a boundaryless, fast company allows us to hang those dreams out there, in view of everyone, so that we can all reach for them.

John F. Welch, Jr.

## LEARNING AS WE GO

Boundaryless people, excited by speed and inspired by stretch dreams, have an absolutely infinite capacity to improve everything. While we are still learning as we go, we have more than 200,000 people who come to work every day intent on finding a better way.

1993

Clarence Randall climbed the executive ranks to become president of Inland Steel, which is now the cornerstone of Ispat International, the seventh-largest steel company in the world, and he was President Eisenhower's special adviser on foreign economic policy. However, he became best known as a writer on business matters, penning several books and numerous articles. He pulled no punches, he said, and spoke from the heart. His down-to-earth attitude was a result of being born and raised in a small upstate New York town of 800. For him, there was nothing better than to have "gone barefoot all day, or caught frogs in a swamp, or trapped muskrats, or shaken chestnuts from a tree with one eye on the farmer's barn." But Randall's mother had bigger plans than muskrat hunting for him; she forced her husband to sell his store and become a coal salesman so that their son could attend Harvard.

Randall went on to Harvard Law School, graduating in 1915, and then joined his cousin's law firm, which provided legal counsel to an iron-ore company in Michigan. During World War I, he served overseas and returned to become a partner with his cousin. Out of the blue, the Inland Steel company invited him to run its iron ore division, which he did in 1925. It was one thing to give legal advice and another to run a business, and he had to rely on gut instinct, which may explain his later disdain for so-called specialists: "Industry today is like Pharaoh of old. We too are threatened with a plague of locusts. . . . Our locusts are the specialists—the men who, with infinite patience, skill, and learning, have completely mastered one minuscule segment of business and can do nothing else."

At age 39, Randall took the helm of the entire company. From his sometimes overwhelming responsibilities, he developed both an honest and a wry perspective. Recognized as having a way with words, Randall wrote a series of articles which he then put together in one of his many books, *The Folklore of Management*. In *The Myth of the Organizational Chart*, an excerpt from that book, he playfully warns against executives who communicate using charts and graphs instead of the English language.

# The Myth of the Organization Chart
## Clarence B. Randall

With the passing of the years, I am impressed by how different management men and management ways are today from those of the prebellum days when I was lucky enough to get my first job.

Not that management itself is any different. It has the same function in any generation under the free enterprise system. Its task is to plan the operation, secure the maximum effort from those who are employed by the enterprise, and coordinate the activities of men and machines. Only the methods and the working tools of management change.

When I began, there were still men who worked ten hours a day at stand-up desks. They wore green eyeshades and had only kerosene lamps to see by. When electric lights first came in, the single unshaded bulb hanging from the ceiling was so dim that they often wished they had the lamps back.

When these men arrived in the morning, they took off their coats and put on alpaca jackets to save the wear and tear on their sleeves. Most of them wore celluloid collars and celluloid cuffs that were attached to their shirts by metal clasps. Everyone that could had a mustache. They wrote with steel pens that were dipped in dirty inkwells. To preserve their correspondence, they made copies with a letter press and pasted the tissues in a large folio volume. Their telephone, when they had one, hung on a wall and had to be cranked by hand.

The boss, who was revered and feared as one who stood on the right hand of the Deity, was driven to work in the morning and taken home at night by a handsome team of horses and, in the summer, a surrey; in the winter, a cutter with jingling bells.

But among these strange characters were fine management men, some of the very best I have ever known. They dreamed great dreams and lived to see them come true. They turned out products in ever-increasing volume for a rapidly growing country. They made money and got ahead. They were the founding fathers of today's great industrial enterprises.

And all of this they did without benefit of organization charts.

Consider the modern counterparts of those earlier strong men.

For the most part, they now come to their executive responsibilities after many years of specialized training. Not only are they college graduates but they have also probably had graduate training at the Harvard Business School or some other fine institution. There they have studied accounting and merchandising and industrial engineering and have done case studies on all sorts of business problems. Their weakness is that, enamored of new methods and still of necessity lacking practical experience, they are prone to confuse the substance of management with its working tools. For example, they tend to disdain the use of the English language, which their forebears employed so pungently, and to adopt instead the representational means of communication. The chart thus takes on such importance in their minds that it becomes an achievement in itself instead of a means to an end.

Upon graduation, these eager young men with highly polished minds arrive in industry on the dead run. They can hardly wait to put into practice the exciting new techniques which they have mastered. When they walk into the office at nine o'clock on any given morning, they are inclined to view the seemingly disorganized state of chaos about them with some disdain.

At heart, they are very good stuff indeed, and so they get ahead fast. It is not long before they receive substantial responsibility, and as they rise in the organization, their yen for the formalities of management persists. When at last their big chance comes, and they are near the top, they surround themselves with staffs who have been similarly trained, and the stamp of the chart-minded executive is placed irrevocably upon the institution that they serve.

---

A chart, as such, is an excellent thing. . . . but it is the beginning of the problem and not the solution. . . . the chart itself will not get things done.

---

Many of these bright young men who make up these new staffs mark the full break with the bold entrepreneurs of the past. They do not want to become president; they are content always to remain staff. Each one of the green-eyeshade boys secretly nursed the hope that one day he could become boss and have his own spanking team of bays, but I am not sure about their successors. Some of them seem to me altogether too ready to stick with their charts if to get the chauffeur-driven Cadillac they must take the responsibility that goes with it.

It is not, of course, the new techniques themselves that I quarrel with, but rather the distorted sense of proportion with which they are employed by some of this new breed of management men. Graphs are fine in their place, but they are not sacrosanct. They should never be lifted above the dignity of useful working tools.

A chart, as such, is an excellent thing. Whatever clarifies thinking and brings a problem into sharp focus is a desirable medium of administration, but it is the beginning of the problem and not the solution. Decisions still have to be taken by an exercise of the will; the chart itself will not get things done.

There must be both selectivity and balanced judgment in the use of the modern management techniques, with choices made that are appropriate to the circumstances. Not all minds react to the same stimuli, for example, and there is no single means of communication which will transmit an idea to all persons with equal effectiveness.

Take blueprints. There is a time and a place for a sketch, but it can never replace the spoken or the written word for the simple reason that there are some men who can never fully comprehend a drawing, no matter how hard they try. The well-rounded management man will, therefore, be master of all the media and will use them appropriately. Above all, he will never forget that it is the idea and not the medium that is important.

There is a touch of sadism in all of us, and the particular form of petty cruelty which I used to delight in practicing was this: When a young engineer was admitted to my august presence, I would ask him a question that called for a reasoned reply. If he reached for a pad and pencil and began to draw, I rebuked him sharply and asked him to tell it to me in words. If he failed that test, I knew that for him ideas had to be expressed on a blueprint or they lacked validity, and doubts about his future rose in my mind. He seemed to be condemning himself to staff work for life.

The most virulent form of this mentality is found in those for whom the organization chart is the quintessence of management, the very end-all of industrial engineering.

In such companies, this imposing document, which is found in every desk and must be consulted frequently by all hands, is as long as the genealogical table of an old New England family and as complete to the smallest detail as the subject of nuclear fission in the *Encyclopaedia Britannica*. For a man not to be squeezed into it somewhere would be a fate worse than death for it could only mean that he was completely unknown. To be connected to only one boss on the chart, and that but by a single line, would be an announcement of inferior status. The men who have really arrived will be spider-webbed off in several directions by mysterious cross-hatching.

Should an outsider chance to see the document and should he advance into the fine print of the job descriptions which will be attached to the chart, he would wonder whether any work is ever done at all, since so much time must obviously be required for study and meditation upon what to do next and how far to go.

---

It is not the preparation of the organization chart that I condemn, but its abuse: this blowing up of its significance to the point where guidance ceases and inhibition sets in.

---

Now, obviously, to know who is to do what and to establish authority and responsibility within an institution are the basic first principles of a good administration, but this is a far cry from handing down immutable tablets of stone from the mountaintop. Not even the Ten Commandments undertook to do more than establish general guidelines of conduct. They contained no fine print and no explanatory notes. Even the Almighty expected us to use our own good judgment in carrying them out.

It is not the preparation of the organization chart that I condemn, but its abuse: this blowing up of its significance to the point where guidance ceases and inhibition sets in. When men turn to it occasionally for broad indications of where responsibility lies so that confusion may be avoided among personnel, all of whom are willing and able, its force is positive. But when men fall into the habit of using it to avoid a task, of saying a pleased "Not me!" to themselves when they consult it, then its force is negative.

Warm human relationships must not be put into cold storage. Situations that are essentially fluid must not be frozen.

Production is, above all else, team play. Before a football game, the varsity may study the sketch of a play which the coach has put on the blackboard, but they don't take the chart into the game with them. When the ball is snapped, if the tackle misses his man, the end gets him, no matter what the chart says.

So it must be in business. Each man must have a sure instinct for adjusting his effort to that of the man alongside him so that the overall objective of the operation will be advanced. He should look at the music when he can, but most of the time he must play by ear.

I remember how shocked I was once when I went to call on the Chicago representative of a large corporation whose main office was in the East. I was a vice president of my company at the time. He was not only a senior vice president of his company but a director as well. I felt entirely at ease in deciding for my company the question before us without even telling my boss that the problem existed. But when I put it to him, he opened his desk, took out a black book, thumbed the pages for a few minutes, and said, "No dice. Home office!" With complete complacency he simply dumped the matter on the desk of a remote boss, because the book told him to. As a consequence, his company missed out on a matter of importance, for I had no intention whatever of going East to pursue it.

Good administration requires flexibility of both mind and method. The infinite variety of the changing pattern of circumstances that affect production and distribution demands it. The most precise organization chart that industrial engineers can draw will be out of date before it can be printed and handed round. A relationship which functions smoothly today may begin to show strain tomorrow because of a new development that could not have been foreseen.

Men of good will who have broad understanding of what their jobs are intended to accomplish can make necessary daily adjustments when circumstances change, but there can be no slippage if the man is harnessed to a chart.

---

Jobs have no vitality of their own. They are parasites. They attach themselves to people and cling tenaciously to particular individuals, no matter what we may do.

---

There is one further difficulty with overemphasis on the formalizing of business relationships, which is this: a chart which suits one group of persons will need revision just as often as there are personnel changes.

Jobs have no vitality of their own. They are parasites. They attach themselves to people and cling tenaciously to particular individuals, no matter what we may do. Take the man away, and the job will never be quite the same again. A relationship which functions smoothly under a particular chart and one set of job descriptions, so long as the original incumbents remain, will begin to show stress when promotion, death, resignation, or retirement intervene. No two individuals will ever bring successively to one job the same complex of strengths and weaknesses, and when a new teammate arrives, some compensating adjustments must be made by those around him. No chart can ever do this for them.

The wise management man, therefore, will follow the golden mean in using the new techniques, mastering them but never letting them master him. He will add them to his kit of working tools but will keep them in their place.

He will remember that the organization chart is a useful scaffold with which to build a house, but will know that it is not the house.

1959

# Patrick J. McGovern

Patrick McGovern is founder and chairman of International Data Group (IDG), which publishes *Computerworld, PC World, Macworld,* and some 290 other computer magazines and newspapers in 75 countries. The formidable Bill Gates once conceded that McGovern's magazines can make or break a product. McGovern first became interested in publishing while a biophysics student at the Massachusetts Institute of Technology, where he did some writing for *Computers & Automation,* one of the first magazines dedicated to computers. Upon graduating in 1959, he became associate publisher. Seeking to fill the void of information on computer users, McGovern founded IDG in 1964 to conduct market research. Three years later he launched his flagship *Computerworld.*

IDG has remained private, but McGovern implemented a profit-sharing program that has handed over about 35 percent of the company to employees. "I wanted to make sure that the future control and direction of the company would be in the hands of the people who built it, the current employees," says McGovern. Although he keeps his nose out of operations and thinks of himself as an investor in his own company, he has spent as much as 20 percent of his time visiting the many offices.

To protect himself, he has kept the company diversified by organizing it as separate corporations. He explained, "As I started to organize entrepreneurial units in which I could give a lot of autonomy to the people involved, I pretty quickly had enough business units so I wasn't turning over my entire business fortune to one person." If one group starts getting too big, he gets out his machete to chop away bureaucracy and create another, smaller unit—a theme that sounds throughout *The Networked Corporation.* Because this essay was written in 1990, some of McGovern's references to such companies as DEC are dated, but his management vision is dynamic: Smaller is better because it creates a greater challenge to the individual, he believes, and he writes that "I learned in biophysics that the performance of an organism is directly related to the challenge to that organism."

# The Networked Corporation
## *Patrick J. McGovern*

When I am driving along Route 128 in Massachusetts or Route 101 in the Silicon valley, I use an eyeball measurement to evaluate the companies that line those highways. The number of cars in the parking lot after 6 P.M. is inversely proportional to the size of the company. The smaller the company, the more cars and lights on in the building. In the large companies, the parking lot is a desert.

This phenomenon is one that reinforces a business lesson I learned right after graduating from MIT. I was associate editor of a computer magazine and my job was to travel around the U.S. and visit computer companies. I noticed immediately that the people I met at the smaller companies were more excited by their work, about product opportunities and contact with customers. The bigger the company, the less satisfied the people were. There was frustration with internal competition to get ahead, not to mention much less contact with the customer.

The conclusion is obvious: small is better. Without a doubt, a small organization creates a greater challenge to the individual to succeed. I learned in biophysics that the performance of an organism is directly related to the challenge to that organism.

Unfortunately, the success of small leads to problems. Companies get bigger; some are already large and cumbersome. But the very success that makes organizations burgeon with revenues and earnings can eventually result in stagnation and lost business opportunities. So the question is, how can you create a small company environment and still continue to grow and prosper?

The answer is the networked corporation and the facilitator is technology. Technology breaks down barriers that blocked the door to the next generation corporate environment. Networked computers, sophisticated but affordable communications capabilities, and strategic use of information systems suddenly create a myriad of possibilities; the possibility of small, for example.

When I started International Data Group in 1964, the lessons I learned from my previous job weren't lost, but the technology simply didn't exist to allow the effective creation of a networked organization. Still, I knew this was a goal to pursue and time and again, I was proved right.

---

I'm convinced that our success is based on a decentralized approach to doing business, on our ability to stay "small."

---

I am hardly surprised that the term "globalization" is suddenly on the lips of CEOs and business school professors. The concept of creating a truly global business organization was at the core of my vision for IDG. When we reached $1 million in sales, I started to view markets outside the United States as the future for the business. I even put International in our name.

Skeptics scoffed at the idea of a publishing company, of all things, being able to operate and flourish on a global basis. Even today, a leading economics columnist stated: "Newspapers will never become a truly global industry."

Perhaps so, as a total industry. But in my opinion, it seems as though companies like the New York Times or McGraw-Hill have simply overlooked this opportunity. No one, myself included, could ever have predicted the impact that technology would have on the advent of true globalization. Without that vision, publishers felt they had a unique product that couldn't be duplicated overseas and preferred licensing their products instead.

I saw it differently, even without a crystal ball on technology's role. We were filling a need in the United States: providing information about a burgeoning computer industry. Other countries would inevitably have those same needs. Readers everywhere want the same thing: to be more effective in business through the use of technology. Throughout the 1970s and 1980s, I was on the road constantly, planting the seeds in Europe, South America, Australia, and the Far East.

My goal was to allow the local publishers, editors, and reporters to determine what their markets required. By the year 2000, I fully expect that up to 70 percent of our business will be generated outside the United States.

Headquarters identifies the mission — in our case, to be the world's leading supplier of information about the information technology industry. We create a set of common values, send the message, provide support, advice, and training . . . but success or failure is determined by the local business unit.

Today, we have 68 business units operating in 40 countries with 3,500 employees. We've grown at a 20 to 30 percent rate per year for 25 years. Headquarters staff is just 18 people and our costs are only 1.5 percent of revenue (as opposed to an average of 3–5 percent).

I'm convinced that our success is based on a decentralized approach to doing business, on our ability to stay "small." By so doing, we can evolve with the market and constantly identify new customer groups.

The most successful business units in the company validate my concept. Those with one goal (i.e., one publication under its wing), perform the best. I've seen units over the years start two or three publications. The first publication does well but the new baby has trouble. It has either too much or not enough love. These struggling publications spring to life when set out on their own in separate business units.

The other side of the equation is that this concept lets me sleep peacefully knowing that our company does not depend on the success of any one business unit to survive. If China's recent crackdown had resulted in the closing of our Beijing operation (it didn't), IDG would go on.

## AUTONOMOUS BUSINESS UNITS

I constantly fight the spread of hierarchy who extol the top-heavy approach. "Why don't you have central paper buying rather than each individual publication finding its own source?" the experts ask. Such economies of scale would certainly produce an immediate increase in margin, they say. That may be true, but taking away operating freedom would cause key people to leave the company and in a few years, stagnation would set in. If you allow a small group of people to take an idea, nurture it, build it and make it happen, the chances of success are enhanced beyond measure.

Ken Olsen saw this clearly at Digital Equipment Corp. in the early '60s when he became frustrated with a suddenly stagnant young company. He found that when things went wrong, everyone turned to him to place the blame. In a stroke of business genius, he restructured the company. Each product group became an autonomous business unit responsible for the individual success or failure of that product. Each unit would compete for corporate resources but would share certain centralized functions such as manufacturing and sales.

Olsen's concept lit a fuse. Digital's sales and earnings took off and throughout the next two decades, this product line strategy propelled the company beyond the $5 billion barrier in revenues. Though he eventually reorganized again in the early 1980s, Olsen never gave up on the concept of individuals having great responsibility and driving their own businesses to success. Today Digital is a $13 billion giant and is fighting IBM toe-to-toe.*

It was no coincidence that as Digital grew, its internal network spread like a giant web around the organization. Top management understood intuitively that such a decentralized approach required a highly refined communications capability. Without information in this environment, one can easily get blindsided by a wave of change or innovation. Today, Digital has a vast international network that allows more than 70,000 of its employees to communicate instantly via computer-based systems.

Adopting a decentralized, networked approach is certainly a lot easier for smaller companies but it is not an untenable concept for giants either. AT&T, for example, recently replaced five of its major business units with 19 business units in order to spread increased responsibility to lower levels of management. Robert Allen, AT&T chairman, simply got tired of the turf wars and endless committee-made decisions. He wants individuals to take responsibility and expects the move to make AT&T much more responsive and quicker to market. This is a reorganization worth keeping an eye on.

T.J. Rogers, head of the highly successful Cypress Semiconductor Corp., has also embraced the concept. Despite its success, Cypress is breaking itself into smaller, independent operations. According to *Electronic Engineering Times*, this marks the first time a healthy electronics company has undertaken such a move. Why do it?

"Cypress would be more vital as ten $100 million companies than as a single $1 billion company," Rogers stated.

---

* Digital's fortunes took a downturn in the 1990s and the company was bought by Compaq in 1998; however, McGovern's message remains poignant.

My advice to *Fortune* 500 CEOs is: Don't be afraid to divide things up, throw out a challenge. Most people are only working at 15 percent of their capacity. If you give them a challenge, their skills and capabilities most definitely will flower. People will be happier and business performance will increase. Best of all, a lot of sour-faced middle managers will disappear.

I saw a clear example of this when I was establishing the first joint publishing venture with the Soviet Union. In Moscow, I met with a group of negotiators who ranged in age from their 30s to 50s. Gorbachev's mandate for change was exciting for those in their 30s. The older bureaucrats, on the other hand, feared the change. They had four-foot-high piles of requests on their desks and perceived *perestroika* as a threat to their careers. It was clear to me that the way to succeed in this venture was to align myself with the people in their 30s.

---

Most people are only working at 15 percent of their capacity. If you give them a challenge, their skills and capabilities most definitely will flower.

---

Of course, breaking down the barrier of overstuffed bureaucracy is no guarantee of success, nor is it the only necessary step to the networked organization. Technology has become the great enabler, the steam roller that is flattening organizations. Ironically, the path of computer technology mirrors the philosophy of the networked corporation.

Like massive, top-heavy bureaucracies, computing was dominated not long ago by huge, powerful mainframes, which controlled the flow of information out into the company. With the advent and proliferation of personal computers and networks, the individual is now empowered with technology at the desktop. More and more, the mainframe is becoming a data repository, no longer in control, but rather a source for information that is turned into knowledge by the end user.

Suddenly the mainframe and the personal computer are partners in the network rather than the master and the slave. Analogous to corporate headquarters, the mainframe can no longer dictate, it must allow other machines to have autonomy in the network.

The combination of networked technology with a small group of talented, motivated professionals is a powerful one. Our flagship publication, *Computerworld*, is a prime example. Long dominant in its market, *Computerworld* started spinning off other publications several years ago while seeking ways to increase market share. Headquarters lost sight of what had made *Computerworld* special. We missed some very important industry trends, had bloated unresponsive management and most important, lost sight of our customer, the reader.

Inevitably, *Computerworld* suffered; readers began to desert, key staff people left as well, and morale was way down. In the past two years, *Computerworld* became its own business unit. Aggressive and talented management was put in place, virtually all the key players coming from within the company. New production technology and graphics equipment was brought in, allowing not only for a complete redesign, but for longer news deadlines, which allow readers to get the very latest information on their desks.

The mission was refocused, the product reevaluated and overhauled, and the tide turned dramatically. With a sleek new look and an ever vigilant ear to the reader, *Computerworld* not only dominates its market but continues to be impressively profitable in a sluggish technology market.

As technology gets lower in cost, it has driven the realization of this organizational structure. We use electronic mail extensively throughout our company, which allows the immediate transmission of news and the sharing of resources around the globe. We've instituted our IDG News Service, which allows stories gathered by our more than 120 computer-related publications to be shared electronically around the world on a daily basis.

## THE GLOBAL NETWORK

All our autonomous units can benefit from the global network; they share market knowledge accumulated by 25 years of publishing experience. Since no business unit has a corner on expertise, knowledge can be and is shared. A technique for improving circulation in Norway works just as well in the United States. The Australian PC publication can acquire essential marketing expertise from *Infoworld* or *PC World*. I wasn't prepared for this when I started out, but I found to my great delight that there is a tremendous amount of transferability of skills around the world.

Indeed, I remember when we set up our first international managers meeting in 1978. Everyone assumed it would be a nice social event but there'd be little exchange of useful information. When I traveled to each country in prior years, they emphasized how unique their market was. Of course, when I'd ask for their four-year plan, they'd set up easy goals so they'd look like heroes to headquarters. We constantly pushed for more aggressive goals.

---

Technology is the vehicle, but it is the people who provide the fuel, who give shape and dimension and power to the concept.

---

I actually expected the individual country managers to be reluctant to share anything for that reason. But at the meeting, just the opposite occurred: The Germans stood up and bragged about how good they were and announced ambitious goals for themselves. Then the Americans, then the French, etc. Soon there was a lively exchange of ideas and information. I saw the benefit of using the forces of natural interpersonal rivalries to work for you. By instituting a worldwide employee stock ownership plan, we've generated even more desire for success. Now the Brazilians have all the more reason to help the French or the Japanese. They all own part of the business.

And this experience puts the networked organization into a different perspective. Technology is the vehicle, but it is the people who provide the fuel, who give shape and dimension and power to the concept. This seemingly obvious tenet is constantly getting lost in corporate hierarchies where CEOs are now asking why they are spending large percentages of budgets on technology and seeing little productivity increase.

Layering on technology offers no strategic advantage if the culture and environment aren't structured to allow individuals to flourish. We are not in business to acquire technology. We are in business to allow people to fulfill their potential, to give them something useful and exciting to do.

I agree with *Boston Globe* economist Robert J. Samuelson, who recently wrote: 'Companies will increasingly flourish—or fail—on how well they become multicultural organizations. They will need to create effective cooperation between people of different nationalities. The marketplace for ideas and technology is now worldwide. Companies are the means of transmission."

1990

# GEORGE N. HATSOPOULOS
## 1927–

Over the years, George Hatsopoulos, founder of Thermo Electron, has won a number of prestigious awards from such organizations as Beta Gamma Sigma (the national business honorary society) and the American Society for Competitiveness. From the time he was a young boy growing up in Greece, he knew that he wanted to be an entrepreneur. "I developed a desire to start a technology-driven company when I was in high school in Greece," he later recalled. "I wanted a company that would not rely on just one invention, but one that could generate businesses in response to societal needs." An early example: When the Germans occupied Greece in World War II, he secretly altered radios so friends could pick up forbidden broadcasts.

Toward the end of high school, Hatsopoulos read about different countries all over the world in order to choose in which to start his business; he picked the United States because it appeared to be the "most receptive to entrepreneurship." He emigrated in 1948 to attend MIT, where he earned a Ph.D. in mechanical engineering. In 1956, he borrowed $50,000 to start the Thermo Electron Corporation and convert his research work to commercial uses. He considers his first genuine hit to be an instrument that measured automobile emissions so that manufacturers could comply with the Clean Air Act of 1970. He reflected, "They [the automobile manufacturers] didn't ask the price. I could charge them anything I wanted."

To keep the entrepreneurial drive alive in his company, Hatsopoulos developed a management philosophy that involves spinning out subsidiaries as opposed to spinning off. As he observed, "The issue was: How do you motivate groups of people in the company to go through all the trouble and risk to create a new area of business?" By spinning out the groups, while still holding a majority of the stock, Hatsopoulos lets the market (i.e., stock price) determine how successful the venture is, and its people are rewarded accordingly. In *A Perpetual Idea Machine,* Hatsopoulos elaborates on his management philosophy and explains why he still considers his company to be "a work in progress."

# A Perpetual Idea Machine
### *George N. Hatsopoulos*

A stock analyst recently described Thermo Electron as *a perpetual idea machine.* I started the company in 1956 with only $50,000. Today, Thermo Electron is a *Fortune* 500 company, a world leader in environmental monitoring and analysis instruments, and a major producer of paper-recycling equipment; biomedical products, including heart-assist devices and mammography systems; alternative-energy systems; and other products and services related to environmental quality, health, and safety. Although Thermo Electron's annual revenues are now well beyond the billion dollar mark, the company remains as it started out—a company dedicated to entrepreneurship based on technology.

Thermo Electron is actually a family of publicly-traded companies, the result of our strategy of "spinning out" promising businesses to bring innovative technologies to commercial markets. We found that this unusual approach affords an ideal climate for sustained growth. It allows us to raise the necessary capital for our diverse new ventures and provides a focus for the creative energies of individuals seeking to apply their ideas to the emerging needs of society. Over the past decade some of our spinout "offspring" have established spinout companies of their own, which we fondly refer to as our "grandchildren."

The evolution of Thermo Electron is perhaps the reflection of an idealized vision of my own life. In my "ideal life" I would first study physics in order to understand its fundamental laws. Then I would make a significant discovery that would lead to an invention, use that invention to start an enterprise, and build an organization that would become the world's largest technology-oriented corporation. And I would accomplish all this in, say, fifty years. Of course, Thermo Electron is not yet the world's largest technology company, but neither has it been fifty years.

I was born in Greece in 1927. Both my grandfathers were politicians, members of the Greek Parliament, and my father was the chief operating officer of the country's electric rail system. As far back as I can remember, I was fascinated with machines. At the age of seven, I "invented" an electric iron, hoping to replace the kind that my mother heated on the stove. Of course, I was disappointed to learn that someone else had already done this twenty years earlier. As a teenager during the Occupation of Greece in 1941, I spent a lot of time in the library reading about other countries. One thing that appealed greatly to me was America's unique quality of entrepreneurship. One of my idols was Thomas Edison. Although he had started General Electric, he lost control of it because of his poor business skills. I began to think seriously about becoming an inventor who would also be a good businessman. I do not pretend today to be as good an inventor as Edison, but I think that I have become a better businessman.

My first experience in combining technology with business came about as a result of the Occupation. The Germans manipulated our radios so that the only station we could receive was the one they used to broadcast their propaganda. They sealed the radios so that the setting could not be changed and inspected them every month; if the seal was tampered with, you were arrested and then sent to a concentration camp. And so the Germans unknowingly created a market for radios that were not sealed.

I started making radios in the basement of our house, giving transmitters to the underground and selling receivers to anyone who dared to buy them. My father did not find out about my "business" until after the war, and even then he nearly had a heart attack after learning about it. I do not consider the Occupation to be the worst years of my life even though many people, including my family, went hungry and lived in constant fear (dead bodies were found daily on our streets). Despite the hardships and the terror, there were some positive elements of the Occupation. One that really stands out is the way people came together. Because we all were "in the same boat," there was no longer any separation of classes by education, wealth, or social position.

---

One of my idols was Thomas Edison. Although he had started General Electric, he lost control of it because of his poor business skills. . . . I do not pretend today to be as good an inventor as Edison, but I think that I have become a better businessman.

---

Those were exciting times, despite the risks, and much that I learned has stayed with me. I think that perhaps the most important thing I learned was to ask myself, what is really going to be *needed* in this society? I knew that when the need is severe enough and arrives unexpectedly, there will be a great opportunity for someone to start a new enterprise. I believe that this is especially true with technology-based ventures. When the war ended, however, I learned another valuable lesson: even the most exciting markets can suddenly disappear. Similarly, even the hottest technologies will eventually be supplanted by more innovative ones.

After the war, I entered the Athens Polytechnic, which my father had attended and where some of my uncles served on the faculty. My original intent was to study electrical engineering, but I became intrigued with thermodynamics. Because I was unable to obtain answers to my questions about certain thermodynamic principles and theories, I decided in 1948 to come to the United States and study at the Massachusetts Institute of Technology (MIT), where I received both my BS and MS degrees. After serving in the U.S. Army, I returned to MIT to earn my doctorate in mechanical engineering, and in 1956 I was appointed an assistant professor.

However, it was still my dream to build an enterprise based on innovative technology. There is tremendous satisfaction in creating something that bears one's own personal imprint. That is why many of us have children, write books, make inventions, develop new scientific theories, and, of course, start our own companies. An important motivation for me is the competition that is involved. I really only enjoy playing tennis when I have a chance to beat my opponent. Competition, especially that which is inherent to business, is something from which I derive great satisfaction. There are people who are averse to risk, but I am not, provided the potential gains are worthwhile. Even if the probability of success for a particular new venture is small, it makes sense to pursue it if the rewards seem big enough. My idea for establishing a new company was to create a broad-based technology enterprise that would work simultaneously on a spectrum of promising innovations, each of which might involve significant risk. Of course, such a collection of fairly risky ventures has considerably less overall risk than does each of its parts.

In April of 1955, I joined my friend, Peter Nomikos, for dinner at the Harvard Business School, from which he was about to graduate. (I often ate dinner with him there; the food was better than at MIT.) For my doctoral thesis at MIT, I had invented a thermionic converter known as a thermoelectron engine, a compact and effective device for converting heat directly into electricity without any moving parts.

At dinner that evening, Peter and I spoke at length about our visions for the future. Eventually, we conceived the idea of forming a company to exploit my invention. My late uncle, Costas Platsis, and Peter's father were bridge partners, so we convinced Costas to lobby Peter's father on our behalf to raise some start-up money for us. In our initial business plan, we asked for $50,000 to build a prototype and achieve proof of principle. The money was granted with an ease that should have given us pause at the time. We learned much later, after Thermo Electron was already a huge success, that upon reading our proposal, and knowing nothing about thermionics, Peter's father had said to Costas: "Listen, Costas, I will give them the $50,000. They will lose it. Then George will go back to teaching at MIT and my son will concentrate on the family business. They will both benefit, and it will be a small price to pay for an important lesson."

The first thing I did was to build a working thermionic converter. Unfortunately, we have yet to find a commercial application for the device. Nevertheless, our research and development experience allowed us to pursue other ventures. We found clients who needed our knowledge of thermodynamics, who were willing to fund us with research contracts. Initially, our main customers were agencies of the federal government and some gas utility companies. To expand our market, we looked for emerging problems in society that might be solved through commercial applications of our growing expertise in thermodynamics and related technologies. We began developing products that could serve such markets and also bring us a healthy return on our R&D investments. Many of our people worked long hours to develop ideas that later became Thermo Electron product lines. In fact, some of our most important lines of business today grew out of those projects initiated in the early 1960s.

By 1966, our annual revenues had grown to about $2 million, and the following year we went public to raise capital for continued R&D and to set up operations for commercializing our first products. We also started acquiring companies that could speed the process of converting our technologies into products and bringing them to market. Some of our research contracts with gas utilities required that we commercialize the technology by a certain time or forfeit our patents and rights. Buying a company with established production facilities and marketing channels was often the only way to meet the deadline.

An example of how we tried to match the company's development efforts to meet the specific needs of society can be seen in our response to the Clean Air Act of 1970. That legislation required automobile manufacturers to limit the nitrogen oxide (NOx) emissions of their vehicles. The problem was that no practical instrument for measuring such pollutants existed at the time. We had been working on an automotive steam engine for the Ford Motor Company and were trying to convince Ford's engineers that our system had very low NOx emissions. In order to confirm our claims, Ford sent two of their employees to measure our engine's exhaust with a laboratory model of a new NOx instrument that could give instantaneous results. After seeing that prototype in action, we decided that it was something that everyone was going to need. When we asked about Ford's plan for this exciting technology, they indicated that they had offered it to the Beckman Corporation, then the world's leader in instruments, but Beckman believed that it would take two years to produce the new device. I told the people at Ford, "Give us an order and we will produce the instruments in three months." They thought I was crazy, but no one else had a device to meet their needs, so they gave us an order for twelve instruments. We succeeded in delivering the instruments in ninety days, and although these first NOx detectors were not perfect, they were the first on the scene. Shortly thereafter, the Environmental Protection Agency designated our technology as the standard to be used for all NOx measurements on automobile exhausts. Suddenly, automobile manufacturers from around the world sought us out. We did not need a marketing staff—just a telephone operator to take the orders. . . .

In developing our business plans for the 1980s, we expected to make major investments in energy conservation technologies. It was assumed that the price of oil would continue to rise for many years; there were even some predictions that by 1990 the price of oil would be $40 to $60 a barrel. In this environment, we planned to focus on developing and producing energy-efficient equipment. But by 1982, there was a major recession underway, and it hit hardest in the basic industries—from automobiles to steel to farm equipment. It created the rust belt. These were the industries that we had expected to be our prime customers for energy-efficient process equipment. At the same time, there was a glut of oil. Energy prices dropped dramatically, pulling the rug out from under industry's incentives to buy more efficient equipment. Almost overnight we found ourselves without a market—our customer base had simply disappeared.

Fortunately, we had simultaneously been working on a number of new ventures. More development was needed, however, before they could be marketed, and we had planned to invest our earnings in that development. This is how we operated—we always had new technologies in the pipeline so we would be able to create additional business ventures. The problem was that in 1982 our earnings dropped by a factor of three. We were suddenly faced with a tough choice: either stop development of any new ventures in order to economize, or wipe out our earnings entirely to pay for accelerated development of the new businesses. We chose the latter, which brought our earnings in 1983 to near zero. In order to minimize the impact of this decision on the price of our stock, we explained our situation to several Wall Street analysts. We told them that if we did nothing, our earnings would drop by 60 percent. If we economized, the drop might be limited to 40 percent. We explained, however, that we were going to spend all of our earnings to speed the development of new businesses. (Fortunately, Thermo Electron has always maintained enough cash to be able to buy our own stock at very low prices and sell later when the price recovers.)

We were at a crossroads in more ways than one. One of our concerns in the late 1970s, when we first created separate divisions, was how to reward the various entrepreneurial groups that were being formed. We tried paying cash bonuses, but basing rewards on short-term financial results cannot reflect the true value of what has been created. We decided that the most effective way of giving our managers incentives was through stock options. But giving options for the parent company to each of those entrepreneurial groups meant that the rewards would be the same regardless of whether any particular group was successful or not. Such options were not tied to specific achievements. So we decided that if we could have a stock price for each of the divisions, we would be able to develop our new enterprises using the same device that had originally built Thermo Electron.

We first put this theory to work by spinning out our artificial heart venture. The company had worked for several years on artificial heart research, with over $70 million of funding provided by the National Institutes of Health. (That is one of the advantages of working on socially important technologies—the government is often willing to subsidize their development.) In 1982, the government drastically cut funding for heart research, and we did not think that we would have a viable product for at least another decade. We needed to raise more capital to support further research on the artificial heart, but we were not sure that investors and analysts who followed the company's stock would understand the heart's potential. They often would say, "I hear you are working on artificial hearts. What does that have to do with energy?"

For these reasons we decided to sell stock in a newly created public subsidiary, Thermedics, Inc. I worried about selling off a core business, but Thermedics was small compared to the whole of Thermo Electron, and so in June 1983, we sold eighty thousand shares of Thermedics to a private venture capital firm for $8.00 a share. In August, we offered seven hundred thousand shares to the public at $9.50 a share. Thermo Electron retained 84 percent of Thermedics.

---

We always had new technologies in the pipeline so we would be able to create additional business ventures.

---

I prefer the word "spinout" to describe what we have been doing because the new companies are no longer divisions or subsidiaries, nor are they "spin-offs," which to me implies companies in which you sell your interest. Spinning out Thermedics not only created a new, smaller company, but also renewed Thermo Electron itself by launching a new venture rather than letting us rest on our laurels. And it gave our managers a chance to be entrepreneurs. We had found the way to give our top people a stake in the business that would directly reflect the value each one added to the company. It is better to let the market determine what value has been created because it provides a highly objective criterion based on real-world conditions. Also, there is a tremendous advantage in having entrepreneurs deal directly with shareholders.

There was also an unexpected dividend for Thermo Electron as a result of spinning out Thermedics: Now that this venture stood alone, investors could see its value as a "pure play." And Thermo Electron was valued even more since it was the majority stockholder in Thermedics. Thermo Electron stock went up, and this was a benefit of the spinout that we had not anticipated. Spinouts became the model for our development as a company throughout the 1980s and up to the present. Whenever a new venture reached a certain point of maturity—typically, when it had a strong management team with a good new idea and the capacity to grow at a compound annual rate of about 30 percent over a long period of time—we would spin it out as a publicly-owned company in which we retained the majority interest.

We even spun out the company's R&D core, which became ThermoTrex. We are now in the process of rebuilding the R&D center while managing ten highly successful public spinouts in which we hold majority stakes; several privately-held, majority-owned spinouts; and seven wholly owned subsidiaries. Currently, our biggest unit, Thermo Instrument Systems, with about $700 million in annual sales, is thinking very seriously of establishing spinouts of its own. I am encouraging them to go ahead.

The only way to obtain capital at a reasonable price in this country is to focus on the entrepreneurial inclinations of certain investors, people who are not interested in a huge conglomerate because they cannot get a feel for anything it does. We repackaged our equities so that investors can buy a piece of any promising technology that excites them. Thermo Electron has gone much further toward decentralization than any company I know. I think that setting up many of our divisions as publicly-owned organizations gives us a highly flexible and responsive structure. Managers of each subsidiary know that their actions will be scrutinized not only by corporate management but also by their own shareholders.

I firmly believe in the benefits of small enterprises. However, small companies standing alone have some big disadvantages—they usually do not have strong financial support, they often lack management know-how, and they do not have market leverage. At Thermo Electron, we have connected a set of small companies into a family that provides financial resources, management support, and strategic direction. At the same time, our companies are able to act independently and respond to the needs of their own customers and shareholders. It is the best of both worlds.

Our companies are autonomous, yet together they actually comprise the larger entity that is Thermo Electron.

There is a core in the sense that our experience and our strong finances originate from the parent company, which can raise capital and consolidate legal and administrative services. We also generate new ideas there and manage businesses that have yet to be spun out. The strategy is central, the financial resources are central, and all the administrative services—from the legal department to the human resources department—are central. The spinouts are implementors of whatever strategy is agreed upon by the parent company.

---

Nobody ever has to leave Thermo Electron to become a great start-up success; they can start their own companies right here.

---

Thermo Electron is now more like an American *keiretsu* than a conglomerate. This is not a coincidence. In studying the advantage that the Japanese have in the cost of capital, I attributed a good deal of that advantage to their *keiretsu* system. When I first presented the spinout strategy to our board, I said, "What we want to do is to build an American *keiretsu.*" Still, there are differences. Our companies are a lot closer than the companies in a *keiretsu.* We transfer employees from one company to another when it is agreed upon by both sides, and there is much more interaction among our companies. We share the same kinds of technologies—energy and instrumentation are the primary foundations upon which virtually all of our businesses have been built.

I do not think that any other large American companies have yet mastered the ability to create new businesses. There are companies that add or buy new businesses, but they do not create them from within. I think our approach represents a way for American companies to become incubators of new business. Traditionally, most new businesses are generated by venture capital, by individuals. That is how *we* started, along with Digital, Polaroid, Data General, Lotus, Apple, and even Hewlett-Packard. All of these companies began as new ventures, where a group of entrepreneurs got together to launch some start-up companies. But none of them were able to duplicate their original success after they grew. Thermo Electron has developed a technique that sustains the entrepreneurial culture. Our growth is driven by inventing new technologies as the need arises, and we do not get into ventures where we do not understand the technology. Our structure provides one-stop shopping for entrepreneurs. Nobody ever has to leave Thermo Electron to become a great start-up success; they can start their own companies right here.

---

I do not think that any other large American companies have yet mastered the ability to create new businesses. There are companies that add or buy new businesses, but they do not create them from within.

---

Thermo Electron's success story probably could not have happened anywhere but in America. I think this country has tremendous competitive advantages but they are not being fully utilized. Many great innovations, for example, originated in the United States but were first commercialized overseas. In the past, Japan has often picked up on our breakthroughs and exploited them in world markets. America's primary advantage, I believe, is the entrepreneurial spirit that pervades our society. Being an entrepreneur is part of the American dream, and that is why we are the only country that has continually created new businesses and industries from scratch. In Massachusetts, for example, the majority of the state's successful companies were started after World War II. In Europe, by contrast, today's top-ranking companies are the same ones that dominated industry before the war. Start-up businesses in America derive great benefit from this country's appetite for exciting new ventures. Venture capital for risky investments is much more readily available here than in other countries. Moreover, our vigorous stock market affords the opportunity to recoup successful investments through initial public stock offerings. The same kind of financial market flexibility and diversity is not available to newly created businesses overseas.

A key question facing America's managers is how to preserve an entrepreneurial climate as companies grow larger. At Thermo Electron, we have found that the spinout approach provides at least part of the answer. Perhaps other companies will wish to adopt similar strategies. I am convinced that only those companies that can continually renew themselves by spawning new businesses will have a chance to go on indefinitely. There are still questions to be answered, and Thermo Electron should be viewed as a "work in progress." We are able to hold our family of companies together now because we all grew up together. Few people who start their careers at Thermo Electron go elsewhere. How will the next generation keep our growing number of businesses working closely after this group retires? When the company becomes very large—say ten times today's size—will they still be able to strike an effective balance between autonomy of operations and close coordination of major strategic decisions? The challenge, not only for Thermo Electron but for American industry at large, is learning how best to capitalize on this country's unique competitive advantages. If we can do this, I am confident that the United States will remain the industrial powerhouse that it has always been.

1996

# PART VIII

# Reengineering and Transformation

Michael Hammer and James Champy's 1993 book, *Reengineering the Corporation*, both diagnosed and perpetuated Corporate America's desire to become more competitive and profitable. John E. Martin, now retired CEO of Taco Bell and highlighted in that book, explains how he changed the company from a "command-and-control" organization into a devoutly customer-focused company. He also acknowledges that change has its enemies and can be painful. The desire for transformation to improve competitiveness is not new, of course. Thomas Watson, Jr., the legendary leader of IBM, had to constantly adapt to rapidly changing technology and changing customer demands. To ease the pain, he preached that "cooperation must outrank self-interest." Also, while structure and goals may change, Watson demanded that the core beliefs, or a philosophy for doing business, must remain strong throughout; otherwise, the company spirit will be killed. Part VIII is about corporate renewal as the evolution of the organization pushes forward.

# GORDON BETHUNE

Gordon Bethune saved the fifth-largest airline in the United States from bankruptcy, turned it around, and three years later had the satisfaction of seeing it named Airline of the Year by *Air Transport World*. When he took over as CEO of Continental Airlines in 1994, the company had been through 10 CEOs and 2 bankruptcies in the last 12 years. One big reason for his success: He had learned the business from the ground up. His father was a crop duster and young Bethune's first job was helping him; for example, he was in charge of lighting the runway with their old car's headlights so his father could land after a long day.

At age 17 and not yet finished with high school, Bethune joined the navy to escape school and boredom. He became a petty officer and found himself supervising eight other men, maintaining airplanes. From his own experience as a mechanic, he knew that "what they want more than anything else is to be left alone to fix things—unless they have a problem, and then they want you to help them solve that." During a stint in Florida in 1965, he finished high school, but college had to wait until he left the navy in the late 1970s and enrolled at Texas A&M. An old navy pal recruited him to join Braniff Airlines as an engine repair manager in 1979. Deregulation had been instituted the year before, and Bethune discovered a company that couldn't adjust to competition.

Over the next few years, he moved through several companies while moving up through the ranks on the operational side, and he also learned to fly. More important, Bethune was learning the airline business from all sides soon he could talk the language of the pilots, the mechanics, and the customers. "As I once told Al Gore in a meeting, it kind of helps to know how a watch works before you try to fix it," he reflected. His varied experience, from helping his dad to witnessing Braniff's struggles, has given him what it takes to boldly wrestle with problems and make business more predictable (such as landing on time). Part of the solution involved burning the employee manual, which he describes in *From Worst to First*.

# From Worst to First
## *Gordon Bethune*

L/et me tell you the story of the ambulance in the valley. There's a little town, and it's about halfway up a mountain in a bend in the road. That hairpin turn is a terrible hazard, and, about once a month, cars go flying off into the valley below. It's awful.

The town council gets together and they look into how much it's going to cost to regrade the road, put in signs, and install a guard rail—in other words, make the thing safe. Well, it's going to be really expensive. In fact, it's going to be so expensive that they decide they just can't afford it. But the cars are still flying off the road and people are getting hurt. They don't like that, and they want to do something, so they solve the problem of the dangerous road in what they believed was a less expensive way.

They put an ambulance in the valley.

It's a great story because it shows how hard people will work to avoid solving their real problem. At Continental before I came here, that kind of thinking was a way of life. The philosophy was that you couldn't solve a problem because it was too expensive to do what would solve the problem.

You know what? If you're asking how much it costs to solve a problem, you'd better ask the other question I've mentioned. You may say it's too expensive to fix the road. But you have to ask the other question: What does it cost *not* to fix it?

When we're talking about the core product of our airline, that question is central. At Continental, I guess I'm the guy who finally said, "You know what? It's *dumb* to put the ambulance in the valley. We gotta fix the road no matter what it costs, and that's all there is to it."

---

People will work to avoid solving their real problem. At Continental before I came here, that kind of thinking was a way of life.

---

That's the difference between success and failure at Continental Airlines. We finally understand that it's dumb to put the ambulance in the valley. The whole point of a road is that you can drive somewhere on it and get there safely. If not, you can put an ambulance wherever you want to, you can put up billboards, and you can talk nice about the road, but it's still going to be a lousy, unreliable road—and sooner or later people are going to stop driving on it.

That's sort of where Continental was: It had become a lousy, unreliable airline and people had stopped using us and for good reason. An airline has no real value at all unless it's predictable and reliable, but for a decade Continental had been cutting costs so much that it not only wasn't improving the road, it had even stopped putting the ambulance in the valley.

So I started asking that question all the time. We know what it costs to do something—get the planes cleaned more often, paint them, hire an extra person to service the engines 10 minutes faster so we can schedule planes to fly when people want them to fly. Those things cost money, and there are always good reasons to avoid doing something that costs money. But what was it costing us not to do those things?

The answer was, it was costing us our business. We had

cut costs so much that we simply had nothing to offer anymore. Our service was lousy, and nobody knew when a
plane might land. We were unpredictable and unreliable,
and when you're an airline, where does that leave you?

It leaves you with a lot of empty planes. You know the
way customers fill stores to buy really crappy products? The
way people line up to see a lousy movie? The way you hurry
to a new restaurant with terrible food and bad service for an
expensive dinner? Well, that's exactly the way people were
lining up to buy Continental Airline tickets. They weren't.
We had a lousy product, and nobody particularly wanted to
buy it. You can't blame them.

*I don't know of any successful company that doesn't have a good
product.* So while we were fixing the marketing, placement,
and organization of our product with Fly to Win, and solving our financial crisis and planning for the future with Fund
the Future, we had to do something even more important.
We had to fix our product.

---

## We had cut costs so much that we simply had nothing to offer anymore.

---

Continental was a terrible airline. For the better part of a
decade, people had said it would cost too much to do things
that would make Continental better. What are the fundamentals of running an airline? Reaching destinations on
time. Being clean, safe, and reliable. To succeed, an airline
has to be good at those things. Until it is, nothing else works.
It's like the pizza—if you want to sell pizza, sooner or later
you're going to have to make a good pizza, with tomato
sauce, and crust. You can have fast delivery, pretty napkins,
and real low prices, but if you don't do that basic pizza stuff,
you can forget the whole thing.

We were an airline. We needed to be clean, safe, and reliable. We needed to operate our planes on time.

## JUST BE ON TIME

Every month the U.S. Department of Transportation measures large airlines according to on-time arrival percentage, lost-baggage claims, complaints received, and number of passengers involuntarily denied boarding.

All of those are important, but we figured out that the most important thing to passengers was getting where they were supposed to get on time. Any survey of airline passengers will tell you that. In fact, the 1997 J.D. Power and Associates Airline Customer Satisfaction Study showed that on-time performance was 22 percent of what determined customer satisfaction. No other single element was judged higher than 15 percent. I've already mentioned that you have to gauge the success of your product by whether it gives your customers what they want. When we chose being on-time as our most important goal at Continental, we were simply choosing what our customers wanted.

Thus, we chose on-time percentage as our macro metric—our basic indicator of whether we were doing well. Don't forget, Continental had been doing terribly for a decade. But we decided that what we were going to do was get our airplanes to land on time.

So we did one more thing.

## WHAT YOU MEASURE AND REWARD
## IS WHAT YOU GET

We told our employees that if our planes landed on time, as our customers desired, we'd pay them extra. Specifically, we told them that every month our on-time percentage was good enough for us to be in the top five nationwide—again, according to those Department of Transportation numbers—every employee would get $65 extra. If the customers won, the employees would win.

Pretty simple, yes? But it was just another one of those things that used to be too expensive at Continental. We couldn't afford to pay employees to make it worth their while to get their jobs done. So we didn't — and they didn't.

## SAVING $5 MILLION BY SPENDING $2.5 MILLION

I've emphasized that what you measure and reward is what you get. Put another way, what gets measured is what gets managed. It's simple: You measure the results you want, and you reward those results. To get Continental to perform better, we were going to have to both measure what we wanted people to do and then reward them for doing it.

---

I've emphasized that what you measure and reward is what you get.

---

So we said to our employees: Get us there on time and it's worth $65 to you — to *each* of you. Don't, and you don't get the dough — none of you. That's all or nobody — we win or lose as a team. Meet the goal and every single employee gets money. Although the pilots operated under their own union contract, this included every other employee — the gate agents, the flight attendants, the baggage handlers, the secretaries, the reservation agents. Every employee got $65 dollars. Simple as that.

Multiply $65 by 40,000 employees (fewer, actually, because we didn't include managers, who had their own bonus plans) and you've got around $2.5 million. Continental was going broke, and I decided to start giving employees an extra $2.5 million per month.

Where we got the figure of $65 is also simple. By being late, we ended up spending a lot of money. Late planes miss connections, which means passengers hang around airports, sometimes even overnight. You have to feed them. Sometimes you have to house them overnight. Sometimes you have to put them on other airlines to get them where you promised to get them.

We took a look at how much we were spending each month on costs associated with being late, and we determined that it was about $5 million dollars. That's $5 million that we were spending every month because we couldn't get our planes in on time. We figured we could take half that and give it right back to our employees if they were on time. Then if it worked, we'd actually be saving money—plus we'd have a product that people might actually want to buy.

This underscores what I said about the ambulance in the valley. It was going to cost us $2.5 million to pay an extra $65 a month to every employee, but an even more important issue was what it would cost us *not* to pay them that. The answer was $5 million or even more—possibly our business. In other words, we were going to save money by spending money—or, as we've learned, save money by motivating our employees to do whatever it takes to succeed.

## YOUR CHECK IS IN THE MAIL— AND IT REALLY WAS!

You don't need me to tell you that it worked, but let me tell you:

It worked.

We announced the new program in January 1995. I'm not sure that every employee truly understood it, and I'm not sure that everyone who understood it believed that anything good would come of it. Remember, these employees didn't trust us, and after the previous decade it was hard to blame them for that. That was one of the reasons we had chosen

Department of Transportation numbers for our goals—in the past, anything to avoid paying promised pay was something employees would have expected from management. Until we re-earned their trust, at least nobody could accuse us of altering numbers supplied by the government.

However, it seemed as if employees gave us the benefit of the doubt right off the bat, because in January 1995, 71 percent of our planes landed on time. That wasn't perfect by any means—we ranked seventh among the top 10 airlines—but it was a lot better than January 1994, when we brought in only 61 percent of our flights on time and came in last. It was a start. We let the employees know we appreciated that and reminded them that if they did better, there was $65 in it for them.

In February 1995, 80 percent of our flights landed on time. That put us in fourth place—and, for the first time in years, better than the industry average of 79 percent.

Fourth. That's top five, and you know what that meant: Checks worth more than $2.5 million went out to our employees.

Please take note of that. We didn't just drop $65 extra dollars into their paychecks and have the whole impact of their bonus disappear. Nor did we let them start calculating how much of it they lost to taxes. We gave each employee $65 in a special check—we took the withholding out of their regular paychecks, so they got $65 actual dollars.

It was exciting to walk the halls during early March, when employees were buzzing about the $65 in what seemed to them to be found money. You would hear stories—one woman wasn't going to tell her husband she got the check, so she could use the $65 of extra-budget money for something special for herself; another employee used the $65 to celebrate by letting his children choose whatever sugary cereal they wanted when they went grocery shopping. For people on tight budgets—and Continental employees were definitely among them, though they've certainly made strides since then—$65 was something.

Do you think they noticed? Well, in March we ranked first. More than 83 percent of our planes landed on time, and nobody did better than that. We were in first place—for the first time in our entire history. They got $65 more.

That said, what did we do to get our planes on time? Yes, it's great that we showed our employees that if they got those planes in on time we'd pay them extra money. That gives them incentive. But surely before we instituted the incentives, our employees weren't getting up in the morning and saying, "What the heck, I'm going to work but who cares whether I do any work today." We couldn't presume that just tossing a little money at them was going to suddenly fix what was wrong. Money could get their attention, but we didn't think it was just lack of money that had been causing our operation to stink.

We burned the employee manual. That's one of the most important things we did, and it had a profound effect on the reliability and predictability of our airline.

Under the old style of management, as symbolized by that authoritarian manual, employees were limited on every side. A passenger with an unusual situation was a dangerous character to be avoided, not a challenge to be resolved. No matter what employees did, the manual probably told them it was wrong—and if the manual didn't, one of their perpetually annoyed supervisors in our generally cranky airline surely would.

Here's an example. We used to have what were called Add-a-Penny-Add-a-Pal fares—you'd buy one ticket at full fare and someone would fly free along with you. Say you're flying with your husband on a companion fare to your daughter's wedding in Chicago. However, there's a problem with the plane, and your flight is canceled. We're going to put you on another flight to Chicago, on another airline. The old manual was crystal clear about procedure in this situation: We put people paying full fares on other airlines; people flying free or paying other special fares had to wait for the next Continental flight. There's no room for interpretation: Mrs. Smith, your flight leaves in 20 minutes, sorry for the trouble, and have a nice flight with our competitor. Mr. Smith? Not so fast—you'll be going out five hours from now.

That's World War III right there in the airport, and if you're Continental's gate agent, you're not any happier than the Smiths. You know it's a stupid policy, but you know that at the old Continental Airlines we followed rules and that was that. So you had a choice: You could take the heat from the Smiths and hate it, or you could break the rule—and maybe lose your job.

---

## We don't want robots, we want team members.

---

Not any more. With the symbolic burning of the manual, we changed that. We set up a committee to reorganize and rewrite that manual. And we don't call it a manual any more, we call it guidelines. The new guidelines are supposed to help employees solve problems—give them a sense of where the boundaries are when they run into trouble. But in the general pursuit of their jobs, we want them to use their heads and use their resources. We don't want robots, we want team members.

Now the guidelines say, for example, that if someone is flying on a special fare or a free fare, we'll try to put them on the next Continental flight, because that makes sense. But if you find yourself in the middle of something complicated, something unusual, something that just doesn't fit, then you use your head and make the best decision that you can. Do what's best for the customer and the airline. Not one or the other—use your head and do what's best for both the customer and the airline.

We want employees to use their judgment. And to be honest, this scared some of our managers to death. "They're going to be giving away the store!" was the basic fear. And there was some grounding to that fear. When you've got irate customers yelling at you in an airport, it may be tempting for an employee to just give them what they want—whatever they want—to make them stop yelling, especially when Continental management has made clear that *we* want to stop yelling, too. Some managers feared that whatever the problems were, employees would solve them by spending money—giving away fares, buying new parts when old ones could be fixed. Given free rein, what would our employees do?

---

We burned the employee manual. That's one of the most important things we did, and it had a profound effect on the reliability and predictability of our airline.

---

I didn't worry. Sure, I figured, 5 percent or so will run wild, take advantage, screw this up. But the other 95 percent are people who probably will be so glad for the opportunity to do their jobs that they'll easily manage the balancing act between the good of the airline and the good of the customer. Then we can let our entire management team worry about managing only 5 percent of our employees, because the other 95 percent will basically be managing themselves.

---

We want employees to use their judgment. And to be honest, this scared some of our managers to death.

---

It's worth making one more point about the employees giving away the store. Once we started making profits, we started writing profit-sharing checks. Each year, around Valentine's Day, 15 percent of our pre-tax profits are distributed to our employees. Therefore, it's their own money they'd be giving away.

Let me tell you, they think twice. And our success shows that I was right. The combination of the freedom to do their jobs and the incentive to get results was the recipe for a miracle.

1998

# STANLEY GAULT

When Stanley Gault accepted the job as CEO and chairman of Goodyear Tire & Rubber, friends told him he was crazy. At age 66, he had nothing else to prove and everything to lose—the ailing company was $3.8 billion in debt, with a dire 70 percent debt-to-equity ratio. However, Gault wanted a shot at turning around the last American-owned major tire company. To symbolize his plans to reinvigorate the company, he had the traditional silver and black colors on its renowned blimps changed to blue and gold. One disturbed employee wrote, "Who the hell do you think you are, changing things that have been that way since 1927?" Gault fired back, "Just who do you think I have to be?"

Gault, born in Ohio, has been many things during his long career. After graduating from the College of Wooster in 1948, he spent the next 31 years toiling at General Electric and rose to the position of senior vice president. He left when Jack Welch became the heir apparent and then spent the next 11 years transforming Rubbermaid into a highly competitive company. While there, he replaced or removed 170 of 172 managers. He retired in 1991, but for only three weeks—Goodyear's board convinced him to take the job. Cynicism was running high among employees—he was the third CEO in four years—but Gault immediately set a new tone (e.g., the blimp repainting).

His number-one priority was reducing the debt, and in less than three years Gault cut it by half. But it took more than just reducing debt to turn the company around: "We've also transformed ourselves from a manufacturing-based company to a marketing-based, customer-oriented enterprise." Instead of the engineers dictating new products as they had in the past, the company now relied on market research. Gault would even take his two grown sons to competitors' parking lots, where they'd ask customers why they had bought the tires they did. Another cultural change was treating even the truck drivers as equals, which Gault describes in *No One Excluded*. He opens his essay by explaining why, after having proven himself at Rubbermaid, he would take on the risky challenge of trying to save Goodyear and become a prime candidate for a Maalox moment.

# No One Excluded
## *Stanley Gault*

People would say, "Why would you undertake this challenge?" Well, frankly, the decision was 98 percent emotional because Goodyear is the last major American-owned tire company. All the other brands, with the exception of a much smaller Cooper, are now owned by foreign companies, and they will never return to this country. Therefore, I decided that I was willing to change my life for three years if there was any way I could lead the charge to rebuild Goodyear. It was mentioned to me more than once that I was a prime candidate for the Maalox moment.

We needed a tremendous cultural change involving everyone in the organization. You have to do many things simultaneously. When you're in this kind of jam, time is not on your side. After I was there about 30 days, I thought I owed it to our people to develop the future objectives for the corporation. For lack of a better title, I wrote "The 12 Objectives for Managing Goodyear Successfully in the '90s." They include having a leadership position in costs, quality, customer service, and innovation. We used film and television around the world. I presented and explained the objectives to all our people. I wanted everyone in the organization to know why these were our objectives, what they meant to each individual position, and how everyone fit into the picture—with no one excluded.

At the same time we discontinued using the word "employee," and we instituted the word "associate" because that was a leveling action. Regardless of your station in the organization, you are an associate. It is particularly important to women and minorities because they feel that the word "employee" means you work for someone. Well, we don't work for each other, we work with each other.

---

I decided that I was willing to change my life for three years if there was any way I could lead the charge to rebuild Goodyear. It was mentioned to me more than once that I was a prime candidate for the Maalox moment.

---

To show you how deeply this word "associate" touches, let me tell you what happened at a meeting of our people. Three or four black associates came up to me—they happened to be all males—and one of them, quite embarrassed, said hesitantly, "Does the word 'associate' apply to me?" Well, I tell you, that really grabs you, doesn't it, when this guy with 35 years of service—and that's how long he had—comes up and says that. He wanted to know, because he was black and worked down in the mill, if the word "associate" applied to him. Well, I told him very quickly where we stood on this word "associate" applying to everybody, his job and my job alike. I made it a point within the next month to go down in the area where he was working to see my new associate down there. With a grapevine like Goodyear has, that was around the world in the next 60 seconds with electronic mail.

The same spirit applies to union relationships. Just before I went to Goodyear, a three-year contract had been formalized by the entire industry. I met with the president of the union and his staff. I respect him. He's a capable, intelligent gentleman. I told him I wanted him to know exactly where I stood, that the settlement they made was unaffordable and we couldn't live with it as such. Therefore, I needed his involvement and support to see if we couldn't work together to bring about productivity improvements to offset the wage increases. We appreciate that we do have our individual responsibilities, but we have a collective responsibility, and that is to his members and to our associates. We have people whose jobs we want to protect in this country and in this company.

---

We discontinued using the word "employee," and we instituted the word "associate" because that was a leveling action.

---

Back at Rubbermaid we had a union at our Wooster, Ohio, headquarters. One day an associate, a union member who drove one of our big over-the-road trucks, said he had heard that my door was never closed and asked if that applied to him. I said, "Sure, when are you going to be around?" He said, "Well, I'm coming into town next Thursday morning. I'll be there at seven." I said, "What time do you really get in?" He said, "Well, I ought to roll in about 5:30." I said, "I'll meet you here at six and I'll make the coffee. I'll be waiting for you."

---

For lack of a better title, I wrote "The 12 Objectives for Managing Goodyear Successfully in the '90s." They include having a leadership position in costs, quality, customer service, and innovation.

---

So he came in. He must have run that rig wide open all night because he was freshly shaved and his hair was still damp. He had been home and showered and had changed clothes. I think he was surprised to see me there. We had a good chat, and he told me some things that were bothering him. One item dealt with backing up trailers at night. We usually had 300 or 400 trailers on a lot. Backing up these rigs at two or three in the morning without proper lighting could possibly pin someone against a trailer or a building. Obviously, I was very interested in that.

---

## We don't work for each other, we work with each other.

---

Another point was that some of the cabs were too old. That following Sunday I went out early in the morning, and I went in every cab we had. Some had 500,000 or 600,000 miles on them, and some had rusty floorboards. I don't want any driver in those kinds of cabs. So I raised hell with our people the following morning. I want those cabs traded, and I want the guys who drive them involved in selecting the vendor. Boy, did that go through the system like wildfire.

After listening to him review his list of topics, I said "Now, I want to share something with you. Together, we have this golden goose here at Rubbermaid, and we don't want anything to screw it up. That means the Rubbermaid family comes first." And did I ever strike a nerve. He looked at me somewhat startled, and I said, "It has to be that way, and you know it. You don't have to acknowledge it to me, but we all have to understand it."

Well, he went back over to the motor pool where all his buddies were waiting because they knew damn well I wouldn't see him that morning. He went over with his list. He said, "I sat down with him in his office. He served me coffee. He took the time for me to go through everything on my list."

414

Well, talk about relationships. We got to be such buddies that I had to be careful when I walked out of the office at night, because I worked long hours and many times I'd be going out to get in my car in the dark, and one of those big rigs would be arriving. The driver could see me, but I couldn't see the driver. I'll tell you, when they get within 50 feet and let that air horn go, it will lift you off the ground. That was their way of saying to you, "He's our friend, and we're all in this together." And we were.

1992

# MARY KAY ASH

Just a month before Mary Kay Cosmetics was to open in 1963, Mary Kay Ash's husband and partner had a fatal heart attack, and all seemed lost. Both Ash's accountant and lawyer advised her to liquidate and cut losses, but she couldn't give up her dream. She was used to toughing it out. When she was growing up in Texas, her father had suffered from tuberculosis and her mother had to support the family. Subsequently, she was required to do more than her share of household chores. When Mary Kay felt overwhelmed, her mother encouraged her with the mantra: "You can do it." In her 1981 autobiography, Ash reflected, "The confidence my mother instilled in me has been a tremendous help."

The impetus to start her own company occurred after 11 years as a sales representative for Stanley Home Products. She quit when a male assistant, who'd been with the company less than two years, was appointed her boss. Not only did Ash open her company on time in 1963, but she went on to build one of the largest direct-sales cosmetics firms in the United States. The women that make up her unique sales force hold in-home "beauty shows" for a half-dozen or so customers. They take a soft-sales approach philosophy, according to Ash, who notes that "we don't sell—we teach." If the customer shows interest, the sales rep is fully prepared to quickly close the sale.

Sales reps are also expected to recruit other reps, and once they do, they then move up the totem pole of command. The formula has been a rousing success, and the company went public in 1968. (In 1985, Ash reacquired the company via a leveraged buyout.) Keeping her people motivated is critical, and she has always been sensitive to her relationship with employees: "Many managers make the mistake of creating a boss-employee relationship between themselves and their people—like student to teacher," she says. Effective communication, according to Ash, is the key to a good rapport; however, when it comes to change, she acknowledges that people will always resist it. Her solution reflects the title of her essay, *People Will Support that Which They Help Create.* Even if it's time-consuming and results in delays, she writes, get your people involved.

# People Will Support That Which They Help Create
## *Mary Kay Ash*

We resist change, even when we are unhappy with the old way of doing things. I've seen people complain vigorously about an old system yet speak out strongly against any recommendation for improvement. After all, change does require people to act—to make adjustments—to do something differently. For many it's much easier to go along with the status quo.

When change is necessary, the way in which you present your case can make a world of difference in the kind of reaction that results. By involving others in the decision—by listening—you can not only avoid bruising egos, but you can raise their levels of self-esteem as well.

However, there is a downside to personnel involvement. The more people who are consulted, the greater the chance that confidential information may be disseminated outside your organization. Increasing the number of those involved is also more time-consuming, so implementation of the change may be delayed. Despite these risks, there is an enormous trade-off in high morale. I think it's of such importance to get people involved in those things that directly affect them that I've always been willing to take the gamble. If you want the full support of your people, you must get them into the act. The sooner the better.

## PEOPLE NATURALLY RESIST CHANGE

I worked for a company whose owner decided to revise the commission schedule paid to his sales managers. All brochures and company literature were changed accordingly. He then made plans for personally announcing the changes during a series of regional sales conferences. I accompanied him to the first conference. I'll never forget it.

---

We resist change, even when we are unhappy
with the old way of doing things. . . . For many
it's much easier to go along with the status quo.

---

To an audience of fifty sales managers he announced that the 2 percent override they were presently earning on their units' sales production was to be reduced to 1 percent. "However," he said, "in lieu of that 1 percent, you will receive a very nice gift for each new person you recruit and train." With that, he lifted a white tablecloth that had been covering a few small appliances such as clock-radios and tape recorders. "You can choose any one of these," he continued, "and the more salespeople you train for the company, the more valuable gifts you will receive."

At that point a sales manager stood up and let him have it with both barrels. She was absolutely furious. "How dare you do this to us? Why, even 2 percent wasn't enough. But cutting our overrides in half and offering us a crummy gift for appeasement insults our intelligence." With that she stormed out of the room. And every other sales manager for that state followed her—all fifty of them. In one fell swoop the owner had lost his entire sales organization in that region—the best in the country. I had never seen such an overwhelming rejection of a change of this kind in my entire life!

The conference had begun on a Friday and was scheduled to last through the weekend. Instead the owner flew back to Texas Saturday morning. Over the weekend he ordered reprints of the sales literature, thus restoring the original 2 percent override. On Monday we attended the next scheduled conference as if nothing had happened. But the sales organization in that region was gone—and not a single one of them ever came back!

---

If you want the full support of your people, you must get them into the act. The sooner the better.

---

That blunder taught me an invaluable lesson about change and how people resist it! People don't like giving up what they've already got. But there is also a more fundamental resistance toward action of *any* kind. Resisting change simply because it's new and different seems to be a natural human response. We become complacent all too easily, and thus change requires a conscious effort.

Some book and record clubs have thrived on the fact that most people avoid taking action. Every month these clubs send their members a card that must be returned if the member does not want to make a purchase. In other words, they have to take action *in order not to buy!* It's called the "negative option." It's easier to buy than to make a decision not to buy.

## SEEK SUPPORT FROM ALL THOSE AFFECTED

A classic example of how people resist even a change for the better occurred when we recently revised the structure of our sales organization. Briefly, we elevated the status of a team leader (an intermediate position between beauty consultant and sales director) by increasing her rate of commission. In addition, upon reaching a certain plateau in sales volume she became eligible to receive a bonus: a VIP (Very Important Performer) automobile. This car is lower-priced than the one available to our sales directors. But both the car and the team leader's new status would have provided excellent incentives for those women who perform well at a mid-managerial level and for those who work with us in a part-time capacity.

There was no question that the team leaders would welcome the new policy. Likewise we anticipated a positive reception from the sales directors, because when their team leaders are motivated to increase sales, the sales directors also profit. (Let me add that the increased commissions and car bonuses would be at company expense.) How could anyone in the field *not* be ecstatic over those changes?

---

Perhaps the best way to introduce change in a company is to keep one foot firmly planted on fundamentals and the other foot searching for better ways to streamline operations.

---

Yet there was resistance! We first presented the new program at a leadership conference held in Dallas. But by the time we were able to relay the plan to the other regions of the country, "the grapevine" had carried misinformation to several sales directors. They feared that by expanding the team leader's position we were diminishing the role of the sales director. Once we met with them and clarified the program, however, it was enthusiastically received. People will support that which they help to create. Keep this in mind whenever you propose changing the status quo. In this case we had worked very closely with our *National* Sales Directors, but we had not included those middle managers who felt threatened by the change.

I suppose an alternative to making important announcements of change at separate leadership conferences could have been to simultaneously make these presentations "live" (via satellite and closed-circuit television) in theaters and auditoriums across the country.

At Mary Kay Cosmetics we want our people's ideas. We encourage them and openly solicit them. Their participation is vital to our growth and health. The more that people are permitted to participate in a new project, the more they'll support it. Conversely, the more they are excluded, the more they will resist it.

Perhaps the best way to introduce change in a company is to keep one foot firmly planted on fundamentals and the other foot searching for better ways to streamline operations. While it's vital to examine potential changes carefully, in the majority of cases you should *stick to the basics*. In our business, we've developed many complementary cosmetics items, including blushers and lip liner pencils in the latest colors and shades. But we always remember that our strongest suit is skin care—not high-fashion cosmetics. Currently we're in a consolidation period, telling our people, "Let's get back to basics." I think this is an important message for all managers. Though every company must be innovative, no company dare allow its foundation to crumble in hurried attempts to adapt to change.

1984

# DAVID ROCKEFELLER
## 1915–

David Rockefeller, grandson of the great John D., was raised in a protective environment that included armed guards around the clock. Among the opulence, the future chairman of Chase Bank managed to learn the value of money from his father, John D., Jr., who said, "I was always so afraid that money would spoil my children, and I wanted them to know its values and not waste it or throw it away on things that weren't worthwhile." Consequently, he made young David keep a ledger book for tracking his spending money and fined him a nickel for any inconsistencies or errors in the entries. Rockefeller emerged from childhood amazingly well-adjusted. Unlike his siblings, who chose to work for one of the family's trusts or foundations, Rockefeller prided himself on taking a real job with Chase and riding the subway to work.

Rockefeller started with Chase in 1946 as an assistant manager in the foreign department, and within two years he was a second vice president for Latin America. Although his family controlled the bank, Rockefeller was not made president until 1960. Under Rockefeller's leadership, Chase expanded rapidly around the world and for some time was the most powerful bank anywhere. Rockefeller, however, was not a flamboyant, globe-trotting executive.

One unusual characteristic: Rockefeller was an avid beetle collector and compiled one of the best collections. This hobby, while quirky, exemplifies his humanistic approach to life. In a 1964 speech, "The Challenge of Leisure," Rockefeller called for businesspeople to "recognize that the achievements of work are not isolated from the experiences of life." In particular, he believed in using leisure time to study and practice the arts, which would in turn help develop the individual's vision, imagination, and resourcefulness. Businesspeople could then better adapt to the swiftly changing environment. For Rockefeller, change is something to take advantage of, and creativity is the operative word. "Creative management, as I envisage it, is one that strives constantly to apply to all areas of a business the concepts of flexibility, receptivity, optism, courage, and social responsibility," he explains in the following selection.

# Managing Change Creatively
## *David Rockefeller*

Business can turn its back on change—and take the consequences.

Or it can manage change creatively—and take advantage of it.

Creative management, as I envisage it, is one that strives constantly to apply to all areas of a business the concepts of flexibility, receptivity, optimism, courage, and social responsibility. In terms of a company's internal environment, this means that management must devise policies to stimulate rather than stifle initiative, inventiveness, and innovation. In organization planning, it means greater emphasis on a structure conducive to individual development and improved communication as well as on new and improved administrative control tools. In personnel, it means a growing demand for broad-gauged individuals capable of independent, original, and critical thought. In operations, it means an up-to-date comprehensive systems approach to the workload. In policy-making, it means greater reliance on integrated, overall planning, particularly long-range planning.

In terms of management philosophy, it means taking cognizance of the fact that the production of goods and services is simply a means to an end. That end is, immediately, earning a profit which gives the enterprise its driving force; but, ultimately and more importantly, providing opportunity for every individual to live a life of dignity, freedom, and fulfillment.

A growing economy by itself is nothing. What is important is what growth and profit can make possible. Sometimes in the quest for private gain, this point is ignored or forgotten. But the ultimate reality on which business enterprise is based is the conversion of earnings into meaningful human advancement and satisfaction.

A creative management philosophy must be one which not only seeks through efficient operation to maximize profit, but which also recognizes its responsibility to render economic service — service by private enterprise to the public interest. The British statesman, Lord Halifax, liked to define service as "the rent we pay for our room on earth." In the case of business enterprises, this rent comes due not once a month but every day of the year. We can pay it by contributing, through creative management, to economic growth at home and abroad. . . .

Regardless of what changes lie ahead, business will always be heavily dependent on talented and creative people. The skills, desires, and ambitions of these people may change, but their contributions to the character, growth, and future of the business will become increasingly vital.

## ENVIRONMENT FOR CREATIVITY

For this reason, management must strive constantly to provide an environment conducive to creativity. Banks and industrial corporations do not innovate. People do. But they will propose new ideas only if they see that the rewards for being right are greater than the penalties for being wrong. They must be encouraged by a proper climate.

A good example of a creative environment was the one I was fortunate enough to experience on my first job. It was in the New York City Hall during Mayor Fiorello LaGuardia's administration. The Mayor was the nearest thing I have ever seen to perpetual motion. Yet busy as he was, he always had time to listen to a fresh idea. As he listened, he might nod, frown, chuckle, shrug, or grimace. But he would seldom reject anything out of hand. Moreover, he had an unusual ability to take a mediocre idea and turn it into something brightly original. He looked upon ideas with enthusiasm rather than suspicion, and this attitude encouraged even junior staff members like myself to speak up whenever we thought an idea had merit.

I remember one occasion on which the Mayor fired a subordinate because he felt the individual was not coming up with enough ideas. Instead of leaving, this fellow went back to his office and began furiously dictating memos. A week passed, then a month, still he heard nothing from Mr. LaGuardia. A persistent fellow, he kept putting his ideas in memo form. Finally, after three months, he received a terse note from the Mayor informing him of a salary increase!

In any organization, whether it be a municipal government, an industrial corporation, or a commercial bank, the manager inevitably sets the creative tone. If he lets it be known that he is receptive to ideas, then he is likely to get them. But this is something he must work at all the time, not on a now-and-then basis.

The manager must review his organization structure regularly to make sure it is not hampering but encouraging creativity and individual development. The difference between success and failure in business often depends on how well the organization brings out the talents of its people. Skillful management can make the work assignments a more satisfying experience for every employee, and at the same time tap the full measure of energy, knowledge, and creativity which he brings to the job.

1964

When Cathleen Black was recruited to become president of Hearst Magazines in January of 1996, the company was under fire—it had just announced advertising rate hikes and lower guaranteed circulation numbers, which needless to say, angered its customers, the advertisers. But Black was familiar with managing in a hostile environment. Back in the 1970s she had helped launch *Ms.*, a feminist magazine that created quite a stir. Black also helped launch another controversial project—*USA Today*, and became publisher. Her fellow newspaper publishers were so impressed that in 1991 she was named president and CEO of the Newspaper Association of America (NAA), a trade association battling to keep readership.

After a successful run at the NAA, Black was tapped for the presidency of Hearst Magazines, where she would oversee 13 publications, including *Cosmopolitan, Esquire, Good Housekeeping,* and *Harper's Bazaar.* She immediately supported the rate hikes and reduced circulation numbers and was not pleased that the competition "sided with the advertising community and hung us out to dry." For long-term financial health and survival of not just Hearst, but the industry, she believed the changes were necessary moves. Magazine competitors, however, love to go after each other. On top of the dog-eat-dog world of glitzy magazines, print media in general has been under attack for years, with readership being lured away first by cable television and now the Internet.

Part of Black's strategy for securing growth is brand-extension and developing multimedia spin-offs of the magazines. "Publishers, more and more, when they look at the kinds of titles they are stewards for, need to think about how to leverage the assets of what their brand stands for." For example, Hearst's *House Beautiful* magazine is now the brand name for house paint, a top seller at Wal-Mart. According to Black, everyone is in the brand-building business, and in *A Brand New Day in the Business World* she explains why every employee must understand his or her company's core identity. "The penalty for those who do not is irrelevancy. Or death," she writes.

# A Brand New Day
# in the Business World
## *Cathleen Black*

T he media world today is packed with predictions. Filled with self-assurance. Awash in new ideas. They may be contradictory, but they are nothing if not confident. "The Internet Is our future!" some of my colleagues and competitors maintain. "Stick to your knitting!" cry others.

For the rest of the nation, though, and that qualifies you, questions about Internet evolution, channel wars, mogul battles, and satellite insanity seem about as relevant as those ancient sectarian disputes. If and when you think of the media and communications, your minds are focused on the big issues: Are the media telling me the truth? Are these new information and entertainment options improving the quality of my life and the lives of my kids? Are they helping me convey the facts about my business to an engaged and aware audience?

These are some of the questions I've been asking myself since I took the helm of Hearst Magazines in January, 1996.

I get up each morning at about 5:30 with a mixture of exhilaration and panic, because one of the first things to pop into my head is: How many Americans will buy and read a Hearst magazine today? Because the fate of my one-thousand-four-hundred employees and our future business depends on how well we inform and entertain the sixty-five million Americans who read our publications.

I've got to tell you: the panic ends pretty quickly after that, because real life takes over. First, my husband, Tom Harvey (he's an attorney) and I have to get the kids ready for school. We have a nine-year-old son and a five-year-old daughter, so you know what that effort involves. Next, I try to work out, usually doing about three miles on a treadmill and read my three daily papers, *The New York Times*, *Wall Street Journal* and my alma mater, *USA Today*.

The first thing that greets me at the office are phone, fax and e-mail messages from my 32 editors and publishers. Their questions range from the qualitative to the financial. Can we get Oprah for the cover of *Good Housekeeping?* Is there too much cleavage on the new cover of *Cosmopolitan?* Can the editor have additional pages? Did the advertising material get here before we went to press?

The executive vice president and general manager, whose job is to keep the next quarter firmly under control, might come in to discuss print runs, the price of paper or which newsstand price test is working. That debate can be interrupted by a phone call from the chief executive of the corporation, who wants my opinion on whether a particular company that has just come up for sale would make a good strategic fit for the company overall. The president of our international division gives a progress report on the forthcoming launch of a Russian edition of *Marie Claire* and our three other Russian editions, *Cosmopolitan*, *Good Housekeeping* and *Harper's Bazaar.* Advertisers call too, from General Motors, to Ralph Lauren, to Procter & Gamble.

Now, some of you may be saying, "That's all very interesting, Cathie, but what does this have to do with me?" It has everything to do with you. Because you are both consumers and potential customers, and you and I, all of you and I, are, to an extent, in the same business. We are in the "brand" business. Our job is to build and market brands. "Uh-uh," some of you are probably thinking. "I'm a banker, a lawyer, a management consultant. I provide professional services to people." Well, you're in the brand business too. "Not me," some of you are still saying. "I own a chain of retails stores. I'm an auto dealer." Well, that's the brand business, as well.

It used to be easy to build a brand in the United States. If you were the first to develop a new product, get it out on the retail shelves, and advertise it in the newspaper, magazines, and television, you'd have a good shot at giving yourself an unassailable market position. But today, it's not so simple. The increasing pace of technology transfer allows your competitors to match your innovations overnight. Markets have gone global, making distribution a more expensive proposition than ever before.

And its harder for your ads to get the audience's attention, what with hundreds of new magazines, scores of television networks, and the Internet competing for time and attention. All these trends require a new way to think about brands and branding. But this begs a very big question. What is a brand? A brand offers a value that transcends the here-and-now. That value can be physical or emotional. Whether actual or perceived, however, that value must be overarching and unique. If it is, the brand can be adapted to other situations, and extended through time. For that's the definition of a well-run-brand. It is a big idea that is immortal. Immortality does not come easy. It's not the product of temporary popularity. I'll bet a lot of you can still sing the Pepsodent jingle, "You'll wonder where the yellow went, when you brush your teeth with Pepsodent." But you'll have a hard time finding it in the store. Yet Crest and Colgate go on and on.

The same is true throughout industry. Studebaker stuttered, but Ford thrives. Burma Shave busted, while Brut soothes. The distinguishing characteristic between brands that flourish and those that die is one thing and one thing only: unceasing attention to consumer-driven innovation. Names like Budweiser, Kodak, Wheaties, and Coke stand out as icons of strong brand identity and continual innovation. And innovation is the key to economic survival. "There is only one valid definition of business purpose," marketing guru Peter Drucker has written: "To create a customer." That means "any business enterprise has two, and only two, basic functions: marketing and innovation."

---

It used to be easy to build a brand in the United States. If you were the first to develop a new product, get it out on the retail shelves, and advertise it . . . you'd have a good shot at giving yourself an unassailable market position.

---

A lot of people talk about innovation. But not too many companies actually do it. Innovation is like former U.S. Supreme Court Justice Lewis Powell's definition of pornography: "You know it when you see it. I've seen it." The minivan that resurrected Chrysler was an innovation. The idea of sharing information across time and space that became Lotus Notes was an innovation.

The graphic rendition of social trends that made *USA Today* a national news phenomenon was an innovation. The psychedelic exploration of digital culture by *Wired* magazine was an innovation.

I mention the latter two because publishing is the business I know the best. But you're all magazine and newspaper readers, so you know it well, too. In fact, to paraphrase a Hollywood maxim, everyone has two businesses, their own, and the publishing business. Yet few people, either inside or outside my industry, think of magazines or newspapers as brands. They should, because history shows some of them to be as potent, if not more so, than such powerhouse brands as IBM and Maxwell House. Indeed, in my field, magazines, some brands have been so robust that they've managed to stamp their names on lifestyles and entire eras. Norman

Rockwell's *Saturday Evening Post* covers still identify not just a magazine, but a way of life. The writings of Tom Wolfe, Norman Mailer and the other "New Journalists" in *Esquire* will forever stand for the tumult of the Sixties. Helen Gurley Brown discovered the independent impulse lurking behind old-fashioned femininity, and her "*Cosmo* Girl" remains a cultural phenomenon to this day. And, yes, *Playboy* Playmates still inhabit the fantasies of men everywhere.

---

What is a brand? A brand offers a value that transcends the here-and-now. That value can be physical or emotional. Whether actual or perceived, however, that value must be overarching and unique.

---

By unleashing the prowess of editors, writers, photographers and designers, trends are communicated to readers. The great brand names of the digital age, Microsoft, Compaq and Lotus, were built almost entirely through coverage by and advertising in magazines like *PC Week* and *Byte*. And it should go without saying that the towering brands of international fashion, from Armani and Chanel, to Calvin Klein and Ralph Lauren, simply would not have existed in a world without *Harper's Bazaar* or *Vogue*.

But, despite history's lessons, the watchword in all industry during the last few years has not been innovation. It's been "replication."

During the 1980s, consumer products companies gave us nineteen new ground coffee brands and twenty-one new toothpaste brands. Big-ticket items have not been spared. In the three decades following 1962, General Motors increased the number of individual Oldsmobile nameplates from three to seventeen. Such look-alike brand proliferation is a recipe for disaster. In a landscape dominated by brand variants of unrelieved sameness, most sales are made on the basis of indistinguishable consumer value. Equal value products are commodities. Commodity products are purchased by consumers on the basis of price. And price-based competition reduces a company's revenues and damages its ability to invest in appealing, original, and profitable new products.

In other words, commoditization kills. As any of you who run a business know too well, get sucked under by the commodity spiral, and you will drown.

Media companies have not been immune from the virus of brand proliferation. Too many have been far more interested in covering our shelf space than in creating consumer value. No better example exists than the television-network business. Now, don't get me wrong. All of us could have learned a lesson about brand development from the television industry in the 1980s. MTV's edgy approach appeals to youth culture; the high-toned attraction of A&E (the Arts & Entertainment network); ESPN'S all-sports, all-the-time offerings; the science-and-nature renaissance on the Discovery Channel; all showed that there were untapped consumer desires waiting to be filled.

---

Despite history's lessons, the watchword in all industry during the last few years has not been innovation. It's been "replication."

---

Yet today, new TV networks are sprouting like weeds, as media companies prepare for an era of unlimited channel choice. And instead of offering singular, appealing new programming concepts, too many companies specialize in repackaging.

There are "Car 54, Where Are You?" episodes from the 1950s on Nick at Nite's TV Land. There are news programs from the 1960s on MSNBC's "Now and Again." And there are prize fights from the 1970s on the Classic Sports Network. The print media, too, have participated avidly in this spiraling cycle of replication. Last year, we disgorged 800 new magazine titles, four times the number produced a decade earlier. When you scan the list of titles and see *Tattoo Guru* and *Whitetail Slug Hunter,* you can't help but think that we're falling into the trap of meaningless segmentation that doesn't grow markets, but simply divides them into a million pieces. This absurd proliferation continues because we have spent far too much time acting like salespeople, and not enough time managing like marketers.

A salesperson has but one goal: to close the sale, here and now. But a marketer, as Peter Drucker says, focuses on creating a customer; a customer for life. A marketer, in other words, is a brand steward. Brand stewardship is a crucial concept that all of us in business must understand, if we are to prosper in a world of instantaneous technology transfer and cutthroat competition. Brand stewardship means recognizing the uniqueness of a brand's equity; adapting it to changing times, customs and desires; and extending it creatively into new geographical, product, and technological territories. The central element of brand stewardship, though, is recognizing that the brand is a relationship. Not the product of a relationship, but the relationship itself.

Some of you here today may be in the auto business. So this lesson about relationships is one you know very well. It's no secret that the economics of automotive retailing have changed dramatically over the past several years. The consumer movement, the wide availability of pricing information, and parity perceptions have combined to erode the dealer's profit margins on the sale of new cars.

Auto dealers today know that profitability comes increasingly from providing after-market service, and from keeping customers satisfied enough that they will return to you every time they want to trade up. In auto retailing, to build your profitability, you must build long-term relationships. Sophisticated marketers have begun to adopt this new attitude toward brands and brand stewardship. They have realized that the key to long-term viability is not through the price-driven search for fickle new customers.

It's through the intensification of the relationship between the brand and its constituencies.

---

The central element of brand stewardship . . . is recognizing that the brand is a relationship. Not the product of a relationship, but the relationship itself.

---

Management consultants Don Peppers and Martha Rogers describe this process in their book, *The One-to-One Future*. Long-term brand-builders don't try to sell one product to as many people as possible, they point out. They try to sell each customer a portfolio of products. That means maintaining an ongoing dialogue with customers, and drawing from this information flow to create real products of real value around core brands. The dialogue, the products, and the relationships in turn form the most powerful tool a marketer can ever have: a community. That's right: a brand community.

Let me give you some examples of companies that have taken their products and turned them into relationships, using brand "experiences" to envelop consumers in feelings of community. Early on, Phil Knight and his brilliant crew of marketers at Nike realized they were not in the business of making shoes. Instead, they saw customers buying into the notion of heroism, as embodied by Nike's celebrity endorsers. So Nike effectively reconfigured itself as a community of heroism, in which consumers and athletes could participate as potential equals. Nike developed unique product lines around different athletic heroes. Around Charles Barkley and his aggressive style of basketball, it built the "Force" line of shoes and clothes. Around high-flying Scottie Pippin it created the "Flight" line.

The Nike Town stores the company is building around the United States (the newest one recently opened in New York a few short blocks from my office) extend this heroic brand experience, in exactly the same way Disney World, Disney stores, Disney movies and the Disney Channel extend the Disney brand experience. In effect, Nike has surrounded consumers with "Nikeism." But it's made the cult open to any and all.

Then, in Atlanta, there's the Coca-Cola Museum: a permanent exhibition of ads and memorabilia from more than 100 years of the company's history. It's not only one of Atlanta's top tourist destinations, it's become a profit center for the softdrink company—one that reinforces, for everyone who stops by, the company's advertising message: "Always Coca-Cola." The ability to create and maintain brand communities has been central to the success of magazines. After all, why do people read a publication? Certainly, they read for information. And of course, they read for entertainment. But in a much more profound way, men and women read magazines and newspapers to be part of a conversation, a dialogue, a community.

This isn't just theory. It's fact. Just look at the developing world of electronic communications.

Local services like Echo in New York and The Well in San Francisco, not to mention America Online and its eight million customers, speak of themselves as on-line communities. So it is with a successful magazine or newspaper. It is not a product to be sold. Instead, it's a commune, a fellowship, a kibbutz.

I learned these lessons about brand stewardship the hard way: I succeeded. And then I failed. The good news—I succeeded again.

But not until I had to do the most difficult thing a business person ever has to do: come to grips with why some enterprises die while others prosper.

I started out in the publishing world selling classified ads for *Holiday* Magazine. I moved up to bigger publications,

*Travel & Leisure,* then *New York* Magazine, and then *Ms.,* where I became the first advertising director. *Ms.* was a very tough sell. Feminism wasn't the most popular item on advertisers' agendas back in the early Seventies. But *Ms.* had a kind of power that made you want to work around the clock to make it succeed. We knew that our readers believed in us. We knew we were successfully planting important new ideas in the American consciousness.

The failure came right after that. I jumped to a job as ad director at *City of San Francisco* magazine. The publication had everything going for it: an affluent market; a famous editor; and most of all, the deep pockets and creative spark of Francis Ford Coppola, its owner. It was only a matter of months before it all came unglued. San Francisco was a city of contrasts in the mid-1970s, from archly conservative to wildly liberal. The magazine tried to bridge those two worlds, unsuccessfully. The readers wanted something different, and the advertisers just would not buy. I left after six months and began to wonder why the magazine fell apart. The answer lay in the comparison between *Ms.* and *City of San Francisco.*

*Ms.* was a community, there was a bond and a relationship between the magazine and its hundreds of thousands of readers. *City* magazine never had a clear identity.

I was able to bring this lesson to bear when I became the publisher of *USA Today.* When I arrived, even though it was the third largest newspaper in the United States, it was losing about $250 million a year, the critics were rampant, journalists still called it "McPaper" because of its color and flashiness, and advertisers complained that we were neither fish nor fowl, neither a newspaper nor a magazine. But what was clear from day one was that reader response was powerful.

How did I know? Because everywhere I went, every city, airport, hotel and even ad agency, I saw men and women, especially young ones, devouring *USA Today.* We had captured the energy of a new generation in our graphics and comprehensiveness, and yes, late sports scores. We had also captured an essential fact about the new American sensibility that our competitors had missed: that an increasingly mobile generation was rooted in a national consciousness that transcended local and regional origins. We were living in a nation where the Atlanta Braves were becoming "America's team." It stood to reason that this nation needed a community newspaper, albeit reinvented.

*USA Today* was founded on that single penetrating idea. It was filling a desperately felt need. I heard it in focus groups. I found it in conversations with readers. I saw it in the energy of our staff, which was constantly tinkering and retooling to make the product better and more relevant to that embedded brand identity. My job was to persuade advertisers that this community of interest existed. And we did. Today, the paper is packed with ads, is profitable and became a new brand.

History taught me a critical lesson that I am reapplying at Hearst Magazines: the brand is king. And a brand steward's role is to facilitate the creation and evolution of a, dare I say it?, interactive community around the brand. Not that there aren't challenges facing us every step of the way. Changes in manufacturing processes, new distribution technologies, and commoditization threaten all of us, no matter what business we're in.

So does concentration among our suppliers and markets.

In the almost 30 years I've been in publishing, the media industries have been utterly reborn by technology and consolidation, no more so than during the last five years. Small and mid-sized advertising agencies, to cite one change, are disappearing into the maws of multinational giants. Just within the past two or three years, we've seen Chiat/Day, the fiercely independent creator of the Energizer Bunny campaign, gobbled up by the Omnicom Group and merged into TBWA, the once-equally independent force behind Absolut vodka's ads. The oldest American ad agency, N. W. Ayer, was acquired by D'Arcy Masius Benton & Bowles, itself the product of a 1980s merger between two other venerable agencies.

Where this leaves creativity will be the question of the next few years. But driving these changes are several inter-related and self-perpetuating trends.

---

The brand is king. And a brand steward's role is to facilitate the creation and evolution of a, dare I say it?, interactive community around the brand.

---

First is the trend toward globalization in consumer prod-uct and service companies. They need to expand beyond maturing markets in developed economies into new markets. And they need to seek efficiencies and scale when entering those markets.

Then there's the trend toward globalization in media, with a handful of companies, like Time Warner, News Corp., Bertelsmann and a few others, seeking worldwide openings for their movies, magazines, television shows, and distribu-tion systems.

Mistakes are made, of course, when you're trying to make your brands relevant in new markets. There's a fasci-nating story told by insiders at Philip Morris, about their efforts to turn Marlboro into a global brand. The company had successfully transformed Marlboro from a women's brand into a men's brand in the 1950s by introducing the image of the cowboy, an image that seemed to work around the world. Until it got to Taiwan.

There, Marlboro just wouldn't sell. The company learned the reason why from a junior art director at its local ad agency. In China, he told them, the cowboy is considered a lower-class worker, little better than a farmhand, and certainly nothing to aspire to. The solution he suggested was to focus the advertisements on the horse, and to use only white horses, a symbol of aristocracy. The change worked to catapult Marlboro into share supremacy in Taiwan.

The point is this: even as it becomes necessary to expand and extend a brand to survive, it is even more crucial that you continue to engage in dialogue with your consumers and adapt to their needs and world view. You cannot rest on past successes. You cannot allow your processes to define who you are.

Branding requires you to understand your core identity, so you can adapt it to changes in form and fashion. The penalty for those who do not is irrelevancy. Or death.

We face this challenge every day at Hearst Magazines. Our company, I'm happy to say, has been an industry leader in developing global brands. Our Russian edition of *Marie Claire* was our 81st international title. Last year, we introduced eight overseas titles, including versions of *Harper's Bazaar* in Russia, Korea, Greece and the Czech Republic. Thanks to our distribution in 100 countries, our international division doubled its revenues last year. The rules we followed? Think global. Act local. And know thyself.

---

Branding requires you to understand your core identity, so you can adapt it to changes in form and fashion. The penalty for those who do not is irrelevancy. Or death.

---

We've also extended our brands carefully into other publications, widening our communities of interest, if you will, while engaging in more specific dialogue. *Cosmopolitan*, for example, tested a publication last year called *Cosmopolitan's All About Men. Country Living Gardener,* an extension of *Country*

*Living,* became a bimonthly. This year, we plan to publish three issues of yet another variation on the theme, *Country Living's Healthy Living.*

After globalization and extension, a third major opportunity to steward a brand is to create brand experiences outside of your existing product lines. Coca-Cola did it with its museum. Our magazines are doing it in various ways. Other media provided one obvious opportunity. *Popular Mechanics* launched a television show on six Hearst-owned stations; it introduced a new line of home videos, *Popular Mechanics for Kids,* as well as books aimed at boys and girls, and a car-repair CD-ROM for their folks. *Redbook* took one of the boldest leaps into alternative media, introducing through Windham Hill Records a five-part compact disc collection, *Redbook Relaxers,* which is now available at record stores and mass retailers around the country.

We've also created events around our brands. *Victoria* magazine produced four one-woman shows featuring Leslie Caron as Colette, a perfect pairing of the publication's stylish identity with an entertainment product. It must have resonated with readers, because audio tapes of the productions, combined with other *Victoria*-branded products that we sell through the magazine and at retail, will generate far more than $1 million in revenue for Hearst this year.

We have broadened our brands into non-media product lines as well. Wal-Mart, the nation's largest retailer, now sells, among other things, *House Beautiful* ceiling fans, *Popular Mechanics* work boots and *Sports Afield* watches.

The biggest opportunity for brand stewardship, however, may be technological. My company is deeply involved in new technologies. Hearst's New Media Division, an R&D "skunk works" under the leadership of former FCC Chairman Al Sikes, has been developing new products and services that are quite exciting. Hearst is a minority investor in Netscape.

Hearst owns or co-owns several enormously successful cable networks, including ESPN, the most valuable of them all. All of my magazines have put together Web sites, many of which are already proving tremendously beneficial to readers and advertisers.

But technology's value is still a big maybe in my business. Right now, there's more eagerness than earnings on that front. Publishers are scurrying around, frantically attempting to repackage existing content for electronic delivery. This has proved enormously costly. In fact, there's a joke making the rounds of Silicon Alley, as New York's downtown "new media" district is called: What is the Information Superhighway? Answer: Its just like cable TV, except a lot more expensive. That joke has a serious point. It says that we err if we look at new media only as something that we can sell to consumers. Instead, media companies must look upon interactivity primarily as a powerful tool for brand stewardship.

---

After globalization and extension, a third major opportunity to steward a brand is to create brand experiences outside of your existing product lines.

---

What's the secret? It comes in four rules, rules that are relevant no matter what business you're in.

First, new-media products must derive from the brand. They must relate to the brand. They must augment the brand experience. And they must use the Internet's truly revolutionary capability, the chance for inexpensive, back-and-forth dialogue with readers, to inculcate and reinforce the brand relationship.

You don't have to be in the media business to benefit from these lessons. Consider Federal Express's World Wide Web site. On it, customers can actually track the progress of their packages across the nation and the world, augmenting the service FedEx provides, and making its customers feel connected to the company in an entirely new way.

At one of my magazines, *Town & Country*, we're throwing a party on the Web, a wedding party. The magazine celebrated its 150th anniversary last year by introducing an on-line bridal registry. The concept is deceptively simple. Couples can register their store and gift preferences, enabling their friends to shop and send messages to them on-line. It's a service for everyone, retailers, guests, and the nervous bride and groom-to-be, with *Town & Country* acting as the facilitator. What better way to use technology to enhance the brand relationship between a magazine, its readers, and its advertisers?

For that's the point. It's not to brainlessly glom on to anything and everything that's new. It's to use innovation, service, dialogue and a brand's special equity to create relationships that can last forever.

---

New-media products must derive from the brand. They must relate to the brand. They must augment the brand experience.

---

But technology can never substitute for the single greatest advantage an enterprise can have, individual creativity. In my business, that's become more important than ever, because we've had to ask our editors to redefine their jobs.

Time was when it was enough for an editor to have a Rolodex full of writers' names and an ability to fix split infinitives. That's still important, but today its also necessary for them to steward their brands into other media, and outside the realm of media. In fact, the editor today has to be something of an impresario, creating an identity for a magazine that can extend across space, time and product lines.

I'll give you an example of which I'm particularly proud. At *Good Housekeeping*, editor Ellen Levine saw an opportunity to take the magazine's historic brand identification with consumer advocacy into the realm of public policy. A little more than a year ago, Ellen published a story about the crisis of "drive-through pregnancies." She asked readers who supported longer hospital stays for mothers and their newborn infants to send an attached coupon to then Senator Bill Bradley.

More than 100,000 did, the most mail Senator Bradley had ever received. Late last year, when President Clinton signed the "Newborns and Mothers Maternity Bill" into law, Senator Bradley publicly credited *Good Housekeeping* with helping to make it happen. And the *"Good Housekeeping Lobby"* has since become a regular brand-extending feature in the magazine.

Which goes a long way to explaining why I wake up every morning thrilled to be in the business I'm in. For magazines are the brands that make things happen. And if they're well stewarded, like *Good Housekeeping*, they can make things happen for a hundred years or more.

1997

There's nothing like a CEO with a penchant for Harley-Davidson motorcycles and Hawaiian shirts—like John Martin, who took over Taco Bell in 1983, and over the next 13 years grew the company from $600 million in sales to $4.5 billion. Martin has been in restauranting throughout his entire career. Back in the 1970s he started off as a management trainee at Burger King, where he rose to regional manager and then to head of European start-up operations. Burger Chef was his next stop, where he became vice president of operations in 1979. Two years later he was elected CEO, but when the company was bought out by Hardee's, he swapped burgers for burritos. When Martin came onboard, Taco Bell had a case of Montezuma's revenge. To turn it around and force the competition to "hang by their fingernails," he introduced value pricing.

To cut prices Martin had to cut costs without hurting quality. "There's 29 cents' worth of labor in a taco. I can't taste labor. Can you?" he observed, and promptly simplified the food preparation processes, reducing the kitchen space from a total of 70 percent of the restaurants down to just 30 percent. The budgets for marketing and other groups were also cut so that Taco Bell could give the consumer more bang for the buck. "The only thing the customer cares about is that final bite," says Martin. After cutting prices and kitchen size, he cut management; store managers were given more independence and supervisors now had to watch 40 or 50 stores instead of 6.

Martin's restructuring experience is featured in *Reengineering the Corporation* by Michael Hammer and James Champy, who write, "The most dramatically drawn lesson is Martin's recognition that the customer must be the starting point for everything in reengineering." But reengineering can take its toll on morale. Martin's answer: "When people can clearly understand that they're doing this for the consumer, that's a lot different from saying, I'm doing it for shareholders or so Martin's office can be nicer. . . . The biggest risk was if we were not bold enough and didn't go far and fast enough." The organizational pain, however, is still apparent in his following story.

# Reengineering the Corporation
## *John E. Martin*

For us, the process of reengineering has been like a voyage of discovery—a voyage we have been on now for nearly a decade, and one that we realize will continue as long as Taco Bell is in the business of serving customers.

Throughout the entire process, our greatest insight has been our most basic—namely, that everything begins with a simple decision to listen to our customer.

When I became CEO in 1983, Taco Bell was much like every other quick-service restaurant business. We were a top-down, "command-and-control" organization with multiple layers of management, each concerned primarily with bird-dogging the layers below them. We were also process-driven, in the old sense of the word, with operational handbooks for everything—including, literally, handbooks to interpret other handbooks.

Like our competitors, we were caught up in the process of processing; we were striving for bigger, better, and more complicated in just about everything we did.

If something was simple, we made it complex. If it was hard, we figured out a way to make it impossible.

We operated this way, because with all our layers of management, we needed to make things difficult so we could keep everybody busy. The more commands and controls we had in the system, the more the system justified its own existence.

Unfortunately, in our ever-increasing efforts to micromanage every aspect of restaurant operations, we became so focused on ourselves and our processes that we forgot to ask a basic question: What the heck do our customers think about all this?

---

Even before taking over as chief executive officer, I had a notion that our customers didn't give a hoot about any of our elaborate systems.

---

Did they care that our assistant restaurant managers could assemble and disassemble the twelve parts of a deep fryer with a blindfold on? Did they care that somebody in our industry probably wrote a handbook on it, including recommendations for the type of blindfold to use? Did they care, in the final analysis, that we managed to turn the relatively simple business of fast food into rocket science, all under the presumption that it was good for them?

Even before taking over as chief executive officer, I had a notion that our customers didn't give a hoot about any of our elaborate systems. My appointment as CEO gave me an opportunity to prove it. It's important to remember that back in the early 1980s, Taco Bell was very much a regional Mexican-American restaurant chain that had enjoyed a fair degree of success in a relatively small niche. In 1982, we had fewer than 1,500 restaurants and did $500 million in total sales; our major competitors, mostly in the hamburger business, were light years ahead of us.

The fast-food world was passing Taco Bell by. In fact, our cumulative real growth from 1978, when PepsiCo acquired Taco Bell, to 1982 was a negative 16 percent compared to the total industry's positive 6 percent.

We were going backwards—fast.

The problem was Taco Bell really didn't know what it wanted to be in those days. So our first order of business was to create a vision for the company. Since we had no place to go but up, we decided to think the unthinkable and create a vision of Taco Bell as a giant in the fast-food industry—not just the leader in the Mexican category, but a competitive force with which all restaurant organizations in all categories would have to contend.

A lot of restaurant people, including many in our own organization, thought that our new vision was something more than farsighted. Farfetched was a word we heard often. But Taco Bell was in an "up or out" situation; there was only one thing we knew for sure, and that was we had to change in a very big way.

Nowadays, when I think back to that early vision and to the massive amount of change we've had to create to fulfill it, I'm reminded of something Robert Kennedy once said: "Progress is a nice word. But change is its motivator, and change has its enemies." His point was that you can't get from Point A to Point B without dealing with some problems.

For Taco Bell to progress from a regional Mexican-American restaurant chain to a national force in the industry, we had to accept the fact that our greatest enemies were the tradition-bound ideas to which many of our employees clung.

In those days, traditional thinkers believed they knew what customers wanted without even asking *them*. Fancier decors, bigger kitchens, more sophisticated equipment, larger staffs, broader menus, outdoor playgrounds. Without asking our customers, in other words, we assumed that what they wanted was bigger, better, and more complex. By following through on this tradition-bound thinking, we were providing slower and costlier service.

So we began our voyage by asking our customers what *they* wanted, and what we found out was encouraging. Our customers, it turned out, didn't want any of those bigger, better, fancier things we assumed they did. What they really wanted was very simple: good food, served fast and hot, in a clean environment, at a price they could afford.

That was it. All the rest meant little to them.

---

We had to accept the fact that our greatest enemies were the tradition-bound ideas to which many of our employees clung.

---

The initial research we did at Taco Bell became our declaration of independence. It helped us look at Taco Bell in an entirely different way and allowed us to turn customer value into the key element of our business proposition.

When a customer walks into a quick-service restaurant and gives us a dollar, a large part of what he or she is paying for has nothing to do with what the customer actually receives for the money. Sure, all the cost factors are important from a business point of view. But what's important from the customer's point of view? Is labor important? No. Is rent important? Not unless you're a PepsiCo shareholder.

In the end, the only important category to customers is food and paper, because that's what they get back for the dollar they give us. Amazingly, though, the percentage of his or her dollar the customer pays for food and paper—in other words, the cost of goods sold—is, historically, the one variable chains have tried to reduce. Even today, restaurant people brag about holding food and paper costs down to twenty-five or twenty-six cents, and putting the extra pennies into marketing, which accounts for about eight cents out of every customer dollar.

One of our well-known, fast-food competitors spends about $1 billion a year marketing its business. That's the cost of about eight billion bean burritos, enough to give every person on this planet one and a half burritos free every year.

So we decided to reduce everything but our cost of goods sold, including the cost of marketing. If we created a better deal for the consumer, we thought, perhaps we wouldn't have to pay so much to twist people's arms to get them to buy our product.

With that decision, we were creating a true paradigm shift that launched our entire reengineering process.

I cannot tell you how exciting and liberating that shift was for our company. By thinking entirely outside the box, by saying to ourselves that the old methods were the way of the dinosaur, we unleashed a power within our company that has produced enormous success, and, in fact, has enabled us now to think realistically about becoming the dominant force in the convenience food industry within the next ten years. Our initial vision has a good chance of becoming reality. Not bad for a sleepy little Mexican-American restaurant organization.

How was that power manifested in the reengineering process?

It took several forms—including a complete reorganization of our human resources and a dramatic redesign of our operational systems to make them more innovative and customer focused.

By traditional restaurant standards the reengineering of our management processes was radical. We eliminated entire layers of management and, in the process, completely redefined nearly every job in the system.

For example, we did away with the "district manager" supervisory layer, which traditionally oversees the management of five or six restaurants. By eliminating that job category, we dramatically changed the job description of our restaurant managers, who had previously reported to the district managers.

For the first time in the fast-food industry, we told restaurant managers that they were responsible for running their own operations without the help—or the hindrance—of another layer of supervision. "You're in charge now," we told them. "How your unit performs in terms of sales, profitability, and customer satisfaction is in your hands, and we will evaluate your performance and decide your compensation based on those very specific business indicators." That was an unheard of move for the command-and-control, quick-service restaurant industry.

The reorganization proved painful for some managers, especially those who still believed the ultimate test of their abilities was assembling the deep-fryer blindfolded. Many managers, however, adapted easily and immediately to the new approach. In fact, they responded so well that eventually we changed their job title from restaurant manager to restaurant general manager. Since they were each responsible for a $1 million to $2 million a year business, they were clearly operating in a general management capacity.

For several years after this reorganization, we saw an exodus of the traditional thinking managers. Most, in fact, wound up working in management positions with our competition, where the area supervisor who oversees a span of five restaurants is still very much the norm.

By contrast, at the Taco Bell supervisory level, our reorganization produced an entirely new job category that we call "market manager." This position exists nowhere else in the restaurant industry.

In 1988, Taco Bell had about 350 area supervisors controlling about 1,800 restaurants. Today, we have just over 100 market managers responsible for about 2,300 company-owned restaurants. Market managers each oversee at least 20 restaurants. Some are in charge of 40, which if you know the restaurant business, you know is an enormous responsibility.

Successful market managers in the new Taco Bell manage by exception, which means they must work only to solve problems, not create them. Equally important, they have to completely reject the old command-and-control style in favor of a model that promotes flexibility, relies on the most advanced management information systems in the business, encourages innovation, and empowers the people around them to do their jobs.

The new market manager position prompted a shake out, as had the previous change.

Some former area supervisors rose to the new challenge, others switched to restaurant general managers and became very productive, while still others left Taco Bell for the more comfortable confines of our competitors.

---

It is when people *stop* taking me aside and saying, "John, these changes will never work," that I'm going to start worrying.

---

Several of those who left, in fact, took me aside and said, in effect, "Hey, John, you're out in left field without a mitt. This new Taco Bell will never work. There are too many changes."

Each time I would listen, smile, shake their hand, and thank them for being an important part of Taco Bell's successful *past*.

After each of those conversations, I was more committed to the reengineering process than ever. Why? Because at Taco Bell, we had accepted that even though change could be painful, it was also an inevitable byproduct of growth and success. It is when people *stop* taking me aside and saying, "John, these changes will never work," that I'm going to start worrying, because that's when Taco Bell is starting to stagnate.

The great American author John Steinbeck once wrote, "It is the nature of man as he grows older to protest against change, particularly change for the better."

1993

"It is quite amazing to me now when I look back and see just how small CBS used to be and how seriously we took our problems then and how hard I worked, as though everything were a matter of life and death," William Paley, the legendary founder of CBS, wrote in his memoir. The Paley family saga is the classic story of rags to riches. Back in 1888, William Paley's grandfather brought his family from Brovary, Russia, to Chicago, Illinois. Although his grandfather lost all his money on bad investments, his father built a successful cigar business, which William was expected to take over.

Paley first became involved with radio as an advertiser, sponsoring a program and promoting La Palina, the family's cigar (note the play on the name). A fateful moment occurred in 1927, when the owner of an ailing radio network that supplied programming and advertisers to a small group of stations approached Paley's father to buy him out. While the elder Paley rejected such an idea, the younger was intrigued. The next year he bought just over a 50 percent interest in the radio company and became president. He reflected, "We needed programs . . . We had to sell time to advertisers. We had to build an organization in a field in which there was little experience to go on. Most important, we had to get control of the finances." The next year Paley changed the name to the Columbia Broadcasting System (CBS).

Back then only 33 percent of American homes had radios, but it was a quickly evolving world that required both building a strong foundation and a vision. "If we had not established a very solid foundation of good principles and concepts at the beginning, I think, we would not have gone as far as we have gone over the years," Paley recalled later. "We developed traditions that have been followed as a matter of course, beyond anything put down formally in writing as rules and regulations." Those concerns are apparent in the following selection from Paley's memoir, in which he focusses on finding a successor. However, the situation becomes complicated when his successor dies of a heart attack after six months in the job.

# Planning for Succession
## *William S. Paley*

In the beginning, when I first came into CBS, there was absolutely nothing in the way of organization. I had to construct the business from the ground up. I was in effect the program manager, sales manager, and financial officer—you name it, I was it. I worked with others, of course, but the responsibility for all those activities was mine. As CBS grew and diversified through the years, my work habits changed and I began to delegate work and authority to more and more people. Nevertheless, for some time the organization of CBS remained the same, not unlike that of a much smaller company. Our management was centralized in myself as top man, aided and backed up by one chief-lieutenant—Klauber, Kesten, and then Stanton. Stanton became CBS's first president and chief operating officer other than myself in 1946. Five years later, with television growing at an enormous rate and as we were about to enter manufacturing, we reorganized the company into six autonomous divisions, each operating like a separate company with its own president and staff, each encouraged to compete with the other divisions.*

---

* The six divisions were CBS Television, CBS Radio, CBS Laboratories, Columbia Records, Hytron Radio & Electronics, and CBS/Columbia.

The plan worked fairly well for fifteen years, but the divisions grew bigger and more numerous so that by 1966 we had ten large divisions, all reporting directly to Stanton and me. After consultations with two management consulting firms and after numerous studies, we proposed to the board of directors a major reorganization of CBS. At the February 1966 meeting of the Board we divided the company into two basic groups—broadcasting and nonbroadcasting activities. John A. Schneider at age thirty-nine was promoted to president of the CBS/Broadcast Group with the tacit understanding that he would then be the number-three man in the corporation, destined to succeed Stanton and me. In June of that year, we made Goddard Lieberson the president of all the nonbroadcasting activities, which we called CBS/Columbia.

At the February meeting, upon a motion of Joseph A. W. Iglehart, the Board voted unanimously that I "be requested and urged" to continue as chairman of the board, and I agreed to continue beyond my sixty-fifth birthday, which would occur that September. It was the first and only exception to the company's mandatory retirement policy, which was introduced by Stanton through the company's personnel office in 1959.

As CBS continued to grow and to diversify, all of the nonbroadcasting activities became too burdensome for one group president and so we evolved the structure of CBS into its present form of sixteen separate divisions reporting to four group presidents—of broadcasting, records, publishing and Columbia.

This reorganization was an ongoing process starting in the last half of the 1960s. It was a complex task, for we needed men for their specific expertise and at the same time we needed men who could span the creative, business and administrative requirements of the various parts of the company.

Once we had Jack Schneider in place in the line of succession, there came a time when Frank Stanton and I discussed the prospect of his succeeding both of us. Stanton and I together had run CBS by that time for more than twenty years. Although we were quite different in personality and disposition, we did make a good team. Stanton was cool, analytical, precise, possessed a high sense of standards and style, and had become known as "the statesman of broadcasting" because of his frequent public appearances before the industry, congressional committees, and the FCC. He was much more than a lobbyist in his public role, for Frank prepared long and hard for each of his public appearances. He spoke from deep knowledge and keen insight upon virtually all aspects of broadcasting and its role in a free society. He was outstanding in maintaining good relations with our affiliated stations, the sinew and backbone of network broadcasting, keeping them informed of network activities as he absorded their views and needs.

I focused my activities upon the business affairs of the company, particularly in planning and developing, which in the sixties were becoming more and more significant. I also gave much of my time to programming, talent and personnel in the important entertainment sections of our broadcasting division. Of course, I reviewed and passed on all policy and important operational decisions of the company as chief executive officer. On most of the problems which confronted CBS, Frank and I saw eye-to-eye and worked together for the good of the company. We had our differences, of course, but we worked them out.

And yet, a strong personal friendship never developed between us. Our bond was business and it never seemed to go beyond that. We shared no outside activity. We never grew close. In fact, as the years went on, we seemed to grow further and further apart. When we came to reorganizing the company in the mid-sixties, I seriously considered for a while the prospect of relieving my own burdens by stepping down as chief executive officer. We tried at one point to work out an arrangement whereby Frank would become chief executive officer of the company as well as president and I would continue as chairman of the board. But that did not work out. I exercised my prerogative to continue on in my own role and despite my age, frankly, I felt just fine, years younger than my age. No doubt, Frank was disappointed. I don't know to what extent, because he was a reticent man and never told me. A year later, Frank signed a new five-year contract with CBS which contained provisions for his consulting services for another sixteen years beyond his own retirement. We continued to work together as we had before, and when the time approached for Frank's retirement, he was instrumental in helping me choose his own successor.

Trying to promote from within, we had moved Jack Schneider up the ladder to executive vice-president of CBS in February, 1969. But that just did not work out. Jack's expertise and fund of knowledge was in broadcasting and he found it difficult to cope with the intricate business and financial decisions incumbent upon anyone involved in running a complex corporation, which CBS was fast becoming. We concluded that what CBS truly needed at the helm was not necessarily a broadcaster but rather someone who was a professional business manager, experienced in handling a multidivisional, diversified corporation like CBS. The outstanding men at CBS had always been broadcasters, for in years past that is what CBS was primarily involved in. Stanton himself was a victim of the CBS transition. I had come by business instincts and know-how at my father's knee and at the Paley family dinner table. So, without fully realizing it, I had developed certain instincts and techniques which served me well in the intricacies of business decisions. In short, both Frank and I came to the conclusion that there was no one else in CBS who could be moved up and that we needed to go to the outside to find a man to replace him as president and me eventually as chairman and chief executive officer of CBS.

Working very closely on the problem, we agreed that we had better find his successor at least a year before his retirement. We wanted the incoming president to get the benefit of Frank's knowledge, experience and guidance. So, in 1971, after some looking around, we hired a top executive search firm to find us a new president for CBS. We spelled out the specifications of the type of man we wanted, and Frank handled most of the preliminary interviews of the candidates brought to us.

---

We concluded that what CBS truly needed at the helm was not necessarily a broadcaster but rather someone who was a professional business manager, experienced in handling a multidivisional, diversified corporation like CBS.

---

He found the man he liked while I was off in Europe, and so the candidate flew over to meet me. This was Charles T. Ireland, Jr., who had had a colorful business career as secretary of the New York Central Railroad Company, president of Allegheny Corporation, chairman of the board of Investors Diversified Services and for the previous four years had served as a right-hand man to Harold S. Geneen of International Telephone and Telegraph, the largest conglomerate in the United States. Chick Ireland was an expert in diversification and acquisitions, and I could see that he was a strong executive of the kind we needed. We talked at great length and agreed that as successful as CBS had been through the years, it also had been rather loosely run. It did not have the controls and checks and balances that modern management requires of a large, diversified company. We had grown so fast, we had not had a chance to fine-tune the operation.

I was impressed with Ireland and told him so, but also said that I could not make a decision on the basis of one meeting and that I could not take the responsibility of his passing up another job that had been offered to him. I could not guarantee that we would hire him until I had had a chance to look into the situation further. He said he was eager to be a contender for the CBS position and would wait for our decision and take his chances.

Upon the recommendation of Stanton and myself, Ireland was elected by the Board as the new president of CBS in September 1971, and started on the job October 1. Stanton was moved up to vice-chairman. Jack Schneider was moved back to his old position as president of the Broadcast Group. Chick Ireland, even though he was still working under the guidance of Stanton, soon demonstrated all the skills of a very well-trained, hard-driving manager. He was a strong, no-nonsense leader who brought about better financial controls, a better flow of information within the executive ranks and better analyses and predictions of what we could expect at CBS. There was some grumbling in CBS ranks as he pushed people rather hard to institute new management controls, but he was doing precisely what was needed at CBS, what we wanted and what he promised to do.

Unfortunately, about six months after he had started on the job, Ireland suffered a heart attack. He was out for five or six weeks and then returned to work, building up his work schedule gradually as he worked one hour a day the first week, then two and gradually to a full schedule. One afternoon, quite late, he came into my office with the good news that his doctor had pronounced him fully recovered: He could take on a full workload at CBS with no restrictions and could even return to playing tennis. I congratulated him. The next morning I received word: Ireland had died of a heart attack in his sleep that night. He had been only fifty-one years of age.

When we recovered from the shock of losing Ireland, we turned to the same executive search firm and asked them to find us another man as quickly as possible. We interviewed quite a few promising candidates and, within one month, Frank and I settled on Arthur R. Taylor, a financial wizard who had risen fast to the position of executive vice-president and chief financial officer of International Paper. He was only thirty-seven years old, tall, good-looking, and extremely articulate, and, above all, it was immediately obvious that here was a man with a very quick mind and a tremendous amount of energy and vitality. We offered the job and Taylor quickly accepted it and won the approval of the CBS Board in July 1972.

There was much surprise and some resentment within the ranks of CBS when Taylor took over as president, particularly because of his age. But I defended him vigorously, pointing out time and again that I had been twenty-six when I took over CBS and Stanton became president when he was thirty-seven. Arthur Taylor represented to me the promise of a long reign at CBS.

Frank worked with Taylor for about eight months before he retired as vice-chairman of CBS on March 31, 1973, which was the last day of the month in which he reached age sixty-five. I had suggested that we give a dinner to salute Frank's achievements and long service to CBS, but he preferred not to have any embellishments added to his retirement. At the Board meeting prior to his retirement, we expressed our sentiments of gratitude for his long service and I presented him with a small Henry Moore sculpture with an inscribed base. He retired from active, everyday duty but served for five more years on the board of directors and continues to serve as a consultant to CBS.

As time went on, it became more and more apparent to me that while Arthur Taylor was indeed brilliant and the company's earnings were at an all-time high, he did not have all of the essential qualities to become my successor. I discussed my analysis of the situation with the outside directors of CBS, singly and then as a group, and they all agreed that Taylor should be replaced so that someone else could be in the position to take over as the chief executive officer of the company.

Once that decision was made, I acted quickly. In preparation I had already looked around for a possible replacement and found the right man with all the qualifications we sought and he was already within the CBS organization. So, on the morning of our scheduled board of directors meeting in October 1976, a little more than four years after Taylor had joined CBS, I summoned him into my office, and in the presence of two Board members, I explained the situation to him and asked for his immediate resignation.

I took his resignation before the Board and proposed a new realignment of management at CBS: I would relinquish my post as chief executive officer of the company after the next stockholders' meeting but would continue as chairman, and as the new president and the next chief executive officer of CBS I proposed John D. Backe, age forty-four, the head of the CBS/Publishing Group.

I had had my eye on John Backe for some time. From the day he came to CBS, I had been impressed with the caliber of his work and, seeing him several times a week in various meetings and conferences, I came to like and admire him personally. I had noted that he thought before he spoke at meetings, was well-prepared, and never overstated his presentations, proposals or estimates. He had a sure hand in everything he did. In one instance he negotiated the acquisition of a company for CBS at several million dollars *less* than the price he had been authorized to pay, a most unusual feat in these times. So, when I realized I needed a good man to replace Arthur Taylor, I settled upon John Backe. I was convinced that in him I had found not only an outstanding business executive but also a good "generalist," a man who could apply his experience, acumen and common sense to a multiplicity of business affairs.

Backe had a master's degree in business administration and, like Ireland and Taylor before him, was a professional business manager with a brilliant career behind him. He got his early training in management at General Electric in Cincinnati, then joined Silver Burdett, the textbook-publishing unit of the General Learning Corporation, a joint venture between General Electric and Time Inc., and within three years became the president of General Learning. He came to CBS as the president of our Publishing Group in 1973, and in the next three years he reorganized that group brilliantly so that its sales increased by about one-third and its profits increased dramatically.

As chief executive officer of CBS since I stepped down after the April stockholders meeting in 1977, Backe has proved himself a strong leader with outstanding skills in managing a multidivisional company. A straightforward man of great integrity, he has been well received by people within and outside CBS, for in addition to his professional qualities, he has a sensitivity for and understanding of the people with whom he works at CBS. He has instituted several innovative practices at our regular corporate planning meetings and our inter-group conferences. Our group presidents can now share their problems and successes with one another on a regular basis. New checks and balances and reporting procedures and corporate strategy sessions have been established under Backe's administration, making for a tighter-knit organization at CBS.

I feel we have made a wise choice in John Backe. He and I have been working well together ever since he took over the active management of CBS. I have stayed on as chairman of the board, in order to make myself available and as helpful as I can be in achieving a smooth transition of executive management, especially in the creative and long-range policy areas. I seem to be working as hard as ever, but now with a feeling of pleasure and comfort because my successor is in place.

1979

Back in 1987 Thomas Watson was named "The Greatest Capitalist in History" by *Fortune* magazine. And to think this was the man who had been called "Terrible" Tom in his youth, who barely graduated from Brown University, and who feared that he could never live up to his father, who had created IBM. Not until World War II did he blossom. While serving in the air force, Watson realized that "I had the force of personality to get my ideas across to others." After the war, he was set on becoming a pilot for United Airlines, until his commanding general convinced him to set his sights on leading IBM, where Watson had been a sales representative.

Watson rejoined his father's company as a vice president in 1946. He quickly rose through the ranks, became president of IBM in 1952, and succeeded his father as CEO in 1956. After taking command, the first order of business was a reorganization. "Prior to the mid-1950s the company was run essentially by one man, T. J. Watson [his father]," he recalled. "Had IBM had an organizational chart at that time, there would have been a fascinating number of lines—perhaps 30 in all—running into his office." Watson distributed responsibilities while at the same time implementing a system of contention management, in which staff and operational people checked each other, and executives were thrown into rough waters to test their mettle.

The postwar period was a time of explosive expansion for IBM, with an annual average growth rate between 1946 and 1955 of 22 percent. Watson built a colossus by pushing the company into computers—the first attempt resulting in a 120-foot monster. He forced his designers to use transistors, hired electronic engineers by the hundreds, and donated a computer to the Massachusetts Institute of Technology to encourage the university to offer a computer science program. In 1963, in the midst of this electronic revolution, Watson wrote what has been called one of the most important business books ever, *A Business and Its Beliefs,* from which the following selection is excerpted. As he details his own company's revolution, Watson concludes, "Beliefs must always come before policies, practices, and goals."

# What Growth and Change Have Taught Us
## *Thomas J. Watson, Jr.*

T echnological change demands an even greater measure of adaptability and versatility on the part of management in a large organization. Unless management remains alert, it can be stricken with complacency—one of the most insidious dangers we face in business. In most cases it's hard to tell that you've even caught the disease until it's almost too late. It is frequently most infectious among companies that have already reached the top. They get to believing in the infallibility of their own judgments.

We had a bout with this disease soon after the war. It had to do with the introduction of the electronic computer—one of the most important single developments in the whole history of our industry. During the late 1940s it had become clear that many large engineering jobs and a good many accounting applications were being hampered by the relatively slow speeds of the calculating machines then available. At about that time J. Presper Eckert and Dr. John W. Mauchly of the Moore School at the University of Pennsylvania had built for the Army a large electronic computer—the Eniac—to make ballistic-curve calculations. Many people in our industry, and I was among them, had seen the machine, but none of us foresaw its possibilities. Even after Eckert and Mauchly left teaching to begin manufacture of a civilian counterpart to the Eniac, few of us saw the potential.

Their company was absorbed by Remington Rand in 1950, and the following year the first production model of Univac was delivered to the Census Bureau, where it replaced some IBM machines.

Throughout this entire period IBM was unaware of the fact that its whole business stood on the threshold of a momentous change. We had put the first electronically operated punched card calculator on the market in 1946. Even in those days we were well aware that electronic computing was so fast that the machine waited nine-tenths of the time of every card cycle for the mechanical parts of the machine to feed the next card. Yet in spite of this we didn't jump to the obvious conclusion that if we could feed data faster we would increase computational speeds 900 per cent. Remington Rand had seen just that—and with Univac they were off to the races.

---

Technological change demands an even greater measure of adaptability and versatility on the part of management in a large organization.

---

The loss of our business in the Census Bureau struck home. We began to act. We took one of our best operating executives, a man with a reputation for getting things done, and put him in charge of everything which had to do with the introduction of an IBM large-scale computer—all the way from design and development through to marketing and servicing. He was so successful that within a short time we were well on our way.

How did we come up from behind so fast? First, we had enough cash to carry the costs of engineering, research, and production. Second, we had a sales force whose knowledge of the market enabled us to tailor our machines very closely to the needs. Finally, and most important, we had good company morale. Everyone realized that this was a challenge to our leadership. We had to respond with everything we had—and we did.

By 1956 it had become clear that in order for us to move rapidly with these technological changes we needed a new organization concept. Prior to the mid-1950s the company was run essentially by one man, T. J. Watson. He had a terrific team around him, but it was he who made the decisions. Had IBM had an organization chart at that time, there would have been a fascinating number of lines—perhaps thirty in all—running into his office.

In the early 1950s the demands of an expanding economy and the Korean War made it necessary for IBM to react more rapidly at all levels than we were able to with our monolithic structure. Increasing customer pressure—to say nothing of a few missteps like the one we made on the electronic computer—caused us to decide on a new and greatly decentralized organization.

---

We decentralized in more or less the usual way and for the usual reasons—that is, to divide the business into more manageable units and to make sure that decisions would be made where and when they should be.

---

We wasted no time in carrying our decision out. In late 1956, after several months of planning, we called the top 100 or so people in the business to a three-day meeting at Williamsburg, Virginia. We went into that meeting a top-heavy, monolithic company and came out of it decentralized.

Today we have eight operating divisions and two wholly owned, but independently operated, subsidiaries. All have a considerable degree of autonomy. Sitting over them and reviewing their long-range plans and major decisions is the Corporate Management Committee, made up of the board chairman, the president, and six other top executives. Available to advise both this committee and the divisions is a corporate staff of specialists in such areas as manufacturing, engineering, personnel, finance, communications, law, and marketing.

We decentralized in more or less the usual way and for the usual reasons—that is, to divide the business into more manageable units and to make sure that decisions would be made where and when they should be.

But in one respect we were quite different from most other companies. IBM is not the kind of business that textbooks say can be decentralized sensibly. We are not, as many large companies are, a grouping of unrelated or merely partly related businesses. We are one business and, for the most part, a business with a single mission.

Our job, and that of each division of IBM, is to help customers solve their problems through the use of data processing systems and other information-handling equipment. There is a close relationship between all the parts of our product line. Any major technological move or marketing decision in any one division is bound to have a direct effect on other segments of the business.

---

Basically all our managers are company-oriented. They think primarily in terms of what is good for IBM rather than what may be good for particular divisions.

---

This means that decisions are being made constantly, all the way down the line, on matters that involve two or more divisions. One might suppose that burdensome machinery would have to be set up throughout the business to settle the thousands of small differences that could be expected to arise among the divisions.

To date it has not been necessary. No matter what division they may be in, basically all our managers are company-oriented. They think primarily in terms of what is good for IBM rather than what may be good for particular divisions. This may be so because many of them were with IBM long before we became a divisional organization. Many of our higher executives have incentive plans in addition to their salaries. But the plans are based on overall IBM performance rather than that of any single division. The arrangement, we believe, has helped to keep everyone pulling together.

Much of this we owe to the company's beliefs. Our people so thoroughly understand the need to give superior service that their concern for the well-being of the customer often overrides whatever differences of opinion there might be among them. Of course I do not mean that we have no differences. It is my responsibility, as it is the president's and that of the Corporate Management Committee, to resolve the major ones. By and large it hasn't been too bad.

As I said earlier, at the time of reorganization we suddenly found that we had need for a great many more staff experts and specialists than were on our rolls. In nearly every case we "made" these experts simply by naming a man to the job. We had some failures, but on the whole our method worked pretty well. The reason, I think, is that these young and relatively inexperienced executives knew three things as well as their own names:

— They knew that any decisions they might make and any actions they might take had to be right for our people.
— They knew that the main aim of our business is service, to help the customer solve his problems no matter how many problems this may create for us.

—And they knew that we will not settle for anything less than a superior effort in everything we do.

In other words, they understood our basic beliefs, and this understanding enabled them to move into unfamiliar jobs and to overcome the shortcomings they may have had in technical skills. This emphasis on beliefs is not meant to downgrade the importance of technical skill. But from the time of our divisional reorganization we have found that an ingrained understanding of the beliefs of IBM, far more than technical skill, has made it possible for our people to make the company successful.

---

Good human relations are easy to talk about. The real lesson, I think, is that you must work at them all the time and make sure your managers are working with you.

---

In looking back on the history of a company, one can't help but reflect on what the organization has learned from its years in business. In thinking specifically of the period since the war when IBM faced the twin challenges of great technological change and growth, I would say that we've come out with five key lessons. They may not be applicable to all companies. All I can do is attest to the great value these five lessons had for us.

1. There is simply no substitute for good human relations and for the high morale they bring. It takes good people to do the jobs necessary to reach your profit goals. But good people alone are not enough. No matter how good your people may be, if they don't really like the business, if they don't feel totally involved in it, or if they don't think they're being treated fairly—it's awfully hard to get a business off

468

the ground. Good human relations are easy to talk about. The real lesson, I think, is that you must work at them all the time and make sure your managers are working with you.

2. There are two things an organization must increase far out of proportion to its growth rate if that organization is to overcome the problems of change. The first of these is communication, upward and downward. The second is education and retraining.

3. Complacency is the most natural and insidious disease of large corporations. It can be overcome if management will set the right tone and pace and if its lines of communication are in working order.

---

The only sacred cow in an organization should be its basic philosophy of doing business.

---

4. Everyone—particularly in a company such as IBM—must place company interest above that of a division or department. In an interdependent organization, a community of effort is imperative. Cooperation must outrank self-interest, and an understanding of the company's particular approach to things is more important than technical ability.

5. And the final and most important lesson: Beliefs must always come before policies, practices, and goals. The latter must always be altered if they are seen to violate fundamental beliefs. The only sacred cow in an organization should be its basic philosophy of doing business.

The British economist Walter Bagehot once wrote: "Strong beliefs win strong men and then make them stronger." To this I would add, "And as men become stronger, so do the organizations to which they belong."

1963

# Acknowledgments

For several years now I have been working on the Business Wisdom series, with this collection being the final installment. It is a great body of work that includes many priceless essays, but it would never have had an audience were it not for the many people who worked on and helped to shape it. As always, Ruth Mills, my editor at John Wiley & Sons, tops the list of those deserving heartfelt thanks. Through the whole process, Ruth never lost her enthusiasm—even when faced with stacks upon stacks of essays. I also greatly appreciate the help of Sasha Kintzler in production and the rest of the Wiley gang, as well as the folks at North Market Street Graphics.

Thanks, too, to Ed Knappman, my agent, for his continuous advice. Input has come from many sources, such as friends and friends of friends and even strangers, and I appreciate it all.

The best is when my kids want to take a book to their schoolteacher; their pride in good old dad makes me particularly pleased. Sometimes I'm even invited for a little "show and tell." (It was pretty funny the time my son's first-grade class tore an entire book to shreds to see how it was made—for some reason the teacher didn't invite me back to discuss writing further.) In the end, it goes without saying that the Business Wisdom series is dedicated to my family, and to my

471

wife Diana in particular. Diana supported the family when I first began this endeavor and she continues to support me in the most important ways. The dream, of course, is that 20 or 30 or even 50 years from now I'll be dedicating yet another book to her and the kids.

# Notes

The biographical sketches were drawn using the following sources:

Giovanni Agnelli:
McQuade, Walter. "The Embattled Prince of Fiat." *Fortune,* August 1971.

Mary Kay Ash:
Ash, Mary Kay. *Mary Kay.* New York: Harper & Row, Publishers, 1981.

Charles Babbage:
"Mr. Babbage's Wonderful Calculating Machine." *Popular Science,* March 1993.
Swaine, Michael. "Paradigms Past: Why Did Babbage Fail?" *Dr. Dobb's Journal,* June 1999.

Jim Barksdale:
"Barksdale Venture Acquires 10% Stake in Respond.com." *The Wall Street Journal,* June 28, 1999.
Copeland, Lee. "James Barksdale: Netscape." *Computer Reseller News,* November 9, 1998.
Darrow, Barbara. "James Barksdale." *Computer Reseller News,* November 17, 1997.
Thibodeau, Patrick, and Elizabeth Wasserman. "Microsoft: Barksdale 'Exaggerated.' " *InfoWorld,* June 7, 1999.

Alexander Graham Bell:
Grosvenor, Edwin S. and Morgan Wesson. *Alexander Graham Bell: The Life and Times of the Man Who Invented the Telephone.* New York: Harry N. Abrams, 1997

Gordon Bethune:
Bethune, Gordon, with Scott Huler. *From Worst to First.* New York: John Wiley & Sons, 1998.

Puffer, Sheila M. "Continental Airlines' CEO Gordon Bethune on Teams and New Product Development." *The Academy of Management Executive,* August 1999.

Cathleen Black:

Calvacca, Lorraine. "Cathleen Black." *Folio: The Magazine for Magazine Management,* April 15, 1999.

Fitzgerald, Mark. "NAA President to Join Hearst." *Editor & Publisher,* December 2, 1995.

Gremillion, Jeff. "Hearst's Fall Color: Basic Black." *Mediaweek,* October 14, 1996.

Arthur Blank and Bernie Marcus:

Harris, Nicole. "Home Depot: Beyond Do-It-Yourselfers." *Business Week,* June 30, 1997.

Hawkins, Chuck. "Will Home Depot Be 'The Wal-Mart of the 90s'?" *Business Week,* March 19, 1990.

Marcus, Bernie, and Arthur Blank with Bob Andelman. *Built from Scratch.* New York: Times Books, 1999.

Jan Carlzon:

Carlzon, Jan. *Moments of Truth.* Cambridge, Massachusetts: Ballinger Publishing Company, 1987.

Marcom, John, Jr. "Moment of Truth." *Forbes,* July 8, 1991.

Odell, Mark. "Swedes Root for Carlzon." *Airline Business,* August 1995.

Andrew Carnegie:

Carnegie, Andrew. "The Road to Business Success." A speech delivered before Curry Commercial College, June 23, 1885.

Wall, Joseph Frazier. *Andrew Carnegie.* New York: Oxford University Press, 1970.

Michael Dell:

Dell, Michael, with Catherine Fredman. *Direct from Dell.* New York: HarperBusiness, 1999.

Kover, Amy. "Never Bet Against Michael Dell." *Fortune,* March 29, 1999.

Esther Dyson:

Dogar, Rana. "Dyson." *Working Woman,* February 1998.

Mills, Elinor. "New Internet Organization Quickly Names Its Board." *InfoWorld,* November 2, 1998.

"Smog Lifters." *Inc.,* January 1999.

Charles R. Flint:

Flint, Charles. *Memories of an Active Life.* New York: G. P. Putnam, 1923.

Henry Ford:

Ford, Henry, with Samuel Crowther. *My Life and Work*. New York: Doubleday, Page & Company, 1922.

Gelderman, Carol. *Henry Ford: The Wayward Capitalist*. New York: The Dial Press, 1981.

John M. Fox:

Klaw, Spencer. "The Entrepreneurial Ego." *Fortune*, August 1956.

"Remade Minute Maid." *Time*, October 13, 1958.

Robert Galvin:

Bettner, Jill. "Underpromise, Overperform." *Forbes*, January 30, 1984.

Galvin, Robert W. "Real Leaders Create Industries." *Research Technology Management*, November/December 1995.

Tamarkin, Bob. "Winning Is Not a Sometime Thing." *Forbes*, April 13, 1981.

Stanley Gault:

Donlon, J. P. "A New Spin for Goodyear." *Chief Executive*, December 1995.

Haas, Nancy. "CEO of the Year: Stanley Gault of Goodyear." *Financial World*, March 31, 1992.

Lubove, Seth. "The Last Bastion." *Forbes*, February 14, 1994.

Harold S. Geneen:

"Double the Profits, Double the Pride." *Time*, September 8, 1967.

Geneen, Harold. *Managing*. Garden City, New York: Double & Company, 1984.

Roberto C. Goizueta:

Greising, David. *I'd Like the World to Buy a Coke: The Life and Leadership of Roberto Goizueta*. New York: John Wiley & Sons, 1998.

Morris, Betsy. "Roberto Goizueta and Jack Welch: The Wealth Builders." *Fortune*, December 11, 1995.

Andrew S. Grove:

"Man of the Year." *Time*, December 29, 1997–January 5, 1998.

Schlender, Brent. "The Incredible, Profitable Career of Andy Grove." *Fortune*, April 27, 1998.

George N. Hatsopoulos:

Hatsopoulos, George. "A Perpetual Idea Machine." *Daedalus*, Spring 1996.

Kahalas, Harvey, and Kathleen Suchon. "Managing a Perpetual Idea Machine." *The Academy of Management Executive*, May 1995.

August Heckscher:
Forbes, B. C. *Men Who Are Making America.* B. C. Forbes Publishing Co., Inc., 1917.

Lee Iacocca:
Iacocca, Lee, with William Novak. *Iacocca: An Autobiography.* New York: Bantam Books, 1984.
Levin, Doron P. *Behind the Wheel at Chrysler: The Iacocca Legacy.* New York: Harcourt Brace & Company, 1995.

Martha Ingram:
Faircloth, Anne. "Minding Martha's Business." *Fortune,* September 29, 1997.
"Mystery Mogul." *Working Woman,* May 1996.

Shelly Lazarus:
Cohen, Elizabeth. "Shelly Lazarus." *People Weekly,* May 5, 1997.
Current Biography Yearbook 1997. New York: H. W. Wilson Company, 1997.

Royal Little:
Little, Royal. *How to Lose $100,000,000 and Other Valuable Advice.* Boston: Little, Brown & Company, 1979.
Little, Royal. "How I'm Deconglomerating the Conglomerates." *Fortune,* July 16, 1979.
Saunders, Dero A. "Royal Little: The Conglomerator." *Forbes,* July 13, 1987.

Klaus Luft:
Foster, Geoffrey. "Nixdorf's Rich Noche." *Management Today,* June 1986.
Roth, Terence. "Luft Resigns Post as Nixdorf Chairman." *Wall Street Journal,* November 21, 1989.
Schares, Gail. "A Rude Shock for One of Europe's High-Tech Successes." *Business Week,* August 22, 1988.

Robert A. Lutz:
"Can Bob Lutz Recharge Exide?" *Business Week,* March 8, 1999.
Lutz, Robert A. *Guts: The Seven Laws of Business that Made Chrysler the World's Hottest Car Company.* New York: John Wiley & Sons, 1998.
"The Car Guy." *Across the Board,* February 1999.

J. Willard Marriott, Jr.:
Marriott, J. Willard, Jr., and Kathi Ann Brown. *The Spirit to Serve.* New York: HarperCollins Publishers, 1997.

Yang, Catherine, et al. "Low Wage Lessons." *Business Week*, November 11, 1996.

John E. Martin:
"1991 Leadership Awards: John E. Martin." *Restaurant Business*, May 20, 1991.
"ASAP Interview: Susan Cramm & John Martin." *Forbes*, August 29, 1994.
Hammer, Michael, and James Champy. *Reengineering the Corporation.* New York: HarperBusiness, 1993.
Martin, Richard. "Ex-Taco Bell Titan Martin Back in the Saddle at Easyriders Cafes." *Nation's Restaurant News*, New York, July 21, 1997.

Mark McCormack:
Feinstein, John. "The King of the Courts." *Tennis*, May 1995.
"Mark McCormack." *Sports Illustrated*, September 19, 1994.
McCormack, Mark. *What They Don't Teach You at Harvard Business School.* New York: Bantam Books, 1984.

Patrick J. McGovern:
IDG corporate Web site.
Hartman, Curtis, and Michael Hopkins. "Publishing Magnate Pat McGovern." *Inc.*, August 1988.
Short, David. "Computing's Paper Emperor." *The European*, May 26, 1995.

Akio Morita:
Morita, Akio. *Made in America: Akio Morita and Sony.* New York: E. P. Dutton, 1986.
Ohmae, Kenichi. "Guru of Gadgets: Akio Morita." *Time*, December 7, 1998.

Edouard Muller:
"Edouard Muller." *Wilson Library Bulletin*, November 1945.
Mirabile, Lisa. *International Directory of Company Histories*, Volume II. Chicago: St. James Press, 1990.
"Swiss Family Nestle." *Fortune*, February 1946.

David Ogilvy:
Bird, Drayton. "David Ogilvy: The Driving Force of O&M's 50 Years." *Marketing*, September 17, 1998.
Bullmore, Jeremy. "The Advertising World Mourns Its Lost Titan." *Marketing*, July 29, 1999.

Ogilvy, David. *Blood, Brains & Beer: The Autobiography of David Ogilvy.* New York: Atheneum, 1978.

Kenichi Ohmae:
Anton, Karen Hill. "Status Quo Buster." *Worldbusiness,* July/August 1996.
Merriden, Trevor. "The Mind of a Strategist." *Management Today,* September 1998.
Ohmae, Kenichi. *The Mind of the Strategist.* New York: McGraw-Hill Book Company, 1982.
Ohmae, Kenichi. "The Myth and reality of the Japanese Corporation." *Chief Executive,* Summer 1981.
Slater, Joanna. "Wired for Strategy." *Far Eastern Economic Review,* May 13, 1999.

William S. Paley:
Paley, William S. *As It Happened: A Memoir.* Garden City, New York: Doubleday & Company, 1979.

Clarence B. Randall:
Randall, Clarence B. *Over My Shoulder.* Boston: Little, Brown and Company, 1956.
Randall, Clarence B. *The Folklore of Management.* Boston: Little, Brown and Company, 1959.

Andrew W. Robertson:
Mirabile, Lisa, editor. *Company Histories,* Volume II. Chicago: St. James Press, 1990.
"State of Business." *Time,* July 15, 1940.
"Westinghouse Electric." *Fortune,* February 1938.

James D. Robinson III:
Grossman, Peter Z. *American Express: The Unofficial History of the People Who Built the Great Financial Empire.* New York: Crown Publishers, 1987.
Saporito, Bill. "The Topping of King James III." *Fortune,* January 11, 1993.

David Rockefeller:
Collier, Peter, and David Horowitz. *The Rockefellers: An American Dynasty.* New York: Holt, Rinehart and Winston, 1976.

Anita Roddick:
O'Byrne, Robert. "Jolly Green Giant." *The Irish Times,* November 4, 1997.

Roddick, Anita. *Body and Soul: Profits with Principles*. New York: Crown Publishers, Inc., 1991.

John Sculley:
Sculley, John. *Odyssey*. New York: Harper & Row, Publishers, 1987.

Alfred P. Sloan, Jr.:
Sloan, Alfred P, Jr. *My Years with General Motors*. Doubleday & Company, Inc., 1964.
Sloan, Alfred P, Jr. "The Most Important Thing I Ever Learned About Business." *System: The Magazine of Business*, August 1924.

Jack Stack:
Stack, Jack. "The Training Myth." *Inc.*, August 1998.
Steinauer, Joan M. "Building Relationships." *Incentive*, April 1998.

Louis F. Swift:
*Dictionary of American Biography*. New York: Charles Scribner's Sons, 1936.
Swift & Company Web site.
Swift, Louis F. "G. F. Swift: I Can Raise Better Men than I Can Hire." *System: The Magazine of Business*, 1927.
Swift, Louis F. "How G. F. Swift Bossed His Own Job." *System: The Magazine of Business*, February 1927.

Charles D. Tandy:
Irwin, Ross. "Charles Tandy Never Stops Selling." *Fortune*, December 1976.
Irwin, Ross. "Charles Tandy's Ghost Can Rest Easy." *Fortune*, November 19, 1979.

Robert Townsend:
*Current Biography Yearbook 1970*. New York: The H. W. Wilson Company, 1970.
Buchalter, Gail. "Up to What?" *Forbes*, March 24, 1986.
Quinn, Judy. "Lessons from a Geezer." *Incentive*, December 1994.
Townsend, Robert. *Up the Organization*. New York: Alfred A. Knopf, 1970.

Sam Walton:
Vance, Sandra S., and Roy V. Scott. *Wal-Mart: A History of Sam Walton's Retail Phenomenon*. New York: Doubleday, 1992.
Walton, Sam, with John Huey. *Sam Walton: Made in America: My Story*. New York: Doubleday, 1992.

Charles B. Wang:

Weld, Royal. "Interview: The Global Marketer: Charles Wang." *Sales and Marketing Management,* May 1999.

Weld, Royal. "Software Giant's Hardware Kings." *Industry Week,* February 15, 1999.

Thomas J. Watson, Jr.:

"The Greatest Capitalist in History." *Fortune,* August 31, 1987.

Watson, Thomas J. Jr., *Father, Son & Co.: My Life at IBM and Beyond.* New York: Bantam Books, 1990.

John F. Welch, Jr.:

Byrne, John A. "How Jack Welch Runs GE." *Business Week,* June 8, 1998.

Morris, Betsy. "Roberto Goizueta and Jack Welch: The Wealth Builders." *Fortune,* December 11, 1995.

Slater, Robert. *The New GE: How Jack Welch Revived an American Institution.* Homewood, Illinois: Business One Irwin, 1993.

Walter B. Wriston:

Serwer, Andrew. "Don't Say Retired: Walter Wriston is Wired." *Fortune,* April 12, 1999.

Zweig, Phillip L. *Wriston: Walter Wriston, Citibank, and the Rise and Fall of American Financial Supremacy.* New York: Crown Publishers, 1995.

# Credits and Sources

"Closing the Management Gap" by Giovanni Agnelli, from the *Conference Board Record*, November 1969. Reprinted by permission of the Conference Board.

"People Will Support That Which They Help Create" from *Mary Kay on People Management* by Mary Kay Ash. Copyright © 1984 by May Kay Cosmetics, Inc. Reprinted by permission of Warner Books, Inc.

"On the Division of Labor" from *On the Economy of Machinery and Manufactures* by Charles Babbage, 1832.

"IT Departments: Getting Down to Business" by James Barksdale, from Netscape's *Netcenter*, July 24, 1998. Reprinted by permission of James Barksdale.

"When Does Profit Become Usury?" by Alexander Graham Bell, from *Outlook*, November/December 1909.

"From Worst to First" from *From Worst to First* by Gordon Bethune with Scott Huler. Copyright © 1998 by Gordon Bethune and Scott Huler. Reprinted by permission of John Wiley & Sons, Inc.

"A Brand New Day in the Business World" by Cathleen Black, from a speech delivered before the Economic Club of Indianapolis, Indiana, March 4, 1997. Reprinted by permission of Hearst Magazines.

"The Invisible Fence" from *Built from Scratch* by Arthur Blank & Bernie Marcus with Bob Andelman. Copyright © 1999 by Homer TLC, Inc. Reprinted by permission of Times Business Books, a division of Random House, Inc.

"Flattening the Pyramid" from *Moments of Truth* by Jan Carlzon. Copyright © 1987 by Ballinger Publishing Company. Reprinted by permission of HarperCollins Publishers, Inc.

"An Employer's View of the Labor Question" by Andrew Carnegie, from *Forum*, April 1886.

"Waging a Campaign of Internal Evangelism" from *Direct from Dell* by Michael Dell with Catherine Fredman. Copyright © 1999 by

Michael Dell. Reprinted by permission of HarperCollins Publishers, Inc.

"Friction Freedom" by Esther Dyson, from *Forbes ASAP,* November 30, 1998. Reprinted by permission of *Forbes ASAP.* Copyright © Forbes Inc., 1998.

"Industrial Consolidation" from *Memories of an Active Life* by Charles R. Flint. Published by G. P. Putnam, 1923.

"Machines and Men" from *My Life and Work* by Henry Ford with Samuel Crowther. Published by Double, Page & Company, 1922.

"What It Takes to Be a Manager" by John M. Fox, from a speech delivered before the sales Executives Club of New York, February 21, 1956.

"Managing Knowledge Towards Wisdom" by Robert Galvin, from *European Management Journal,* August 1996. Reprinted with permission from Elsevier Science.

"No One Excluded" by Stanley Gault, from *Fortune,* December 14, 1992. Copyright © 1992 Time Inc. Reprinted by permission.

"The Essential Element" from *Managing* by Harold S. Geneen and Alvin Moscow. Copyright © 1984 Harold S. Geneen and Alvin Moscow. Used by permission of Doubleday, a division of Random House, Inc.

"Globalization: A Soft Drink Perspective" by Roberto C. Goizueta, from a speech delivered before the Town Hall of California, February 9, 1989. Reprinted by permission of The Goizueta Foundation.

"How to Make Confrontation Work for You" by Andrew S. Grove, from *Fortune,* July 23, 1984. Copyright © 1984 Time Inc. Reprinted by permission.

"A Perpetual Idea Machine" by George N. Hatsopoulos, from *Daedalus,* Spring 1996. Reprinted by permission of *Daedalus,* Journal of the American Academy of Arts and Sciences, from the issue entitled, "Managing Innovation," Spring 1996, Vol. 125, No. 2.

"Can Good Management Be Reduced to Simple Rules?" by August Heckscher, from *System: The Magazine of Business,* 1923.

"Skip Meetings" from *Talking Straight* by Lee Iacocca with Sonny Kleinfeld. Copyright © 1988 Lee Iacocca. Used by permission of Bantam Books, a division of Random House, Inc.

"Community Involvement Key to Profits, Productivity" by Martha Ingram, from *Computer Reseller News,* January 20, 1997.

"Global Branding" by Shelly Lazarus, from *Adweek,* November 9, 1998. Reprinted by permission of *Adweek.*

"Conglomerates Are Doing Better than You Think" by Royal Little, from *Fortune,* May 28, 1984. Copyright © 1984 Time Inc. Reprinted by permission.

"What American CEOs Can Learn from German Management" by Klaus Luft, from *Chief Executive*, Winter 1981–82. Reprinted by permission of *Chief Executive*.

"Lutz's Immutable Laws" by Robert A. Lutz, a speech delivered before the University of Michigan Automotive Management Briefing Seminar, August 7, 1996. Reprinted by permission of Robert A. Lutz.

"Room at the Revenue Inn" by J. Willard Marriott, Jr. and Robert G. Gross, from *Chief Executive*, July 1997. Reprinted by permission of *Chief Executive*.

"Reengineering the Corporation" by John E. Martin, from *Reengineering the Corporation* by Michael Hammer and James Champy. Copyright © 1993 by Michael Hammer and James Champy. Reprinted by permission of HarperCollins Publishers, Inc.

"How to Make or Break a Hire" by Mark McCormack. Copyright © 1997 Mark McCormack. Reprinted by permission of Mark McCormack.

"The Networked Corporation" by Patrick J. McGovern from *Chief Executive*, April 1990. Reprinted by permission of *Chief Executive*.

"Morita Shock" by Akio Morita, from *Tokyo Business Today*, March 1992. Reprinted by permission of *Tokyo Business Today*.

"Personality in Business" by Edouard Muller, from a speech delivered before the Nestle Christmas Party, December 16, 1945.

"Managing Crown Princes" from *Ogilvy on Advertising* by David Ogilvy. Copyright © 1983 by David Ogilvy. Compilation copyright © 1983 by Multimedia Publications, Ltd. Reprinted by permission of Crown Publishers.

"The Mind of the Strategist" from *The Mind of the Strategist* by Kenichi Ohmae. Copyright © 1982 Kenichi Ohmae. Reprinted by permission of The McGraw-Hill Companies.

"Planning for Succession" from *As It Happened* by William S. Paley. New York: Doubleday, 1979.

"The Myth of the Organization Chart" from *The Folklore of Management* by Clarence B. Randall. Copyright © 1961 by Clarence B. Randall; copyright © renewed 1989 by Mary Gilkey and Miranda Hunter. Reprinted by permission of Little, Brown and Company, Inc.

"Management's responsibilities to the Public" by Andrew W. Robertson, from *A Handbook for Business Speakers*. Published by Dartnell Publications, Inc., 1940.

"Managing Technology Through People" by James D. Robinson III, from *Chief Executive*, Spring 1981. Reprinted by permission of *Chief Executive*.

"Managing Change Creatively" from *Managing Change Creatively* by David Rockefeller. New York: McGraw-Hill Book Company, 1964.

# Chronology

# Author Index

# Subject Index